MW00834085

"Second Maccabees presents the reader with some of the most challenging Greek in the Septuagint. It is far more complex than almost all of the Greek of the New Testament and poses frequent difficulties that have given rise both to ancient textual variants and modern scholarly emendations in an attempt to make the Greek more intelligible. All who attempt to study 2 Maccabees in its original language will be grateful to Seth Ehorn for providing such a detailed analysis of the grammar and syntax as well as his consistently thorough treatment of the syntactical and textual problems. This two-part work will prove an invaluable *vade mecum*."

—**DAVID A. DESILVA**, *Trustees' Distinguished Professor of New Testament and Greek, Ashland Theological Seminary*

"It is a delight to see the first volume in the Baylor Handbook on the Septuagint series. Seth Ehorn has provided an exceptional guide to the reading of 2 Maccabees 1–7 that will be indispensable for anyone wishing to explore in depth the Greek grammar of the book. A rich introduction provides an overview of the literary structure, dating, and language features of this book and should be consulted by everyone working on 2 Maccabees. The translation and commentary provide an informed guide to the syntax and semantics of the Greek text, explaining in a clear and concise way any difficulties within the text. Students of Greek can now explore for themselves one of the more difficult Greek texts in the Septuagint."

—**JIM K. AITKEN**, *Reader in Hebrew and Early Jewish Studies, University of Cambridge*

BHLXX

Baylor Handbook on the Septuagint
Sean A. Adams and Seth M. Ehorn
General Editors

2 MACCABEES 1–7
A Handbook on the Greek Text

Seth M. Ehorn

BAYLOR UNIVERSITY PRESS

Cover design by Kasey McBeath
Cover image: Shiloh Byzantine basilica mosaic, © Todd Bolen/BiblePlaces.com
Book design by Baylor University Press; typeset by Scribe Inc.

Paperback ISBN: 978-1-4813-1382-7
Library of Congress Control Number: 2020023160

NATIONAL
ENDOWMENT
FOR THE
HUMANITIES

2 Maccabees 1–7 has been made possible in part by a major grant from
the National Endowment for the Humanities: NEH CARES. Any views,
findings, conclusions, or recommendations expressed in this book do not
necessarily represent those of the National Endowment for the Humanities.

Printed in the United States of America on acid-free paper with a
minimum of thirty percent recycled content.

CONTENTS

SERIES INTRODUCTION

There has been something of a renaissance in Septuagint studies among biblical scholars in the twentieth and twenty-first centuries, evidenced by the production of critical editions of the Septuagint, new translation projects, commentaries on individual books, new reading tools and introductions, and the induction of various centers for study of the Septuagint. Yet despite this growing international interest in the Septuagint, there is a dearth of language resources that are aimed at helping facilitate rapid reading and translation of the Septuagint. The Baylor Handbook on the Septuagint (BHLXX) is designed to fill this lacuna and meet the needs of students, teachers, and scholars who are interested in reading the Septuagint.

Each volume of the BHLXX treats a septuagintal book (or portion of a book) verse-by-verse, guiding the reader through the Greek text of the Septuagint. Contributors cannot comment on every aspect of the text, but every significant grammatical or syntactical issue will receive attention. In this respect, the BHLXX differs from the Brill Commentary on the Septuagint and *La Bible d'Alexandrie*, which provide historical, theological, and literary comments rather than detailed comments on the Greek text itself.

There is need to clarify what is meant by "Septuagint." It is widely acknowledged that *septuaginta*, from which the English transliteration "Septuagint" derives, was originally a designation used to refer to the Greek Pentateuch. However, the name "Septuagint" has been extended and applied more broadly than these first five books, encompassing the entire Greek versions of the Hebrew Bible as well as a selection of so-called Apocryphal books. In accordance with this standard usage, the BHLXX includes books from this widest grouping and often employs the term "Septuagint" or "LXX" in this general sense. For additional discussion on terminology, interested readers should consult Jobes and Silva (14–17).

Greek-Based Approach

Septuagint studies has been dominated by investigations that have used the Greek text primarily as a way to understand better the Hebrew *Vorlage* (or source text) or ancient approaches to translation (e.g., Boyd-Taylor). Although these are valid approaches to the Septuagint, they are by no means the only ways to engage critically with the text. Recently, there has been a move to understand the Septuagint as a Greek text on its own terms and not only as a derivative text. Tessa Rajak (143–44) provides two strong reasons for understanding the text in this way:

1. Greek translations in due course *did* stand alone, in fact sooner rather than later, and they therefore rapidly proved usable and fully intelligible in their ancient context.
2. The degree of interference from the source language is sometimes overstated. While sometimes Septuagint Greek can be awkward, it is very rarely unintelligible.

This approach fits with a growing movement within Septuagint scholarship that seeks to prioritize the Greek text and to understand how the Septuagint would have been understood in its wider Greek context (see, e.g., Aitken; Lee 2004; 2018). This perspective requires a rethinking of the linguistic and grammatical approaches to the text as well as a new set of tools that understands the Greek of the Septuagint as a *text* and not just as a *translation*.

The BHLXX operates on the assumption that the Septuagint represents one aspect of post-classical Greek. This claim needs qualification, but represents a growing trend in Septuagint studies to prioritize the Greek text that expresses natural idioms. In a significant study on *The Greek of the Pentateuch*, John Lee (2018, 22) claimed that

> It is too easy to assume that anything in the LXX that is not immediately recognizable as normal Greek is due to Semitic interference. Our procedure ought rather to be to assume that it *might* be normal Greek, that is, to begin with the presumption of innocence, and not decide on a verdict until the evidence on both sides has been fully investigated.

Lee's point is not that the Septuagint is free from Hebrew interference. Rather, he rightly points out that foreign or unusual constructions have, all too often, been explained away as examples of Semitic interference without much evidence. But as our knowledge of post-classical Greek has grown, many alleged instances of Semitic interference have turned out to be idiomatic Greek. In agreement with Lee's arguments, the BHLXX is a resource that attempts to take the Greek of the Septuagint seriously before assuming that it represents translation Greek.

As a result of this adopted perspective, BHLXX series authors will make limited recourse to the Hebrew, mainly doing so when it is necessary to understand the Greek grammar or syntax. The difference in approaches can be illustrated by an example from Exod 1:1-5a:

> ¹Ταῦτα τὰ ὀνόματα τῶν υἱῶν Ισραηλ τῶν εἰσπεπορευμένων εἰς Αἴγυπτον ἅμα Ιακωβ τῷ πατρὶ αὐτῶν — ἕκαστος πανοικίᾳ αὐτῶν εἰσήλθοσαν — · ²Ρουβην, Συμεων, Λευι, Ιουδας, ³Ισσαχαρ, Ζαβουλων καὶ Βενιαμιν, ⁴Δαν καὶ Νεφθαλι, Γαδ καὶ Ασηρ. ⁵Ιωσηφ **δὲ** ἦν ἐν Αἰγύπτῳ.

> ¹These are the names of the sons of Israel who had entered into Egypt with Jacob their father. Each with their whole household went in: ²Reuben, Simeon, Levi, Judah, ³Issachar, Zebulun and Benjamin, ⁴Dan and Nephtali, Gad and Asher. ⁵**But** Joseph was in Egypt.

In this passage the translator(s) of LXX Exodus rendered the Hebrew connective *vav* (ו) in several different ways. As Muraoka (§72j) observes more generally, recourse to Hebrew in *this* passage shows that *vav* (ו) is left untranslated (3 times), translated as καί (3 times), and translated as δέ (1 time). But one could also approach the text by reading it as a Greek document, observing that the connective δέ (rather than καί) is a common way to signal a change of subject (cf. Smyth §2836). Whereas 1:1-4 concerns the sons of Israel, 1:5 introduces a new subject, Joseph, and this development in the narrative is marked by δέ. The grammar is understandable to a Greek reader and we should seek to read it as such.

In addition to grammar and syntax, we must also ask a similar question about Septuagint lexicography. Should vocabulary be studied in relationship to underlying Hebrew terms or studied discretely as Greek terms? Because the aim of the BHLXX is to facilitate reading of the Greek text of the Septuagint, we have opted for the latter approach, generally preferring definitions that are derived from Muraoka's *A Greek-English Lexicon of the*

Septuagint (*GELS*) or the *Brill Dictionary of Ancient Greek* (*GE*). Mura-oka's lexicon is a welcome new resource that focuses on the meaning of Greek terms, distinct from Hebrew terms, building upon his prior meth-odological work on the relationship between Greek and Hebrew in Sep-tuagint studies. In a programmatic essay, Muraoka (1990, 44–45) stated,

> Notwithstanding one's recognition of the basic character of the LXX for most of its parts as a work of translation, it is equally important to recognise that the LXX *is* a Greek document, and one must attempt to read it as such, and it has been so read down the ages. . . . Before one concludes, out of despair per-haps, that a particular rendition is merely an attempt mechani-cally to reproduce the Hebrew, every attempt ought to be made to comprehend the translation as a Greek document.

By treating the Septuagint as Greek literature itself and not as a transla-tion document, the BHLXX focuses on the unique aspects of the Greek language. As such, Muraoka's lexicon as well as other Greek lexicons covering Hellenistic literature provide the most logical choice for ref-erence tools that focus on reading the Septuagint itself. Readers may also want to consult the lexicon produced by Johan Lust, Erik Eynikel, and Katrin Hauspie, *A Greek-English Lexicon of the Septuagint* (LEH), which adopts a different theoretical approach and is also full of rich data. The differences between these two lexica are informative of how methodological approaches influence decisions at even a lexical level. For important critiques of the methodological weaknesses of each lexi-con, see Aitken (9–15).

Another major difference between *GELS* and LEH is that the for-mer attempts to place lexical items in their literary context, not only identifying the part of speech the item typically holds, but also high-lights collocations and words that are grammatically, contextually, and semantically linked. This additional information provides a more robust understanding of how Greek words work in context as well as a wider perspective of how the language functions as a whole.

Septuagint lexicography is one of the big scholarly topics at the moment and new works are expected to be available soon. Arguably the most important in this field will be E. Bons and J. Joosten, *Historical and Theological Lexicon of the Septuagint*. This multivolume work will be published by Mohr Siebeck with the first volume expected in 2020. Readers with very little knowledge of the Septuagint will find the intro-duction by Karen Jobes and Moisés Silva, *Invitation to the Septuagint*, to be the best point of entry into the field. Now in its second edition, the book introduces readers to key questions and provides up-to-date bibliographic entries on many important topics in Septuagint studies.

Greek Text and Translations of the Septuagint

Volumes in the BHLXX use the Rahlfs-Hanhart (R-H) 2006 edition of the Septuagint as a base text. The rationales for this decision are that this text is complete, it is the most widely accessible edition of the Septuagint, and it is traditionally the one most used by those initially interested in the LXX. However, contributors to the BHLXX will also consult the Göttingen edition on text-critical matters and, where beneficial, variation units from volumes in that edition are considered in the handbook. This critical edition focuses on individual books of the LXX and represents the best attempts at reconstructions based on extant Greek manuscripts. Unfortunately, not all of the LXX books have been completed and published. As a result, some BHLXX volumes will not be able to engage with this significant resource.

A further difficulty occurs when determining which text to produce. As is well known in septuagintal studies, certain LXX books have multiple, distinct Greek texts (e.g., Judges, 1–4 Kingdoms, Daniel, Tobit, etc.). In these books the amount of textual overlap between the different versions is often significant, although the number of pluses and minuses create distinctive characteristics in each recension. It is not possible for each handbook to treat every version, and so the decision has been made to follow one version in its entirety—to be determined by the handbook author and discussed in their introduction—and to include the additional material found in the other version where appropriate. This additional material will be marked in the text of the handbook for ease of identification. The goal of this decision is to allow for maximum coverage with minimal redundancy.

The BHLXX also serves an important scholarly function in providing a fresh translation of the R-H Septuagint from a Greek-language perspective. Previous translations, such as *A New English Translation of the Septuagint* (NETS), adopt a different approach to the Greek text. Specifically, NETS adopts an "interlinear" approach, which aims "to bring the Greek reader to the Hebrew original" (Pietersma and Wright, xiv). Lancelot Brenton's translation, now quite dated, is a diplomatic text based on Codex Vaticanus. Most recently, *The Lexham English Septuagint*, edited by Ken Penner (2019), provides a fresh translation of the LXX without recourse to the Hebrew text. For the ease of reading, the BHLXX standardizes the spelling of proper names in translation following the NRSV.

Getting Started

Each volume of the BHLXX offers a verse-by-verse discussion of the Septuagint text, guiding the reader through the intricacies of the Greek text. This work is not designed to be an exhaustive resource for discussions of grammar, syntax, or lexicography, but each author will seek to provide commentary on any significant questions arising from the Greek text. The goal of this series is to support students of Greek as they navigate their way through unfamiliar and sometimes difficult texts. The handbooks are thus designed to serve as companions to the Septuagint and complement standard commentaries, where they exist, which may or may not discuss the intricacies of the primary language.

A reasonable level of knowledge of Greek grammar is presupposed by this tool. Students should be aware of a few Greek grammars that focus on the Septuagint. The first is that of F. C. Conybeare and St. George Stock, *Grammar of the Septuagint*. Second, Henry St. J. Thackeray, *A Grammar of the Old Testament in Greek According to the Septuagint*. These grammars may prove useful in helping to solve difficult issues of syntax or morphology; however, as they are over a century old, they are not informed by modern linguistic study or the deeper understanding of the Septuagint that has emerged in recent decades. More recently, Muraoka has completed his *A Syntax of Septuagint Greek*, a comprehensive work on the morphosyntax and syntax of Septuagint Greek that compares the LXX text with contemporary Greek literature. Although not without its flaws, this is a significant contribution to Septuagint scholarship and will no doubt be a foundational resource for future scholarship. Beyond these grammars that explicitly focus on the Septuagint, we recommend the following grammars of classical Greek: Herbert Smyth's *Greek Grammar*; Evert van Emde Boas, Albert Rijksbaron, Luuk Huitink, and Mathieu de Bakker, *The Cambridge Grammar of Classical Greek*; Heinrich von Siebenthal, *Ancient Greek Grammar*. Additionally, the following grammars on Greek papyri are useful: Mayser, *Grammatik der griechischen Papyri aus der Ptolemäerzeit*; Palmer, *A Grammar of the Post-Ptolemaic Papyri*; Gignac, *A Grammar of the Greek Papyri of the Roman and Byzantine Periods*.

Contributors to the BHLXX typically employ standard grammatical labels such as those found in intermediate and advanced Greek grammars. These labels (e.g., a participle of *manner* or *subjective* genitive) represent not only a morphological determination, but also a contextual judgment about the function of the word. These categories are contested with different scholars categorizing the Greek text differently. Although one system will be adopted in each volume, we would recommend examining a range of resources to understand alternate viewpoints.

Each handbook consists of the following features. The Introduction draws the readers' attention to some of the distinctive features of the Greek text in question and treats some of the broader issues relating to the text as a whole in a more thorough fashion. The handbook proper consists of two parts. The text is divided into sections based on the overall structure of the book and each section is introduced with a translation that illustrates how the insights gleaned from the analysis that follows may be expressed in natural English. Following the translation is the heart of the handbook, which offers a detailed analysis of the Greek text. The Greek text of each verse is followed by comments on syntactic, lexical, text-critical, and other significant issues.

Each page of the handbook includes a header to help readers quickly locate comments on a particular passage. Terminology used in the comments that is potentially unfamiliar to many users is included in a glossary at the end of each handbook. Each volume also includes an index that provides an exhaustive list of grammatical or syntactical phenomena occurring in the text. This feature provides a valuable resource for Greek teachers wanting to illustrate a particular phenomenon or develop exams or exercises. Finally, each handbook concludes with a bibliography of works cited, providing helpful guidance in identifying resources for further research on the Greek text.

It is our hope that through engagement with the BHLXX volumes students will be better suited to engage with and understand the unique context(s) of the Septuagint as a text in its own right. Along the way, students will encounter readings that differ from what they know to be derived from the Hebrew Bible. Such discoveries will be well worth the effort.

Sean A. Adams
University of Glasgow, Scotland

Seth M. Ehorn
Wheaton College, USA

PREFACE

I do not remember the first time I read 2 Maccabees. However, I do remember reading the book very closely during my postgraduate studies at the University of Edinburgh in a "Classics Reading Group." As I read through the book, I made extensive notations in my latest Moleskine® notebook. Little did I know that these notes would form the basis of my notes years later for a lecture on Second Temple Judaism and for a course on Intermediate Greek Grammar. When the opportunity to write a handbook for Baylor University Press emerged, the choice seemed obvious.

This handbook is the fruit of several years of labor, often in the nooks and crannies of my teaching schedule. In addition to the countless hours spent in the Greek text of 2 Maccabees, I have found several volumes in the Baylor Handbook on the Greek New Testament (BHGNT) series to be useful models in preparing my own handbook on 2 Maccabees. While this debt is owed to many contributors in that series, I have found Brookins and Longenecker (1 Corinthians), Decker (Mark), and Olmstead (Matthew) to be particularly helpful when preparing my own handbook. While they are rarely explicitly cited in the following pages, I gladly acknowledge the significant role these authors played in modeling *how* to comment on the Greek text throughout this handbook.

Carey Newman, former director of Baylor University Press, supported the Baylor Handbook on the Septuagint (BHLXX) and my contribution to it from the start. Upon Carey's departure from Baylor, David Aycock and Cade Jarrell picked up the proverbial baton and proved equally supportive and helpful. They, as well as the entire team at Baylor University Press, deserve thanks for their tireless work in bringing this handbook to publication.

Several colleagues and former students assisted me by reading chapters of this handbook in draft form. Jerusha Crone read several chapters and made many valuable comments, as did Alex Long, Katie Marcar, Teresa McCaskill, Josiah Brake, and John Canty. Ellen Howard deserves a special word of thanks. In her capacity as my teaching assistant at Wheaton College Graduate School, she carefully read chapters 1–4, providing many comments on the utility of the handbook, making helpful observations on verbal aspect (her emerging area of expertise), and saving me from numerous errors. Frank Shaw also read the Introduction and provided detailed comments that have improved the final version. Finally, my coeditor for the BHLXX series, Sean Adams, read and commented on the entire manuscript. Of course, any errors that remain are my own responsibility.

Seth M. Ehorn

ABBREVIATIONS

(Abbreviations of primary sources follow the *Society of Biblical Literature Handbook of Style*)

1st	first person
2nd	second person
3rd	third person
A	Codex Alexandrinus
acc	accusative
act	active
aor	aorist
AT	Alpha Text (of Esther)
BDAG	Danker, *A Greek-English Lexicon of the New Testament*, 2000
BDF	Blass, Debrunner, and Funk, *A Grammar of the New Testament*
BHGNT	Baylor Handbook on the Greek New Testament
BHLXX	Baylor Handbook on the Septuagint
cf.	compare (*confer*)
ch(s).	chapter(s)
CGCG	van Emde Boas, *Cambridge Grammar of Classical Greek*
dat	dative
DCH	Clines, *Dictionary of Classical Hebrew*, 8 vols.
EDG	Beekes, *Etymological Dictionary of Greek*
e.g.	for example (*exempli gratia*)
fem	feminine

fut	future
GE	Montanari, *The Brill Dictionary of Ancient Greek*
GELS	Muraoka, *A Greek-English Lexicon of the Septuagint*
gen	genitive
HALOT	Koehler and Baumgartner, *The Hebrew and Aramaic Lexicon of the Old Testament*, 5 vols.
H-R	Hatch and Redpath, *A Concordance to the Septuagint*
i.e.	that is (*id est*)
impf	imperfect
impv	imperative
ind	indicative
inf	infinitive
L	manuscripts grouped under the recension *L*
LCL	Loeb Classical Library
LDAB	Leuven Database of Ancient Books
LEH	Lust, Eynikel, and Hauspie, *A Greek-English Lexicon of the Septuagint*, 2003
lit.	literally
LN	Louw and Nida, *Greek-English Lexicon of the New Testament*
LSJ	Liddell, Scott, and Jones, *A Greek-English Lexicon*, 1996
LXX	Septuagint
masc	masculine
MAMA	Calder, *Monumenta Asiae Minoris Antiqua*, 8 vols., 1928–1962
MBG	Mounce, *The Morphology of Biblical Greek*
MHT	Moulton, Howard, and Turner, *A Grammar of New Testament Greek*, 4 vols.
mid	middle
MS(S)	manuscript(s)
Muraoka	Muraoka, *A Syntax of Septuagint Greek*
NETS	New English Translation of the Septuagint
neut	neuter
NewDocs	Horsley, *New Documents Illustrating Early Christianity*, 10 vols.
nom	nominative

NP	noun phrase
NRSV	New Revised Standard Version
NT	New Testament
OCD	Hornblower, *Oxford Classical Dictionary*, 4th ed.
OGIS	Dittenberger, *Orientis graeci inscriptiones selectae*, 2 vols., 1903–1905
opt	optative
pass	passive
pl	plural
plprf	pluperfect
PP	prepositional phrase
pres	present
prf	perfect
ptc	participle
q	manuscripts grouped under the recension *q*
R-H	Rahlfs-Hanhart, *Septuaginta*, 2006
SIG	Dittenberger, *Sylloge inscriptionum graecarum*, 4 vols., 3rd ed., 1915–1924
sg	singular
subj	subjunctive
THB	Lange, *Textual History of the Bible*, vol. 2C: *Deuterocanonical Scriptures*
TLG	*Thesaurus Linguae Graecae: Canon of Greek Authors and Works*
V	Codex Venetus
voc	vocative

INTRODUCTION

In accordance with the aims of the Baylor Handbook on the Septuagint (BHLXX) series, this handbook on 2 Maccabees is primarily a grammatical and syntactical analysis of the Greek text and not a full-scale commentary. Accordingly, historical and theological comments are addressed only minimally throughout the handbook proper. In many instances alternative ways of understanding the Greek syntax are outlined in the handbook and, in most cases, a preferred understanding is stated.

While writing this handbook I have read and interacted primarily with commentaries by Félix-Marie Abel, Christian Habicht, Jonathan Goldstein, Carl Grimm, Robert Doran, Daniel Schwartz, and Tobias Nicklas. While each of these commentaries has its own strengths, this handbook is distinguished by its particular attention to the Greek text of 2 Maccabees. For further historical, rhetorical, and theological commentary, users of this handbook may benefit from reading Doran (2012) or D. Schwartz while working through the Greek text. *The Brill Dictionary of Ancient Greek* (*GE*) and Muraoka's *Greek–English Lexicon of the Septuagint* (*GELS*) are the primary lexicons cited throughout this handbook, although other lexicons (e.g., LSJ, LEH, and BDAG) were consulted and cited when they provided useful discussion or helpful glosses.

The remainder of this introduction considers (1) the Greek edition and translation of 2 Maccabees in this handbook, (2) the books of the Maccabees and the structure of 2 Maccabees, (3) the literary integrity of 2 Maccabees and its dating, (4) Greek verbs in 2 Maccabees, and (5) the language, style, and syntax of 2 Maccabees. These topics will help orient users of this handbook to 2 Maccabees more generally as well as to some of the specific issues arising from the Greek text.

Greek Edition and Translation of 2 Maccabees

Greek Edition. The BHLXX utilizes the Rahlfs-Hanhart (R-H) 2006 edition of the Septuagint because, unlike the Göttingen edition (which is
essential for scholarly work), R-H provides a complete edition of the
LXX and it is the edition most users of the BHLXX will have at hand.
While this handbook on 2 Maccabees utilizes the R-H text, the Göttingen edition completed by Robert Hanhart (1959, 1976², 2008³, 2017⁴)
was consulted for text-critical matters and, at times, significant variation
units are discussed in the textual comments of the handbook. Hanhart's
edition built upon the work of his predecessor, Werner Kappler, whose
dissertation on 2 Maccabees remains useful for serious textual study.
Significant text-critical work on 2 Maccabees was also undertaken by
Peter Katz (1960) and Habicht, both of whom provide lists of their disagreements with Hanhart's critical text (cf. *THB* §10.2.2.3), especially
with respect to conjectural emendations. Hanhart (1961) also responded
to Katz's criticism in a short book.

   In order to aid the user of this handbook, I have compiled the following list of all the differences between the R-H edition (2006) and the
most recent Göttingen edition (4th edition, 2017). (Note: this list was
generated using the print editions and not electronic editions, which
in my experience have more errors.) Two kinds of differences *are not
included* in the list. First, proper names are not included when, characteristically, they lack breathing marks and/or accents found in the
R-H text. Second, words that lack the moveable *nu* are not included
when they differ between the two editions. The following list serves as
a pointer to the handbook proper, where many (but not all) of these
differences are mentioned and sometimes discussed.

   1. Punctuation difference (1:4, 7, 8, 11, 13, 19, 20, 22, 23², 27, 32,
      33, 36; 2:1, 2², 4², 6, 7, 8, 9, 14, 18, 21, 22, 30; 3:2, 6, 9, 11³, 19²,
      20, 24², 32², 33, 36, 37; 4:3, 4, 13, 14, 22, 28², 32, 34, 38, 46; 5:8,
      17, 18, 22; 6:6, 7, 9, 12, 13, 19², 20², 23, 29, 30; 7:16², 18, 22²,
      26, 28², 36, 37²; 8:8, 18², 20², 27, 32; 9:4, 9, 15, 16, 18², 20², 23,
      24², 25; 10:6, 13, 16, 17, 19², 21, 22, 29², 30; 11:3², 11, 24, 28,
      31, 36, 37; 12:4, 8, 9, 14, 15, 16, 22, 24, 27, 35, 36, 37, 39, 43,
      44; 13:7, 14, 15³, 16, 19, 24, 25; 14:3, 4, 6, 7, 9, 17, 18, 21², 22,
      24, 25, 31, 32, 35², 38, 39, 41; 15:2, 3², 4, 5², 8, 12, 13, 14, 17, 21,
      22, 30², 38).
   2. Inflection difference (1:8; 2:22; 3:28, 33; 4:9, 20, 30; 5:13, 18; 6:4;
      8:20, 30; 9:8, 24; 10:2; 11:5, 14, 24, 26²; 12:3, 6, 11, 13, 22, 35;
      13:19; 14:3, 17; 15:12).

3. Versification difference (1:9/10, 20/21; 5:2/3; 11:13/14; 13:10/11, 22/23).
4. Simple vs. compound verb form (1:17; 3:19; 14:20).
5. Paragraphing difference (1:18, 24, 30; 4:43; 5:27; 7:39, 41; 8:16; 10:9/10).
6. Omission or addition of word(s) (1:18[2], 20, 22; 2:8; 3:28; 4:19, 20, 33; 5:13, 18, 27; 6:11, 30; 8:11, 16, 27; 9:20, 21; 10:28, 30; 11:16, 20; 12:3, 6, 7, 23, 26, 27, 35; 13:5; 15:3).
7. Spelling variation (2:6, 18, 23; 4:9, 13, 19[2], 21, 22, 24; 5:2, 8, 16; 6:17; 8:2, 7, 19, 23, 24, 30, 35; 9:13; 10:4; 11:3, 34, 36; 12:9, 13, 19, 24, 35; 13:5; 14:3, 19, 36, 38[2]; 15:22, 26, 32).
8. Different word choice(s) (2:7, 3:4, 5, 11, 13, 18, 28; 4:5, 10, 19, 20; 5:7, 8, 16, 23; 6:2, 29; 7:14, 30, 40; 8:11, 20; 9:9, 12; 10:30; 11:2, 5; 12:3, 4, 27, 28, 43; 13:15, 25, 26; 14:13, 15, 20, 22, 26, 31; 15:12, 11, 12, 20, 39).
9. Variation in word order (5:27; 8:13; 11:25; 13:4, 5; 14:4, 26, 33).

The Göttingen edition of 2 Maccabees includes the obelus (†) several times in the text, marking places where the text is judged to be corrupt (4:34; 6:29; 7:30; 8:33; 9:20-21; 10:13; 11:14; 12:13; 13:15). For additional discussion of possible corruptions, see especially Katz (1960).

Following the Göttingen edition of 2 Maccabees, the handbook proper sometimes refers to q or L in text-critical discussions. These abbreviations refer to recensions that group together manuscripts as follows:

q = LXX[29, 71, 74, 98, 107, 120, 130, 243, 370, 731]
L = LXX[64, 236, 381, 534, 728] and, less completely preserved,
        in LXX[19, 62, 93, 542]

In addition to consulting the critical edition of 2 Maccabees, necessary discussion of the extant Greek witnesses is located in the critical edition of 1 Maccabees by Kappler (1990). A useful summary of the extant Greek witnesses is also found in *THB* §10.2.1.3.

Two other editions of the Greek text of 2 Maccabees merit mention. The valuable edition of 2 Maccabees by Henry Swete (1905) is not systematically cited in the handbook for text-critical purposes. However, Swete's punctuation and paragraphing decisions were considered in the preparation of this handbook. Abel's *Les Livres des Maccabées* contains not merely a useful French translation and commentary, but also a critical edition of the Greek text with useful text-critical comments.

Noteworthily, Abel engages seriously with de Bruyne's scholarship on the Latin witnesses of 2 Maccabees.

Translation. Because the goal of this handbook is to help readers understand the grammar and syntax of the Greek text, the translation of 2 Maccabees in the handbook attempts to follow the general phrase and clause order of the Greek text. This was not always possible (or desirable) when rendering it into English, but hopefully this decision will help readers follow along with the Greek text as they work through the handbook. Although rare or unusual vocabulary is frequent in 2 Maccabees, glosses are not always included in the entries in the handbook. In cases where a gloss is not included in the grammatical entry, the translation should function to clarify the meaning of the word.

I regularly consulted the New English Translation of the Septuagint (NETS) while producing the translation for this handbook. However, I have departed from its decisions in virtually every verse for reasons of style, clause order, lexicography, text-critical determinations, or translation philosophy. Nevertheless, NETS represents some of the best LXX scholarship and its influence is felt and is here gratefully acknowledged on virtually every page of this handbook.

The sections into which the text has been divided for comment are informed by the critical editions cited above. Yet, in many instances, the longer paragraphs in these editions required breaking the text into smaller, more manageable units for comment. When breaking up these larger units, I have sometimes followed the judgments of other scholars. The reader of this handbook should not read too much into these textual divisions. More often than not, the decision to divide the text was simply a matter of size and practicality.

The Books of the Maccabees and the Structure of 2 Maccabees

The Books of the Maccabees. Although this handbook covers only 2 Maccabees, it is useful to situate briefly 2 Maccabees within the "books of the Maccabees." Here the *plural* "books" helps clarify that 2 Maccabees is not a continuous story with other books of a similar namesake. For example, the main material of 2 Maccabees considers the period from 175 BCE to 160 BCE and, thus, runs roughly parallel to many events found in 1 Maccabees 1–7. Those interested in exploring the similarities and differences between 1 and 2 Maccabees may find the following chart of parallel sections useful (cf. Abel, xxxix–xl):

1 Maccabees	2 Maccabees
The precursors of the Seleucids (1:1-10)	Seleucus IV, the parties at Jerusalem. Heliodorus at the temple (3:1-4, 6)
The advance of Antiochus IV Epiphanes (1:10)	The advance of Antiochus IV Epiphanes (4:7)
Led by apostates (1:11-15)	Led by apostates (4:7-50)
Expedition of Antiochus Epiphanes to Egypt. Looting the temple (1:16-28)	Expedition of Antiochus Epiphanes to Egypt. Sedition in Jerusalem. Capture of the city and looting of the temple (5:1-23)
Capture of Jerusalem and founding of Acra by Apollonius (1:29-40)	Capture of Jerusalem by the Mysarch Apollonius (5:24-26). Judas Maccabeus leaves Jerusalem (5:27)
Profanation of the temple. Persecution (1:41-59)	Profanation of the temple. Persecution (6:1-9)
Martyrs (1:60-65). Mattathias leaves Jerusalem and begins war against persecutors (2:1-70)	Martyrs (6:10–7:42)
Judas' First Successes (3:10-26)	Judas' first successes (8:1-7)
Nicanor and Gorgias (3:27–4:25). Judas' victory over Gorgias (4:26-35)	Judas' victories over Nicanor. Timothy and Bacchides (8:8-36)
Campaign of Lysias (4:26-35)	The death of Antiochus Epiphanes (9:1-29)
Purification of the temple (4:36-61)	Purification of the temple (10:1-9)
War with neighbors (5:1-68). The death of Antiochus Epiphanes (6:1, 17)	War with neighbors (10:10-38). Campaign of Lysias. Letters (11:1-38). War with neighbors (12:1-45)
Antiochus V's campaign. Peace (6:18-63)	Antiochus V's campaign. Peace (13:1-26)
Demetrius I. The high priest Alcimus against Judas (7:1-21)	Demetrius I. The high priest Alcimus against Judas (14:1-10)
Judas' victory over Nicanor (7:23-48)	Judas' victory over Nicanor (14:11-15, 35)
Institution of the festival in memory of the death of Nicanor (7:49)	Institution of the festival in memory of the death of Nicanor (15:36)

Although 1 and 2 Maccabees tell overlapping stories (cf. Josephus, *J.W.* 1.41-45; *Ant.* 12.237-412; 12.413–13.214), they were written from very different perspectives. Most notably, 2 Maccabees includes miraculous accounts within the story (e.g., 3:24-26; 5:2-4; 10:29; 11:8; 12:22; 14:15; 15:27), showing not only the tragedy of Jewish persecution but also a perspective on divine judgment. Because this handbook does not explore the parallels between the two books, interested readers may wish to consult Sievers' *Synopsis of the Greek Sources for the Hasmonean Period: 1–2 Maccabees and Josephus, War 1 and Antiquities 12–14*. Additionally, the introduction to D. Schwartz's commentary on 2 Maccabees provides several useful discussions that bear upon the relationship between 1 and 2 Maccabees.

The other books that bear the name "Maccabees"—3, 4, and 5 Maccabees—differ dramatically from 1–2 Maccabees. The work called "3 Maccabees" is a misnomer because the text narrates the persecution of Alexandrian Jews during the time of Ptolemy IV Philopator (221–204 BCE). That is, the story is set before the Maccabean period began. Fourth Maccabees is a philosophically minded treatise that seeks to demonstrate the superiority of reason over passion. Because it draws upon the very same martyrdom narratives found in 2 Macc 6:18–7:42 (probably in direct dependence upon 2 Maccabees), the title of "Maccabees" is slightly more appropriate. However, it is noteworthy that Judas Maccabaeus is not mentioned anywhere in the work. Fifth Maccabees narrates the period from Heliodorus to Herod (184–6 BCE) and is perhaps a conflation of the other Maccabean books, writings from Josephus, and a Jewish work called *Yosippon*. The compositional character is a matter of debate. For short summaries of 3, 4, and 5 Maccabees, see Evans (55–56, 66–67).

Structure of 2 Maccabees. Two letters are prefixed to 2 Maccabees (1:1-9; 1:10–2:18). The book has a prologue (2:19-32), an epilogue (15:37-39), and is structured around three major attacks on the Jerusalem temple: (1) by Heliodorus under Seleucus IV (3:1-40); (2) under Antiochus IV Epiphanes (4:1–10:9); and (3) the final assault by Nicanor under Demetrius I (10:10–15:36). An alternative and more simple division of the chapters distinguishes between (1) events prior to the Maccabean revolt (chs. 3–7) and (2) the Maccabean revolt (chs. 8–15). Following this latter structure and for reasons of practicality, this handbook on 2 Maccabees is divided into two sections: chapters 1–7 and chapters 8–15.

Literary Integrity of 2 Maccabees and Dating

Literary Integrity. Although a full-scale analysis of the literary integrity of 2 Maccabees is beyond the scope of this introduction, a few brief comments are in order because the grammatical and syntactical analysis

that follows has a direct bearing on this question. First, the relationship between the opening letters (1:1-9; 1:10–2:18) and the epitome
(3:1–15:36) is the subject of considerable debate. The difference between
the account of the death of Antiochus Epiphanes IV in 1:13-16 and
9:1-17 presents an obvious problem for assuming the unity of the book
(see discussion in the handbook on 1:10-17). Additionally, the language
and style of the opening letters differs from each other and from the
rest of the book, suggesting that the letters derive from (a) Semitic *Vor-
lage(n)*. Based on the noticeably different style of the letters, it is unlikely
that the two letters were translated by the same person or group. But what
impact did appending these letters have upon the existing narrative?

Source critical determinations are complex, but it is striking that the
opening letters seek to establish Hanukkah as a central holiday whereas
the main narrative of 2 Maccabees focuses on the campaigns against
Nicanor (e.g., 8:1-36; 15:1-35) and the narrative closes by calling for the
commemoration of Nicanor's Day (15:36). The exception to this is 10:1-
8, which some scholars argue has been relocated from elsewhere in the
text (e.g., Habicht, 199–200, 249–50; Goldstein, 24–26, 345–48) or was
added to the narrative (e.g., Schwartz, 371–79; Wheaton, 260–62; *THB*
§10.2.1.1.3). While it is true that the narrative focuses mainly on Nicanor, it would be a mistake to ignore the explicit statement in the prologue
that the writer desires to epitomize the story concerning "the cleansing
of the greatest temple and the dedication of the altar" (2:19b). Without
10:1-8 in the narrative, this desire remains unfulfilled. Thus, although
Hanukkah occupies only a small part of the narrative, it plays an important part in the epitomizer's stated purpose and should probably be taken
as original to the text. The arguments for and against including 10:1-8 in
the text are discussed more fully in the handbook proper.

Second, there is also some discussion about the originality of the
martyrdom narratives in 6:18–7:42. While the martyrdom stories play
an important role in the overall theological argument (*THB* §10.2.1),
the martyrdom section also lacks expected political terminology that
would align it with the rest of the book. As a result, scholars have argued
multiple options, including that Jason's original used a different source
for the martyrdom account (e.g., Engel, 4) or that the epitomizer used
a different source here (e.g., D. Schwartz, 20, 24–25). Less tenable is the
option that the martyrdom account was a later addition (e.g., Habicht,
176–77). On the assumption that the epitomizer included this section (using some traditional source), the many linguistic connections
between the martyrdom account and the rest of the narrative make more
sense (Domazakis, 341–50). Additionally, the Deuteronomic theme of
God hiding his face due to sin that pervades the authorial reflections

(4:16-17; 5:17-20; 6:12-16) emerges in the form of a quotation from
Deut 32:36 as well as echoes of this theme in 7:33. Whatever the source
underlying the martyrdom traditions, the text as we have it has been
carefully integrated into the larger narrative. For more on this, see the
brief discussion in the handbook on 7:1-6.

The handbook proper occasionally engages these source critical
questions. However, both here and in the handbook, discussion of these
important questions should not distract from reading the Greek text as
we now have it. Doran (1981, 22–23) concludes that

> the epitome is a unified piece, separate from the prefixed letters
> and not a patchwork quilt of sources. This is not to deny that the
> epitome shows that information was gained from many quar-
> ters. The application of the methods of source-criticism, how-
> ever, has failed to turn up 'sources' in the technical sense. The
> epitome, therefore, must be considered as a whole and analyzed
> accordingly.

Those interested in more discussion of the literary integrity of 2 Maccabees should consult D. Schwartz (1–37), Doran (1981, 3–23; 2012, 1–3),
and especially the relevant entries in Brill's *Textual History of the Bible*,
vol. 2C: *The Deuterocanonical Scriptures* (*THB* §10.2).

Linguistic Issues and the Dating of 2 Maccabees. The complex compositional character of 2 Maccabees makes it difficult to fix a date to
the work with any certainty. It is generally conceded that Jason's five-
volume work, which forms the basis for the epitome, was written shortly
after the events it narrates (cf. D. Schwartz, 15). Thus, Jason's work can
be no earlier than 161 or 160 BCE, the likely date of Nicanor's defeat
(15:20-36). Moreover, because the opening letters (1:1-9; 1:10–2:18)
likely date later than the epitome, they are less helpful for determining
when the epitome was written. Based on the linguistic data, Domazakis
(354) demonstrates that the epitome of 2 Maccabees is at home in the
Greek of the second or first century BCE. This broad range generally
aligns with what other scholars have concluded, although some scholars
still prefer to date the epitome to the first century CE (e.g., Zeitlin and
Tedesche, 27–28).

Although nothing in the handbook depends on this determination,
the earlier dating—generally in the second or first century BCE—and,
specifically, something prior to the fall of Hasmonean rule (63 BCE)
makes the most sense of the generally positive description of relations
with the Romans in 4:11; 8:10, 36; 11:34-36 (cf. van Henten 1997, 51).
If the epitome was written during the reign of John Hyrcanus and his

successors, this would narrow the window to 125–63 BCE (cf. Shaw 2015, 276). For additional discussion of dating, see the works cited at the end of this Introduction and also the entry at 1:9 on ἔτους ἑκατοστοῦ ὀγδοηκοστοῦ καὶ ὀγδόου.

Greek Verbs in 2 Maccabees

Given both the significance of and the considerable scholarly interest in the Greek verbal system, it seems wise to discuss the Greek verbs in 2 Maccabees in some detail prior to a more general description of the language, style, and syntax of 2 Maccabees. First, given the confusion that sometimes pertains to such discussion, an explanation of some of the key terms employed in this handbook follows. Following this there is a discussion of the use of Greek verbs in 2 Maccabees.

Tense. Because Greek is often labeled and described using the language of tense, it is important to define precisely what is meant by this term. In the indicative mood, I understand tense labels as descriptions of how verbal action is located within time (often in relation to the time of writing or speaking). Although some anomalies exist, the past, present, and future tenses are each grammaticalized in the indicative mood (e.g., the augment[s]) to mark their temporal significance. Although several NT scholars have argued that Greek verbs do not encode time in the indicative mood (e.g., McKay, 39–40; Porter 1989, 107–8; Campbell, 239–40), the evidence best supports the view that indicative verbs grammaticalize both tense *and* verbal aspect (*CGCG* §33; Siebenthal §193a; Fanning, 420–22). Nevertheless, to the extent that verbal aspect has been emphasized in recent studies, these contributions have been valuable and repay close study. For an up-to-date discussion of the significance of both tense and aspect, see the various studies in the edited volume by Runge and Fresch (2016).

Aspect. No less significant than tense is verbal aspect, which concerns how the writer or speaker presents the action unfolding in time. I follow many scholars in seeing a distinction between three verbal aspects: imperfective (present, imperfect), perfective (aorist), and stative (perfect, pluperfect). The perfective aspect (aorist) presents action in summary fashion or as a complete whole. As such, the perfective aspect is the default choice to narrate events. Meanwhile, the imperfective aspect (present, imperfect) presents action as unfolding, progressing, or continuing. In narrative texts, imperfective aspect is typically used to provide background information to the main narrative and, thus, takes on a more global significance. That is, the imperfective aspect presents information that is "incomplete" from the perspective of the larger textual unit or narrative (cf. *CGCG* §33.51). The third aspectual category is more debated than the first two. The stative aspect (perfect, pluperfect) presents a state or effects of an action that are in some way relevant in the present or, in the case of the pluperfect, in the past. Additionally, the future tense is notably absent from this categorization because many grammarians and linguists consider the future to be "aspectually neutral" (*CGCG* §33.6; cf. Porter 1999, 43–46). Because the aorist is the most common verb in narrative contexts to carry the storyline, it is unmarked (for prominence). As indicated above, the imperfect often provides background information and is more marked for prominence. The lesser used perfect and pluperfect are both grammatically marked and more prominent than the aorist and imperfect. In each of these instances, "prominence" helps distinguish between what is central and what is supportive within the discourse (see a fuller definition in the glossary). For an insightful discussion of verbal aspect, including its relation to temporal and spatial categories, see the up-to-date study by Thomson (13–80).

Verbs and Narrative. Based on the R-H text, there are 2,302 verbs in 2 Maccabees, including finite verbs, participles, and infinitives. When only the indicative verbs are counted, there are 789 verbs. Comparison of the distribution of these verbs across the tenses is instructive:

	All Verbs (2,302)	**Indicative Verbs (789)**
Aorist	1,090 (47.4%)	428 (54.2%)
Present	723 (31.4%)	80 (10.1%)
Imperfect	208 (9.0%)	208 (26.4%)
Perfect	186 (8.1%)	23 (2.9%)
Future	81 (3.5%)	36 (4.6%)
Pluperfect	14 (0.6%)	14 (1.8%)

As expected, the aorist and the imperfect indicative are the most common verb tenses in 2 Maccabees because these are the main tenses used to locate action in the past. The plotline of the story typically occurs in the aorist indicative. According to Rijksbaron (11), "[s]ince the *imperfect* characterizes the state of affairs as 'not-completed' it creates a framework within which other states of affairs may occur, while the *aorist indicative* characterizes the state of affairs as 'completed', as a mere event." The variation between the aorist and imperfect within a narrative is significant for the way that the plotline of the narrative unfolds.

Whereas the aorist presents actions as events that simply occurred, the imperfect creates an expectation that some related action will occur (cf. Rijksbaron, 11).

This dynamic can be illustrated briefly in the opening of the narrative (3:1-4). The first three verses set up the background of the story and, as expected, the only indicative verb is an imperfect.

> ¹While the holy city was governed in complete peace and while the laws were observed as best as possible on account of both the piety and hatred of wickedness of Onias, the high priest, ²*it also came about* [συνέβαινεν] [that] the kings themselves honored the place and glorified the temple with the most excellent gifts ³with the result that even Seleucus, the king of Asia, provided out of his own revenues all the expenses associated with the ministries of the sacrifices. ⁴Now a certain Simon, of the tribe of Benjamin, who had been appointed captain of the temple, **had a difference of opinion** [διηνέχθη] with the high priest about the office of the market overseer in the city.

The entirety of 3:1 is a circumstantial frame for the main clause in 3:2. Then in 3:2-3, the text switches to the imperfect to introduce a new state of affairs that came about. This sets the stage for the introduction of a new character, Simon (3:4), who helps accomplish the first step in the narrative plotline of 2 Maccabees 3 (using the aorist). Much of the narrative of 2 Maccabees uses the aorist and imperfect in this manner.

Although 2 Maccabees employs the imperfect with a frequency comparable with contemporary Hellenistic narratives (cf. Muraoka §28.ca.i), it also uses the imperfect in places where the aorist would be expected. For example, in chapter 3 there is a long stretch of imperfect verbs from 3:9b-23 that cannot be classified easily as providing off line material (i.e., material that does not advance the main plotline) or a framework within which the main plotline of the story must be understood. It is possible, as Shaw (2016, 412) suggests, that the epitomizer overuses the imperfect tense here. However, in my view it is likely that the extended use of the imperfect is part of the narrative strategy of the epitomizer (see discussion in the handbook under 3:13-23).

The present indicative is typically employed in sections containing direct or indirect discourse. For example, in 3:37-39, the text reads as follows:

> ³⁷But when the king asked Heliodorus what sort of person might be suitable to be sent once more to Jerusalem, **he said**

[ἔφησεν], ³⁸"If _you have_ [ἔχεις] any enemy or plotter of things, send him there, and after he has been flogged, you shall welcome him back, if he should even come through safely, because there is truly some divine power around the place. ³⁹For he, the one who has a heavenly dwelling, _is_ [ἐστίν] the overseer and helper of that place, and _he destroys_ [ἀπολλύει] those who come on the basis of ill intent by striking [them] down."

Note the shift from the aorist (3:37) to the present (3:38-39) as soon as the discourse starts. Here we see the normal use of the present indicative to "refer to actions that occur at the moment of speaking" (_CGCG_ §33.14). This is a regular pattern of verb tense shifts throughout the narrative (e.g., 7:2, 6, 9, 11, 16, 18, 23, 28, 30, 32, 37). The historic present is also used, although not in great frequency (e.g., 15:5).

The perfect indicative is used (23 times) to convey a past action and effects that are, in some way, relevant in the present. Often the perfect "expresses a more or less permanent state in the present which exists as the result of a completed action" (_CGCG_ §33.34). A few verbs have specific meanings in the perfect stem that cannot be related either textually or by inference to a preceding action (cf. _CGCG_ §33.36). For example, in two uses of a perfect form of πείθω in 2 Maccabees (8:18²), the verb is basically indistinguishable in meaning from the present. Another example is the use of the perfect form of ἀποργίζομαι (5:17), which is an atelic verb that marks "an extreme degree of the state" (_CGCG_ §33.37). In 5:17 the verb does not seem to indicate that Israel's God was angered in the past and he remains in a state of anger. Rather, ἀποργίζομαι is qualified by the adverb βραχέως, which indicates that "the Sovereign was angered _briefly_."

The pluperfect (including pluperfect periphrastic constructions) is used as many as 17 times in 2 Maccabees (3:17, 29, 30, 36; [4:1²], 26; 6:5; 9:7, 18; 12:39; 13:17; 14:17, 24, 38², 15:7, 9), often to provide supplemental, descriptive, and explicatory material (cf. Campbell, 237). Shaw (2016, 413) notes that in several instances the pluperfect is used where a simple aorist would have sufficed. The related form, the perfect, was itself losing some of its distinction from the aorist in Hellenistic Greek (cf. Jannaris §1874; Caragounis, 154–55; Mayser, II 2.1.139–41). On analogy with the perfect, it seems likely that the pluperfect was at times used when the aorist would have been the more precise choice. For a detailed discussion on the possible function of the pluperfect, see the entry at 3:29 in the handbook on ἔρριπτο.

Finally, the future indicative is used in specific contexts to express intentions (e.g., 2:23), predictions (e.g., 6:26), deliberations (e.g., 7:7), threats (e.g., 7:14), and announcements (e.g., 9:4). As expected, the future appears regularly in direct and indirect discourse (cf. Campbell, 159–60).

Language, Style, and Syntax

Second Maccabees, along with a few other books (e.g., 3–4 Maccabees, Wisdom), is rightly considered to be among the best literary Greek in the LXX corpus. The language and style of 2 Maccabees is also quite different from other LXX books—both because the main epitome is not the result of a translation and also because the author is generally well-educated and at home in the Hellenistic Greek of his day (cf. D. Schwartz, 67). Comparison with Polybius' *Histories*, Diodorus Siculus' *Library of History*, and Dionysius of Halicarnassus' *Roman Antiquities* is instructive. For example, shared vocabulary and phrase similarities with these works suggests that they belong to the same linguistic milieu (cf. Domazakis, 354). Additionally, the dramatic presentation of suffering and persecution as well as the motif of "just deserts" (i.e., the punishment fits the crime) is seen in 2 Maccabees (e.g., 4:38, 42; 8:33; 13:6-8) as well as some of the works mentioned above (Doran 1981, 92–94). Paradoxically, 2 Maccabees is "an example of Jewish historiography that on the one hand vehemently turns against the Hellenization of Judaism and on the other hand participates in the literary world of Hellenism" (Nicklas 2015, 173). That is, the epitomizer is a linguistic product of the very Hellenistic influence he claims to despise.

The best study currently available on the language and syntax of 2 Maccabees is Doran (1981, 24–46). Additionally, Shaw (2016, 407–15) published a chapter on "The Language of Second Maccabees" that provides a helpful overview of some of the grammatical and syntactical issues in 2 Maccabees. In that study, Shaw also mentions a forthcoming book project titled *A New Direction in 2 Maccabean Studies: Text, Language, and Style*, which promises to be a valuable and much fuller examination of the linguistic features of 2 Maccabees. The following discussion takes cues from both Doran (1981) and Shaw (2016) and draws upon the analysis found in the handbook proper.

The Prefixed Letters (1:1-9; 1:10–2:18). Before turning to the prologue (2:19-32) and the epitome (3:1–15:36), I offer very brief comments on the language and syntax of the prefixed letters (1:1-9; 1:10–2:18). It is interesting that there are no uses of the μέν/δέ construction in the letters, not only when compared with the rest of 2 Maccabees (see, e.g., 2:25, 2:26, 2:28, 2:30-31, 2:32, 3:8) but also given that some LXX books (that are translations of a Hebrew *Vorlage*) include the μέν/δέ construction.

Because there is no Hebrew lexical equivalent for μέν, the introduction of the μέν/δέ construction in other LXX books should be understood as the translator's representation of how the discourse functions (cf. Fresch 2017a, 313–16; Lee 2018, 98–101). The lack of μέν/δέ constructions in the opening letters of 2 Maccabees certainly suggests something about the particular translation technique of the prefixed letters or, additionally, something about the time when these letters were translated and affixed to the rest of the book.

Other interesting features of the opening letters must be discussed separately because the letters themselves differ from one another. As Shaw (2016, 407) notes, in many ways the Greek of the first letter (1:1-9) resembles the Greek of many other LXX books. The paratactic style of the letter is marked by the frequent use of καί. This is further underscored by the single example of hypotaxis in 1:7, where a genitive absolute construction occurs. Finally, although declining in post-classical Greek, the use of the optative (7 times) in the first letter follows the standard classical usage of the mood to convey wishes.

The second letter (1:10–2:18) is much longer and represents a higher register of Greek than the first. Shaw (2016, 407–9) draws attention to three distinct features. First, the varied use of ὡς (18 or 19 times, depending on a text-critical judgment in 1:18) provides evidence of both classical and post-classical constructions. In addition to consulting the grammatical index at the end of this handbook, the following examples illustrate the variety. Temporal (e.g., 1:15, 20, 21, 22, 32, 33; 2:7) or comparative (1:23; 2:1, 8[2]) uses of ὡς are the most common. But, ὡς also introduces indirect discourse (2:2, 9, 13), conveys purpose/intention (1:14), and (with ἄν) has a causal function (1:11). Second, as Shaw notes, there are multiple correlative constructions (e.g., 1:14, 18, 21, 23; 2:10) that coordinate clauses together. However, as noted above, the second letter never uses the μέν/δέ construction to coordinate clauses. Third, the more sophisticated Greek style of the second letter is illustrated by the use of brachylogy (1:18), solecism (1:31), ellipsis (1:34), prolepsis (2:1), and hyperbaton (2:13). Additionally, the second letter employs the genitive absolute construction after a main clause (1:13), which may be an example of *varatio* (μεταβολή) when compared with its usual placement prior to a main clause (cf. *CGCG* §60.32). A few other examples of the genitive absolute construction following a main verb appear in the epitome. However, in these cases the placement appears to be conditioned by the presence of another genitive absolute construction in the same verse (see 7:4 on συνορώντων) or other syntactical constraints in context (see 4:38 on ἀποδόντος). Finally, as most commentators observe, the grammar and logic of 2:17-18a are awkward. There is no main verb in these verses, either due to anacoluthon, loss of a verb from the textual tradition, or the need to supply the verb ἐστίν (see handbook for further discussion). The logic is also strained because of the use of two γάρ clauses, one of which may introduce a parenthetical clause (cf. Shaw 2016, 408) or may modify a more remote clause.

The Prologue (2:19-32), Epitome (3:1–15:36) and Epilogue (15:37-39). Because of the length of the epitome, it is not possible to offer extensive comments on every aspect of Greek language and style. The handbook proper provides some additional discussion of both and, hopefully, will provide data for future analysis of the Greek of 2 Maccabees. The agenda of 2 Maccabees is set out clearly in several places in the prologue of the work: Jason of Cyrene's five-volume work "we shall attempt to epitomize into a single treatise" (πειρασόμεθα δι᾿ ἑνὸς συντάγματος ἐπιτεμεῖν, 2:23; cf. 2:26, 28). Thus, we see that 2 Maccabees is an epitome (2:26, 28). Although scholars debate the sources that underlie the epitome, this need not deter comments on the Greek text of 2 Maccabees. It is impossible to pull apart Jason's original work from the epitomizer's work, especially when there is evidence of epitomizer's reworking. The only workable procedure is to treat the Greek text of the epitome as a unit (cf. Shaw 2016, 409). The remaining section includes a discussion of neologisms, hyperbaton, transitional use of the μέν/δέ construction, and verbal periphrasis.

Neologisms. The presence of neologisms has long been observed by readers of 2 Maccabees. In the LEH lexicon, a number of dictionary entries relevant to 2 Maccabees are marked by either "neol." (marking words that occur first in the LXX) or "neol.?" (marking words that occur in the LXX and roughly contemporary literature or documentary texts). Yet, it was not until 2018 that a full-scale study of these alleged neologisms was published. Domazakis' significant study investigated: (1) words first attested in 2 Maccabees that do not recur anywhere else in extant Greek literature (i.e., *absolute hapax legomena*); (2) words first attested in 2 Maccabees that recur elsewhere in the LXX (including both so-called apocryphal and canonical books); (3) words first attested in the LXX that were taken up in 2 Maccabees; (4) words first attested in 2 Maccabees that were taken up in non-literary and extra-septuagintal texts; and (5) words first attested in Greek literature contemporary with 2 Maccabees that were (presumably) adopted by 2 Maccabees. In the conclusion of his study, Domazakis (354) states that the language of 2 Maccabees

> combines, in different proportions, elements drawn from sources as diverse as Homer and tragic poetry, Greek historiography of the Classical and Hellenistic periods, Hellenistic

honorific decrees, the Greek translations of the Hebrew Bible, and other Jewish-Greek writings.

According to Domazakis, there are 68 neologisms in 2 Maccabees (many of these are discussed in the handbook). The rich variety of language in 2 Maccabees demonstrates the author's ability to draw from both Jewish and Greek literature.

Hyperbaton. One common characteristic of 2 Maccabees' style is hyperbaton (ὑπέρβατον, "transposition"), which refers to the "separation of two or more syntactically closely connected words or groups of words, for signaling or reinforcing the end of syntactical and semantic units in the Greek (and, by analogy, Latin) literary sentence" (Markovic, 127). Although hyperbaton was often employed for metrical reasons in Greek poetry (cf. Quintilian, *Inst.* 8.6.63-64), in prose it often throws emphasis on the word that is separated from its syntactical pair (BDF §473). There are many and diverse examples of discontinuous syntax in 2 Maccabees, but here I will focus on two types.

First, in some examples, hyperbaton "is achieved by fixing the material 'sandwiched' between the article and substantive as modifiers of the substantive and not some other item in the text" (Baugh, 196). For example, in 2:20: ἔτι τε **τοὺς** πρὸς Ἀντίοχον τὸν Ἐπιφανῆ καὶ τὸν τούτου υἱὸν Εὐπάτορα **πολέμους** ("additionally, both **the wars** against Antiochus Epiphanes and the son of this one, Eupator"). Here τοὺς . . . πολέμους has an embedded phrase (πρὸς Ἀντίοχον τὸν Ἐπιφανῆ καὶ τὸν τούτου υἱόν) that modifies it. Because prepositional phrases (PP) are often adverbial, the use of hyperbaton helps clarify that it modifies the noun phrase (NP). This type of hyperbaton does not only occur with PPs, as is seen in 2:19: καὶ **τὸν** τοῦ ἱεροῦ τοῦ μεγίστου **καθαρισμόν** ("and **the cleansing** of the greatest temple"). Here the Greek article and its head (τὸν . . . καθαρισμόν) surround the genitive modifiers. The interpositional placement clarifies that the genitive phrase modifies τὸν . . . καθαρισμόν. This kind of hyperbaton is extremely common in 2 Maccabees (cf. Doran 1981, 44).

Second, in some examples of hyperbaton, the modifier precedes the head. In such cases there is typically "strong emphasis on the modifier" (*CGCG* §60.18). For example, in 3:25: **φοβερὸν** ἔχων **τὸν ἐπιβάτην** ("having **a frightful rider**"). Here the modifier (φοβερόν) precedes the head (τὸν ἐπιβάτην), both of which surround the participle ἔχων. The effect is that "frightful[ness]" of the rider is emphasized in the construction. An additional example is found in 3:14: ἦν δὲ **οὐ μικρὰ** καθ᾽ ὅλην τὴν πόλιν **ἀγωνία** ("and there was no **small distress** throughout the whole city"). Here the modifier (μικρά) is separated from the head noun (ἀγωνία) and the emphasis is on the "small[ness]" of the distress in a litotic statement (an understatement).

Digressions. The epitomizer employs digressions (παρέκβασις) at several places in the work (4:16-17; 5:17-20; 6:12-17; 7:20-29). There appear to be two main reasons for this. First, in many instances, digressions are "an attempt to guide the reader's understanding of events" (Coetzer, 250). This is seen quite clearly in the digressions of 4:16-17 and 5:17-20, where the author interjects his own understanding that departing from the law results in disaster for the Jews. Here again we see the epitomizer employing a common feature of Greek literature but using that feature to present Jewish ways of thinking.

Second, Cicero (d. 43 BCE) emphasized that "arousing emotion" is a major reason to employ digressions. Cicero (*De or.* 2.77.311–312) stated that

> it is often useful to digress from the subject one has put forward and is dealing with, for the purpose of arousing emotion; and accordingly very often either a place is given to a digression devoted to exciting emotion after we have related the facts and stated our case, or this can rightly be done after we have established our own arguments or refuted those of our opponents, or in both places, or in all the parts of the speech, if the case is one of this importance and extent; and the cases that are the weightiest and fullest for amplification and embellishment are those that give the greatest number of openings for a digression of this kind, so allowing the employment of the topics which either stimulate or curb the emotions of the audience. (LCL)

Cicero's text offers a useful discussion for analyzing the longest digression in 2 Maccabees. Following the description of the martyrdom of six brothers, the epitomizer interrupts the discourse with an extended digression concerning their mother (7:20-29). After this, the story returns to a speech by the seventh son followed by his death (7:30-40). According to Perry (172), "[e]motion seems to be a primary reason for the location of the mother's speeches between the sixth and seventh deaths. The mother exhorts her son to accept death with courage, trusting in God's justice and the promise of resurrection."

Transitional μέν/δέ. The most common use of μέν is "to correlate a clause with one that follows introduced by δέ or ἀλλά [or καί]" (Runge, 74). The discourse function of μέν is clear: "anticipation of a related sentence that follows" (Runge, 75). This can take multiples forms, including *listing* ideas (2:25) or *contrasting* ideas (e.g., 4:26-27; 8:18; 14:8). Perhaps the most interesting use of the μέν/δέ construction in 2 Maccabees is the use of μέν at the conclusion of a narrative section followed by δέ in the following section (3:40–4:1; 7:42–8:1; 10:9-10; 15:24-25). As Shaw (2016, 410) notes, this use of μέν/δέ dates to Herodotus (e.g., *Hist.* 4.205–5.1) and, according to Hornblower (94), is "used as a device to stress both continuity and the element of transition" (cf. Brock, 7). Thus, the use of μέν at the end of major discourse units pushes the reader along to the following section.

Verbal Periphrasis. The construction of periphrases using ποιέω with an abstract noun is characteristic of Attic Greek (cf. Horrocks, 41). As Dhont (152) notes, this construction is "not typically Septuagintal," but is occasionally encountered in books that reflect a higher linguistic register and/or more natural Greek idiom (e.g., Job 14:3; 22:3). While the first usage of such a periphrasis in 2 Maccabees appears in the second letter at 1:23, the majority of uses occur in the prologue and epitome with the following nouns: περίπατον (2:30), μετάφρασιν (2:31), ἐκκομιδήν (3:7), πορείαν (3:8), λιτανείαν (3:20; 10:16), ἱλασμόν (3:33), πρεσβείαν (4:11), ἀπαίτησιν (4:28), τραυματίας (4:42), δικαιολογίαν (4:44), σφαγάς (5:6), παράκλησιν (7:24), ἱκετεία (8:29), ἀσχήμων (9:2), πορείαν (12:10), σφαγή (12:16), διωγμός (12:23), ἐξιλασμός (12:45), ἱεροσυλία (13:6), στρατοπεδεία (13:14), and κοινολογία (14:22). It is not surprising that a book composed in Greek uses this periphrasis, but its frequency shows that the epitomizer is fond of this construction.

Another type of verbal periphrasis in 2 Maccabees is comprised of εἰμί + participle. There are several examples of periphrasis of this sort, used to create present (1:6), imperfect (3:11; 10:6), pluperfect (3:36; [4:1²]; 11:16; 14:17, 38²; 15:7, 9), perfect (4:1²), and future (6:28) periphrastic constructions. According to Bentein (12–18), periphrastics are motivated by several possible concerns: (1) morphology, (2) syntax, (3) semantics, and (4) pragmatics. Periphrasis due to *morphology* refers to periphrastics as "replacement forms" or avoidance strategies (e.g., when a particular form is morphologically complex). Periphrasis due to *syntax* is motivated by a concern to coordinate the participle with one (or more) nominal(s) in the context. Periphrasis due to *semantics* refers to periphrastics having an intensified or emphatic meaning. As Bentein notes, this sense is possible, but highly subjective (cf. Rijksbaron, 127). Periphrasis due to *pragmatic* concerns refers to motivations that fundamentally affect the construction. In the LXX, is the construction because of an underlying Hebrew *Vorlage*? Is the construction used to imitate classical authors (i.e., Atticizing construction)? These motivations are considered when periphrastic constructions are discussed in the handbook proper.

This discussion of the language and style in 2 Maccabees has been far from comprehensive. However, some of the significant issues encountered in the handbook proper have been introduced. Readers interested in these issues should look for additional discussion(s) following the translations in the handbook as well as any of the following introductory resources for an overview of critical issues on 2 Maccabees:

1. Frank Shaw, "2 Maccabees," in *T&T Clark Companion to the Septuagint*, ed. James K. Aitken (London: Bloomsbury T&T Clark, 2015), 273–91;

2. Johannes Schnocks, "2 Maccabees," in *Textual History of the Bible*, vol. 2: *Deuterocanonical Scriptures*, ed. Frank Feder and Matthias Henze (Leiden: Brill, 2019), 142–53 (§10.2);

3. Tobias Nicklas, "Makkabaion II / 2 Maccabees," in *Introduction to the Septuagint*, ed. Siegfried Kreuzer (Waco, Tex.: Baylor University Press, 2019), 271–78 (German edition: *Handbuch zur Septuaginta: Einleitung in die Septuaginta* [Gütersloh: Gütersloher Verlaghaus, 2016], 306–13).

A HANDBOOK ON THE GREEK TEXT OF
2 MACCABEES 1-7

2 Maccabees 1:1-9

¹To the Jewish brothers throughout Egypt, greetings, [from] the Jewish brothers in Jerusalem and those in the Judean countryside. Good peace. ²And may God do good to you, and may he remember his covenant in favor of Abraham and Isaac and Jacob, who are his faithful slaves. ³And may he give you all a heart to worship him and to do his will eagerly and with a willing spirit. ⁴And may he open your heart with respect to his law and the commandments, and may he establish peace. ⁵And may he heed your prayers and be reconciled to you, and may he not forsake you in an evil time. ⁶And now we are praying for you here. ⁷When Demetrius reigned, in the one hundred sixty-ninth year, we Jews wrote to you in the oppression and in the distress that came upon us in those years after Jason and those with him left the holy land and the kingdom ⁸and set fire to the gate and shed innocent blood. We prayed to the Lord and we were heard, and we offered a sacrifice and grain offering, and we lit the lamps and set out the loaves. ⁹And now see that you celebrate the days of tent-pitching in the month of Chislev. In the one hundred eighty-eighth year.

The opening letter of 2 Maccabees (1:1-9) includes standard features of epistolography: letter opening (1:1), expansion of salutation (1:2-5), letter body (1:6-8), and letter closing, including an exhortation and date (1:9). Key transitions in the letter (1:6 and 1:9) are marked by καὶ νῦν (Doering, 161; *pace* Klauck, 262–63). The purpose for the letter is stated in 1:9: encouragement for Egyptian Jews to celebrate the feast of tent-pitching (i.e., Tabernacles), thereby offering diasporan Jews a meaningful alternative to Greek ritual and forging a stronger tie to Jews in Judea (Simkovich, 293–310). Although the text refers to Tabernacles, most scholars rightly note that the letter intends to refer to Hanukkah, which at the time of composition would not have its own name (see 1:9 on τὰς ἡμέρας τῆς σκηνοπηγίας). The establishment of a connection between the Diaspora and Palestine is a common theme in Jewish literature and there are other letters requesting that Jews in the Diaspora observe Jewish festivals (e.g., the colophon of Greek Esther). On the question of the authenticity and independence of this letter, see discussion in Doran (2012, 1–3), D. Schwartz (1–15), and especially Doering (160–62).

Because of the frequent use of καί to render apodotic ו in the LXX (Aejmelaeus, 126–47), the repetition of καί in 1:1-9 is usually taken as evidence of a Semitic *Vorlage* for the letter. But, M. Miller (210) suggests an additional consideration: "the translators may have been considering the rhythmic presentation of a list of elements in the text. Each wish is short, without a hint of admonition or reproach, and displays a clear oral pattern, which can be represented well by a 'measured' verse presentation." In particular, M. Miller (105–40) notes that καί was used repeatedly in the Elephantine Hermopolis letters as an indicator of performance. Accordingly, on the assumption that the letter contained in 1:1-9 would have been read aloud, it is possible that the repetition of καί represents both a Semitic *Vorlage* and idiomatic Greek in performance contexts.

1:1 Τοῖς ἀδελφοῖς τοῖς κατ᾽ Αἴγυπτον Ιουδαίοις χαίρειν οἱ ἀδελφοὶ οἱ ἐν Ιεροσολύμοις Ιουδαῖοι καὶ οἱ ἐν τῇ χώρᾳ τῆς Ιουδαίας εἰρήνην ἀγαθήν.

Τοῖς ἀδελφοῖς τοῖς . . . Ιουδαίοις. Dative of recipient. The typical order for a letter greeting is: "from A χαίρειν to B." Here we find: "to B χαίρειν from A." By fronting the addressee, the author may be portraying himself with less significance (D. Schwartz, 135). This notion is further supported by the way this letter ends with a petition because the ones who are being petitioned usually held higher status than those making requests (M. Miller, 218). See 9:19 for the same construction. ἀδελφός refers to a "relative, compatriot, comrade" (*GE*, 28) or, better, to a "fellow member of faith community" (*GELS*, 9).

Whether Ιουδαίος should be understood as "Jew" or "Judean" is a subject of much debate. For example, Mason (2007, 457) argues that "there was no category of 'Judaism' in the Greco-Roman world, no 'religion' too, and that the *Ioudaioi* were understood until late antiquity as an ethnic group comparable to other ethnic groups." Conversely, S. Schwartz (238) argues that "the corporate identity of the Jews was much more conspicuously and obviously religious in nature, as early as the Hellenistic period and probably even earlier, than that of any other national or ethnic group in the Mediterranean world and the Near East, and this corporate identity was unusually simplified, pared down, integrated, portable and in fact ripe for an act of abstraction." Schwartz's understanding is preferable here and makes better sense with the PP (κατ᾽ Αἴγυπτον) that modifies τοῖς Ιουδαίος.

κατ᾽ Αἴγυπτον. Locative ("*in* Egypt") or, more precisely, extension ("*throughout* Egypt"; cf. Smyth §1690). The placement of the PP between the article and noun clarifies that it has the adjectival function in attributive position (cf. Smyth §1156). Because geographic names definitionally refer to unique entities, the use (or lack) of the article is not predictable. Muraoka (§5cb) notes that within a PP, Αἴγυπτος is almost always anarthrous (cf. 3 Macc 2:25; 3:20).

χαίρειν. Pres act inf χαίρω. The infinitive in a letter opening formula may originate from the so-called imperatival infinitive (Muraoka §30bh; Siebenthal §218d). Doering (136) notes that "χαίρειν did not always replace 'peace' but could appear side by side with it" in Jewish epistolography.

οἱ ἀδελφοὶ οἱ . . . Ιουδαῖοι. Nominative absolute. Smyth (§940; cf. §942) notes that "[t]he nominative may be used independently in the citing of names of persons and things." On the syntax of the letter opening, see comments on Τοῖς ἀδελφοῖς τοῖς . . . Ιουδαίοις.

ἐν Ιεροσολύμοις. Locative. Variation between κατά + accusative (see above) and ἐν + dative is common when expressing location. On the syntax of the PP, see comments on κατ᾽ Αἴγυπτον above. In general, Greek city names often appear in the plural, either because cities are comprised of many parts (LSJ, 32 on Ἀθῆναι) or, more likely, because "every *polis* seems to have used the plural of the city-ethnic as the name of the state" (Hansen, 193; cf. Smyth §1005).

ἐν τῇ χώρᾳ. Locative. A distinction between the city (Ιεροσολύμοις) and the countryside (τῇ χώρᾳ τῆς Ἰουδαίας) is observed (cf. 1 Esd 6:8; Josephus, *Ant.* 13.284). Mason (2016, 124) notes that "each *polis* was assumed to anchor a dependent territory known as its *chōra* or countryside (Latin *territorium*), which is where many citizens lived on their land." In accordance with Apollonius' Canon, both the head noun (χώρᾳ) and its genitive modifier (Ιουδαίας) are articular (Wallace, 250).

τῆς Ιουδαίας. Attributive genitive, qualifying τῇ χώρᾳ ("the *Judean* countryside"). As noted above, the use (or lack) of the article with place names is not predictable. However, in the LXX, Ιουδαία is almost always articular.

εἰρήνην ἀγαθήν. Because the nominative would be more conventional in the letter opening, the use of the accusative requires explanation (although see Smyth §940, who suggests that the accusative is also possible). Some suggest taking it as the object of ἀγαθοποιῆσαι in 1:2 (Goldstein, 141), but this does not explain the (now) redundant καὶ εἰρήνην ποιῆσαι in 1:4. Others suggest adding καί before εἰρήνην ἀγαθήν to link it with χαίρειν earlier in 1:1 (Habicht, 200; cf. D. Schwartz, 129), but this does not explain adequately the use of the accusative. Another solution is that it is used because of the inverted structure of the opening (see comments on τοῖς ἀδελφοῖς above). Because the sender is placed in the nominative case, the greeting cannot also be placed in the nominative case (Doran 2012, 25). The best solution was offered by Bickermann (1933, 233–54), who argued that this compound "reflects the attempt to combine a Greek epistolary salutation and a Semitic 'peace' greeting, literally translated" (cf. Doering, 136).

An expression of "peace" is a typical health wish found near the opening of Greco-Roman letters. At least one textual tradition (L) adds the equivalent of ὑμῖν (i.e., "peace *to you*"), which, although common in letter openings and improving the sense of the text, is judged to be a later addition.

1:2 καὶ ἀγαθοποιῆσαι ὑμῖν ὁ θεὸς καὶ μνησθείη τῆς διαθήκης αὐτοῦ τῆς πρὸς Αβρααμ καὶ Ισαακ καὶ Ιακωβ τῶν δούλων αὐτοῦ τῶν πιστῶν.

ἀγαθοποιῆσαι. Aor act opt 3rd sg ἀγαθοποιέω. While somewhat rare in the LXX (5 times), the meaning of ἀγαθοποιέω is relatively straightforward: "to do good" (*GE*, 6). The opening letter includes 8 uses of the optative (1:2-5; cf. 3:7; 4:1; 11:28; 15:24) and here it expresses a wish or desire (Muraoka §29db.i; Smyth §1814). Moreover, because in postclassical Greek the optative was declining in use, the relative frequency of the optative is an indication of the literary and stylistic level of the opening letter (cf. Muraoka §29da).

ὑμῖν. Dative of advantage. Based on the putative Semitic *Vorlage* of this letter, Abel (286) suggests that the dative case is used after ἀγαθοποιῆσαι because that is how Greek translators tended to represent the *Hiphil* of יטב with ל-preposition (cf. Gen 12:16).

ὁ θεὸς. Nominative subject of ἀγαθοποιῆσαι.

μνησθείη. Aor mid opt 3rd sg μιμνήσκω. Following ἀγαθοποιῆσαι, the verb μνησθείη indicates that God will remember favorably (cf. *GELS*, 462). Although θε- (or θη-) is typically understood to mark passive morphology, it is actually a dual-voice form and here it is middle (cf. Aubrey, 563–625; Caragounis, 153). Verbs that describe cognitive events (e.g., forgetting, remembering) often use middle-voice morphology (cf. *GE*, 1349).

τῆς διαθήκης. Genitive complement of μνησθείη. Verbs of remembering often take the genitive case (Smyth §1356; BDF §175; Muraoka §22p).

αὐτοῦ. Possessive genitive, qualifying τῆς διαθήκης.

τῆς πρὸς Αβρααμ καὶ Ισαακ καὶ Ιακωβ τῶν δούλων αὐτοῦ τῶν πιστῶν. The article functions as an adjectivizer, changing the PP (πρὸς Αβρααμ . . .) into an attributive modifier of τῆς διαθήκης.

πρὸς Αβρααμ καὶ Ισαακ καὶ Ιακωβ τῶν δούλων αὐτοῦ τῶν πιστῶν. The most important grammatical ambiguity to resolve is the case that πρός governs. Because the names Αβρααμ, Ισαακ, and Ιακωβ are indeclinable, it is difficult to decide how to construe this PP with the genitive phrase (τῶν δούλων αὐτοῦ τῶν πιστῶν) that follows it (see esp. Goldstein, 142; Doran 2012, 25). This ambiguity led to the secondary reading περί (MS 19-62) or, as noted below, to shift the genitive phrase into the accusative case.

πρὸς Αβρααμ καὶ Ισαακ καὶ Ιακωβ. Spatial or advantage. Because the collocation of διαθήκη + πρός usually employs the accusative case (cf. Gen 6:18; Exod 6:2; 2 Macc 8:15; Sir 44:18; etc.), it is tempting to take the text that way here. However, taking the names in the accusative would make the following genitive modifiers (τῶν δούλων αὐτοῦ τῶν πιστῶν) difficult to understand. Rather than assume the text contains a mistake, it is preferable to understand πρός + genitive communicating either a *spatial* sense ("before, in the presence of," *GE*, 1787.II.A.C) or *advantage* ("on the side of, in favor of," *GE*, 1787.II.A.B; GELS, 588.I.1). Both senses are used in comparable contexts (e.g., oaths, supplications, etc.) in Greek literature (e.g., Homer, *Il.* 1.339; Herodotus, *Hist.* 1.75.2). On the spatial sense, Doran (2012, 25) states that "Abraham, Isaac, and Jacob were witnesses to the compact that God established with his people." Even though this is a plausible reading of the grammar, it is not clear why stressing that they were "in the presence of" Israel's God is useful or necessary. On the contrary, a favorable covenant for Abraham (and his descendants) would be relevant to many readers of 2 Maccabees.

τῶν δούλων . . . τῶν πιστῶν. Genitive in apposition to Αβρααμ καὶ Ισαακ καὶ Ιακωβ. The modifier τῶν πιστῶν is attributive: "who are his *faithful* slaves." The Göttingen edition also lists the variant readings τοὺς δούλους αὐτοῦ τοὺς πιστούς (MSS 46-52 55) or τὸν δοῦλον αὐτοῦ τὸν πιστόν (MSS 29-107), converting the syntax into appositional structure. Both readings appear to be secondary, generated in light of the grammatical ambiguities mentioned above.

αὐτοῦ. Possessive genitive, qualifying τῶν δούλων . . . τῶν πιστῶν.

1:3 καὶ δῴη ὑμῖν καρδίαν πᾶσιν εἰς τὸ σέβεσθαι αὐτὸν καὶ ποιεῖν αὐτοῦ τὰ θελήματα καρδίᾳ μεγάλῃ καὶ ψυχῇ βουλομένῃ.

καὶ. The conjunction that links the verb δῴη to ὁ θεός, the subject in 1:2.

δῴη. Aor act opt 3rd sg δίδωμι. The implied subject of the verb is ὁ θεός from the previous verse. On the use of the optative in 2 Maccabees, see 1:2 on ἀγαθοποιῆσαι.

ὑμῖν . . . πᾶσιν. Dative indirect object of δῴη. Other aspects of 1:1–2:18 stress that *all* Jews in Egypt are being addressed (cf. 2:17).

καρδίαν. Accusative direct object of δῴη.

σέβεσθαι. Pres mid or pass inf σέβω. Used with εἰς τό to denote purpose (see Burk, 99–105; MHT 3:143). Morphologically, the verb may be either middle or passive, depending on how one understands the verbal action and the accusative αὐτόν (see below). It is preferable to understand the middle here, because the action implied in the verb affects the subject. The present infinitive (imperfective verbal aspect) suggests habitual practice. On the meaning of the verb, see *GE* (1900): "to venerate, honor, revere."

αὐτὸν. Either the accusative direct object of σέβεσθαι (middle: "to honor *him*") or the accusative subject of the infinitive σέβεσθαι (passive: "*he* might be honored"). See the previous entry.

ποιεῖν. Pres act inf ποιέω. Linked by καί to εἰς τό to denote purpose (see σέβεσθαι above).

αὐτοῦ. Subjective genitive, qualifying τὰ θελήματα.

τὰ θελήματα. Accusative direct object of ποιεῖν.

καρδίᾳ μεγάλῃ καὶ ψυχῇ βουλομένῃ. Datives of manner. The collocation of καρδίᾳ μεγάλῃ (lit. "with a strong heart") is best understood as "eagerly" (cf. *GELS*, 363). This is probably reinforced by the following ψυχῇ βουλομένῃ, which is taken as hendiadys (cf. Smyth §3025). These datives may modify ποιεῖν, σέβεσθαι, or both.

βουλομένῃ. Pres mid ptc dat fem sg βούλομαι (attributive).

1:4 καὶ διανοίξαι τὴν καρδίαν ὑμῶν ἐν τῷ νόμῳ αὐτοῦ καὶ ἐν τοῖς προστάγμασιν καὶ εἰρήνην ποιῆσαι.

καὶ. The conjunction that links the verb διανοίξαι to ὁ θεός, the subject in 1:2.

διανοίξαι. Aor act opt 3rd sg διανοίγω. The implied subject of the verb is ὁ θεός from 1:2. On the use of the optative in 2 Maccabees, see 1:2 on ἀγαθοποιῆσαι.

τὴν καρδίαν. Accusative direct object of διανοίξαι.

ὑμῶν. Possessive genitive, qualifying τὴν καρδίαν.

ἐν τῷ νόμῳ. The preposition ἐν is difficult to understand within the larger clause. The collocation of (δι-) ἀνοίγω + ἐν may be used to convey instrumentality (e.g., Ps 48:5), but this sense is not implied here (cf. Doran 2012, 26; Dommershausen, 109). Moreover, the translation "[may he open your heart] *to his law*" (NETS) would be better communicated with the dative case alone (unless there is simply a mismatch in language, on par with English "*on* the plane" vs. "*in* the car"). The spatial sense of the dative (metaphorically extended) is, perhaps, intended, suggesting that one's heart is opened when one spends time "in the law."

If a Semitic origin is presumed for 1:1-9, then it is possible that ἐν τῷ νόμῳ parallels a Hebrew construction similar to *b. Ber.* 17a:

תהיהפתח לבי <u>בתורתך</u> ובמעוותיך תרדוף נפשי

"May you open my heart <u>in your law</u>, and may my soul pursue your commandments."

H-R indicates that the ‭ב‬-preposition is commonly translated by ἐν.

αὐτοῦ. Genitive of source, qualifying τῷ νόμῳ and τοῖς προστάγμασιν.

ἐν τοῖς προστάγμασιν. Because πρόσταγμα is a standard term for "command" or "law" in Hellenistic Greek, the term "compares the commands of the Torah to those of Hellenistic kings" (D. Schwartz, 137). There are parallel uses of πρόσταγμα and νόμος both in reference to God's "laws" and "commands," including the variation between the singular (νόμος) and the plural (προστάγματα) in Exod 18:16, 20; Lev 19:37; 1 Macc 10:14; etc. In 2:2, πρόσταγμα refers to "the commandments of the Lord" (τῶν προσταγμάτων τοῦ κυρίου), which the people are to remember.

καί. The conjunction that links the verb ἐπακοῦσαι to ὁ θεός, the subject in 1:2.

εἰρήνην. Accusative direct object of ποιῆσαι.

ποιῆσαι. Aor act opt 3rd sg ποιέω. The collocation of ποιέω + εἰρήνη (Josh 9:15; 1 Macc 6:49, 58; 11:51; 13:37; 14:11; Isa 27:5; 45:7; Jer 40:6) means "establish peace" (BDAG, 839).

1:5 καὶ ἐπακοῦσαι ὑμῶν τῶν δεήσεων καὶ καταλλαγείη ὑμῖν καὶ μὴ ὑμᾶς ἐγκαταλίποι ἐν καιρῷ πονηρῷ.

καί. The conjunction that links the verb ἐπακοῦσαι to ὁ θεός, the subject in 1:2.

ἐπακοῦσαι. Aor act opt 3rd sg ἐπακούω. The implied subject of the verb is ὁ θεός from 1:2. On the use of the optative in 2 Maccabees, see 1:2 on ἀγαθοποιήσαι.

ὑμῶν. Subjective genitive, qualifying τῶν δεήσεων.

τῶν δεήσεων. Genitive complement of ἐπακούω. The verb (ἐπί-) ἀκούω often takes the genitive as its complement (e.g., Gen 17:20; 21:17).

καταλλαγείη. Aor pass opt 3rd sg καταλλάσσω. Porter (1994, 16–17, 61–62) observes that, prior to 2 Maccabees, the verb is rarely used to refer to reconciliation between humans and gods (cf. Sophocles, *Ajax* 744). In particular, Porter defines the use in 1:5 as when "[t]he subject effects reconciliation by giving up its own anger against another party" (1994, 17). Nicklas (2011, 1379) notes that, after 2 Maccabees, καταλλάσσω is found in soteriological contexts in the NT (e.g., 2 Cor 5:19; Rom 5:10) and early Christian literature (e.g., *1 Clem.* 48:1). Cf. uses in 5:20; 7:33; 8:29.

ὑμῖν. Dative of association. The passive form of καταλλάσσω often appears with the dative, denoting the person who is reconciled with the (implied) subject of the verb (cf. BDAG, 521.b.α).

μή. The basic distinction between οὐ and μή is that οὐ and its compounds allow a writer or speaker to reject the reality of an affirmation (objective negation). By contrast, μή and its compounds allow the writer or speaker to reject a possibility, wish, or hypothesis (subjective negation) (cf. Muraoka §83a; *CGCG* §56.2). Here, μή negates the optative ἐγκαταλίποι.

ὑμᾶς. Accusative direct object of ἐγκαταλίποι. The pronoun is fronted for emphasis (Muraoka §76ee).

ἐγκαταλίποι. Aor act opt 3rd sg ἐγκαταλείπω. The idea of God abandoning his people is found in 2 Chr 15:2; 24:20; Pss 21:2; 37:22; 70:11; Isa 49:14. Cf. 2 Macc 6:16: παιδεύων δὲ μετὰ συμφορᾶς οὐκ ἐγκαταλείπει τὸν ἑαυτοῦ λαόν ("while he disciplines us with calamities, he does not forsake his own people"). Ps 36:28: ὅτι κύριος ἀγαπᾷ κρίσιν καὶ οὐκ ἐγκαταλείψει τοὺς ὁσίους αὐτοῦ, εἰς τὸν αἰῶνα φυλαχθήσονται ("because the Lord loves justice and will not forsake his devout, they shall be kept safe forever") (cf. Pss 118:8; 139:9; Sir 23:1; 51:10).

ἐν καιρῷ πονηρῷ. Temporal. The preposition indicates the "point of time when someth[ing] occurs" (BDAG, 329).

1:6 καὶ νῦν ὧδέ ἐσμεν προσευχόμενοι περὶ ὑμῶν.

καὶ νῦν. A combination of the conjunction and adverb that serves as a logical marker, indicating a transition in the letter from "the general introduction to the practical part of the letter" (D. Schwartz, 139). See

2 John 5, which uses καὶ νῦν to mark a transition (cf. Acts 3:17; 13:11; O.Ber. 2.195; esp. 2 Macc 14:36; cf. *GE*, 1410).

ὧδέ. Adverb of place. The adverb has two accents, the circumflex and acute, because it is followed by an enclitic (ἐσμεν). When following a word with a circumflex on the penult, the enclitic surrenders its accent, and it appears as an additional acute accent on the preceding word (Smyth §183.c).

ἐσμεν προσευχόμενοι. Present periphrastic construction, taking the person, number, and mood from ἐσμεν; aspect, voice, and lexical form from προσευχόμενοι. Thus, the synthetic form would be: προσευχόμεθα, pres mid ind 1st pl. On motivations for periphrastic constructions, see comments in the Introduction. There are 59 uses of the equivalent form, προσευχόμεθα, attested in the *TLG*, suggesting that it has not been morphologically replaced (e.g., 2 Thess 1:11; Lysias, *Orat.* 51.5; Plutarch, *Mor.* 435b; 654c). Likewise, the syntactical and semantic explanations do not explain the use here. The periphrastic construction is probably motivated by pragmatic concerns, particularly the letter writer's attempt to convey high literary style. Moreover, Levinsohn (2016, 323) argues that copular imperfectives portray "iterative events, with the actor portrayed as performing the action from time to time during the period envisaged, rather than continuously."

ἐσμεν. Pres act ind 1st pl εἰμί.

προσευχόμενοι. Pres mid ptc nom masc pl προσεύχομαι (present periphrastic).

περὶ ὑμῶν. Advantage. The meaning of περί encroaches on ὑπέρ (Doran 2012, 28).

1:7 βασιλεύοντος Δημητρίου ἔτους ἑκατοστοῦ ἑξηκοστοῦ ἐνάτου ἡμεῖς οἱ Ἰουδαῖοι γεγράφαμεν ὑμῖν ἐν τῇ θλίψει καὶ ἐν τῇ ἀκμῇ τῇ ἐπελθούσῃ ἡμῖν ἐν τοῖς ἔτεσιν τούτοις ἀφ᾽ οὗ ἀπέστη Ἰάσων καὶ οἱ μετ᾽ αὐτοῦ ἀπὸ τῆς ἁγίας γῆς καὶ τῆς βασιλείας.

βασιλεύοντος. Pres act ptc gen masc sg βασιλεύω (genitive absolute, temporal). Fuller (151) notes that "[t]he function of the form of participle and noun/pronoun in the Genitive (without any other formal cause, such as a preposition) is to draw the reader's attention to certain information in a more detached way than other circumstantial participles. . . . The information in the [genitive absolute] acts as an essential frame in which to interpret the information of the main clause, or of an even larger discourse." In 1:7 the genitive absolute clause describes the circumstances (e.g., time within which) of the action of the main verb occurs. For additional nuances of the genitive absolute, see Smyth (§2070).

Δημητρίου. Genitive subject of the participle βασιλεύοντος.

ἔτους ἑκατοστοῦ ἑξηκοστοῦ ἐνάτου. Genitive of time (cf. Gen 11:10; 1 Macc 3:37; 2 Macc 11:21, 33, 38). "The genitive of a [noun phrase] may be used to indicate a period within which something takes place" (Muraoka §22h). The stated year "169" corresponds to 143 BCE, which would situate the letter during the reign of the Seleucid king Demetrius II (ca. 145–139 BCE). On dating issues, see Bar-Kochva (166–67). See Smyth (§347) on numerals.

ἡμεῖς. Nominative subject of γεγράφαμεν.

οἱ Ἰουδαῖοι. Substantized adjective in apposition to ἡμεῖς. On the issue of translating "Jews" rather than "Judeans," see 1:1 on Τοῖς ἀδελφοῖς τοῖς . . . Ἰουδαίοις.

γεγράφαμεν. Prf act ind 1st pl γράφω. Perhaps this is an epistolary perfect ("we *write* to you"), where "[t]he writer of a letter or book . . . may put himself in the position of the reader or beholder who views the action as past" (Smyth §1942). Alternatively, it may be translated simply as a perfect ("we *wrote* to you"). On the latter sense, Torrey (123) notes that the perfect verb refers to the letter itself.

ὑμῖν. Dative indirect object of γεγράφαμεν.

ἐν τῇ θλίψει καὶ ἐν τῇ ἀκμῇ τῇ ἐπελθούσῃ. D. Schwartz (140–41) suggests that these PPs are an allusion to Prov 1:27: ἔρχηται ὑμῖν θλῖψις καὶ πολιορκία ("affliction and siege came upon you").

ἐν τῇ θλίψει. Temporal.

ἐν τῇ ἀκμῇ τῇ ἐπελθούσῃ. Temporal. The word ἀκμή occurs six times in the LXX. It refers to a "point, edge; culminating point, prime, zenith" of something (*EDG*, 52). In several LXX uses it refers to the "highest point" of something: beauty (Esth 15:5, 7), age/maturity (4 Macc 18:9), tip of a weapon (2 Macc 12:22), [height of] hellenization (2 Macc 4:13). It can also be used to refer to a "climactic *or* opportune moment" (*GE*, 69), such as here in 1:7 (cf. Sophocles, *Phil.* 12; Euripides, *Herc. fur.* 532).

τῇ ἐπελθούσῃ. Aor act ptc dat fem sg ἐπέρχομαι (attributive).

ἡμῖν. Dative of disadvantage.

ἐν τοῖς ἔτεσιν τούτοις. Temporal.

ἀφ᾽ οὗ. Temporal (see BDAG, 105.2.b.γ; *GE*, 241.2.B.c). This is a fixed expression that denotes the point of time from which something begins (cf. 1:33; 12:40; 13:21).

ἀπέστη. Aor act ind 3rd sg ἀφίστημι. Although NETS and some scholars prefer to translate ἀφίστημι as "revolt" in 1:7 (cf. *GE*, 357; D. Schwartz, 141, translates as "revolt," presuming the Hebrew *Vorlage* סרר), when the verb is used in collocation with ἀπό + location (e.g., city) it indicates movement away from a location (Josh 8:15-16; 1 Esd

1:28; Sir 47:24; BDAG, 157.2). This suggests that "Jason and those with him *left* . . ." is the basic sense here (cf. Doran 2012, 30–31). Ἰάσων καὶ οἱ μετ᾽ αὐτοῦ. Compound nominative subject of ἀπέστη. On the use of a singular verb with compound subjects, McKay (18) notes that "[i]f one of the subjects is more important than the others a singular verb may be attached to it, especially when the verb precedes its subject" (cf. 1 Macc 2:14, 39, 45; 3:23, 42; 4:16; Thucydides, *Hist.* 4.38.2; Xenophon, *Anab.* 7.2.29).

οἱ. The nominative article functions as a nominalizer (cf. 5:27; 6:19; 12:28, 37, 45; 15:24), changing the following PP (μετ᾽ αὐτοῦ) into the second element of the compound nominative subject of ἀπέστη.

μετ᾽ αὐτοῦ. Association.

ἀπὸ τῆς ἁγίας γῆς καὶ τῆς βασιλείας. Separation ("*away from* the holy land and the kingdom"). The PP is better taken as modifying the verb ἀπέστη ("they left . . . from the holy land and the kingdom") than οἱ μετ᾽ αὐτοῦ ("those with him from the holy land and the kingdom").

τῆς ἁγίας γῆς. Elsewhere 2 Maccabees focuses upon the holy *city* (cf. 1:12; 3:1; 9:14; 15:14) rather than the land. "Holy land" can have a range of meanings (cf. Zech 2:16; Wis 12:3; LAB 19:10), but it probably refers to the same thing as "the kingdom" that follows. For brief discussion on "holy land" by diaspora Jews, see Barclay (421–22).

τῆς βασιλείας. The identity of "kingdom" is somewhat ambiguous. Following the discussion of ἀφίστημι + ἀπό above, it is likely that the kingdom refers to the Seleucid kingdom (cf. Doran 2012, 31). This understanding is further reinforced by the referencing to the "reign of Demetrius" (βασιλεύοντος Δημητρίου) earlier in 1:7.

1:8 καὶ ἐνεπύρισαν τὸν πυλῶνα καὶ ἐξέχεαν αἷμα ἀθῶον· καὶ ἐδεήθημεν τοῦ κυρίου καὶ εἰσηκούσθημεν καὶ προσηνέγκαμεν θυσίαν καὶ σεμίδαλιν καὶ ἐξήψαμεν τοὺς λύχνους καὶ προεθήκαμεν τοὺς ἄρτους.

ἐνεπύρισαν. Aor act ind 3rd pl ἐμπυρίζω. *GE* (678) suggests the gloss "to set fire to."

τὸν πυλῶνα. Accusative direct object of ἐνεπύρισαν. It is not certain what gate of the Jerusalem temple is intended by this term. For descriptions of the temple gates, see Josephus (*J.W.* 5.198-206; *Ant.* 15.410-20).

ἐξέχεαν. Aor act ind 3rd pl ἐκχέω.

αἷμα ἀθῶον. Accusative direct object of ἐξέχεαν. The adjective ἀθῶον is attributive.

ἐδεήθημεν. Aor mid ind 1st pl δέομαι. On θη- middle morphology, see 1:2 on μνησθείη.

τοῦ κυρίου. Genitive of person with the verb ἐδεήθημεν (GELS, 143; BDAG, 218.b). Cf. 1 Esd 8:53; Esth 13:8; 14:1; Jdt 12:8; 3 Macc 1:16; 5:25; etc.

εἰσηκούσθημεν. Aor pass ind 1st pl εἰσακούω.

προσηνέγκαμεν. Aor act ind 1st pl προσφέρω.

θυσίαν καὶ σεμίδαλιν. Accusative direct objects of προσηνέγκαμεν. The Göttingen edition reads θυσίας (plural) rather than θυσίαν (singular), departing from MSS A' V 19 311 La^VBM (Sy III). The singular is probably modeled off of biblical language (e.g., Isa 19:21; Jer 17:26; Ps 40:7): זבח ומנחה ("*sacrifice* and burnt offering") (cf. Torrey, 142; D. Schwartz, 142). In either case, the point of the passage is that ritual sacrifices have begun again.

ἐξήψαμεν. Aor act ind 1st pl ἐξάπτω. As with the basic form ἅπτω, the compound form ἐξάπτω can have the sense "to light a fire, set fire" depending on its direct object (GE, 715). For contexts of lighting lamps or fires, see Exod 30:8; Num 8:3; Judg 15:5; 1 Macc 4:50; Sir 32:16; Ezek 21:3.

τοὺς λύχνους. Accusative direct object of ἐξήψαμεν.

προεθήκαμεν. Aor act ind 1st pl προτίθημι.

τοὺς ἄρτους. Accusative direct object of προεθήκαμεν.

1:9 καὶ νῦν ἵνα ἄγητε τὰς ἡμέρας τῆς σκηνοπηγίας τοῦ Χασελευ μηνός. ἔτους ἑκατοστοῦ ὀγδοηκοστοῦ καὶ ὀγδόου.

The Göttingen edition and R-H differ in versification. Although I follow R-H here, I note that Göttingen begins 1:10 with ἔτους ἑκατοστοῦ ὀγδοηκοστοῦ καὶ ὀγδόου ("In the one hundred eighty-eighth year").

καὶ νῦν. A combination of the conjunction and adverb that serves as a logical marker, indicating a transition to the final request of the letter. See comments in 1:6; 14:36; 15:23. M. Miller (212–13) notes that this "signals to the audience that the letter is coming to a close and a decision needs to be made." Doran (2012, 33) argues that καὶ νῦν is "best understood here not in terms of a transitional formula . . . but rather, as used frequently in the Hebrew Scriptures, to introduce an imperative." Doran is correct that καὶ νῦν is a common rendering of עתה + [ו], and this is often followed by an imperative. The standard Hebrew lexicons support the idea that עתה is used "often introducing a new subject or section" (HALOT 2:902.3.a) or "introducing a command or suggesting or wish" (DCH 6:634.8). Assuming a Semitic *Vorlage* for 1:1-9, the use of καὶ νῦν fits this function well.

ἵνα. Introduces a content clause, which may serve as the subject of an implied verb: παρακαλοῦμεν: "*we urge you* . . . that (ἵνα)" (cf. Muraoka §66b). It is possible that παρακαλέω was elided because its function as a transitional formula was required due to the use of καὶ νῦν. More preferably, ἵνα may be used with the subjunctive as a periphrasis for the imperative (BDAG, 477.2.g; Wallace, 476–77; BDF §387). Although an independent use of ἵνα is rare, this usage is to be expected following the transition marked by καὶ νῦν. GE (977) notes that ἵνα appears sometimes in the main (rather than subordinate) clause (cf. Tob 8:12; Arrianus, *Epict. diss.* 4.1.41). MHT (3:95) argue that imperatival ἵνα is a Semitism, citing several LXX examples (e.g., Gen 18:21; 44:34; Num 11:15; Deut 5:14; Josh 22:24; etc.) and noting the "secular poverty of examples." However, Cadoux (165–73) discusses some examples from LSJ (e.g., P.Cair.Zen. 240.12; PSI 4.412.1), suggesting it is an acceptable though rare Greek construction attested as early as the third century BC.

An alternative construal of the grammar, although far less compelling given the presence of καὶ νῦν in 1:9, is to connect ἵνα with γεγράφαμεν in 1:7: "we wrote to you . . . in order that." On this reading, much of 1:7-8 would be parenthetical and ἵνα would denote the purpose for writing.

ἄγητε. Pres act subj 2nd pl ἄγω (imperatival). Although rare, the injunctive value of the subjunctive is found also in Judg 9:15; Dan 12:10; Tob 8:12 (cf. Muraoka §29ba.ii). Here the verb means something like "to celebrate" because it is paired with a festival (cf. 1:18; 10:6; 15:3; 1 Esd 1:17; 5:50; 7:14; Esth 16:22). See GE (25.1.g) for the meaning of "celebrate . . . [a festival]." The imperfective aspect of the verb suggests that a habitual practice is being commended.

τὰς ἡμέρας τῆς σκηνοπηγίας. Literally, "The days of tent-making" = "[the Festival of] Tabernacles." This description differs from the standard combination of ἑορτή + σκηνοπηγία: "Feast of Tabernacles" (cf. Deut 16:16; cf. Deut 31:10; 1 Esd 5:50; Zech 14:16, 18, 19). D. Schwartz (9) observes that Tabernacles and Hanukkah are linked in 1:9 and 1:18. Moreover, 10:6 highlights that Hanukkah was celebrated by "remembering . . . the Feast of Booths" (μνημονεύοντες . . . τὴν τῶν σκηνῶν ἑορτήν). This may explain why the text refers to this holiday during the month of Chislev (December) even though Tabernacles is celebrated in September–October (see Klauck, 263–64). Other Jewish authors refer to Tabernacles with other titles: e.g., "Lights" (Josephus, *Ant.* 12.325) and "Renewal" (John 10:22).

The best explanation for why the opening letter refers to "Tabernacles" rather than "Hanukkah" is because at the time of writing, Hanukkah did not have its own, distinct name. This led the author(s) of this letter to refer to a festival that resembled it most closely (cf. Regev, 4). In particular, VanderKam (1987, 32) notes the following similarities: an eight-day period, rejoicing, and the way of life forced upon participants in the festival.

τὰς ἡμέρας. Accusative direct object of ἄγητε.

τῆς σκηνοπηγίας. Genitive of apposition, qualifying τὰς ἡμέρας.

τοῦ Χασελευ μηνός. Genitive of time, qualifying τὰς ἡμέρας τῆς σκηνοπηγίας. According to Zech 7:1 and 1 Macc 4:52, Chislev is the ninth month in the Jewish calendar.

ἔτους ἑκατοστοῦ ὀγδοηκοστοῦ καὶ ὀγδόου. Genitive of time. The number "188" corresponds to 124 BCE (Shaw 2015, 276). There is a significant variation unit in the Göttingen edition, which lists several iterations of the number "188," but also the number "148": ἑκατοστοῦ τεσσαρακοστοῦ καὶ ὀγδόου (62 65; *169* La^X; *138* La^B; *179* La^M; *178* La^P). Orthographically, the numbers are similar when written as abbreviations: ΡΠΔ ("188") and ΡΜΔ ("148"). This similarity may be cause of the variation units in the textual tradition (cf. D. Schwartz, 143–44). Because 188 is less important than 148 (the year of the temple's rededication), it is the *lectio difficilior* (Doran 2012, 33) and should probably be adopted. See the balanced discussion of this issue in *THB* (§10.2.1.1.2).

There is also the oddity that the letter that comprises 1:1-9 contains different dates in 1:7 and 1:9. As D. Schwartz (521–22) notes, this problem has generally been resolved either (1) by positing that 1:1-9 is a composite of two original letters; (2) the dating in 1:9 (1:10 in Göttingen) belongs with what follows (i.e., 1:10–2:18). But, Goldstein (153) plausibly suggests that "188" refers to the date of the letter, not the date of the festival (cf. Doran 2012, 33). For Greek numerals, see Smyth (§347).

2 Maccabees 1:10-17

[10]Those in Jerusalem and in Judea and the senate and Judas, to Aristobulus—teacher of King Ptolemy, who is of the family of the anointed priests—and to the Jews in Egypt, greetings and good health. [11]Because we have been saved by God from grave dangers, we give thanks to him greatly as if he was drawing up in battle-order against the king, [12]for he drove out those who drew up in battle-order in the holy city. [13]When the leader and his seemingly invincible army reached Persia, they were cut to pieces in the temple of Nanea when the priests of the goddess Nanea used a deception. [14]For, as if for the purpose of marrying her, both Antiochus and the friends with him came to the place in order to take its many treasures for a pledge of a dowry. [15]And when the priests [of the temple] of Nanea had set out these things and that man entered with a few men inside the wall of the sacred precinct, [the priests] closed the temple, when Antiochus had entered [it]. [16]After opening a secret door in the ceiling, throwing stones, they struck down the leader, and

after cutting off the limbs and removing his head, they threw [them] to those outside. [17]Blessed in every way be our God, who delivered up those who have behaved impiously.

This second letter (1:10–2:18) includes standard epistolary features: letter opening (1:10), an extensive proem (1:11-17), letter body (1:18b–2:15), and letter closing (2:16-18). Like the first letter (1:1-9), this letter is also designed to encourage diaspora Jews to remain connected to Jerusalem, particularly through the celebration of festivals. The letter purports to be from "Judas," presumably Judas Maccabeus (1:10), following the death of Antiochus Epiphanes (1:13-17).

The authenticity of this letter as well as its composition are much debated. Goldstein (157–59) discusses the issues that complicate dating the letter to the historical period it purports to represent. A succinct discussion of the various theories about the composition of the second letter is found in Shaw (2015, 276–77) or Parker (388). To summarize the key issue, the account of Antiochus Epiphanes' death in 1:11-17 contradicts the account found in 9:1-17. In 1:11-17 Antiochus is attacked and "cut to pieces" by priests after entering a Persian temple, but in 9:1-17 Antiochus dies from a combination of factors: Israel's God inflicts Antiochus with an "invisible blow" (9:5), Antiochus falls from his chariot (9:7), and his body begins to deteriorate (9:9-12). This difference has contributed to the debate about the unity of the 2 Maccabees. Some defend the unity of the work, but most scholars posit that a later redactor is responsible for adding 1:10–2:18. See the Introduction for additional discussion of the literary integrity of 2 Maccabees.

Whatever one decides on these critical issues, it seems clear that the purpose of the second letter is "to illustrate the continuity between the first and the second temple" (Lange, 165), in particular, legitimizing the Hasmonean temple. This is accomplished through the retelling of various legends about the temple sacrifices and sacred fire. Specifically, Nehemiah (1:18-36), Jeremiah (2:1-8), and Solomon (2:9-12) each emerge within the story in relationship to fire from Israel's first temple.

1:10 Οἱ ἐν Ἱεροσολύμοις καὶ οἱ ἐν τῇ Ἰουδαίᾳ καὶ ἡ γερουσία καὶ Ἰουδας Ἀριστοβούλῳ διδασκάλῳ Πτολεμαίου τοῦ βασιλέως, ὄντι δὲ ἀπὸ τοῦ τῶν χριστῶν ἱερέων γένους, καὶ τοῖς ἐν Αἰγύπτῳ Ἰουδαίοις χαίρειν καὶ ὑγιαίνειν.

See comments in 1:9 on location of ἔτους ἑκατοστοῦ ὀγδοηκοστοῦ καὶ ὀγδόου ("In the one hundred eighty-eighth year") in the Göttingen and R-H editions.

Οἱ . . . οἱ. Nominative absolutes. The articles function as nominalizers of the PPs (ἐν Ἱεροσολύμοις and ἐν τῇ Ἰουδαίᾳ). Wallace (236) notes this is a common use of the article.

ἐν Ἱεροσολύμοις. Locative. See 1:1 on ἐν Ἱεροσολύμοις.

ἐν τῇ Ἰουδαίᾳ. Locative.

ἡ γερουσία καὶ Ἰουδας. Nominative absolutes. It must be decided whether ἡ γερουσία refers here to a formalized group (e.g., "the senate") or is a product of translation, perhaps from זקנים ("elders"). Given the source critical issues related to this prefixed letter (1:10–2:18), it is difficult to decide. Tentatively, I prefer "senate" (cf. 4:44; 11:27), even if this is more a "reflection of Greek perceptions and not of actual Judean institutions" (Sharon, 284). Cf. γερουσία in 1 Macc 12:6 and Josephus, *Ant.* 12.138-44.

Ἀριστοβούλῳ. Dative of recipient. On the possible identity of Aristobulus as "a Jewish scholar interpreting the wisdom of the Torah to Gentiles," see the brief discussion in Doran (2012, 43).

διδασκάλῳ. Dative in apposition to Ἀριστοβούλῳ.

Πτολεμαίου τοῦ βασιλέως. Objective genitive, qualifying διδασκάλῳ.

ὄντι. Pres act ptc dat masc sg εἰμί (attributive, modifying Ἀριστοβούλῳ). However, Muraoka (§31df) notes that a circumstantial clause in an oblique case will take a participle in the oblique case, expressing agreement: "to Aristobulus, teacher of King Ptolemy, *as he is* of the family of the anointed priests."

δὲ. Development, moving beyond the description of Aristobulus as a teacher and noting the connection to the priests. The conjunction δέ is used 462 times in 2 Maccabees, predominantly in the main history (438 out of 462 uses appear in 2:19–15:39) and is always postpositive. As Runge (31) argues, δέ "represents the writer's choice to explicitly signal that what follows is a new, distinct development in the story or argument, based on how the writer conceived it." In practice, this often means a switch of grammatical subject or a logical development in the narrative. On the role of δέ in Greek narratives, see also Black (142–78).

ἀπὸ τοῦ . . . γένους. Source.

τῶν χριστῶν ἱερέων. Partitive genitive, qualifying τοῦ . . . γένους. On the language of "anointed priests," see Lev 4:5, 16; 6:15.

τοῖς . . . Ιουδαίοις. Dative of recipient. On the issue of translating "Jews" rather than "Judeans," see 1:1 on Τοῖς ἀδελφοῖς τοῖς . . . Ιουδαίοις.

ἐν Αἰγύπτῳ. Locative.

χαίρειν. Pres act inf χαίρω. See 1:1 on χαίρειν.

ὑγιαίνειν. Pres act inf ὑγιαίνω.

1:11 ἐκ μεγάλων κινδύνων ὑπὸ τοῦ θεοῦ σεσωσμένοι μεγάλως εὐχαριστοῦμεν αὐτῷ ὡς ἂν πρὸς βασιλέα παρατασσόμενοι·

ἐκ μεγάλων κινδύνων. Separation.

ὑπὸ τοῦ θεοῦ. Agency.

σεσωσμένοι. Prf pass ptc nom masc pl σώζω (causal). The perfect (stative verbal aspect) presents the state in which the Jews find themselves presently.

μεγάλως. Adverb of manner. Technically the adverb could modify σεσωσμένοι ("because we have been *greatly* saved"), but it is better taken to modify εὐχαριστοῦμεν ("we give thanks *greatly*"). Elsewhere in 2 Maccabees, μεγάλως typically precedes the word it modifies (3:21; 10:38; 15:27; but see 2:8 where it follows) and it is typical to see an adverb modify εὐχαριστέω to express frequency or manner.

εὐχαριστοῦμεν. Pres act ind 1st pl εὐχαριστέω. Although εὐχαριστέω is rare in the LXX (6 times), it is a standard epistolary feature in Hellenistic letters (cf. White, 66). See also Rom 1:8; 1 Cor 1:4; Phil 1:3; 1 Thess 1:2; Phlm 4; etc.

αὐτῷ. Dative complement of εὐχαριστοῦμεν. The antecedent is τοῦ θεοῦ.

ὡς ἄν. Cause. In accordance with other Hellenistic authors (e.g., Polybius), here ὡς ἄν denotes the reason or cause for thanksgiving (cf. *GE*, 2427.H.A).

πρὸς βασιλέα. Opposition. With the verb παρατασσόμενοι, the PP has the sense of "against the king" (BDAG, 874.3.d.α). The noun lacks the article, which was typical when referring to kings in some classical literature (cf. Doran 2012, 39).

παρατασσόμενοι. Pres mid ptc nom masc pl παρατάσσω (causal). Used with ὡς ἄν, the participle has a causal function. It is difficult to understand how this verb describing the people being "battle-ready" explains why they are to "give thanks" to God. Nicklas (2011, 1379) notes that some scholars (e.g., Abel, 290; Habicht, 202) propose reading παρατασσομένῳ (singular) here to improve the sense: "as if *he* was drawing up in battle-order." Orthographically, this would involve only a small shift from OI to Ω at the end of the word and is further supported by the Syriac tradition of 2 Maccabees: "we very greatly give thanks to God who helped us and delivered us from all the afflictions which came upon us." This explanation is argued convincingly by Doran (2012, 39), who further notes the connection between 1:11 and 1:12 and God's role in throwing out those who are "battle-ready" against the holy city.

1:12 αὐτὸς γὰρ ἐξέβρασεν τοὺς παραταξαμένους ἐν τῇ ἁγίᾳ πόλει.

αὐτὸς. Nominative subject of ἐξέβρασεν. The referent of αὐτός is difficult to discern. Antiochus (cf. 1:14) is a possible candidate, but D. Schwartz (146–47) argues that it may refer to Jason. This reading has the added benefit of aligning the second letter's (1:10–2:18) villain with the first letter's (1:1-9) villain.

γὰρ. Causal conjunction, supplying the reason for giving thanks in 1:11. Runge (52) notes that γάρ "signals close continuity with what precedes . . . [but] differs from καί by adding the semantic constraint of strengthening/support." That is, γάρ does not serve to advance the argument, but "introduces explanatory material that strengthens or supports what precedes. This may consist of a single clause, or it may be a longer digression. Although the strengthening material is important to the discourse, it does not advance the argument or story" (54).

ἐξέβρασεν. Aor act ind 3rd sg ἐκβράζω.

τοὺς παραταξαμένους. Aor mid ptc acc masc pl παρατάσσω (substantival). Direct object of ἐξέβρασεν.

ἐν τῇ ἁγίᾳ πόλει. Locative. Although many commentators understand the collocation of παρατάσσω + ἐν with the meaning "against" (cf. Abel, 291; Goldstein, 154) and this is a possible sense (cf. Zech 14:3: παρατάξεται ἐν τοῖς ἔθνεσιν ἐκείνοις, ["the Lord will draw up in battle *against* those nations"]), the locative sense of ἐν ("in") is also common (cf. Judg 8:1; 9:45; 11:9, 12; 12:1, 3; 20:33; Neh 4:2).

1:13 εἰς τὴν Περσίδα γενόμενος γὰρ ὁ ἡγεμὼν καὶ ἡ περὶ αὐτὸν ἀνυπόστατος δοκοῦσα εἶναι δύναμις κατεκόπησαν ἐν τῷ τῆς Ναναίας ἱερῷ, παραλογισμῷ χρησαμένων τῶν περὶ τὴν Ναναίαν ἱερέων.

εἰς τὴν Περσίδα. Locative. 2 Maccabees uses two words to refer to "Persia": Περσίς (1:13, 20; 9:1, 21), Περσική (1:19). The distinction between these terms should probably not be pressed too far. Goldstein (170) notes that "Jews writing in the late second century referred to any part of the territory then controlled by the Parthian empire as [Περσίς]."

γενόμενος. Aor mid ptc nom masc sg γίνομαι (temporal). When used with an adverbial predicate, "to make a change of location in space" (BDAG, 198.6.a; cf. *GE*, 429).

γὰρ. Introduces an explanation of the details from 1:12. *Pace* D. Schwartz (147), who believes that the repetition of γάρ (cf. 1:12) indicates the "secondary nature of this passage." See 1:12 on γάρ.

ὁ ἡγεμὼν καὶ ἡ περὶ αὐτόν. Compound nominative subject of κατεκόπησαν.

ὁ ἡγεμών. Refers to a "leader, . . . commander" (GE, 901), specifically to Antiochus.

ἡ. The article functions as a nominalizer, changing the PP (περὶ αὐτόν) into the second element of the compound nominative subject of κατεκόπησαν. The article is feminine, most likely, because the elided word στρατιά ("army") is feminine (cf. 8:24; 12:20; 15:20).

περὶ αὐτόν. Association. See BDAG (798.2.δ): "of persons who are standing, sitting, working or staying close to someone . . . [t]he central person in the group can be included." Cf. 1:13; 1:33; 1:36; 4:41; 8:16, 30, 32; 9:3; 10:35; 11:6; 12:5, 11, 14, 19, 20, 24, 37, 39; 13:1, 15, 22; 14:1, 18, 30; 15:1, 6, 13, 18.

ἀνυπόστατος . . . δύναμις. Predicate of εἶναι. GELS (61) glosses ἀνυπόστατος as "armed forces" (cf. 8:5), but the sense of ἀνυπόστατος is probably "unstoppable" or "invincible" (GE, 214).

δοκοῦσα. Pres act ptc nom fem sg δοκέω (adjectival). Agrees with the article in the phrase ἡ περὶ αὐτόν.

εἶναι. Pres act inf εἰμί (indirect discourse with a verb of cognition).

κατεκόπησαν. Aor pass ind 3rd pl κατακόπτω. Although in a military context, the verb often means "to be routed" (GE, 1057; cf. NETS), when used with "stones" (see 1:16; cf. Mark 5:5) it has the sense of "cut to pieces" (GELS, 373; cf. Mic 1:7; 4:3; Isa 2:4; 27:9).

ἐν τῷ . . . ἱερῷ. Locative.

τῆς Ναναίας. Possessive genitive, qualifying τῷ . . . ἱερῷ.

παραλογισμῷ. Dative complement to χρησαμένων.

χρησαμένων. Aor mid ptc gen masc pl χράομαι (genitive absolute, temporal). Less typically, the genitive absolute follows the main verb (cf. CGCG §60.32). On the meaning of the verb, see GE (2371): "to use" + dative. On the genitive absolute, see 1:7 on βασιλεύοντος.

τῶν . . . ἱερέων. Genitive subject of the participle χρησαμένων.

περὶ τὴν Ναναίαν. Association. GELS (546) notes that περί occurs in the place of the genitive.

1:14 ὡς γὰρ συνοικήσων αὐτῇ παρεγένετο εἰς τὸν τόπον ὅ τε Ἀντίοχος καὶ οἱ σὺν αὐτῷ φίλοι χάριν τοῦ λαβεῖν τὰ χρήματα πλείονα εἰς φερνῆς λόγον.

ὡς. Purpose/intention. Used with a future participle (ἀναψύξοντα) to mark a purpose (GELS, 749.12). Sim (82) notes that "[w]hen this particle occurs with a participle it alerts the reader to interpret the following presentation as a potential situation, perhaps even one being presented as true by others but without being endorsed as such by the author."

γὰρ. Provides an explanation of the preceding statement in 1:13 about the massacre of the leader (ὁ ἡγεμών), Antiochus. See 1:12 on γάρ.

συνοικήσων. Fut act ptc nom masc sg συνοικέω (purpose). See comments on ὡς. On the meaning of the verb, see *GE* (2048): "to dwell together, live together" = "to marry," used with the dative (cf. *GELS*, 658).

αὐτῇ. Dative complement of συνοικήσων. Refers to the goddess Nanea (cf. 1:13).

παρεγένετο. Aor mid ind 3rd sg παραγίνομαι. On the use of a singular verb with compound subjects (ὁ . . . Ἀντίοχος καὶ οἱ σὺν αὐτῷ φίλοι), see 1:7 on ἀπέστη. The verb is followed by εἰς + accusative of place (cf. BDAG, 760.1).

εἰς τὸν τόπον. Locative.

ὅ τε Ἀντίοχος καὶ οἱ σὺν αὐτῷ φίλοι. Compound nominative subject of παρεγένετο.

τε . . . καὶ. Correlative construction. τε . . . καί connects words more closely than καί alone: "*both* Antiochus *and* those with him" (BDF §444.2; BDAG, 933.2.c).

ὅ . . . Ἀντίοχος. Nominative subject of παρεγένετο. The article ὁ appears here with the accent because τέ, an enclitic particle, loses its accent to the preceding word (Smyth §181–82).

οἱ . . . φίλοι. Nominative subject of παρεγένετο. The word φίλος was used "as a title in the court of the Ptolemies" (*GE*, 2285). This sense for φίλος becomes clear in 2 Maccabees as "friends" are entrusted with public affairs (7:24), appointed for military service (8:9), and executing judgment at trials (10:13). For further discussion of this sense of φίλοι, especially in light of numismatic evidence, see Theophilos (2018, 38–43), who concludes that: "the ΦΙΛ- lexeme . . . includes not merely an emotional or personal dimension of friendship, but also the dimension of obligation."

σὺν αὐτῷ. Association.

χάριν. Purpose. Accusative of χάρις, used as a preposition with the infinitive (*GELS*, 729; cf. 1 Macc 11:11; 13:4; Sir 19:25; Dan 2:13). *GELS* (729), "with final force . . . 'in order to secure its treasures.'"

τοῦ λαβεῖν. Aor act inf λαμβάνω (purpose). The article indicates the case of the infinitive and marks the infinitive as the object of the preposition (Burk, 83). It is well-documented that Antiochus Epiphanes looted from temples (e.g., Polybius, *Hist.* 30.26.9), so it is not surprising that this plan to "take its many treasures" was anticipated by the priests of Nanea (D. Schwartz, 149).

τὰ χρήματα πλείονα. Accusative direct object of λαβεῖν. The comparative adjective from πολύς (*GELS*, 574), used elatively ("very much, many"). On the morphology, see Thackery (81–82). On the meaning of χρήματα, see 3:6 on χρημάτων ἀμυθήτων.

εἰς... λόγον. Purpose. λόγος refers to "an account which may be credited or debited" (*GELS*, 434).

φερνῆς. Genitive of apposition, explaining λόγον. Because the immediate context refers to marriage (συνοικήσων αὐτῇ), λόγος is further defined as a "dowry."

1:15 καὶ προθέντων αὐτὰ τῶν ἱερέων τοῦ Ναναίου κἀκείνου προσελθόντος μετ᾽ ὀλίγων εἰς τὸν περίβολον τοῦ τεμένους, συγκλείσαντες τὸ ἱερόν, ὡς εἰσῆλθεν Ἀντίοχος.

προθέντων. Aor act ptc gen masc pl προτίθημι (genitive absolute, temporal). On the genitive absolute, see 1:7 on βασιλεύοντος.

αὐτὰ. Accusative direct object of προθέντων. Agrees with τὰ χρήματα in 1:14.

τῶν ἱερέων. Genitive subject of the participle προθέντων. Both in Jewish and so-called pagan cults, τὸ ἱερόν (lit. "sacred") was a designation for sacred space, especially after the Maccabean revolt (cf. Bickermann 2007, 484). Thus, as a substantive τὸ ἱερόν denotes "sacred place, sanctuary, temple" (*GE*, 968.C).

τοῦ Ναναίου. Possessive genitive.

κἀκείνου. Due to crasis: καί + ἐκεῖνος (*GELS*, 352; *GE*, 1009). The genitive demonstrative pronoun refers to Antiochus (cf. 1:14) and is the subject of προσελθόντος.

προσελθόντος. Aor act ptc gen masc sg προσέρχομαι (genitive absolute, temporal). On the genitive absolute, see 1:7 on βασιλεύοντος.

μετ᾽ ὀλίγων. Association.

εἰς τὸν περίβολον. Locative.

τοῦ τεμένους. Partitive genitive.

συγκλείσαντες. Aor act ptc nom masc pl συγκλείω (temporal).

τὸ ἱερόν. Accusative direct object of συγκλείσαντες.

ὡς. Temporal conjunction, used with the aorist to communicate a temporal idea: "when, after" (BDAG, 1105.8.a).

εἰσῆλθεν. Aor act ind 3rd sg εἰσέρχομαι.

Ἀντίοχος. Nominative subject of εἰσῆλθεν.

1:16 ἀνοίξαντες τὴν τοῦ φατνώματος κρυπτὴν θύραν βάλλοντες πέτρους συνεκεραύνωσαν τὸν ἡγεμόνα καὶ μέλη ποιήσαντες καὶ τὰς κεφαλὰς ἀφελόντες τοῖς ἔξω παρέρριψαν.

ἀνοίξαντες. Aor act ptc nom masc pl ἀνοίγω (temporal).

τὴν . . . κρυπτήν θύραν. Accusative direct object of ἀνοίξαντες.

τοῦ φατνώματος. Genitive of place/location (Muraoka §22i). Refers to a "coffered ceiling" (*GE*, 2259). On ceiling architecture in Greek buildings, see Coulton (148).

βάλλοντες. Pres act ptc nom masc pl βάλλω (means). The participle explains the means by which the action is completed: "*throwing* stones, they struck down the leader."

πέτρους. Accusative direct object of βάλλοντες.

συνεκεραύνωσαν. Aor act ind 3rd pl συγκεραυνόω.

τὸν ἡγεμόνα. Accusative direct object of συνεκεραύνωσαν. See 1:13 on ὁ ἡγεμών.

μέλη. Accusative direct object of ποιήσαντες.

ποιήσαντες. Aor act ptc nom masc pl ποιέω (temporal). The collocation of ποιέω + μέλος means "to cut a body into pieces" (see *GE*, 1307).

τὰς κεφαλὰς. Accusative direct object of ἀφελόντες. Katz (1960, 12) plausibly suggests that the plural is "a thoughtless adaptaion to μέλη." While it is reasonable to think that Antiochus' friends were with him (1:14-15), the singular τὸν ἡγεμόνα requires the reading τὴν κεφαλήν (MS 55 La^P Sy). As is typical in Greek (cf. *CGCG* §28.4; Wallace, 215), because the possessor of the body part is obvious in context, only the Greek article is used to convey this relationship: τὴν κεφαλήν = "*his* head."

ἀφελόντες. Aor act ptc nom masc pl ἀφαιρέω (temporal). On the meaning of the verb, see BDAG (154.1): "to detach someth[ing] by force."

τοῖς ἔξω. The article functions as a nominalizer, changing the adverb ἔξω into the dative complement of παρέρριψαν.

παρέρριψαν. Aor act ind 3rd pl παραρρίπτω. On the meaning of the verb, see *GE* (1564): "to cast away."

1:17 κατὰ πάντα εὐλογητὸς ἡμῶν ὁ θεός, ὃς παρέδωκεν τοὺς ἀσεβήσαντας.

κατὰ πάντα. Reference.

εὐλογητὸς. Predicate adjective. Alternatively, εὐλογητός may be understood as a verbal adjective with ὁ θεός taken as a predicate nominative after an implied copula: "*blessed be* our God" (cf. BDF §412.2; Wallace, 40).

ἡμῶν. Genitive of subordination.

ὁ θεός. Nominative subject of an implied verb.

ὅς. Nominative subject of παρέδωκεν. Its antecedent is ὁ θεός.

παρέδωκεν. Aor act ind 3rd sg παραδίδωμι. The Göttingen edition reads the simple form ἔδωκε(ν), which is less forceful than παραδίδωμι ("to consign [to justice], hand over," *GE*, 1546.1.B). Nevertheless, δίδωμι can be used with the sense of "to give as booty, leave to the mercy of" (*GE*, 521). As Doran (2012, 39) notes, Greek manuscripts of the Bible sometimes show variation between these two verbs, demonstrating that they can be similar in meaning, depending on context.

τοὺς ἀσεβήσαντας. Aor act ptc acc masc pl ἀσεβέω (substantival). Direct object of παρέδωκεν.

2 Maccabees 1:18-23

[18]Because we are intending to celebrate the Purification of the temple on the twenty-fifth of Chislev, we thought it necessary to notify you in order that you yourselves also may celebrate [the days] of Tabernacles and of the fire, when Nehemiah, the one who built both the temple and the altar, offered sacrifices. [19]For when our fathers were being brought into Persia, the pious priests of that time took some of the fire of the altar and secretly hid [it] in a hollow that had the appearance of a waterless cistern, in which they kept [it] safe with the result that the place was unknown to all. [20]Now, after many years had passed, when it seemed right to God, Nehemiah, having been commissioned by the king of Persia, sent the descendants of the priests who had hidden [it] to the fire. When they reported to us that they had not found fire but thick water, he ordered them after drawing [it] up to bring [it]. [21]When the materials of the sacrifices were presented, Nehemiah ordered the priests to sprinkle with water both the wood and the things sitting upon it. [22]When this had been done and time had passed and when the sun shone out, even though it was clouded over earlier, a great fire was lit so that everyone marveled. [23]And the priests offered prayer while the sacrifice was being consumed—both the priests and everyone [prayed], with Jonathan leading and the rest responding, as [did] Nehemiah.

On the function of this part of the letter, see the brief comments following the translation of 1:10-17.

1:18 Μέλλοντες ἄγειν ἐν τῷ Χασελευ πέμπτῃ καὶ εἰκάδι τὸν καθαρισμὸν τοῦ ἱεροῦ δέον ἡγησάμεθα διασαφῆσαι ὑμῖν, ἵνα καὶ αὐτοὶ ἄγητε σκηνοπηγίας καὶ τοῦ πυρός, ὅτε Νεεμιας ὁ οἰκοδομήσας τό τε ἱερὸν καὶ τὸ θυσιαστήριον ἀνήνεγκεν θυσίας.

Although R-H links 1:18 with the preceding section by keeping the text of 1:18 in the same paragraph, the Göttingen edition is probably correct to begin a new paragraph here.

Μέλλοντες. Pres act ptc nom masc pl μέλλω (causal).

ἄγειν. Pres act inf ἄγω (complementary). Here the verb means something like "to celebrate" because it is paired with the Festival of Tabernacles. See 1:9 on ἄγητε for further comments on the verb and the verbal aspect of the present infinitive.

ἐν τῷ Χασελευ. Temporal. BDAG (329.10): "marker of a period of time, *in, while, when*." Although Chislev was indicated as τοῦ Χασελευ μηνός in 1:9, it is common without μήν ("month") in the LXX (1 Macc 14:27; Esth 9:15) and papyri (cf. Muraoka §5h; MHT 3:16–18).

πέμπτῃ καὶ εἰκάδι. Dative of time, indicating the time when the action of the main verb occurs (Wallace, 155). For Greek numerals, see Smyth (§347).

τὸν καθαρισμὸν. Accusative direct object of ἄγειν. Goldstein (171) notes that following ἄγω, this denotes "the proper name of a festival."

τοῦ ἱεροῦ. Objective genitive.

δέον. Pres act ptc acc neut sg δεῖ (substantival). Accusative subject of the infinitive διασαφῆσαι, used to express necessity. Muraoka (§94dd) notes that here "we find a bare δέον in lieu of δέον εἶναι."

ἡγησάμεθα. Aor mid ind 1st pl ἡγέομαι.

διασαφῆσαι. Aor act inf διασαφέω (indirect discourse). An assumption may be expressed with an infinitive clause (Muraoka §69ba). Further, Muraoka (§69g) notes this is an example of "an infinitive clause as the subject of an underlying nominal clause serving as the object."

ὑμῖν. Dative indirect object of διασαφῆσαι.

ἵνα. May indicate the content of the notification, but better indicates the purpose.

καὶ. Adverbial.

αὐτοὶ. Intensive adjective, agreeing with the second person plural subject implied in ἄγητε.

ἄγητε. Pres act subj 2nd pl ἄγω. Subjunctive with ἵνα.

σκηνοπηγίας καὶ τοῦ πυρός. The two uses of the genitive here have puzzled readers. The manuscript tradition of 2 Maccabees has the following variants: τὰς σκηνοπηγίας (MS 106), ὡς σκηνοπηγίας (MSS q *L*-62 58 Lat Syr Arm), and the Göttingen edition prints ὡς. Doran

(2012, 46) suggests that σκηνοπηγίας and τοῦ πυρός are in the genitive case because they are governed by διασαφῆσαι (understanding δία + genitive), but this is unlikely because the genitives appear within the subordinate ἵνα clause. It is best to consider this an example of brachylogy, specifically an example where "an object is frequently omitted when it can readily be supplied from the context" (Smyth §3018.k; cf. Muraoka §74). This suggests that τὰς ἡμέρας should be supplied in thought/ translation because it is implicit in the prior expression ἐν τῷ Χασελευ πέμπτῃ καὶ εἰκάδι ("twenty-fifth [day] of Chislev"). Thus, ἵνα καὶ αὐτοὶ ἄγητε αὐτὸν [τὰς ἡμέρας] σκηνοπηγίας καὶ τοῦ πυρός ("in order that you yourselves also celebrate [the days] of Tabernacles and of the fire"). For a parallel syntactical problem, see the Hebrew text of Esth 9:19 and 9:22, which also speaks of days of a festival elliptically. Goldstein (172) argues that this brachylogy "is a very strong indication that [2 Macc 1:10–2:18] was originally written in Hebrew." However, MHT (3:16-17) indicate that the ellipse of ἡμέρα is a common phenomenon in Greek, citing papyri from the third century BCE. Thus, it is possible that the construction both represents a Semitic *Vorlage* and that it represents idiomatic Greek.

ὅτε. Introduces a temporal clause, marking "a point of time that coincides with another point of time" (BDAG, 731.1).

Νεεμιας. Nominative subject of ἀνήνεγκεν. Readers familiar with the biblical narrative will expect Zerubbabel rather than Nehemiah to be mentioned here (cf. Ezra 2:1-2; 3:1-13; 6:14-17; Sir 49:11-13). This is an obvious historical anachronism, but one that can be explained in various ways. Some scholars, following the Babylonian Talmud, believe that Zerubabbel should be identified with Nehemiah: "Zerubbabel [was so called] because he was sown in Babylon. But [his real name was] Nehemiah the son of Hachaliah" (*b. Sanh.* 38a). Others argue that this is a generic chronological reference, where the entire Persian period is briefly summarized and Nehemiah's association with building in Jerusalem links him to this building project (cf. D. Schwartz, 151). Bergren (260–63) argues that the author(s) of this letter "wished to cultivate a direct comparison between Nehemiah and Judas Maccabee." This desire to forge a connection may explain why Nehemiah is portrayed carrying out building, dedication, and purification plans. See Bergren (249–70) for fuller discussion.

ὁ οἰκοδομήσας. Aor act ptc nom masc sg οἰκοδομέω (attributive, modifying Νεεμιας). Although R-H (following MSS A V), reads ὁ οἰκοδομήσας, the Göttingen edition lacks the article. The anarthrous construction could still function attributively. But the sense is altered if the participle is read adverbially, which would now suggest that rebuilding the temple and offering sacrifices happened concurrently (cf. Goldstein, 173). The repetition of *omicron* in ὁ οἰκοδομήσας may be an example of unintentional *haplography*. A few MSS (*L*⁻⁶² 311) read ᾠκοδόμησε(ν), which converts this into a parallel clause: "Nehemiah *built* . . . [and] offered sacrifices."

τε . . . καὶ. Correlative construction: "both . . . and." See 1:14 on τε . . . καί.

τό . . . ἱερὸν. Accusative direct object of οἰκοδομήσας.

τὸ θυσιαστήριον. Accusative direct object of οἰκοδομήσας.

ἀνήνεγκεν. Aor act ind 3rd sg ἀναφέρω. Due to suppletion, ἤνεγκα supplies the aorist forms of φέρω and compound-φέρω verb forms.

θυσίας. Accusative direct object of ἀνήνεγκεν.

1:19 καὶ γὰρ ὅτε εἰς τὴν Περσικὴν ἤγοντο ἡμῶν οἱ πατέρες, οἱ τότε εὐσεβεῖς ἱερεῖς λαβόντες ἀπὸ τοῦ πυρὸς τοῦ θυσιαστηρίου λαθραίως κατέκρυψαν ἐν κοιλώματι φρέατος τάξιν ἔχοντος ἄνυδρον, ἐν ᾧ κατησφαλίσαντο ὥστε πᾶσιν ἄγνωστον εἶναι τὸν τόπον.

καὶ γὰρ. Introduces an additional statement that "explains the preceding" (*GELS*, 125; cf. Denniston, 108; BDF §452.3; Mayser II 3.122–23).

ὅτε. Introduces a temporal clause.

εἰς τὴν Περσικὴν. Locative. See 1:13 on εἰς τὴν Περσίδα.

ἤγοντο. Impf pass ind 3rd pl ἄγω. The imperfect indicative (imperfective verbal aspect) describes the ongoing action of "being brought" into Persia.

ἡμῶν. Genitive of relationship.

οἱ πατέρες. Nominative subject of ἤγοντο.

οἱ . . . εὐσεβεῖς ἱερεῖς. Nominative subject of κατέκρυψαν.

τότε. Temporal adverb, modifying the nominative subject like an attributive adjective. It is possible that ὅτε . . . τότε form a correlative construction (cf. Shaw 2016, 407), but the placement of τότε suggests that it modifies οἱ.

λαβόντες. Aor act ptc nom masc pl λαμβάνω (attendant circumstance).

ἀπὸ τοῦ πυρὸς τοῦ θυσιαστηρίου. Verbs of "taking" often take a genitive object or a preposition with the genitive in place of an accusative direct object when what is taken is only part of the whole (cf. the partitive genitive; *GE*, 1209; Siebenthal §184e). Similar constructions with λαμβάνω are found in 4:6 (οὐ λημψόμενον τῆς ἀνοίας) and 12:35 (λαβόμενος τῆς χλαμύδος).

τοῦ θυσιαστηρίου. Genitive of source or, better, separation.

λαθραίως. Adverb of manner. It is possible that λαθραίως modifies either λαβόντες ("*secretly* taking . . .") or κατέκρυψαν ("*secretly* hid . . . ," cf. NETS). The latter is more likely because it would be difficult to take fire secretly from the temple.

κατέκρυψαν. Aor act ind 3rd pl κατακρύπτω.

ἐν κοιλώματι. Locative.

φρέατος τάξιν ἔχοντος ἄνυδρον. This expression and its meaning are the subject of much discussion. Hanhart's (1961, 30–31) text, printed in both R-H and the Göttingen edition, might be translated as follows: "[in the hollow] of a cistern having a waterless condition" (cf. D. Schwartz, 152; Doran 2012, 46). But even this translation is fraught (cf. Schaper, 229). At the center of the debate is the use of τάξις, which often appears in the following collocation: ἔχω + τάξις + genitive (of comparison/similarity) (cf. BDAG, 989.4). For example,

> Let. Aris. 69 κρηπῖδος ἔχουσα τάξιν
>
> having the appearance of a shoe
>
> 2 Macc 9:18 ἱκετηρίας τάξιν ἔχουσαν
>
> having the appearance/form of a supplication

This regular collocation led Wilhelm (16–17) to emend ἔχοντος ἄνυδρον to ἔχοντι ἀνύδρου, converting ἔχοντι into apposition with κοιλώματι and ἀνύδρου into apposition with φρέατος: "in a hollow that had the appearance of a waterless cistern." Taking into consideration the parallel construction in 9:18, this emendation makes good sense of the Greek text and is to be preferred (cf. Katz 1960, 12–13; Schaper, 228–29). Alternatively, Doran (2012, 46–47) admits that ἔχοντος is "less usual" and that the writer who produced it was "not completely sure how to use the word τάξις." In the textual discussion below, these different understandings of the clause are taken into consideration.

φρέατος. Genitive of apposition (i.e., "hollow *which is a well*") or, following Wilhelm's reconstructed text, genitive of comparison.

τάξιν. Accusative direct object of ἔχοντος.

ἔχοντος. Pres act ptc gen masc sg ἔχω (apposition, with φρέατος). Taking Wilhelm's emendation, ἔχοντι, the parsing would be: pres act ptc dat masc sg ἔχω (apposition, with κοιλώματι).

ἄνυδρον. Accusative in apposition to τάξιν or, following Wilhelm's reconstructed text, ἀνύδρου (genitive) is appositional with φρέατος.

ἐν ᾧ. Locative. The relative pronoun agrees with κοιλώματι φρέατος, both of which are neuter singular.

κατησφαλίσαντο. Aor mid ind 3rd pl κατασφαλίζομαι.

ὥστε. Result. The particle is built from ὡς + τέ ("and so") and is a consecutive conjunction. This could modify the preceding clause (ἐν ᾧ κατησφαλίσαντο), but it is better taken to modify κατέκρυψαν.

πᾶσιν. Dative indirect object of εἶναι.

ἄγνωστον. Predicate adjective preceding εἶναι, in agreement with τὸν τόπον.

εἶναι. Pres act inf εἰμί. Used with ὥστε to indicate a consequence or result.

τὸν τόπον. Accusative subject of the infinitive εἶναι.

1:20 διελθόντων δὲ ἐτῶν ἱκανῶν, ὅτε ἔδοξεν τῷ θεῷ, ἀποσταλεὶς Νεεμιας ὑπὸ τοῦ βασιλέως τῆς Περσίδος τοὺς ἐκγόνους τῶν ἱερέων τῶν ἀποκρυψάντων ἔπεμψεν ἐπὶ τὸ πῦρ· ὡς δὲ διεσάφησαν ἡμῖν μὴ εὑρηκέναι πῦρ, ἀλλὰ ὕδωρ παχύ, ἐκέλευσεν αὐτοὺς ἀποβάψαντας φέρειν.

R-H differs from the Göttingen edition in versification. The Göttingen edition (and derivative translations) begin(s) 1:21 at ὡς δὲ διεσάφησαν.

διελθόντων. Aor act ptc gen neut pl διέρχομαι (genitive absolute, temporal). For other uses of the verb to express the idea of time elapsing, see Exod 14:20; Amos 8:5; Jer 8:20; Ps 89:4; 4 Kgdms 11:26 (cf. *GELS*, 168.4). On the genitive absolute, see 1:7 on βασιλεύοντος.

δὲ. Development, marking a change of grammatical subject from "the pious priests" in 1:19 to "Nehemiah" in 1:20. It is best translated as "now." See 1:10 on δέ.

ἐτῶν ἱκανῶν. Genitive subject of the participle διελθόντων. The adjective ἱκανός refers to "*considerable* in quantity" (*GELS*, 339). Cf. "mature in years" (ἱκανοί ἐστε ἐν τοῖς ἔτεσιν, 1 Macc 16:3; 13:49), "quite a sum of money" (χρήματα ἱκανά, 2 Macc 4:45; cf. 8:25), and "many years" (ἱκανὰ ἔτη, Zech 7:3).

ὅτε. Introduces a temporal clause.

ἔδοξεν. Aor act ind 3rd sg δοκέω. On the meaning of the verb, see *GELS* (174): "*to be thought good and right* by [somebody] or in his or her judgement (τινι) to act in a certain way." Cf. 2:29.

τῷ θεῷ. Ethical dative ("[it seemed right] *to God*" = "[it seemed right] *as far as God is concerned*").

ἀποσταλεὶς. Aor pass ptc nom masc sg ἀποστέλλω (temporal or, perhaps, causal).

Νεεμιας. Nominative subject of ἔπεμψεν.

ὑπὸ τοῦ βασιλέως. Agency.

τῆς Περσίδος. Genitive of subordination ("king *over Persia*"). See 1:13 on εἰς τὴν Περσίδα.

τοὺς ἐκγόνους. Accusative direct object of ἔπεμψεν. The adjective (BDAG, 300: "descendants") is used as a substantive.

τῶν ἱερέων. Genitive of relationship.

τῶν ἀποκρυψάντων. Aor act ptc gen masc pl ἀποκρύπτω (attributive, modifying τῶν ἱερέων).

ἔπεμψεν. Aor act ind 3rd sg πέμπω.

ἐπὶ τὸ πῦρ. Direction, indicating movement toward an object (cf. GELS, 266.3.2). Here it denotes movement toward the fire that was hidden (cf. 1:19) and modifies ἔπεμψεν ("Nehemiah sent the priests . . . to the fire," cf. 5:18).

ὡς. Temporal conjunction, used with the aorist to communicate "when, after" (BDF §455; BDAG, 1105.8.a).

δὲ. Development, marking a change of grammatical subject from "Nehemiah" (1:20a) to "the descendants of the priests" (implied subjects of διεσάφησαν). See 1:10 on δέ.

διεσάφησαν. Aor act ind 3rd pl διασαφέω. On the meaning of the verb, see BDAG (236.2): "to inform by relating someth[ing] in detail, *tell plainly, tell in detail, report.*"

ἡμῖν. Dative indirect object of διεσάφησαν. The Lucianic recension (MSS L⁻⁵³⁴⁻⁹³⁻⁵⁴² 311 Sy) omits ἡμῖν, most likely, due to its obvious difficulty in context. How could priests from Nehemiah's day report what they found *to us* (i.e., readers of 2 Maccabees)? Goldstein (177) discusses several interpretive options for this variation unit, including textual corruption (ἢ μήν, "truly," rather than ἡμῖν, followed by Doran 2012, 46–47, and Nicklas 2011, 1380) and the possibility of the writer shifting a direct quotation (e.g., "we did not find fire," ἡμῖν οὐ εὕρηται πῦρ) into indirect speech. Cf. Katz (1960, 13).

μὴ . . . ἀλλὰ. One of many point/counterpoint sets in 2 Maccabees (e.g., μηκέτι . . . ἀλλά in 4:14; 10:4; οὐ[κ] . . . ἀλλά in 4:17; 9:22; μή . . . ἀλλά in 5:18-19; 6:12, 13; 7:29; 8:15; 11:24). This type of construction is used to cancel out an idea and replace it with another one (Runge, 92–100). Because the priests hid fire from the temple in a dry cistern (1:19), this construction reminds us that though they expected to find the fire, they found only water. On the negation, see 1:5 on μή.

εὑρηκέναι. Prf act inf εὑρίσκω (indirect discourse). As the object of a verb of perception (διεσάφησαν), the infinitive is used to convey indirect speech (Smyth §937). The subject does not need to be named explicitly because it is the same subject implied in the main verb. Although the aorist (perfective aspect) is expected here, Muraoka (§28ed) suggests that "the perfect devoid of its proper aspectual value [was] beginning to double for the aorist."

πῦρ. Accusative direct object of εὑρηκέναι.

ὕδωρ παχύ. Accusative direct object of an implied εὑρηκέναι. Ellipsis is common in contrasting statements using ἀλλά (see BDF §479.1). παχύς refers to *"having a large quantity of components tightly packed"* (*GELS*, 541.1). Thus, ὕδωρ παχύ probably refers to "thick liquid" or "marsh water" (NETS). Despite the ambiguity of this expression, many scholars connect this to the substance discussed in 1:36 (Goldstein, 177; D. Schwartz, 153).

ἐκέλευσεν. Aor act ind 3rd sg κελεύω. The verb κελεύω is often followed by an infinitive, which supplies the intended action that should be carried out (BDAG, 538).

αὐτοὺς. Accusative direct object of ἐκέλευσεν.

ἀποβάψαντας. Aor act ptc acc masc pl ἀποβάπτω (accusative absolute, temporal). Alternatively, when paired with a verb of communication and a pronoun (in the accusative), an accusative anarthrous participle may indicate indirect discourse (Smyth §2106–9; Wallace, 645–46). The participle is in the accusative case because it describes action related to αὐτούς. MS A reads ἀποβάψαντες, which agrees with the implied subject of ἐκέλευσεν, but is probably a transcription error introduced because most adverbial participles are nominative.

φέρειν. Pres act inf φέρω (indirect discourse).

1:21 ὡς δὲ ἀνηνέχθη τὰ τῶν θυσιῶν, ἐκέλευσεν τοὺς ἱερεῖς Νεεμιας ἐπιρρᾶναι τῷ ὕδατι τά τε ξύλα καὶ τὰ ἐπικείμενα.

See comments in 1:20 on the different versification of the Göttingen edition and R-H in 1:21.

ὡς. Temporal conjunction, used with the aorist to communicate "when, after" (BDAG, 1105.8.a).

δὲ. Development, marking a change of grammatical subject from Nehemiah (1:20b) to "the things of sacrifice" (τὰ τῶν θυσιῶν). See 1:10 on δέ.

ἀνηνέχθη. Aor pass ind 3rd sg ἀναφέρω. In the aorist passive, the verb is built upon the sixth principal part, (αν)ἠνέχθην. *MBG* (§14.5) notes that "[w]hen a velar stop (κ γ) is immediately followed by a θ, the first stop is aspirated." Thus: ενεκ → ηνεκ → ηνεχθην. See also 1:18 on ἀνήνεγκεν.

τὰ. The neuter nominative article functions substantively (Wallace, 235), as the subject of ἀνηνέχθη. Neuter plural subjects are used commonly with a singular verb (Smyth §958).

τῶν θυσιῶν. Because the neuter article (τά) has a broad scope of reference, it is difficult to define the genitive more narrowly. Wallace's (79) category of aporetic genitive is applicable.

ἐκέλευσεν. Aor act ind 3rd sg κελεύω. See 1:20 on ἐκέλευσεν.

τοὺς ἱερεῖς. Accusative direct object of ἐκέλευσεν.

Νεεμιας. Nominative subject of ἐκέλευσεν.

ἐπιρρᾶναι. Aor act inf ἐπιρραίνω (indirect discourse). On the meaning of the verb, see *GE* (785) suggests "to sprinkle (on), scatter."

τῷ ὕδατι. Dative of means.

τά . . . ξύλα. Accusative direct object of ἐπιρρᾶναι.

τε . . . καί. Correlative construction: "both . . . and." See 1:14 on τε . . . καί.

τὰ ἐπικείμενα. Pres mid ptc acc neut pl ἐπίκειμαι (substantival). Direct object of ἐπιρρᾶναι.

1:22 ὡς δὲ ἐγένετο τοῦτο καὶ χρόνος διῆλθεν ὅ τε ἥλιος ἀνέλαμψεν πρότερον ἐπινεφὴς ὤν, ἀνήφθη πυρὰ μεγάλη ὥστε θαυμάσαι πάντας.

ὡς. Temporal conjunction, used with the aorist to communicate "when, after" (BDAG, 1105.8.a).

δὲ. Development, marking a change of grammatical subject from Nehemiah (1:21).

ἐγένετο. Aor mid ind 3rd sg γίνομαι.

τοῦτο. Nominative subject of ἐγένετο. The Göttingen edition omits τοῦτο from the text. However, on the strength of the manuscript evidence (MSS V *L* 46-52 55 58), it should probably be included in the text. Without τοῦτο, the meaning is virtually the same and the syntax is a little smoother.

χρόνος. Nominative subject of διῆλθεν.

διῆλθεν. Aor act ind 3rd sg διέρχομαι. See 1:20 on διελθόντων.

ὅ . . . ἥλιος. Nominative subject of ἀνέλαμψεν. Regarding the accent on ὅ, see 1:14 on ὅ . . . Ἀντίοχος.

τε. The particle τέ is typically placed "immediately after the word (or first word of a phrase or clause) which it joins to what precedes or to what follows" (LSJ, D.1).

ἀνέλαμψεν. Aor act ind 3rd sg ἀναλάμπω.

πρότερον. Adverb of comparison, modifying the participle clause. BDAG (888.1.b): "earlier, formerly."

ἐπινεφὴς. Predicate nominative preceding ὤν, in agreement with the singular subject.

ὤν. Pres act ptc nom masc sg εἰμί (concessive; "the sun shone . . . *even though* it was clouded over").

ἀνήφθη. Aor pass ind 3rd sg ἀνάπτω. In the aorist passive, the verb is built upon the sixth principal part, ἥφθην.

πυρά μεγάλη. Nominative subject of ἀνήφθη.

ὥστε. Introduces a result clause, which modifies what immediately precedes.

θαυμάσαι. Aor act inf θαυμάζω. Used with ὥστε to indicate a result.

πάντας. Accusative subject of the infinitive θαυμάσαι.

1:23 προσευχὴν δὲ ἐποιήσαντο οἱ ἱερεῖς δαπανωμένης τῆς θυσίας, οἵ τε ἱερεῖς καὶ πάντες, καταρχομένου Ιωναθου, τῶν δὲ λοιπῶν ἐπιφωνούντων ὡς Νεεμιου.

προσευχὴν. Accusative direct object of ἐποιήσαντο.

δὲ. Development, marking a change of grammatical subject from "a great fire" (πυρὰ μεγάλη, 1:22) to "the priests" (οἱ ἱερεῖς). See 1:10 on δέ.

ἐποιήσαντο. Aor mid ind 3rd pl ποιέω. When the middle of ποιέω is used with a verbal noun (προσευχήν), this can be a periphrasis for the verb derived from the noun itself: προσεύχομαι (GELS, 570.II; BDF §310.1; BDAG, 839.2.d; Smyth §1722). See the Introduction for further comments on verbal periphrases comprised on an abstract noun with ποιέω.

οἱ ἱερεῖς. Nominative subject of ἐποιήσαντο.

δαπανωμένης. Pres pass ptc gen fem sg δαπανάω (genitive absolute, temporal). The present participle, as well as the placement of the genitive absolute construction following the main verb, implies contemporaneous time in relation to the main verb ἐποιήσαντο. On the genitive absolute, see 1:7 on βασιλεύοντος.

τῆς θυσίας. Genitive subject of the participle δαπανωμένης.

οἵ . . . ἱερεῖς καὶ πάντες. These words clearly modify the earlier grammatical subject, οἱ ἱερεῖς. This is an example of right-dislocation for emphasis, namely "a delayed appositional reference to an entity that was referred to earlier in the clause" (Runge, 326). On the accent on οἵ, see 1:14 on ὅ . . . Ἀντίοχος.

τε . . . καὶ. Correlative construction. See 1:14 on τε . . . καί.

καταρχομένου. Pres mid ptc gen masc sg κατάρχω (genitive absolute, manner). While the genitive absolute participial construction is typically temporal, "[a]ll the varieties of the circumstantial participle can appear in the absolute participle" (Robertson, 1130). Thus, the manner in which they prayed was: "Jonathan leading. . . ." On the genitive absolute, see 1:7 on βασιλεύοντος.

Ιωναθου. Genitive subject of the participle καταρχομένου.

δὲ. Development, marking a change of grammatical subject from "Jonathan" (Ιωναθου) to "the rest" (τῶν . . . λοιπῶν). See 1:10 on δέ.

τῶν . . . λοιπῶν. Genitive subject of the participle ἐπιφωνούντων.

ἐπιφωνούντων. Pres act ptc gen masc pl ἐπιφωνέω (genitive absolute, manner). On the genitive absolute, see 1:7 on βασιλεύοντος.

ὡς. Introduces a comparative clause, involving ellipsis: "the rest responded *as* Nehemiah (responded)."

Νεεμιου. Subject of an implied form of ἐπιφωνέω. The noun Νεεμιου is genitive because it agrees with τῶν . . . λοιπῶν ἐπιφωνούντων (cf. Muraoka §26n).

2 Maccabees 1:24-29

[24]The prayer was in this manner: "O Lord, Lord God, Creator of all, [who] is awe-inspiring and strong and just and merciful; [who] alone is king and kind; [25][Who] alone is bountiful; [who] alone is just and almighty and everlasting. [Who] rescues Israel from every evil; [who] made the fathers to be chosen and [who] sanctified them. [26]Accept the sacrifice on behalf of all your people Israel, and preserve your portion, and make [it] holy. [27]Gather together our scattered [people]; set free those who are slaves among the gentiles; look on those who have been rejected and despised, and let the gentiles know that you are our God. [28]Torture those who oppress and are insolent with pride. [29]Plant your people in your holy place, as Moses said".

The prayer begins with an accumulation of epithets for God, which was common in Greek religious practice as well as Jewish tradition. In this context, the epithets express faith in the omnipotence of Israel's God (cf. Abel, 295). On the significance of prayer, Newman (201–18) has shown that Jews often turned to prayer when temple worship was not easily accessible. Thus, prayer is a key form of Jewish piety in the diaspora.

1:24 ἦν δὲ ἡ προσευχὴ τὸν τρόπον ἔχουσα τοῦτον Κύριε κύριε ὁ θεός, ὁ πάντων κτίστης, ὁ φοβερὸς καὶ ἰσχυρὸς καὶ δίκαιος καὶ ἐλεήμων, ὁ μόνος βασιλεὺς καὶ χρηστός.

ἦν. Impf act ind 3rd sg εἰμί.

δὲ. Development; see 1:10 on δέ.

ἡ προσευχὴ. Nominative subject of ἦν. The article is anaphoric, pointing back to the prayer (προσευχήν) mentioned in 1:23.

τὸν τρόπον . . . τοῦτον. Accusative direct object of ἔχουσα. The collocation ἔχω + τρόπος means "in this manner" (*GELS*, 688.2.a). On the separation of the demonstrative from the noun phrase, see the discussion of hyperbaton in the Introduction.

ἔχουσα. Pres act ptc nom fem sg ἔχω (attributive, modifying ἡ προσευχή). Greek often employs ἔχω as a surrogate for εἰμί, especially in idioms where ἔχω is followed by an adverb expressing manner (e.g., Josephus, *Ant.* 1.26, 66, 74; Matt 4:24; 2 Cor 12:14). Although not the exact idiom, the collocation of ἔχω + τρόπος (expressing manner) has the same meaning.

Κύριε κύριε. Vocatives of direct address. The repetition of the divine name is probably a sign of fervor (cf. Abel, 295) and here may echo Exod 34:6.

ὁ θεός. Nominative substituting for vocative (cf. Muraoka §22yb; Smyth §1288). Conybeare and Stock (§50) note that "when [the nominative for the vocative is] . . . employed, the nominative usually has the article. As in Hebrew the vocative is regularly expressed by the nominative with the article, it is not surprising that the LXX translators should often avail themselves of this turn of speech" (cf. Robertson, 264, 462–63; Zerwick §33). Moreover, the vocative form θεέ is extremely rare in the LXX (2 Kgdms 7:25; 3 Macc 6:2; 4 Macc 6:27; Odes Sol. 14:12; Wis 9:1; Sir 23:4; Hos 14:4; Ezek 4:14). For brief discussion of the vocative in classical Greek, see *CGCG* (§30.55).

Following the mention of God comes a series of several further epithets that are each governed by the article (cf. Doran 2012, 49).

ὁ . . . κτίστης. Nominative (substituting for vocative) in apposition to ὁ θεός. In other prayer contexts in 2 Maccabees, Israel's God is evoked as "the creator" (7:23; 13:14). Additionally, numismatic evidence from the Roman period indicates that κτίστης was used to describe an emperor founding a city. This may suggest that reference to Israel's God as ὁ κτίστης should also be understood against this background, asserting a claim of superiority over other powers (cf. Theophilos 2015, 191–205).

πάντων. Objective genitive ("the one who created *all*"). Elsewhere in 2 Maccabees, God is described as creator "of the world" (τοῦ κόσμου, 7:23; 13:14).

ὁ φοβερὸς καὶ ἰσχυρὸς καὶ δίκαιος καὶ ἐλεήμων. Nominatives in apposition to ὁ θεός. The article governs each adjective (cf. MS A adds ὁ prior to ἰσχυρός).

ὁ μόνος. Nominative (substituting for vocative) in apposition to ὁ θεός and the subject of an implied verb. Alternatively, μόνος may be used attributively with the sense of "the *only* king and kind one . . ." (cf. *CGCG* §29.47; Muraoka §38b.iv). In its diasporan context, the appellation μόνος is both religious and political.

βασιλεὺς καὶ χρηστός. Predicate nominative of an implied verb.

1:25 ὁ μόνος χορηγός, ὁ μόνος δίκαιος καὶ παντοκράτωρ καὶ αἰώνιος, ὁ διασῴζων τὸν Ισραηλ ἐκ παντὸς κακοῦ, ὁ ποιήσας τοὺς πατέρας ἐκλεκτοὺς καὶ ἁγιάσας αὐτούς.

ὁ μόνος. Nominative (substituting for vocative) in apposition to ὁ θεός in 1:24 and the subject of an implied verb. This is the second (of three) uses of μόνος in 1:24-25, emphasizing the uniqueness of the God of Israel.

χορηγός. Predicate nominative of an implied verb. The substantive χορηγός is an LXX *hapax legomena*, but the corresponding verb χορηγέω is more common and has the basic sense of "to give" (e.g., Sir 1:10, 26; 39:33). *GE* (2369) lists four main meanings for χορηγός: head of the chorus, underwriter of the expenses of the chorus, one who supports the expenses [of something], protector. Thus, the sense of "generous giver, bestower" is suggested in this context where God is extolled (*pace* Doran 2012, 50).

δίκαιος καὶ παντοκράτωρ καὶ αἰώνιος. Predicate nominatives. Each adjective is governed by the article that precedes the second ὁ μόνος in 1:25. παντοκράτωρ ("almighty") is an epithet for Israel's God that "must be placed alongside passages in the condensed narrative that imply a tolerant view of other gods and religions" (Doran 2012, 49; cf. van Henten 1996, 126).

ὁ διασῴζων. Pres act ptc nom masc sg διασῴζω (substantival). Nominative (substituting for vocative) modifying ὁ θεός in 1:24.

τὸν Ισραηλ. Accusative direct object of ὁ διασῴζων.

ἐκ παντὸς κακοῦ. Separation ("*from* every evil" or "*out of* every evil").

ὁ ποιήσας. Aor act ptc nom masc sg ποιέω (substantival). Nominative (substituting for vocative) modifying ὁ θεός in 1:24. *GELS* (212) notes that ποιέω τινα ἐκλεκόν is functionally equivalent to ἐκλέγομαι.

τοὺς πατέρας. Accusative direct object of ποιήσας in an object-complement double accusative construction.

ἐκλεκτούς. Complement in an object-complement double accusative construction.

ἁγιάσας. Aor act ptc nom masc sg ἁγιάζω (subtantival). Nominative (substituting for vocative) modifying ὁ θεός in 1:24.

αὐτούς. Accusative direct object of ἁγιάσας.

1:26 πρόσδεξαι τὴν θυσίαν ὑπὲρ παντὸς τοῦ λαοῦ σου Ισραηλ καὶ διαφύλαξον τὴν μερίδα σου καὶ καθαγίασον.

πρόσδεξαι. Aor mid impv 2nd sg προσδέχομαι. The aorist imperative is often used to make a request of a superior (Wallace, 487;

Muraoka §29e), such as a human being to a deity (e.g., Ps 70:2). On the meaning of the verb, see BDAG (877.1): "to receive favorably" + accusative of thing.

τὴν θυσίαν. Accusative direct object of πρόσδεξαι.

ὑπὲρ παντός. Advantage ("on behalf of all"). See the similar constructions of θυσία + ὑπέρ in 3:32; 1 Kgdms 15:22; Ezek 44:29; 45:17.

τοῦ λαοῦ. Partitive genitive ("[all] *who are of* your *people*").

σου. Possessive genitive.

Ισραηλ. Genitive in apposition to τοῦ λαοῦ. The word is indeclinable, but here it agrees with τοῦ λαοῦ.

διαφύλαξον. Aor act impv 2nd sg διαφυλάσσω.

τὴν μερίδα. Accusative direct object of διαφύλαξον. As D. Schwartz (155) notes, it is possible that διαφύλαξον *τὴν μερίδα σου* ("[preserve] *your portion*") echoes Deut 32:9, which states that "his people became the Lord's portion" (ἐγενήθη μερὶς κυρίου λαὸς αὐτοῦ).

σου. Possessive genitive.

καθαγίασον. Aor act impv 2nd sg καθαγιάζω. While ἁγιάζω appears frequently in the LXX (196 times), the compound form, καθαγιάζω, appears only six times, three of which are in 2 Maccabees (1:26; 2:8; 15:18). Elsewhere in the LXX, καθαγιάζω appears in connection with animals (Lev 27:26) and cultic objects (Lev 8:9; 1 Chr 26:20; 2 Macc 2:8; 15:18), but here καθαγιάζω appears in a construction that parallels 1:25:

> 1:25   ὁ ποιήσας τοὺς πατέρας ἐκλεκτοὺς καὶ *ἀγιάσας* αὐτούς
>
> [who] chose the fathers and [who] *sanctified* them
>
> 1:26   διαφύλαξον τὴν μερίδα σου καὶ *καθαγίασον*
>
> preserve your portion, and *make* [it] *holy*

Both verbs take human beings, either explicitly stated or implied, for a direct object.

1:27 ἐπισυνάγαγε τὴν διασπορὰν ἡμῶν, ἐλευθέρωσον τοὺς δουλεύοντας ἐν τοῖς ἔθνεσιν, τοὺς ἐξουθενημένους καὶ βδελυκτοὺς ἔπιδε, καὶ γνώτωσαν τὰ ἔθνη ὅτι σὺ εἶ ὁ θεὸς ἡμῶν.

ἐπισυνάγαγε. Aor act impv 2nd sg ἐπισυνάγω. On the aorist imperative for making requests of a superior, see 1:26 on πρόσδεξαι.

τὴν διασπορὰν. Accusative direct object of ἐπισυνάγαγε.

ἡμῶν. Partitive genitive ("[the scattered] *of us*").

ἐλευθέρωσον. Aor act impv 2nd sg ἐλευθερόω.

τοὺς δουλεύοντας. Pres act ptc acc masc sg δουλεύω (substantival). Direct object of ἐλευθέρωσον.

ἐν τοῖς ἔθνεσιν. Locative. The plural (rather than the singular) of ἔθνος is typically used to denote a large group of people. The noun ἔθνος is typically translated as "nation" (Doran 2012, 47) or "gentile" (D. Schwartz, 156). That latter is especially the case in the LXX when ἔθνος is set in contrast with λαός, as is the case in the present context (cf. 1:29). In earlier Greek usage, ἔθνος meant something like "nation" (e.g., Herodotus, *Hist.* 1.101; 9.106), but in later usage it was used to refer to "foreign, barbarous nations" (LSJ, 480) as opposed to Greeks (e.g., Aristotle, *Pol.* 1324b10). A similar (negative) connotation seems to be implied here where the Jews are described in favorable terminology (e.g., 1:25) and the "gentiles" need to come to knowledge of Israel's God.

τοὺς ἐξουθενημένους. Prf pass ptc acc masc sg ἐξουθενέω (substantival). Direct object of ἔπιδε. The verb ἐξουθενέω is ultimately derived from ἐξουδενίζω (ἐξ οὐδείς), which has the sense of "to hold of no account at all, scorn" (*GE*, 729).

βδελυκτούς. Accusative direct object of ἔπιδε. See *GELS* (116): "loathed."

ἔπιδε. Aor act impv 2nd sg ἐφοράω. Due to suppletion, most grammars list this word as the aorist principal part of ὁράω. But, εἶδον is from the root *ϝιδ (cf. Smyth §431), which is a form slowly replacing the aorist forms of ὁράω (cf. *MBG* §31.5b; 44.5).

γνώτωσαν. Aor act impv 3rd pl γινώσκω. The sense is probably not permissive ("permit the gentiles *to know*") but hortatory. This seems more likely because the means by which the gentiles will know God is expressed through the prior imperative verbs.

τὰ ἔθνη. Nominative subject of γνώτωσαν.

ὅτι. Introduces a content clause that is the clausal complement (indirect discourse) of γνώτωσαν.

σὺ. Nominative subject of εἶ. When a copula is used, if one of the words in the nominative is a pronoun, it will be the subject (Wallace, 43).

εἶ. Pres act ind 2nd sg εἰμί.

ὁ θεὸς. Predicate nominative.

ἡμῶν. Genitive of subordination.

1:28 βασάνισον τοὺς καταδυναστεύοντας καὶ ἐξυβρίζοντας ἐν ὑπερηφανίᾳ.

βασάνισον. Aor act impv 2nd sg βασανίζω. On the meaning of the verb, see BDAG (168.1): "to subject to punitive judicial procedure, *torture*." Cf. similar uses in 7:13, 17; 9:6.

τοὺς **καταδυναστεύοντας**. Pres act ptc acc masc pl καταδυναστεύω (substantival). Direct object of βασάνισον. On the meaning of the verb, see *GELS* (371.1): "*to cause . . . unjust hardship*, often from a position of power."

ἐξυβρίζοντας. Pres act ptc acc masc pl ἐξυβρίζω (substantival). Linked by καί to the article τούς as a second direct object of βασάνισον.

ἐν ὑπερηφανίᾳ. Reference. On the meaning of the noun, *GE* (2202) suggests "arrogance, pride, haughtiness." The PP + ἐξυβρίζω communicates what someone is hubrisitic *in*.

1:29 καταφύτευσον τὸν λαόν σου εἰς τὸν τόπον τὸν ἅγιόν σου, καθὼς εἶπεν Μωυσῆς.

καταφύτευσον. Aor act impv 2nd sg καταφυτεύω. The verb occurs only here in 2 Maccabees, but it is commonly used with the figurative sense of "to plant [people in a location]" in the LXX (cf. Exod 15:17; 2 Kgdms 7:10; 1 Chr 17:9; Ps 43:3; Amos 9:15; Jer 11:17; 24:6; 38:28; Ezek 17:22-23; 36:36; cf. *GE*, 1090).

τὸν λαόν. Accusative direct object of καταφύτευσον.

σου. Possessive genitive.

εἰς τὸν τόπον τὸν ἅγιόν. Locative.

σου. Possessive genitive.

καθὼς εἶπεν Μωυσῆς. The citation formula follows an inexact citation of LXX Exod 15:17a: εἰσαγαγὼν καταφύτευσον αὐτοὺς εἰς ὄρος κληρονομίας σου ("Lead them in, and plant them in the mountain of your inheritance," NETS).

εἶπεν. Aor act ind 3rd sg λέγω.

Μωυσῆς. Nominative subject of εἶπεν.

2 Maccabees 1:30-36

[30]And the priests were singing the hymns. [31]When the materials of the sacrifices had been consumed, Nehemiah ordered [them] to pour the remaining water on very large stones. [32]When this was done, a flame blazed up, but when the light from the altar shone back, it was consumed. [33]When this situation became known and it was reported to the king of the Persians that, in the place where the exiled priests had hidden the fire, the water had appeared, with which those with Nehemiah had purified the things of the sacrifice, [34]erecting a fence around [the place], the king made [it] a sacred [place], after investigating the situation. [35]And to those whom the king favored, he was receiving a large sum of money and sharing [it]. [36]And those with Nehemiah designated it

"nephthar," which translated means "purification," but by most people it is called "nephthai."

On the function of this part of the letter, see the brief comments following the translation of 1:10-17.

1:30 Οἱ δὲ ἱερεῖς ἐπέψαλλον τοὺς ὕμνους.

Οἱ . . . ἱερεῖς. Nominative subject of ἐπέψαλλον.

δὲ. Development; see 1:10 on δέ.

ἐπέψαλλον. Impf act ind 3rd pl ἐπιψάλλω. The term is a *hapax legomenon* in the LXX, but is attested in wider Greek literature with the sense "to accompany on a stringed instrument" or, by extension, "to sing" (*GE*, 806). The simple form ψάλλω is well attested, especially in the Greek Psalms. For descriptions of Levitical priests as singers, see 1 Chr 25:7; Josephus, *Ant.* 20.216–18.

τοὺς ὕμνους. Accusative direct object of ἐπέψαλλον.

1:31 καθὼς δὲ ἀνηλώθη τὰ τῆς θυσίας, καὶ τὸ περιλειπόμενον ὕδωρ ὁ Νεεμιας ἐκέλευσεν λίθους μείζονας καταχεῖν.

καθὼς. Temporal conjunction (= καθ᾽ ὡς), used with the aorist, meaning "when" or "after" (*GE*, 1009).

δὲ. Development, marking a change of grammatical subject from "the priests" (Οἱ . . . ἱερεῖς) in 1:30 to the Nehemiah in 1:31. See 1:10 on δέ.

ἀνηλώθη. Aor pass ind 3rd sg ἀναλίσκω.

τὰ. The article functions as a nominalizer, making τῆς θυσίας the subject of ἀνηλώθη. The neuter plural subject is used commonly with a singular verb (cf. Smyth §958).

τῆς θυσίας. Because the neuter article (τά) has a broad scope of reference, it is difficult to define the genitive more narrowly. Wallace's (79) category of aporetic genitive is applicable.

τὸ περιλειπόμενον ὕδωρ. Accusative direct object of καταχεῖν. Refers to the thick water (1:20) that was found in the cistern where the priests hid the fire taken from the temple (1:18).

τὸ περιλειπόμενον. Pres pass ptc acc neut sg περιλείπομαι (attributive, modifying ὕδωρ). The verb is rare in the LXX, appearing only in the Maccabean literature to refer to: "*remaining* property" sold from a town that was invaded (2 Macc 8:14), "the *remaining* son" (of seven) who was martyred (4 Macc 12:6), "*those who remained*" were left behind when others were dragged off (4 Macc 13:18). It is used in here to refer to "the *remaining* water" that was left behind after hiding the fire (see 1:19-20).

ὁ Νεεμίας. Nominative subject of ἐκέλευσεν.

ἐκέλευσεν. Aor act ind 3rd sg κελεύω.

λίθους μείζονας. Solecism, i.e., a grammatical mistake, unless the preposition ἐπί has fallen out of the textual tradition here (cf. Abel, 297) (see below). The comparative adjective ("*larger* stones") should probably be construed as superlative ("*very large* stones"), which is a common pattern in Greek (cf. Muraoka §23ba-bb).

καταχεῖν. Pres act inf καταχέω (indirect discourse). This verb often takes a genitive (or sometimes dative) complement (e.g., Gen 39:21; Josephus, *Ant.* 6.54; *J.W.* 3.271, 272; *Ag. Ap.* 2.256; Mark 14:3) and not the accusative. D. Schwartz (157–58; cf. Goldstein, 180; Shaw 2016, 407) notes that the Greek text seems to require the addition of ἐπί to make sense: "to pour out *upon* very large stones" (cf. Job 41:15). Katz (1960, 13) argues that an original ἐπί dropped out prior to λίθους due to haplography: ΕΚΕΛΕΥΣΕΝ ΕΠΙΛΙΘΟΥΣ. This may be preferable. Alternatively, Muraoka (§60a) discusses examples of "doubly transitive verbs" (e.g., in Gen 21:19; 24:43) where "it appears that the two accusative objects are not of equal standing and their respective syntactic behavior differs."

1:32 ὡς δὲ τοῦτο ἐγενήθη, φλὸξ ἀνήφθη· τοῦ δὲ ἀπὸ τοῦ θυσιαστηρίου ἀντιλάμψαντος φωτὸς ἐδαπανήθη.

ὡς. Temporal conjunction, translated "when, after" with the aorist (BDAG, 1105.8.a).

δὲ. Development, marking a change of grammatical subject from Nehemiah in 1:31 to τοῦτο in 1:32. See 1:10 on δέ.

τοῦτο. Nominative subject of ἐγενήθη. The neuter singular demonstrative pronoun may refer to a unit of thought and "take up a substantive idea not expressed by a preceding neuter word" (Smyth §1253). Here the anaphoric use, also signaled by the use of δέ, refers to the preceding clause: "Nehemiah ordered [them] to pour the remaining water on very large stones."

ἐγενήθη. Aor pass ind 3rd sg γίνομαι.

φλὸξ. Nominative subject of ἀνήφθη.

ἀνήφθη. Aor pass ind 3rd sg ἀνάπτω. See 1:22 on ἀνήφθη.

τοῦ . . . φωτὸς. Genitive subject of the participle ἀντιλάμψαντος.

δὲ. Development; see 1:10 on δέ.

ἀπὸ τοῦ θυσιαστηρίου. Source. The origin or source of the light (τοῦ . . . φωτός) is "the altar" (cf. Sir 33:7, where the origin of light is "from the sun," ἀφ᾽ ἡλίου).

ἀντιλάμψαντος. Aor act ptc gen neut sg ἀντιλάμπω (genitive absolute, temporal). This word is a *hapax legomenon* in the LXX, but appears in wider Greek literature with the meaning "to shine a flame (*as signal*) in response" or "to reflect light, shine" (*GE*, 200). On the genitive absolute, see 1:7 on βασιλεύοντος.

ἐδαπανήθη. Aor pass ind 3rd sg δαπανάω. See 1:23 on δαπανωμένης. The grammatical subject of this verb is not specified, which suggests either that something has been lost in transmission (Goldstein, 180) or that something, like *nephthar* (1:36), must be supplied from the literary context (Doran 1981, 8).

1:33 ὡς δὲ φανερὸν ἐγενήθη τὸ πρᾶγμα, καὶ διηγγέλη τῷ βασιλεῖ τῶν Περσῶν ὅτι εἰς τὸν τόπον, οὗ τὸ πῦρ ἔκρυψαν οἱ μεταχθέντες ἱερεῖς, τὸ ὕδωρ ἐφάνη, ἀφ' οὗ καὶ οἱ περὶ τὸν Νεεμιαν ἥγνισαν τὰ τῆς θυσίας,

ὡς. Temporal conjunction, used with the aorist to communicate "when, after" (BDAG, 1105.8.a).

δὲ. Development, marking a change of grammatical subject from the "flame" in 1:32 to τὸ πρᾶγμα in 1:33. See 1:10 on δέ.

φανερὸν. Predicate adjective in agreement with πρᾶγμα.

ἐγενήθη. Aor mid ind 3rd sg γίνομαι. "[An examination] of the forty-five occurrences of the -θη- forms of γίνομαι in the GNT has shown that the voice of these forms is ambiguous. Here, the sense is middle, not 'was made,' but 'became,' i.e., by coming into the world" (Brookins and Longenecker, 40).

τὸ πρᾶγμα. Nominative subject of ἐγενήθη. See *GE* (1732): "state of affairs, circumstances, situation."

διηγγέλη. Aor pass ind 3rd sg διαγγέλλω.

τῷ βασιλεῖ. Dative indirect object of διηγγέλη.

τῶν Περσῶν. Genitive of subordination ("*over* the Persians").

ὅτι. Introduces either a content clause or, more loosely, indirect discourse.

εἰς τὸν τόπον. Locative.

οὗ. The genitive relative pronoun appears here without a grammatical antecedent and functions as an adverb: "where."

τὸ πῦρ. Accusative direct object of ἔκρυψαν.

ἔκρυψαν. Aor act ind 3rd pl κρύπτω.

οἱ . . . ἱερεῖς. Nominative subject of ἔκρυψαν.

μεταχθέντες. Aor pass ptc nom masc pl μετάγω (attributive, modifying οἱ . . . ἱερεῖς). The sixth principal part of ἄγω is ἤχθην.

τὸ ὕδωρ. Nominative subject of ἐφάνη.

ἐφάνη. Aor pass ind 3rd sg φαίνω.

ἀφ᾽ οὗ. Temporal. See 1:7 on ἀφ᾽ οὗ.

οἱ. The article functions as a nominalizer, changing the PP (περὶ τὸν Νεεμιαν) into the nominative subject of ἥγνισαν.

περὶ τὸν Νεεμιαν. Association. See 1:13 on ἡ περὶ αὐτόν.

ἥγνισαν. Aor act ind 3rd pl ἁγνίζω. Goldstein (180) notes that the author of the letter "took advantage of the ambiguity of the verb [ἁγνίζω], which can mean both 'purify' and 'burn [as an offering]'" (cf. Doran 2012, 51).

τὰ. The neuter accusative article functions substantively (Wallace, 235), as the accusative direct object of ἥγνισαν. The neuter plural subject is used commonly with a singular verb (cf. Smyth §958).

τῆς θυσίας. Because the neuter article (τά) has a broad scope of reference, it is difficult to define the genitive more narrowly. Wallace's (79) category of aporetic genitive is applicable.

1:34 περιφράξας δὲ ὁ βασιλεὺς ἱερὸν ἐποίησεν δοκιμάσας τὸ πρᾶγμα.

περιφράξας. Aor act ptc nom masc sg περιφράσσω (manner). The verbs means "*to build a fence around* [something] *to prevent entry into it*" (*GELS*, 545; cf. 12:13). The Greek is elliptical, but some MSS (*L*[-62] 46-52 58 La[P] [Sy] Arm) supply τὸν τόπον (cf. τὸν τόπον in 1:33) as the accusative direct object of περιφράξας. D. Schwartz (158) notes that fencing off was "a crucial step in the foundation of any temple" (cf. 3 Kgdms 9:15).

δὲ. Indicates a change of grammatical subject from "Nehemiah and all those with him" in 1:33 to the king in 1:34. See 1:10 on δέ.

ὁ βασιλεὺς. Nominative subject of ἐποίησεν.

ἱερὸν. Accusative direct object of ἐποίησεν. Used as a substantive because the implied head noun (τόπον) can be supplied easily in context (Muraoka §23f). The adjective ἱερός has the sense of "sacred" or "consecrated" (*GE*, 968).

ἐποίησεν. Aor act ind 3rd sg ποιέω. The collocation of ποιέω + ἱερός [accusative] is rare.

δοκιμάσας. Aor act ptc nom masc sg δοκιμάζω (temporal). On the meaning of the verb, see *GELS* (174): "to subject to scrutiny" (cf. Zech 13:9; Ps 65:10; Sir 2:5; Jer 11:20). The same word is used with a different sense in 4:3. Shaw (2016, 409) rightly notes that this participial construction is awkward and "appears hastily thrown in."

τὸ πρᾶγμα. Accusative direct object of δοκιμάσας. See 1:33 on τὸ πρᾶγμα.

1:35 καὶ οἷς ἐχαρίζετο ὁ βασιλεύς, πολλὰ διάφορα ἐλάμβανεν καὶ μετεδίδου.

There are several critical issues in 1:35 that affect how the passage is understood. Nicklas (2011, 1380) notes the possibility of a textual corruption in this verse, but does not suggest a better alternative (cf. Habicht, 205). Several critical issues are discussed below, but it is worth summarizing them: (1) the referent of οἷς ("those whom") is underspecified, leading to multiple text-critical emendations as well as modern proposals from scholars about *who* these people were; (2) the syntax of πολλὰ διάφορα is difficult to determine; and (3) the verbs ἐχαρίζετο, ἐλάμβανεν, and μετεδίδου have textual variants in order to improve their senses in context.

οἷς. Dative of reference or, better, advantage. The antecedent of the demonstrative pronoun is disputed. Goldstein (180–81) suggests οἱ περὶ τὸν Νεεμιαν ("Nehemiah's men") from 1:33, but D. Schwartz (159) and Doran (2012, 51) argue that it refers to those who drew out the liquid in 1:21: τοὺς ἱερεῖς (see comments on Schwartz's emendation of ἐχαρίζετο below, which supports this understanding).

ἐχαρίζετο. Impf mid ind 3rd sg χαρίζομαι. Following the reading in R-H and the Göttingen edition, the idea is that the king took money and gave it to those whom he *favored*. Codex A omits the verb altogether, perhaps by accident or, more likely, due to the difficulty of construing it in context (cf. Goldstein, 180–81, who follows MS A). However, Risberg (17–18), followed by D. Schwartz (158–59), follows an emendation to ἐξηρύσαντο ("who had drawn out") and translates 1:35 as "And the king took large sums of money and bestowed them upon the people *who had drawn out* (the liquid)." This imperfect verb (imperfective verbal aspect) and the ones that follow suggest habitual or regular practice of the king.

ὁ βασιλεύς. Nominative subject of ἐχαρίζετο.

πολλὰ διάφορα. Accusative direct object of ἐλάμβανεν and μετεδίδου. NRSV and NETS, in agreement with the punctuation of R-H and the Göttingen edition, construe πολλὰ διάφορα as the direct object of ἐλάμβανεν and μετεδίδου ("[the king] was receiving and giving πολλὰ διάφορα"). It is also possible, even if less likely, to read these words as the direct object of ἐχαρίζετο: "[the king] was bestowing πολλὰ διάφορα." Regarding meaning, Hellenistic authors used διάφορα to refer to "a large sum of money" (*GE*, 517).

ἐλάμβανεν. Impf act ind 3rd sg λαμβάνω. Here NETS translates the collocation of λαμβάνω and μεταδίδωμι as "exchange [gifts]," which does not quite capture the nuance of μεταδίδωμι as "sharing" a portion of something (cf. T. Zeb. 6:6). Some MSS (*L*-534 19 62 311) read plural (ἐλάμβανον καὶ μετεδίδουν) rather than singular verbs (ἐλάμβανεν καὶ μετεδίδου), providing the sense "to those whom the king was bestowing much money *used to accept and share it.*"

μετεδίδου. Impf act ind 3rd sg μεταδίδωμι.

1:36 προσηγόρευσαν δὲ οἱ περὶ τὸν Νεεμιαν τοῦτο νεφθαρ, ὃ διερμηνεύεται καθαρισμός· καλεῖται δὲ παρὰ τοῖς πολλοῖς νεφθαι.

προσηγόρευσαν. Aor act ind 3rd pl προσαγορεύω. The verb means "to . . . designate (*with a certain name*)" (*GE*, 1789).

δὲ. Development, marking a change of grammatical subject from the king in 1:35 to "Nehemiah and all those with him" (οἱ περὶ τὸν Νεεμιαν) in 1:36. See 1:10 on δέ.

οἱ. The article functions as a nominalizer, changing the PP (περὶ τὸν Νεεμιαν) into the nominative subject of προσηγόρευσαν.

περὶ τὸν Νεεμιαν. Association. See 1:13 (cf. 1:33) on περὶ αὐτόν.

τοῦτο. Accusative direct object of προσηγόρευσαν in an object-complement double accusative construction. The demonstrative pronoun refers to the "thick water" from 1:20 and referenced in 1:31, 33.

νεφθαρ. Complement in an object-complement double accusative construction. The word is indeclinable, but here it agrees with τοῦτο. LEH (416) suggests the word derives from Hebrew נפתא, but provides no further analysis. More fruitfully, Plutarch (*Alex.* 35:1) uses the similar word νάφθα to refer to a highly flammable substance: "This *naphtha* is in other ways like asphaltum, but is so sensitive to fire that, before the flame touches it, it is kindled by the very radiance about the flame and often sets fire also to the intervening air. To show its nature and power, the Barbarians sprinkled the street leading to Alexander's quarters with small quantities of the liquid" (LCL).

ὃ. Nominative subject of διερμηνεύεται. The relative pronoun agrees with τοῦτο νεφθαρ.

διερμηνεύεται. Pres pass ind 3rd sg διερμηνεύω. The verb occurs only once in the LXX. On the meaning of the verb, see BDAG (244.1): "to translate from one language to another, *translate*" (cf. Acts 9:36; 1 Cor 12:30; 14:5, 13, 27).

καθαρισμός. Nominative in apposition to the relative pronoun ὅ.

καλεῖται. Pres pass ind 3rd sg καλέω.

δὲ. Development; see 1:10 on δέ.

παρὰ τοῖς πολλοῖς. Sphere. παρά marks someone "whose viewpoint is relevant, in the sight or judgment of someone" (BDAG, 757.2).

νεφθαι. Predicate nominative. The indeclinable word (cf. νεφθαρ above) has been given the nominative case ending. It agrees with the (implied)

subject of the passive verb καλεῖται (see BDF §412.2). For similar constructions of καλέω with the nominative, see Gen 11:9; Hos 2:18; Isa 35:8; etc.

2 Maccabees 2:1-3

[1]Now it is found in the records that the prophet Jeremiah ordered those
being deported to take some of the fire, as has been mentioned [2]and
that the prophet commanded those being deported, after giving the law
to them, not to forget the commandments of the Lord and not to be
led astray in thoughts when seeing the gold and silver statues and their
adornment. [3]And by speaking other similar things, he was exhorting
[them] that the law should not depart from their heart.

Jeremiah is an important figure in 2:1-8 and he also returns later in the
narrative of 2 Maccabees (15:11-16), forging a connection between
the letter and the epitome.

**2:1 Εὑρίσκεται δὲ ἐν ταῖς ἀπογραφαῖς Ιερεμιας ὁ προφήτης ὅτι
ἐκέλευσεν τοῦ πυρὸς λαβεῖν τοὺς μεταγενομένους, ὡς σεσήμανται.**

Εὑρίσκεται . . . ἐν ταῖς ἀπογραφαῖς. The tradition that Jeremiah
ordered Jewish deportees to take objects from the first temple and hide
them is not part of any known biblical text, but it is found in several
other later sources. In 4 Bar. 3:8-11 Jeremiah is ordered to "take [the
holy vessels] and deliver them to the earth." See also 2 Baruch, which
describes the seer witnessing an angel removing "the veil, the holy
ephod, the mercy seat, the two tables, the holy raiment of the priests,
the altar of incense, the forty-eight precious stones . . . and all the holy
vessels of the tabernacle" (2 Bar. 6:7).

Εὑρίσκεται. Pres mid or pass ind 3rd sg εὑρίσκω. It is possible to
understand the verb as either middle ("one finds") or passive ("[it] is
found"), depending on how one handles Ιερεμιας. On the meaning of
the verb, see *GELS* (304.5): "*to discover* a fact after examination" + ὅτι.
This is a common word for "ascertaining a fact from documents" (Goldstein, 181; 2 Esd 4:15, 19; 6:2; Neh 13:1; Esth 6:2; Dan 12:1). Goldstein
(181–82) notes that εὑρίσκω is often used with an impersonal ("it is
found") or editorial ("we find that") sense.

δὲ. Development; see 1:10 on δέ.

ἐν ταῖς ἀπογραφαῖς. Locative. Usually plural, ἀναγραφή refers to a
"public archive" or "record" (cf. *GE*, 131.A). Here, as well as in 2:4 and
2:13, the letter's claims are supported by appealing (however vaguely) to
public records (cf. D. Schwartz, 166).

Ιερεμιας. Nominative subject of εὑρίσκεται (passive) or, more likely, of ἐκέλευσεν. The clause could be translated "*Jeremiah the prophet is found in the records. . . .*" This results in an awkward phrase in English idiom. The placement of Ιερεμιας ὁ προφήτης in the main clause was resolved in the Vulgate by converting the nominatives to genitives: "in the writings *of Jeremiah the prophet.*" Alternatively, this is likely an example of prolepsis, where "the substantive is placed out of its right place before the conjunction in a subordinate clause" (Robertson, 423; cf. Smyth §2182). The NP is fronted for the sake of prominence or emphasis (Muraoka §84c; Siebenthal §128b.d). *GE* (1498) provides a similar example of prolepsis from Xenophon, *Anab.* 3.2.29:

ἐπιστάμεθα Μυσούς . . . ὅτι μεγάλας πόλεις οἰκοῦσιν

We know that the Mysians inhabit large cities

Because the name Ιερεμιας is being established in the narrative it is anarthrous (Smyth §1136; Muraoka §1b). Compare this use with the following articular uses of the name in 2:5 and 2:7, where the article defines "[o]bjects already mentioned or in the mind of the speaker or writer" (Smyth §1120.b).

ὁ προφήτης. Nominative in apposition to Ιερεμιας.

ὅτι. Introduces the clausal complement (indirect discourse) of εὑρίσκεται.

ἐκέλευσεν. Aor act ind 3rd sg κελεύω.

τοῦ πυρός. Partitive genitive ("[some] *of the fire*"). Wallace (85) notes that "[o]ccasionally, the noun to which the genitive is related is absent, understood from the context" (cf. *CGCG* §30.25).

λαβεῖν. Aor act inf λαμβάνω (indirect discourse).

τοὺς μεταγενομένους. Aor mid ptc acc masc pl μεταγίνομαι (substantival). Subject of λαβεῖν. The Göttingen edition notes several variants here (and in 2:2, where the same word appears), including a shift into the present tense (μεταγινομένους, L'–[62 542]) as well as another lexeme, μετάγω (μεταγομένους, V 29-71-107-130-370 62 46-52 311[mg] 771 La[VBM]). The *TLG* records that μεταγίνομαι occurs only 22 times in extant Greek literature; the usage here in 2:1 is the earliest. Perhaps this explains the reading μετάγω ("to be transferred," cf. *GE*, 1322), which is taken by many commentators to be the earliest recoverable text (cf. Habicht, 205; Doran 2012, 54; Goldstein, 182; Nicklas 2011, 1380). *GE* (1322) glosses μεταγί(γ)νομαι as "to be transferred" or "deported," however, only 2:1-2 is cited as evidence for this meaning (cf. *GELS*, 453). It is very likely that μεταγενομένους has been confused for μεταγομένους.

ὡς. Introduces a clause of comparison.

σεσήμανται. Prf pass ind 3rd sg σημαίνω. The perfect indicative (stative verbal aspect) expresses the present state that is the result of completed action (Wallace, 574–76; cf. *CGCG* §33.11). In 11:17 the same word is used to refer to matters "indicated" or "mentioned" in a letter, suggesting that σημαίνω is also used here to refer back to something written. BDAG (920) refers to "speech that simply offers a vague suggestion of what is to happen," but this sense cannot explain many instances (e.g., Esth 2:22). On the meaning of the verb, see *GELS* (620.3): "to name, mention" (1 Esd 8:48).

2:2 καὶ ὡς ἐνετείλατο τοῖς μεταγενομένοις ὁ προφήτης δοὺς αὐτοῖς τὸν νόμον, ἵνα μὴ ἐπιλάθωνται τῶν προσταγμάτων τοῦ κυρίου, καὶ ἵνα μὴ ἀποπλανηθῶσιν ταῖς διανοίαις βλέποντες ἀγάλματα χρυσᾶ καὶ ἀργυρᾶ καὶ τὸν περὶ αὐτὰ κόσμον·

ὡς. Introduces another clausal complement (indirect discourse) of εὑρίσκεται in 2:1. Functions like ὅτι (see *GELS*, 304.5) in 2:1.

ἐνετείλατο. Aor mid ind 3rd sg ἐντέλλομαι.

τοῖς μεταγενομένοις. Aor mid dat masc pl μεταγίνομαι (substantival). Indirect object of ἐνετείλατο. See 2:1 for discussion of this word.

ὁ προφήτης. Nominative subject of ἐνετείλατο.

δοὺς. Aor act ptc nom masc sg δίδωμι (temporal). The participle may be temporal ("[the prophet . . . commanded] *after giving* the law to them") or, less likely, means ("*by giving* the law to them"). On the latter sense, see D. Schwartz (160).

αὐτοῖς. Dative indirect object of δοὺς.

τὸν νόμον. Accusative direct object of δοὺς.

ἵνα μὴ. Introduces a negative imperatival clause following ἐνετείλατο (cf. BDF §387.3) or, better, a content clause that serves as the direct object of ἐνετείλατο: ἐνετείλατο . . . ἵνα μὴ ἐπιλάθωνται = "he commanded . . . not to forget" (Muraoka §66b). It is also possible, but less likely, to construe ἵνα with δοὺς. See 1:5 on μή for further comments on negation.

ἐπιλάθωνται. Aor mid subj 3rd pl ἐπιλανθάνομαι. Subjunctive with ἵνα.

τῶν προσταγμάτων. Genitive complement of ἐπιλάθωνται. Verbs of remembering often take the genitive case (Smyth §1356; BDF §175; Muraoka §22p). See 1:4 on πρόσταγμα.

τοῦ κυρίου. Genitive of source.

καὶ. The conjunction links the ἵνα μὴ to ἐνετείλατο as a second content clause.

ἀποπλανηθῶσιν. Aor pass subj 3rd pl ἀποπλανάω. Subjunctive with ἵνα.

ταῖς διανοίαις. Dative of sphere or, perhaps, means.

βλέποντες. Pres act ptc nom masc pl βλέπω (temporal or, less certainly, causal).

ἀγάλματα χρυσᾶ καὶ ἀργυρᾶ καὶ τὸν . . . κόσμον. Accusative direct objects of βλέποντες. The adjectives χρυσᾶ ("golden") and ἀργυρᾶ ("silver") are attributive modifiers of ἀγάλματα (*GE*, 7: "statue, esp. of gods").

περὶ αὐτά. Reference. The neuter plural pronoun agrees with ἀγάλματα.

2:3 καὶ ἕτερα τοιαῦτα λέγων παρεκάλει μὴ ἀποστῆναι τὸν νόμον ἀπὸ τῆς καρδίας αὐτῶν.

ἕτερα τοιαῦτα. Accusative direct object of λέγων.

λέγων. Pres act ptc nom masc sg λέγω (means). Although λέγων often signals direct speech when it follows the main verb, in this context it denotes the means by which Jeremiah exhorted those with him.

παρεκάλει. Impf act ind 3rd sg παρακαλέω.

μὴ. See 1:5 on μή for further comments on the negation.

ἀποστῆναι. Aor act inf ἀφίστημι (indirect discourse). Although 2:1 introduces indirect discourse with ὅτι, and 2:2 introduces indirect discourse with ὡς, here the author uses the bare infinitive. Because indirect discourse can be constructed in each of these ways (Smyth §2579), it is likely that this represents the stylistic variation of the letter or, perhaps, the translator.

τὸν νόμον. Accusative subject of the infinitive ἀποστῆναι. It is also possible to construe τὸν νόμον as the object of the infinitive: "not to send away *the law*."

ἀπὸ τῆς καρδίας. Separation.

αὐτῶν. Possessive genitive.

2 Maccabees 2:4-8

[4]And it was in the writing that the prophet ordered the tent and the ark to follow him because an oracle came about. [And it was in the writing] that he went out to the mountain where Moses went up and saw the inheritance of God. [5]And Jeremiah came and found a cave-like house and he brought there the tent, the ark, and the altar of incense; and he sealed up the entrance. [6]And some of those who followed [him], even though they came forward so that they could mark the way, nevertheless could not find [it]. [7]But, when Jeremiah learned [this], rebuking them he said, "The place will be unknown until God gathers together a meeting of people and he shall be merciful. [8]And then the Lord will disclose these things, and the glory of the Lord and the cloud will appear, as it was shown to Moses, as also Solomon prayed that the place be completely sanctified."

On the function of this part of the letter, see the brief comments following the translation of 1:10-17.

2:4 ἦν δὲ ἐν τῇ γραφῇ ὡς τὴν σκηνὴν καὶ τὴν κιβωτὸν ἐκέλευσεν ὁ προφήτης χρηματισμοῦ γενηθέντος αὐτῷ συνακολουθεῖν· ὡς δὲ ἐξῆλθεν εἰς τὸ ὄρος, οὗ ὁ Μωυσῆς ἀναβὰς ἐθεάσατο τὴν τοῦ θεοῦ κληρονομίαν.

ἦν. Impf act ind 3rd sg εἰμί.

δὲ. Development; see 1:10 on δέ.

ἐν τῇ γραφῇ. Locative. The construction without the article, ἐν γραφῇ, is far more common (1 Chr 28:19; 2 Chr 2:10; 1 Macc 12:21; Ps 86:6; Sir 39:32; 42:7; 44:5; 45:11; Ezek 13:9), suggesting that the article is anaphoric: "in the [previously mentioned] writing" (cf. Nicklas 2011, 1381). See 2:1 on ἐν ταῖς ἀπογραφαῖς.

ὡς. Introduces another clausal complement (indirect discourse) of εὑρίσκεται in 2:1. Functions like ὅτι (see GELS, 304.5) in 2:1 and expresses the content of what "was in the writing" (ἦν . . . ἐν τῇ γραφῇ). See similar uses in 4:1; 7:17.

τὴν σκηνὴν καὶ τὴν κιβωτὸν. Accusative subjects of the infinitive συνακολουθεῖν. Obviously, the prophet's command was not given to "the tent and the ark." Some person is the implied recipient of the command (Muraoka §69e).

ἐκέλευσεν. Aor act ind 3rd sg κελεύω.

ὁ προφήτης. Nominative subject of ἐκέλευσεν.

χρηματισμοῦ. Genitive subject of the participle γενηθέντος. See GE (2376): "oracular response, divine revelation."

γενηθέντος. Aor pass ptc gen masc sg γίνομαι (genitive absolute, temporal or, better, causal). Whereas the genitive absolute is traditionally used when the subject of the participle is different from the subject of the main clause, this may be an example of "loose syntax" (Muraoka §31ha; Mayser II 3.67–71). Thus, Goldstein (156) translates χρηματισμοῦ γενηθέντος as "on receiving a divine revelation," where the prophet and χρηματισμοῦ is the predicate. But, this requires an unusual sense for γίνομαι as "receive" rather than "come about" (cf. GE, 429). It is better to understand this as a true genitive absolute, with the sense of "because an oracle came about." On the genitive absolute, see 1:7 on βασιλεύοντος.

αὐτῷ. Dative of accompaniment. The verb συνακολουθέω is used with a dative to indicate who accompanies the grammatical subject (cf. BDAG, 964).

συνακολουθεῖν. Pres act inf συνακολουθέω (indirect discourse).

ὡς. Introduces a second object clause.

δὲ. Development; see 1:10 on δέ.

ἐξῆλθεν. Aor act ind 3rd sg ἐξέρχομαι.

εἰς τὸ ὄρος. Locative.

οὗ. Adverb of place. Historically, οὗ was the genitive singular of ὅς. However, it came to have the function of an adverb of place: "where" (*GE*, 1492).

ὁ Μωυσῆς. Nominative subject of ἐθεάσατο.

ἀναβὰς. Aor act ptc nom masc sg ἀναβαίνω (attendant circumstance).

ἐθεάσατο. Aor mid ind 3rd sg θεάομαι. Because the grammatical subject is the center of emphasis, verbs of sensory perception are often middle (cf. N. Miller, 429).

τὴν . . . κληρονομίαν. Accusative direct object of ἐθεάσατο.

τοῦ θεοῦ. Possessive genitive or, better, source ("the inheritance [to be granted] *by God*").

2:5 καὶ ἐλθὼν ὁ Ιερεμιας εὗρεν οἶκον ἀντρώδη καὶ τὴν σκηνὴν καὶ τὴν κιβωτὸν καὶ τὸ θυσιαστήριον τοῦ θυμιάματος εἰσήνεγκεν ἐκεῖ καὶ τὴν θύραν ἐνέφραξεν.

ἐλθὼν. Aor act ptc nom masc sg ἔρχομαι (attendant circumstance). Due to suppletion, ἦλθον (active) supplies the aorist forms of ἔρχομαι (middle-only). Even though most verbs of translational bodily motion are morphologically middle, this mismatch is common because ἦλθον encodes different features than ἔρχομαι with regard to grammatical voice.

ὁ Ιερεμιας. Nominative subject of εὗρεν. Having established the subject, Ιερεμιας, in 2:1, the subsequent references in 2:5 and 2:7 are articular, indicating anaphoric use of the article.

εὗρεν. Aor act ind 3rd sg εὑρίσκω.

οἶκον ἀντρώδη. Accusative direct object of εὗρεν. On the meaning of ἀντρώδης, see *GELS* (60): "similar to a cave."

τὴν σκηνὴν καὶ τὴν κιβωτὸν καὶ τὸ θυσιαστήριον. Accusative direct objects of εἰσήνεγκεν.

τοῦ θυμιάματος. Attributive genitive. "The altar *of incense*" refers to the temple's altar.

εἰσήνεγκεν. Aor act ind 3rd sg εἰσφέρω. See 1:8 on ἀνήνεγκεν.

ἐκεῖ. Adverb of place.

τὴν θύραν. Accusative direct object of ἐνέφραξεν.

ἐνέφραξεν. Aor act ind 3rd sg ἐμφράσσω.

2:6 καὶ προσελθόντες τινὲς τῶν συνακολουθούντων ὥστε ἐπιση-μάνασθαι τὴν ὁδὸν καὶ οὐκ ἐδυνήθησαν εὑρεῖν.

προσελθόντες. Aor act ptc nom masc pl προσέρχομαι (temporal or, perhaps more likely, concessive). The concessive idea would be that "*even though some came forward to mark the way . . .* they were not able to find it." This understanding is suggested by the fact that those unable to locate the cave were "those who followed [Jeremiah]" (2:6) to the cave.

τινὲς. Nominative subject of ἐδυνήθησαν.

τῶν συνακολουθούντων. Pres act ptc gen masc pl συνακολουθέω (substantival). Partitive genitive.

ὥστε. Purpose. When used with the infinitive it conveys "consequence presented as intention or expectation" (*GE*, 2428). Here it introduces the intention or aim of "those who followed [Jeremiah]," namely, "so that they could mark the way."

ἐπισημάνασθαι. Aor mid inf ἐπισημαίνω (purpose). Cf. Job 14:17 for the only other LXX use of ἐπισημαίνω.

τὴν ὁδὸν. Accusative direct object of ἐπισημάνασθαι.

καὶ. The two phrases linked by καί are contrasted. They were intending to "mark the way *nevertheless* they could not find it." This usage is in alignment with Runge's explanation of the function of καί: "καί constrains the connected element to be closely associated with what comes before, regardless of whether there is semantic continuity or not" (26).

οὐκ. See 1:5 on the use of οὐ versus μή.

ἐδυνήθησαν. Aor pass ind 3rd pl δύναμαι. The Göttingen edition reads ἠδυνήθησαν, which is a common variation between ε and η for the augment of δύναμαι in both the imperfect and the aorist.

εὑρεῖν. Aor act inf εὑρίσκω (complementary).

2:7 ὡς δὲ ὁ Ιερεμιας ἔγνω, μεμψάμενος αὐτοῖς εἶπεν ὅτι Καὶ ἄγνωστος ὁ τόπος ἔσται, ἕως ἂν συναγάγῃ ὁ θεὸς ἐπισυναγωγὴν τοῦ λαοῦ καὶ ἵλεως γένηται·

ὡς. Temporal conjunction, used with the aorist to communicate "when, after" (BDAG, 1105.8.a). See 1:15.

δὲ. Development, marking a change of grammatical subject from "some" (τινές) in 2:6 to Jeremiah in 2:7. See 1:10 on δέ.

ὁ Ιερεμιας. Nominative subject of ἔγνω. On the article, see 2:5.

ἔγνω. Aor act ind 3rd sg γινώσκω.

μεμψάμενος. Aor mid ptc nom masc sg μέμφομαι (manner). The word has the sense of "to blame, criticize, reproach, disapprove of, find fault with" (*GE*, 1309). Cf. Sir 11:7; 41:7. Although the participle precedes the main verb (εἶπεν), it does not indicate anterior action (cf. Muraoka §31dd).

αὐτοῖς. Dative complement of μεμψάμενος. While it is possible to construe αὐτοῖς with εἶπεν ("he said *to them*"), the verb μέμφομαι can take the dative for its complement (cf. *GE*, 1309; BDAG, 629; Sir 41:7; Josephus, *Ag. Ap.* 1.142).

εἶπεν. Aor act ind 3rd sg εἶπον.

ὅτι. Introduces direct discourse.

Καί. Possibly a case of apodotic καί where the Greek imitates (or possibly translates) the parataxis of Hebrew by using the coordinating conjunction at the beginning of the clause preceded by one (or more) subordinate clauses (cf. Le Moigne, 267). See Muraoka (§90g) on the use of καί in various constructions, including constructions reflecting apodotic conjunction ו.

ἄγνωστος. Predicate adjective, agreeing with ὁ τόπος.

ὁ τόπος. Nominative subject of ἔσται.

ἔσται. Fut mid ind 3rd sg εἰμί.

ἕως ἄν. Temporal conjunction. See *GELS* (312.B.b): "until" + aorist subjunctive (cf. Gen 24:14, 19: Exod 15:16; 33:22; 34:35; Lev 16:17; 23:14; Isa 6:11).

συναγάγῃ. Aor act subj 3rd sg συνάγω.

ὁ θεὸς. Nominative subject of συναγάγῃ.

ἐπισυναγωγὴν. Accusative direct object of συναγάγῃ.

τοῦ λαοῦ. Genitive of material ("a meeting [consisting] *of people*") or, perhaps, partitive ("a meeting *of* [some] *people*").

ἵλεως. Predicate adjective, agreeing with the implied singular subject of γένηται. The Göttingen edition reads ἔλεος, "there shall be *mercy*" (cf. Nicklas 2011, 1381), but parallels with 2:22 and 7:37 support the reading ἵλεως here (Habicht, 206).

γένηται. Aor mid subj 3rd sg γίνομαι.

2:8 καὶ τότε ὁ κύριος ἀναδείξει ταῦτα, καὶ ὀφθήσεται ἡ δόξα τοῦ κυρίου καὶ ἡ νεφέλη, ὡς ἐπὶ Μωυσῇ ἐδηλοῦτο, ὡς καὶ ὁ Σαλωμων ἠξίωσεν ἵνα ὁ τόπος καθαγιασθῇ μεγάλως.

τότε. Temporal adverb.

ὁ κύριος. Nominative subject of ἀναδείξει.

ἀναδείξει. Fut act ind 3rd sg ἀναδείκνυμι.

ταῦτα. Accusative direct object of ἀναδείξει.

ὀφθήσεται. Fut pass ind 3rd sg ὁράω. Due to suppletion, the future forms of ὁράω are formed from the stem *οπ. Moreover, when a labial stop is followed by *theta*, the following pattern occurs: πθ → φθ.

ἡ δόξα... καὶ ἡ νεφέλη. Compound nominative subject of ὀφθήσεται. On the use of a singular verb with compound subjects, see 1:7 on Ἰάσων καὶ οἱ μετ᾽ αὐτοῦ.

τοῦ κυρίου. Possessive genitive or, better, source ("glory *from the Lord*").

ὡς. Introduces a comparative clause. The Göttingen edition reads ὡς καὶ ἐπί, following several Greek manuscripts (MSS A´ 62 46-52 311).

ἐπὶ Μωυσῆ. Reference. ἐπί is a "marker indicating the one to whom, for whom, or about whom someth[ing] is done" (BDAG, 366.14.a).

ἐδηλοῦτο. Impf pass ind 3rd sg δηλόω.

ὡς. Introduces a comparative clause.

καὶ. Adverbial.

ὁ Σαλωμων. Nominative subject of ἠξίωσεν.

ἠξίωσεν. Aor act ind 3rd sg ἀξιόω. Often in 2 Maccabees the verb ἀξιόω has the sense of "to put a request to" (*GELS*, 61), especially in contexts where God is the (implied) recipient (5:4; 8:14, 29; 10:4, 16; 12:42). Thus, here the verb means "to pray."

ἵνα. Either purpose or complementary, introducing the content ("that") of the prayer.

ὁ τόπος. Nominative subject of καθαγιασθῇ.

καθαγιασθῇ. Aor pass subj 3rd sg καθαγιάζω. Subjunctive with ἵνα. See 1:26 on καταγίασον.

μεγάλως. Adverb of manner. On the sense of "completely," see *GE* (1293).

2 Maccabees 2:9-12

[9]It was also told that, because he possessed wisdom, he offered a sacrifice for the dedication and completion of the temple. [10]Just as also Moses prayed to the Lord and fire came down from heaven and ate up the materials of the sacrifice, so also Solomon prayed and after fire came down and consumed the whole burnt offerings. [11]And Moses said, "Because the sin offering had not been eaten, it was consumed." [12]Likewise, Solomon also celebrated the eight days.

On the function of this part of the letter, see the brief comments following the translation of 1:10-17.

2:9 διεσαφεῖτο δὲ καὶ ὡς σοφίαν ἔχων ἀνήνεγκεν θυσίαν ἐγκαινισμοῦ καὶ τῆς τελειώσεως τοῦ ἱεροῦ.

διεσαφεῖτο. Impf pass ind 3rd sg διασαφέω.

δέ. Development; see 1:10 on δέ.

καί. Adverbial.

ὡς. Introduces the clausal complement (indirect discourse) of διεσαφεῖτο. Both ὡς and ὅτι can function to introduce content after a verb of knowing or speaking: "it was also being explained *that*" (cf. *GE*, 2426).

σοφίαν. Accusative direct object of ἔχων.

ἔχων. Pres act ptc nom masc sg ἔχω (causal).

ἀνήνεγκεν. Aor act ind 3rd sg ἀναφέρω. See 1:18 on ἀνήνεγκεν.

θυσίαν. Accusative direct object of ἀνήνεγκεν.

ἐγκαινισμοῦ . . . τῆς τελειώσεως. Genitives of destination/purpose ("sacrifice *for the dedication* and *completion*") or, less likely, epexegetical ("sacrifice, *namely* [the sacrifice] *of dedication* and *completion*") (Wallace, 100). Doran (2012, 58) notes that "[t]he author has neatly chosen to have depend on a single substantive two genitives, one of which has the sense of 'newness, beginning' and the other the sense of 'end, completion, perfection.'" For details of such a sacrifice, see especially 4 Kgdms 7:5-7.

τοῦ ἱεροῦ. Objective genitive.

2:10 καθὼς καὶ Μωυσῆς προσηύξατο πρὸς κύριον, καὶ κατέβη πῦρ ἐκ τοῦ οὐρανοῦ καὶ τὰ τῆς θυσίας ἐδαπάνησεν, οὕτως καὶ Σαλωμων προσηύξατο, καὶ καταβὰν τὸ πῦρ ἀνήλωσεν τὰ ὁλοκαυτώματα.

καθὼς . . . οὕτως. Correlative construction, introducing a clause of comparison: "*just as* also Moses . . . *so* also Solomon" (*GE*, 1508; BDAG, 741.1).

καί. Adverbial.

Μωυσῆς. Nominative subject of προσηύξατο. Doran (2012, 58) notes that the specific biblical reference of this story is unclear because Moses never prays with the result that fire comes down (cf. Deut 9:26; Num 11:2; 21:7). The best possible background for this story is Lev 9:23-24, when Moses and Aaron exit the tent of meeting and "fire comes down and consumes what is on the altar" (NETS).

προσηύξατο. Aor mid ind 3rd sg προσεύχομαι.

πρὸς κύριον. Because the dative case is often used with (προσ-) εύχομαι to indicate manner (BDAG, 879), the PP provides the functional equivalent of an indirect object of προσηύξατο (cf. 9:13; Jdt 11:17; Neh 2:4; etc.).

κατέβη. Aor act ind 3rd sg καταβαίνω.

πῦρ. Nominative subject of κατέβη.

ἐκ τοῦ οὐρανοῦ. Source.

τά. The article τά functions as a nominalizer, making τῆς θυσίας the accusative direct object of ἐδαπάνησεν.

τῆς θυσίας. Because the neuter article (τά) has a broad scope of reference, it is difficult to define the genitive more narrowly. Wallace's (79) category of aporetic genitive is applicable.

ἐδαπάνησεν. Aor act ind 3rd sg ἐδαπάνησεν.

καί. Adverbial.

Σαλωμων. Nominative subject of προσηύξατο.

προσηύξατο. Aor mid ind 3rd sg προσεύχομαι.

καταβάν. Aor act ptc nom neut sg καταβαίνω (attendant circumstance).

τὸ πῦρ. Nominative subject of ἀνήλωσεν. The article is used to point back to the "fire" mentioned earlier in 2:10 (Smyth §1120).

ἀνήλωσεν. Aor act ind 3rd sg ἀναλίσκω.

τὰ ὁλοκαυτώματα. Accusative direct object of ἀνήλωσεν. This refers to "a cultic sacrifice in which the animal was entirely consumed by fire" (BDAG, 703.1).

2:11 καὶ εἶπεν Μωυσῆς Διὰ τὸ μὴ βεβρῶσθαι τὸ περὶ τῆς ἁμαρτίας ἀνηλώθη.

καὶ εἶπεν Μωυσῆς. There is no known text that corresponds to the saying that follows this introductory formula. The quoted speech would fit perfectly into the narrative of Lev 10:16-19, yet it reproduces very little from that context (cf. τὸ περὶ τῆς ἁμαρτίας). While it is possible that there is another source that might explain the wording of this saying, it is more likely that the quotation is a summary of the content of Lev 10:16-19. In that context, Moses expresses his anger with the priests, questioning them as to why they did not eat the goat that had been offered for sin.

εἶπεν. Aor act ind 3rd sg λέγω.

Μωυσῆς. Nominative subject of εἶπεν.

μή. See comment on the negation in 1:5.

βεβρῶσθαι. Prf pass inf βιβρώσκω. Used with διὰ τό to denote cause. The neuter article τό indicates the case of βεβρῶσθαι (Burk, 27–46). The perfect infinitive (stative verbal aspect) describes the state of the sin offering.

τό. The article functions as a nominalizer, changing the PP (περὶ τῆς ἁμαρτίας) into the accusative subject of the infinitive βεβρῶσθαι.

περὶ τῆς ἁμαρτίας. Reference. The noun ἁμαρτία is used to refer to the "slaughtered animal offered to atone" = "sin offering" (*GELS*, 31).

ἀνηλώθη. Aor pass ind 3rd sg ἀναλίσκω. For other examples of things "destroyed" or "consumed" by fire, see Gen 41:30; Ezek 5:12; Joel 1:19-20; 2:3. Cf. the use of the same verb in 1:31.

2:12 ὡσαύτως καὶ ὁ Σαλωμων τὰς ὀκτὼ ἡμέρας ἤγαγεν.

ὡσαύτως καὶ. "Likewise also" (*GE*, 2427–28), comparing Solomon's actions (2:12) with Moses' (2:11).

ὁ Σαλωμων. Nominative subject of ἤγαγεν.

τὰς ὀκτὼ ἡμέρας. Accusative direct object of ἤγαγεν. The cardinal number ὀκτώ ("eight") is indeclinable. "The eight days" refers to the eight-day celebration in 2 Chr 7:9-10/3 Kgdms 8:66 as a precedent for Hanukkah. As D. Schwartz (165) notes, the fact that Hanukkah is an eight-day celebration is here assumed even though this fact is only explicitly stated in 10:6.

ἤγαγεν. Aor act ind 3rd sg ἄγω. On the collocation of ἄγω + ἡμέρας, see 1:9 on ἄγητε.

2 Maccabees 2:13-15

[13]Now the same things were reported also in the records and in the memoirs of Nehemiah, and that, establishing a library, he collected the book rolls about the kings and prophets, and the writings of David, and letters of kings about votive offerings. [14]Likewise, Judas also collected everything for us that had been lost because of the war that had come, and it is in our possession. [15]So, then, if you have need of them, send those who will bring them back for you.

2:13 ἐξηγοῦντο δὲ καὶ ἐν ταῖς ἀναγραφαῖς καὶ ἐν τοῖς ὑπομνηματισμοῖς τοῖς κατὰ τὸν Νεεμιαν τὰ αὐτὰ καὶ ὡς καταβαλλόμενος βιβλιοθήκην ἐπισυνήγαγεν τὰ περὶ τῶν βασιλέων βιβλία καὶ προφητῶν καὶ τὰ τοῦ Δαυιδ καὶ ἐπιστολὰς βασιλέων περὶ ἀναθεμάτων.

ἐξηγοῦντο. Impf pass ind 3rd pl ἐξηγέομαι.

δὲ. Development; see 1:10 on δέ.

καὶ. Thematic addition ("also"). Alternatively, it is possible that this καί should be construed with the following καί in a "both . . . and" construction: "Now the same things were reported *both* in the records *and* in the memoirs of Nehemiah." However, reference to "the same things" (τὰ αὐτά) suggests the former.

ἐν ταῖς ἀναγραφαῖς. Locative. See 2:1 on ἐν ταῖς ἀπογραφαῖς.

ἐν τοῖς ὑπομνηματισμοῖς τοῖς κατὰ τὸν Νεεμιαν. Locative. It is possible, but unlikely, that the καί that links this PP to the previous clause is epexegetical: "in the records, *that is*, in the memoirs of Nehemiah." Ὑπομνηματισμοί is best understood as a reference to "historical records" (D. Schwartz, 166).

τοῖς. The article functions as a nominalizer, turning the PP (κατὰ τὸν Νεεμιαν) into a substantive that modifies τοῖς ὑπομνηματισμοῖς.

κατὰ τὸν Νεεμιαν. Reference. BDF (§224) notes that "κατά as a circumlocution for the possessive or subjective gen[itive] is generally Hellenistic" (cf. Mayser II 1.11; 2.343; Muraoka §22v.iv; MHT 3:268). Based on the grammar alone, it is difficult to say whether the "memoirs of Nehemiah" refers to something written *by Nehemiah* or *about Nehemiah* (Habicht, 206).

τὰ αὐτά. Nominative subject of ἐξηγοῦντο. Here τὰ αὐτά functions as a substantival identical adjective. The referent of "the same things" is likely (much of) the content mentioned in 2:1-12.

ὡς. Possibly epexegetical, introducing a clause that explains τὰ αὐτά: "now the same things were reported . . . namely, upon founding a library, he collected the books." But, more likely, ὡς introduces a clausal complement (indirect discourse) of ἐξηγοῦντο.

καταβαλλόμενος. Pres mid ptc nom masc sg καταβάλλω (temporal; or, possibly, attendant circumstance). Because the participle is present tense, it is best translated as expressing action contemporaneous with the action of the main verb ἐπισυνήγαγεν.

βιβλιοθήκην. Accusative direct object of καταβαλλόμενος. On the meaning of βιβλιοθήκη, see Lange (166), who argues that "the library in question must have been the Jerusalem temple library."

ἐπισυνήγαγεν. Aor act ind 3rd sg ἐπισυνάγω. The verb forms the basis for the rest of 2:13 and has three accusative direct objects that modify it (τὰ βιβλία, τὰ [βιβλία], ἐπιστολάς), indicating what was "collected."

τὰ . . . βιβλία. Accusative direct object of ἐπισυνήγαγεν. Doran (2012, 55), following MS q, omits βιβλία in his translation, arguing that "[t]he present position of βιβλία breaks up the connection, formed by the single article, between 'kings and prophets' as well as the parallel with the following τὰ τοῦ Δαυιδ." The syntax is awkward, but the evidence for the omission is slim.

According to the LDAB, *all* ancient books that date between 400 BCE and 50 BCE (i.e., within a reasonable window of the composition of 2 Maccabees) *are in the form of book rolls* (cf. Roberts and Skeat). Therefore, βιβλία refers here to a book roll.

περὶ τῶν βασιλέων . . . καὶ προφητῶν. Reference.

τὰ τοῦ Δαυιδ. On the possible reference to a tripartite Hebrew canon in 2:13, see Lange (155–67). However, this is most likely a reference to the Psalms and not *pars pro toto* to all the Writings (Bergren, 265; *pace* D. Schwartz, 166).

τὰ. The article resumes βιβλία without repeating it. Accusative direct object of ἐπισυνήγαγεν.

τοῦ Δαυιδ. Genitive of source ("the writings *derived from* David") or subjective genitive ("*David's* writings").

ἐπιστολὰς βασιλέων περὶ ἀναθεμάτων. This could refer to letters incorporated into 2 Maccabees (e.g., 11:22-26, 27-33) or, more likely, to letters that have not survived.

ἐπιστολὰς. Accusative direct object of ἐπισυνήγαγεν.

βασιλέων. Genitive of source ("the letters *derived from* kings") or subjective genitive ("*kings'* letters").

περὶ ἀναθεμάτων. Reference. Denotes votive offerings, which are "are voluntary dedications to the gods, resulting not from prescribed ritual or sacred calendars but from *ad hoc* vows of individuals or communities in circumstances usually of anxiety, transition, or achievement" (*OCD*, 1564–65).

2:14 ὡσαύτως δὲ καὶ Ιουδας τὰ διαπεπτωκότα διὰ τὸν γεγονότα πόλεμον ἡμῖν ἐπισυνήγαγεν πάντα, καὶ ἔστιν παρ' ἡμῖν·

ὡσαύτως . . . καὶ. See 2:12 on ὡσαύτως καί.

δὲ. Development, marking a change of grammatical subject from Nehemiah (implied subject of ἐπισυνήγαγεν) in 2:13 to Judas in 2:14.

Ιουδας. Nominative subject of ἐπισυνήγαγεν.

τὰ . . . πάντα. Accusative direct object of ἐπισυνήγαγεν. The separation of the article from the adjective is an example of hyperbaton where most of the interpositional words modify τὰ πάντα.

διαπεπτωκότα. Prf act ptc acc neut pl διαπίπτω (attributive, modifying πάντα). Refers to the books mentioned in 2:13. The meaning of διαπίπτω is difficult to determine, but *GE* (502) lists "to fall apart" as a possibility, which would refer to books that are damaged or, generally, in bad shape. Josephus uses the term in this sense in reference to books: "those [books] that are *damaged* [τῶν διαπεπτωκότων] shall be given the necessary care" (*Ant.* 12.2.4). Alternatively, the context, specifically the reference to having the books "in our possession," suggests the possible meaning "to lose" = "go missing" (*GELS*, 156). Thus, the translation "everything . . . *that had been lost.*" On the reconstruction of the temple's archives, see Josephus, *Ag. Ap.* 1.34–35.

διὰ τὸν γεγονότα πόλεμον. Causal.

γεγονότα. Prf act ptc acc masc sg γίνομαι (attributive). The perfect participle (stative verbal aspect) describes a state of war as something that happened.

ἡμῖν. Dative of advantage, modifying ἐπισυνήγαγεν. It is also possible to connect ἡμῖν with γεγονότα ("the war which had come upon *us*," cf. Abel, 308–9). In that case, it would be a dative of disadvantage (cf. Habicht, 207; Goldstein, 187; Doran 2012, 55). The use of a dative pronoun to modify a verb elsewhere in 2 Maccabees is inconclusive (e.g., 1:14, 18, 19, 20, 35; 2:2, 4, 7, 14, 15, 16).

ἐπισυνήγαγεν. Aor act ind 3rd sg ἐπισυνάγω. Elsewhere, ἐπισυνάγω is used to refer to gathering up God's people (1:27; 2:18) and "a resonance is set up" between Judas' action of collecting books and the ingathering of the people (Doran 2012, 60).

ἔστιν. Pres act ind 3rd sg εἰμί.

παρ᾽ ἡμῖν. Locative. Literally, "with us" = "in our possession."

2:15 ὧν οὖν ἐὰν χρείαν ἔχητε, τοὺς ἀποκομιοῦντας ὑμῖν ἀποστέλλετε.

ὧν. Either an objective genitive ("if you [have] need [of] *them*") or genitive of source ("if you have need of anything *from them*").

οὖν. Inferential. The postpositive conjunction signals continuity and development. Runge (43) notes that οὖν "differs from the other development markers by adding the constraint of close continuity with what precedes. In this sense, it resembles καί by closely linking discourse elements together, but with the added constraint of a new development." Thus, οὖν is often used to draw an inference from preceding discourse or to resume a narrative plotline.

ἐὰν. Introduces a third-class conditional clause (Smyth §2323), which uses ἐάν + subjunctive in the protasis. The third-class conditional introduces prospective conditions where the writer or speaker "presents fulfillment of the condition as very well possible/likely" (*CGCG* §49.6; cf. Porter 1999, 262).

χρείαν. Accusative direct object of ἔχητε.

ἔχητε. Pres act subj 2nd pl ἔχω. The collocation of χρείαν + ἔχω conveys necessity.

τοὺς ἀποκομιοῦντας. Fut act ptc acc masc pl ἀποκομίζω (substantival). Direct object of ἀποστέλλετε. This rare word has the sense of "*to carry back* [something] to where it belongs" (*GELS*, 76).

ὑμῖν. Dative of advantage.

ἀποστέλλετε. Pres act impv 2nd pl ἀποστέλλω. An imperative in the apodosis of prospective conditions has future reference. See above.

2 Maccabees 2:16-18

[16]Therefore, because we are about to celebrate the Purification, we write to you. Therefore, you would do well by celebrating the days. [17]And the God who saved all the people and who returned the inheritance to all and [who returned] the kingship and the priesthood and the consecration, [18]just as he promised through the law, for we hope in God that soon he will show mercy to us and will gather [us] from everywhere under heaven to the holy place. For he rescued us from great evils and has cleansed the place.

2:16 Μέλλοντες οὖν ἄγειν τὸν καθαρισμὸν ἐγράψαμεν ὑμῖν· καλῶς οὖν ποιήσετε ἄγοντες τὰς ἡμέρας.

Μέλλοντες. Pres act ptc nom masc pl μέλλω (causal). See the nearly identical phrase in 1:18.

οὖν. Resumptive. Returns to the main topic introduced in 1:18, which was interrupted (or supported) by stories about Nehemiah (1:18-36), Jeremiah (2:1-8), and Solomon (2:9-12) that were meant to legitimize the Hasmonean temple. Runge (43) notes that "[o]ne often finds οὖν at high-level boundaries in the discourse, where the next major topic is drawn from and builds upon what precedes." See also 2:15 on οὖν.

ἄγειν. Pres act inf ἄγω (complimentary). On the meaning "celebrate," see 1:9 on ἄγητε.

τὸν καθαρισμὸν. Accusative direct object of ἄγειν.

ἐγράψαμεν. Aor act ind 1st pl γράφω. An epistolary aorist ("we *write* to you"), where "[t]he writer of a letter or book . . . may put himself in the position of the reader or beholder who views the action as past" (Smyth §1942). See also MHT (3:73) on this verb.

ὑμῖν. Dative indirect object of ἐγράψαμεν.

καλῶς. Adverb of manner.

οὖν. Inferential. Rhetorically, the conjunction may form part of a question: "will you *therefore* please keep the days?" (NRSV; cf. *CGCG* §59.34; BDAG, 736.1.c.α).

ποιήσετε. Fut act ind 2nd pl ποιέω. The combination of καλῶς + ποιέω is a common way of making a polite request at the conclusion of a letter body (White, 204). The formula is typically employed by those in authority rather than those petitioning someone in authority (Habicht, 207; Doran 2012, 60).

ἄγοντες. Pres act ptc nom masc pl ἄγω (complementary to ποιήσετε). Verbs that express "a certain manner of being or acting" (e.g., ποιέω) sometimes take a supplementary participle (*CGCG* §52.8). On the collocation of ἄγω + ἡμέρας, see 1:9 on ἄγητε.

τὰς ἡμέρας. Accusative direct object of ἄγοντες.

2:17 ὁ δὲ θεὸς ὁ σώσας τὸν πάντα λαὸν αὐτοῦ καὶ ἀποδοὺς τὴν κληρονομίαν πᾶσιν καὶ τὸ βασίλειον καὶ τὸ ἱεράτευμα καὶ τὸν ἁγιασμόν,

Both the grammar and logic of 2:17-18a require two general comments. First, there is no main verb in 2:17-18a. It is possible that a verb has fallen out of the textual tradition (cf. Goldstein, 187) or that this is an example of anacoluthon (cf. Abel, 309–10; D. Schwartz, 132). Alternatively, it is possible that a form of εἰμί should be understood in 2:17. On this reading, ὁ σώσας becomes the predicate: "God [*is*] *the one who saved*." Most likely is that 2:17-18a is an appositional modifier defining "God" in 2:18b: "God, the one who saved . . . we hope in this God" (Doran 2012, 61).

Second, the first use of γάρ in 2:18 requires explanation. If εἰμί is understood in 2:17 there is now a problem because in 2:18b, present "hope in God" seems to be offered as an explanation (γάρ) for God's past actions. Accordingly, it is desirable to take the first γάρ clause as parenthetical (Smyth §2812; Denniston, 68–69; *CGCG* §59.15; cf. Shaw 2016, 408), where a large clause is inserted into the main clause (cf. e.g., Thucydides, *Hist.* 1.87; Polybius, *Hist.* 4.34.1). More preferably, following Doran's reading, hope in God (2:18) provides the reason (γάρ) why Jews should celebrate purification (2:16).

ὁ . . . θεὸς. Nominative subject of ἐλπίζομεν (2:18). See above for an alternative explanation.

δὲ. Development, marking a change of grammatical subject from "you" (the implied subject in ποιήσετε) in 2:16 to God in 2:17. See 1:10 on δέ.

ὁ σώσας. Aor act ptc nom masc sg σῴζω (attributive, modifying ὁ . . . θεός). See above.

τὸν πάντα λαὸν. Accusative direct object of σώσας. In contrast with ἔθνος (cf. 1:27), here λαός denotes Jews. The word πᾶς, which occurs two times in 2:17, clarifies that all Jews are to be the recipients of God's action (cf. Doran 2012, 61).

αὐτοῦ. Possessive genitive or, possibly, subordination.

ἀποδοὺς. Aor act ptc nom masc sg ἀποδίδωμι (attributive, modifying ὁ . . . θεός). Linked by καί to the article ὁ.

τὴν κληρονομίαν . . . καὶ τὸ βασίλειον καὶ τὸ ἱεράτευμα καὶ τὸν ἁγιασμόν. Accusative direct objects of ἀποδοὺς. Cf. Exod 19:6.

πᾶσιν. Dative of advantage. It is unusual that πᾶσιν occurs after τὴν κληρονομίαν rather than prior to or after the entire string of accusative direct objects of ἀποδούς. This is one reason that Goldstein (187) believes that an additional verb must be supplied in 2:17. Muraoka (§78e) notes that when πᾶς refers "to separate entities, πᾶς may be added with the first term and need not be repeated further." However, none of Muraoka's examples parallel 2:17 exactly, where πᾶσιν appears after (not prior to) the first noun in the sequence.

2:18 καθὼς ἐπηγγείλατο διὰ τοῦ νόμου· ἐλπίζομεν γὰρ ἐπὶ τῷ θεῷ ὅτι ταχέως ἡμᾶς ἐλεήσει καὶ ἐπισυνάξει ἐκ τῆς ὑπὸ τὸν οὐρανὸν εἰς τὸν ἅγιον τόπον· ἐξείλατο γὰρ ἡμᾶς ἐκ μεγάλων κακῶν καὶ τὸν τόπον ἐκαθάρισεν.

καθὼς. Introduces a clause of comparison.

ἐπηγγείλατο. Aor mid ind 3rd sg ἐπαγγέλλομαι.

διὰ τοῦ νόμου. Means. On the promise in the Law, see Exod 19:6: ὑμεῖς δὲ ἔσεσθέ μοι βασίλειον ἱεράτευμα καὶ ἔθνος ἅγιον. In a PP, νόμος appears 57 times with the article and 28 times without the article in the LXX.

ἐλπίζομεν. Pres act ind 1st pl ἐλπίζω. The present indicative (imperfective verbal aspect) likely suggests a general truth that is continuously in effect (cf. *CGCG* §33.16).

γὰρ. Causal conjunction, supplying the reason why Jews in Egypt should celebrate (cf. 1:16). See 1:12 on γάρ.

ἐπὶ τῷ θεῷ. Basis (cf. BDAG, 364.6). The preposition ἐπί is commonly used with ἐλπίζω to indicate what one hopes *in* (e.g., 1 Macc 2:61; 2 Macc 7:20; Pss 4:6; 5:12; 7:2; 9:11; 12:6; 15:1; 16:7; 17:3, 31; 20:8; 21:5-6, 9; 24:20; 25:1; etc.). The article is anaphoric, pointing back to the God described in 2:17.

ὅτι. Introduces a clausal complement of ἐλπίζομεν. The entire clause functions as the direct object of ἐλπίζομεν.

ταχέως. Temporal adverb.

ἡμᾶς. Accusative direct object of ἐλεήσει.

ἐλεήσει. Fut act ind 3rd sg ἐλεέω.

ἐπισυνάξει. Fut act ind 3rd sg ἐπισυνάγω.

ἐκ τῆς ὑπὸ τὸν οὐρανὸν. Source.

τῆς. The article functions as a nominalizer, changing the PP (ὑπὸ τὸν οὐρανόν) into a substantive. Alternatively, Conybeare and Stock (§45) suggests that the "use of the feminine article with same case of χώρα or γῆ [is] understood."

ὑπὸ τὸν οὐρανὸν. Locative.

εἰς τὸν ἅγιον τόπον. Locative.

ἐξείλατο. Aor mid ind 3rd sg ἐξαιρέω. *GE* (710) notes that the middle form means "to take away (*for oneself*)."

γάρ. Causal conjunction. The reason why one should hope that Israel's God will show mercy and gather his people is *because* God has rescued his people from great evils. See 1:12 on γάρ.

ἡμᾶς. Accusative direct object of ἐξείλατο.

ἐκ μεγάλων κακῶν. Separation.

τὸν τόπον. Accusative direct object of ἐκαθάρισεν.

ἐκαθάρισεν. Aor act ind 3rd sg καθαρίζω. The Göttingen edition reads ἐκαθέρισεν, which is an alternate spelling. On such spelling variations, see Caragounis (517–46).

2 Maccabees 2:19-25

[19]Now, the story concerning Judas Maccabeus and the brothers of this one and the cleansing of the greatest temple and the dedication of the altar; [20]additionally, both the wars against Antiochus Epiphanes and the son of this one, Eupator; [21]and the appearances that came from heaven to those who behaved heroically for [the sake of] Judaism so that even though few in number they plundered the whole country and pursued the barbarian hordes [22]and they regained possession of the most famous temple throughout the inhabited world and liberated the city and re-established the laws that were about to be abolished, while the Lord with all equity became merciful to them—[23][all this] that has been displayed by Jason of Cyrene through five book rolls, we shall attempt to epitomize through a single treatise. [24]For, considering the great quantity of numbers involved and the difficulty there is for those who wish to dig into the stories about the history because of the mass of material, [25]we sought to bring about amusement for those wishing to read, to make it easy for those who are well-disposed to memorize, and to profit all those who chance upon [this].

Up until now 2 Maccabees has consisted of prefixed letters (1:1-9; 1:10–2:18). Thus, 2:19-23 is the epitomizer's first contribution. In terms of style and excitement, the epitomizer does not disappoint. The prologue includes some of the standard *topoi* of Greek literature, including the pleasure of reading history and the effort involved in producing the narrative (cf. D. Schwartz, 171). The purpose of the main narrative of 2 Maccabees is clearly stated in 2:23: "to epitomize" (ἐπιτεμεῖν). Although presented as a story about "Judas and his brothers" (2:19), Judas' brothers are hardly mentioned in the narrative: e.g., Joseph/John

(8:22; 10:19), Jonathan (8:22), and Simon (8:22; 10:19-20). Moreover, the work is supposed to cover the campaigns against Antiochus Epiphanes and Eupator, his son (2:20), but the narrative itself extends beyond this period (cf. 2 Maccabees 12–15).

In terms of Greek style, the syntax of 2:19-23 is "a skillful exploitation of the rich linguistic resources available" to the writer (Muraoka §81). In particular, 2:19-23 form a long period: "now the story about Judas Maccabeus [Τὰ δὲ κατὰ τὸν Ιουδαν τὸν Μακκαβαῖον, 2:19] . . . we shall attempt to epitomize [πειρασόμεθα ἐπιτεμεῖν, 2:23]." This example of hyperbaton accords with what Longinus describes in *Subl.* 22.4: "For [Demosthenes] often suspends the sense which he has begun to express, and in the interval manages to bring forward one extraneous idea after another in a strange and unlikely order, making the audience terrified of a total collapse of the sentence, and compelling them from sheer excitement to share the speaker's risk: then unexpectedly, after a great interval, the long-lost phrase turns up at the end, so that he astounds them all the more by the very recklessness and audacity of the transpositions" (LCL). Similarly, Plutarch (*Mor.* 7b) notes that "a discourse composed of a series of short sentences I regard as no small proof of lack of culture" (LCL). On hyperbaton in 2 Maccabees, see the Introduction.

2:19 Τὰ δὲ κατὰ τὸν Ιουδαν τὸν Μακκαβαῖον καὶ τοὺς τούτου ἀδελφοὺς καὶ τὸν τοῦ ἱεροῦ τοῦ μεγίστου καθαρισμὸν καὶ τὸν τοῦ βωμοῦ ἐγκαινισμόν.

Τὰ. The neuter article functions as a nominalizer, changing the PP (κατὰ τὸν Ιουδαν τὸν Μακκαβαῖον . . .) into the accusative direct object of ἐπιτεμεῖν (2:23). "*The things* concerning [κατά] . . ." refers to "*the story* concerning [κατά] . . ." (cf. BDAG, 689.2.h.α; Muraoka §6a.i). See 3:40; 9:3; 10:10.

δὲ. Development, suggesting that the prologue (2:19-32) is connected to the prefixed letters (1:1–9; 1:10–2:18). See 1:10 on δέ.

κατὰ τὸν Ιουδαν τὸν Μακκαβαῖον. Reference. See 2:13 on κατὰ τὸν Νεεμιαν. The name Μακκαβαῖος probably means "hammer" or "mallet," as suggested by the meaning of מקבתא in Aramaic (cf. Ilan, 438). On the use of alternative names by Jews in antiquity, see Williams (317–35).

τοὺς . . . ἀδελφοὺς. Linked by καί to κατά. On the possible meaning(s) of ἀδελφούς, see 1:1. Despite the paucity of references to Judas' "brothers" in 2 Maccabees (cf. 8:22; 10:19-20; 14:17), it is likely that the sense is familial.

τούτου. Genitive of relationship. The genitive of a demonstrative pronoun "may substitute for αὐτοῦ, αὐτῆς, or αὐτῶν and be inserted between the article and a substantive" (Muraoka §34c; cf. Mayser II 2:66).

τὸν . . . καθαρισμὸν. Linked by καί to κατά.

τοῦ ἱεροῦ τοῦ μεγίστου. Objective genitive. The superlative of μέγας ("greatest") is used multiple times in 2 Maccabees (3:35, 36; 5:6; 14:13, 31; 15:18). See esp. 14:13, 31 for descriptions of the *"greatest* temple."

τὸν . . . ἐγκαινισμὸν. Linked by καί to κατά. In the LXX ἐγκαινισμός is used of the "dedication" *of the altar* (Num 7:10, 11, 84; 2 Chr 7:9; 1 Macc 4:56, 59), *of the temple* (1 Esd 7:7; 2 Macc 2:9), and *of the house [of God?]* (Ps 29:1). The noun refers to "inauguration" or "renewal" of an object or structure (*GE*, 582), typically through sacrifices or offerings (cf. Num 7:10, 11, 84). 2 Maccabees 10:3 states that they "made another altar of sacrifice" (NETS), suggesting the *inauguration* of a new altar in the summary of 2:19.

τοῦ βωμοῦ. Objective genitive. Given 2 Maccabees' use of θυσιαστήριον elsewhere (e.g., 1:18-19, 32; 2:5; 3:15; 4:14; 6:5; 10:3, 26; 14:3, 33; 15:31), the use of βωμός for "altar" is curious. Although βωμός is most commonly used in the LXX to refer to idolatrous altars, there are examples where it is synonymous with θυσιαστήριον (cf. Sir 50:12-14). The most relevant data is that in 10:2 the Maccabees tore down the foreign "altars" (βωμούς); but in 13:8 Menelaus dies justly because he committed many sins "against [Israel's] altar" (περὶ τὸν βωμόν). The data may be explained by noting that the rigid terminological divide between βωμός (pagan altar) and θυσιαστήριον (Israel's altar) became less significant over time, perhaps as language users became less sensitive to immediate threats of hellenization (cf. D. Schwartz, 172). Additionally, Doran (2012, 66) suggests that βωμοῦ was chosen in 2:19 to resonate with ἱεροῦ.

2:20 ἔτι τε τοὺς πρὸς Ἀντίοχον τὸν Ἐπιφανῆ καὶ τὸν τούτου υἱὸν Εὐπάτορα πολέμους.

ἔτι. Adverb, used to add an additional comment: "additionally" (see *GE*, 835). Cf. 6:4.

τε . . . καὶ. Correlative construction. See 1:14 on τε . . . καί.

τοὺς . . . πολέμους. Accusative object of κατά (reference) from 2:19. The separation of the article from the adjective is an example of hyperbaton. The placement of the PP between the article and its head clarifies that the PP modifies the NP.

πρὸς Ἀντίοχον τὸν Ἐπιφανῆ. Opposition (Smyth, §1695.3.c). On the syntax of the honorific Ἐπιφανής, see Wilson (238–67). On the wordplay with ἐπιφανεία, Novenson (2012, 90) states that "[the author] exploits the king's honorific for polemical purposes by ironically using the cognate noun ἐπιφανεία, 'manifestation' or 'appearance,' throughout for the wondrous acts of God by which the wicked Seleucid rulers are laid low." In other words, the "epiphanies" of God are more powerful than Antiochus "Epiphanes," who is the enemy of God's people. Cf. 2:11; 3:24; 5:4; 12:22; 14:15; 15:27.

τὸν . . . υἱὸν. Linked by καί to πρός.

τούτου. Genitive of relationship. See 2:19 on τούτου.

Εὐπάτορα. Accusative in apposition to υἱόν.

2:21 καὶ τὰς ἐξ οὐρανοῦ γενομένας ἐπιφανείας τοῖς ὑπὲρ τοῦ Ἰουδαϊσμοῦ φιλοτίμως ἀνδραγαθήσασιν, ὥστε τὴν ὅλην χώραν ὀλίγους ὄντας λεηλατεῖν καὶ τὰ βάρβαρα πλήθη διώκειν.

καὶ. The conjunction that links τὰς ἐξ οὐρανοῦ γενομένας ἐπιφα-νείας with κατά (reference) in 2:19.

τὰς . . . γενομένας ἐπιφανείας. Accusative object of κατά from 2:19. These "appearances" comprise a significant part of the later narrative (e.g., 3:24-26; 5:2-4; 10:29; 11:8; 12:22; 14:15; 15:27). On the wordplay with Antiochus *Epiphanes*, see 2:20 on πρὸς Ἀντίοχον τὸν Ἐπιφανῆ.

γενομένας. Aor mid ptc acc fem pl γίνομαι (attributive, modifying τὰς ἐπιφανείας).

ἐξ οὐρανοῦ. Source/origin.

τοῖς . . . ἀνδραγαθήσασιν. Aor act ptc dat masc pl ἀνδραγαθέω (sub-stantival). Indirect object of γενομένας. On the meaning of the verb, see *GE* (162): "to behave like an honest man, act well, behave heroically."

ὑπὲρ τοῦ Ἰουδαϊσμοῦ. Advantage ("on behalf of Judaism" or, better, "for [the sake of] Judaism"). Although many understand Ἰουδαϊσμός as simply "Judaism" (i.e., the religion of the synagogue), the term refers more strictly to "the defense and promotion of Jewish customs by Jew-ish people" (Novenson 2014, 33). Moreover, 2 Maccabees uses (and, perhaps, even invents) the word Ἰουδαϊσμός as a term in contrast to Ἑλληνισμός ("to hellenize," i.e., adopt Greek customs) in 4:13. In the other uses of Ἰουδαϊσμός in the book, Judas and his companions travel around Judea "enlisting those who had persevered in Ἰουδαϊσμός" (8:1). The elder Razi "was accused of Ἰουδαϊσμός and risked body and life for the sake of Ἰουδαϊσμός" (14:38). Commenting on the term, Novenson (2014, 35) notes that "to practice [Judaism in the Hellenistic period] at all meant to choose it, which had not been the case for Jews before, and this choice warranted a name. Of course, there was already a name for gentiles who chose to observe Jewish customs: the verb ἰουδαΐζω, 'judaizing.' The neologism Ἰουδαϊσμός, 'judaization,' is a morphological twist on that existing term, a new word used to signify the suddenly radical choice by Jews to follow their own ancestral ways."

φιλοτίμως. Adverb of manner, modifying ἀνδραγαθήσασιν. On the meaning of the adverb, see *GE* (2288): "with courage, bravely."

ὥστε. Introduces result clauses, modifying ἀνδραγαθήσασιν: "those who behaved heroically . . . *so that.*" Five infinitives (λεηλατεῖν, διώκειν, ἀνακομίσασθαι, ἐλευθερῶσαι, ἐπανορθῶσαι) follow ὥστε in 2:21-22, providing multiple results of Judas' and his men's heroic actions.

τὴν ὅλην χώραν. Accusative direct object of λεηλατεῖν. Although ὅλος typically occurs in predicate structure (Muraoka §38b.ii; cf. BDF §275), the epitomizer uses it in attributive structure (2:21, 29; 3:14; 4:38, 47; 5:2; 6:3; 7:5; 8:18; 14:35). Similar patterns are found in classical authors and Ptolemaic papyri (Mayser II 2:95–96).

ὀλίγους. Predicate adjective of ὄντας.

ὄντας. Pres act ptc acc masc pl εἰμί (concessive).

λεηλατεῖν. Pres act inf λεηλατέω. Used with ὥστε to indicate a result.

τὰ βάρβαρα πλήθη. Accusative direct object of διώκειν. Although βάρβαρος was typically reserved for non-Greeks, the epitomizer used it here to describe the Greek rulers Antiochus Epiphanes and Eupator. By employing the term in reference to Greek rulers, the epitomizer is "attempting to present himself as a good Greek (of the Jewish type), hoping to gain the sympathies of Greek readers" (D. Schwartz, 174; cf. Habicht, 208).

διώκειν. Pres act inf διώκω. Used with ὥστε to indicate a result.

2:22 καὶ τὸ περιβόητον καθ᾽ ὅλην τὴν οἰκουμένην ἱερὸν ἀνακομίσασθαι καὶ τὴν πόλιν ἐλευθερῶσαι καὶ τοὺς μέλλοντας καταλύεσθαι νόμους ἐπανορθῶσαι, τοῦ κυρίου μετὰ πάσης ἐπιεικείας ἵλεω γενομένου αὐτοῖς.

τὸ περιβόητον . . . ἱερόν. Accusative direct object of ἀνακομίσασθαι. On the language of "the most famous temple," cf. Josephus, *Ant.* 13.77. The separation of the modifier from the head is an example of hyperbaton where the modifier (περιβόητον) is emphasized.

καθ᾽ ὅλην τὴν οἰκουμένην. Extension. The substantive οἰκουμένη derives from the present feminine participle of οἰκέω. The meaning of οἰκουμένη is disputed, but it may refer to the "the inhabited world" or "the world as an administrative unit" (BDAG, 699).

ἀνακομίσασθαι. Aor mid inf ἀνακομίζω. Used with ὥστε (cf. 2:21) to indicate a result.

τὴν πόλιν. Accusative direct object of ἐλευθερῶσαι. The epitomizer often refers to ἡ πόλις rather than Ἱεροσολύμα (cf. 3:1, 14; 4:38, 39, 48; 5:2, 5, 17; 8:3, 17; 9:14; 10:1; 11:2; 13:14; 15:14, 17), providing "a generic spin, perhaps to encourage his audience to identify with the book's heroes" (Simkovich, 307).

ἐλευθερῶσαι. Aor act inf ἐλευθερόω. Used with ὥστε (cf. 2:21) to indicate a result. Cf. 9:14, where Antiochus Epiphanes declares the city to be "free" (ἐλευθέραν).

τοὺς μέλλοντας ... νόμους. Accusative direct object of ἐπανορθῶσαι. The separation of the modifier from the head is an example of hyperbaton where the modifier (μέλλοντας) is emphasized.

μέλλοντας. Pres act ptc acc masc pl μέλλω (attributive).

καταλύεσθαι. Pres pass inf καταλύω (complementary, modifying μέλλοντας).

ἐπανορθῶσαι. Aor act inf ἐπανορθόω. Used with ὥστε (cf. 2:21) to indicate a result.

τοῦ κυρίου. Genitive subject of the participle γενομένου.

μετὰ πάσης ἐπιεικείας. Manner. The meaning of ἐπιείκεια relates to God's forbearance or equity. In 10:4, God's ἐπιείκεια is appealed to as a basis for lesser discipline if the people sin. For the collocation of ἐπανορθόω + μετὰ πάσης, see 5:20.

ἵλεω. Predicate genitive of γενομένου. Following the principle of *lectio difficilior potior*, the Göttingen edition's ἵλεως (nominative), which is less grammatically correct, may be preferable.

γενομένου. Aor mid ptc gen masc sg γίνομαι (genitive absolute, temporal). On the genitive absolute, see 1:7 on βασιλεύοντος.

αὐτοῖς. Dative of advantage.

2:23 ὑπὸ Ἰάσωνος τοῦ Κυρηναίου δεδηλωμένα διὰ πέντε βιβλίων πειρασόμεθα δι᾽ ἑνὸς συντάγματος ἐπιτεμεῖν.

ὑπὸ Ἰάσωνος. Agency. The Göttingen edition reads Ἰάσονος, which likely reflects a common spelling variation of the O-sound (Caragounis, 517–46).

τοῦ Κυρηναίου. Genitive of source/origin. As D. Schwartz (175) notes, "Cyrene" may denote either the city or the entire region of Cyrenaica.

δεδηλωμένα. Prf pass ptc acc neut pl δηλόω (substantival). The participle agrees with the neuter article τά in 2:19. On the meaning of the verb, see *GE* (474.2): "to be displayed, be demonstrated [in writing]." The perfect participle (stative verbal aspect) emphasizes the present state produced by prior action.

διὰ πέντε βιβλίων. Locative ("*in* five book rolls") or, perhaps, means ("*through* five book rolls"). On the translation "book roll," see 2:13 on τὰ . . . βιβλία.

πειρασόμεθα. Fut mid ind 1st pl πειράζω. The future stresses intention (cf. *CGCG* §33.43). Smyth (§1008) refers to this as a "plural of modesty," where "[a] speaker in referring to himself may use the first-person plural as a modest form of statement."

δι' ἑνὸς συντάγματος. Locative or means. On the meaning of σύνταγμα, *GE* (2051) suggests "treatise, work." On the desire to provide a shorter narrative that is easier to follow, see Aristotle, *Pol.* 1260b40.

ἐπιτεμεῖν. Fut act inf ἐπιτέμνω (complementary). There are 22 future infinitives in 2 Maccabees (2:23, 32; 7:14, 19, 24³, 26; 8:10, 11²; 9:8, 15²; 16³, 17², 22, 27; 11:2, 3; 12:11², 12; 13:3, 13; 14:14; 15:33), which account for approximately 25 percent of LXX uses. Many grammarians consider the future aspectually vague, including the future infinitive (cf. Muraoka §28he); however, some scholars argue that the -σ- suffix denotes the (non-past) perfective aspect (Ellis, 138–39). The future infinitive denotes "future time *relative* to the main verb" when the context shows that stress is laid on the idea of futurity (Smyth §1865d; cf. Muraoka §28he; BDF §350).

According to the *OCD* (529), "[t]he Hellenistic age was the first to feel the growth of recorded literature as a burden; and the age which cast doubt on the propriety of a 'big book' (Callim[achus] fr. 465 Pf.) also pioneered the abridgement of long works." See 2:32, where the same verb is repeated at the end of the preface.

2:24 συνορῶντες γὰρ τὸ χύμα τῶν ἀριθμῶν καὶ τὴν οὖσαν δυσχέρειαν τοῖς θέλουσιν εἰσκυκλεῖσθαι τοῖς τῆς ἱστορίας διηγήμασιν διὰ τὸ πλῆθος τῆς ὕλης,

συνορῶντες. Pres act ptc nom masc pl συνοράω (causal).

γὰρ. Introduces an explanation of 2:23, in particular the things written "through five book rolls."

τὸ χύμα. Accusative direct object of συνορῶντες. Doran (2012, 68–69) and others suggest(s) that τὸ χύμα τῶν ἀριθμῶν refers to "a great number of pages," referring to the length of Jason's work, which was five book rolls according to 2:23. D. Schwartz (176) believes it refers to "the great quantity of numbers" referenced in 2 Maccabees. Bar-Kochva (178) counted more than 50 such numbers in 2 Maccabees, suggesting that Jason's text had at least this many, if not more numbers.

τῶν ἀριθμῶν. Genitive of apposition or descriptive (aporetic) genitive.

τὴν οὖσαν. Pres act ptc acc fem sg εἰμί (substantival). Linked by καί as a second direct object of συνορῶντες.

δυσχέρειαν. Accusative subject of the participle οὖσαν. When the subject of the participle differs from the main subject of the sentence, it generally appears in the accusative case (CGCG §52.13). The word δυσχέρεια (δυσ + χείρ) includes the inseparable prefix δυσ-, which "negates the good sense of a word, w[ith] notion of hard, bad, difficult" (BDAG, 265). On the etymology, EDG (361) suggests that δυσχέρεια is "[n]ot related to χείρ . . . [but rather] with χαίρω." The epitomizer has an affinity for δυσ-compound words: δυσημερία (5:6), δυσμένεια (6:29; 12:3; 14:39), δυσμενῶς (14:11), δυσπέτημα (5:20), δυσπολιόρκητος (12:21), δυσπρόσιτος (12:21), δυσσέβεια (8:33), δυσσεβέω (6:13), δυσσέβημα (12:3), δυσσεβής (3:11; 8:14; 9:9; 15:33), δύσφημος (13:11; 15:32), δυσφορέω (4:35; 13:25), δυσφόρως (14:28), δυσχέρεια (2:24; 9:21), δυσχερής (6:3; 9:7, 24; 14:45).

τοῖς θέλουσιν. Pres act ptc dat masc pl θέλω (substantival). Ethical dative, where the "dative substantive indicates the person whose feelings or viewpoint are intimately tied to the action (or state) of the verb" (Wallace, 146–47).

εἰσκυκλεῖσθαι. Pres mid inf εἰσκυκλέω (complementary). On the meaning of the verb, see GE (616): "go in, plunge in" + dative. The verb is extremely rare, appearing only three times (according to the TLG) prior to 2 Maccabees (Aristophanes, Thesm. 265; Vesp. 1475; Menander, Dysk. 758). Like other middle verbs (e.g., ἔρχομαι), where the verbal concept inheres in the subject, the reflexive nature of εἰσκυκλεῖσθαι is a metaphorical extension of the more basic meaning, referring to "digging into" or "diving into" historical records to be studied (GELS, 200).

τοῖς . . . διηγήμασιν. Dative complement of εἰσκυκλεῖσθαι. See GE (527): "narration, recount" = "stories."

τῆς ἱστορίας. Topical, where the head noun (τοῖς διηγήμασιν) is about the dependent noun (τῆς ἱστορίας): "the stories about the history" (cf. Muraoka §22v.xi). It is possible that the article refers back to Jason's work (Doran 2012, 69).

διὰ τὸ πλῆθος. Cause. The phrase τὸ πλῆθος τῆς ὕλης ("the mass of material") is roughly parallel to τὸ χύμα τῶν ἀριθμῶν mentioned earlier in 2:24.

τῆς ὕλης. Genitive of material.

2:25 ἐφροντίσαμεν τοῖς μὲν βουλομένοις ἀναγινώσκειν ψυχαγωγίαν, τοῖς δὲ φιλοφρονοῦσιν εἰς τὸ διὰ μνήμης ἀναλαβεῖν εὐκοπίαν, πᾶσιν δὲ τοῖς ἐντυγχάνουσιν ὠφέλειαν.

ἐφροντίσαμεν. Aor act ind 1st pl φροντίζω. This verb forms the basis for all of 2:25 and has three accusative direct objects that modify it (ψυχαγωγίαν, εὐκοπίαν, ὠφέλειαν). On the meaning of the verb, see *GELS* (721): "to think and devise," thus the translation "we sought to bring about." On the use of the plural, see 2:23 on πειρασόμεθα.

μὲν ... δὲ ... δὲ. The use of the μέν creates the expectation that a related element will follow; i.e., μέν is forward-pointing or anticipatory (Runge, 76). One often finds μέν/δέ sets, implicating a point and counterpoint. On the repetition of δέ, Smyth (§2905) notes that "[i]f more than two clauses are contrasted, only the first clause has μέν, while each of the following clauses has δέ." Here the construction allows the epitomizer to use the main verb (ἐφροντίσαμεν) once.

τοῖς ... βουλομένοις. Pres mid ptc dat masc pl βούλομαι (substantival). Dative of advantage.

ἀναγινώσκειν. Pres act inf ἀναγινώσκω (complementary).

ψυχαγωγίαν. Accusative direct object of ἐφροντίσαμεν.

τοῖς ... φιλοφρονοῦσιν. Pres act ptc dat masc pl φιλοφρονέω (substantival). Dative of advantage. On the meaning of the verb, see *GELS* (717): "to be favourably and well disposed." Although φιλοφρονέω occurs only here in the LXX, the adverb φιλοφρόνως appears in 3:9 and 4 Macc 8:5. Habicht (208) believes that φιλοπονοῦσιν should be read (as a conjecture) here: "those who love work" (cf. *GE*, 2283). While the conjecture does provide a clearer sense of the text, it is not necessary.

διὰ μνήμης. Means.

ἀναλαβεῖν. Aor act inf ἀναλαμβάνω. Although the infinitive is used with εἰς τό most often to convey purpose, this sense does not make sense here. Beckwith (159) provides examples where εἰς τό + infinitive is joined with "verbs, adjectives, and even nouns to denote the respect in which the limited word is to be understood." Thus, the basic sense "*to take up* through memory" (cf. *GELS*, 41), relates to τοῖς φιλοφρονοῦσιν: "those who are well-disposed *with respect to memorization*" = "those who are well-disposed to memorize."

εὐκοπίαν. Accusative direct object of ἐφροντίσαμεν. See *GELS* (301): "*easiness* of execution."

πᾶσιν τοῖς ἐντυγχάνουσιν. Dative of advantage. As expected, πᾶς stands in predicate position but functions attributively (see Smyth §1174.b).

ἐντυγχάνουσιν. Pres act ptc dat masc pl ἐντυγχάνω (substantival). On the meaning of the verb, see *GE* (706): "to meet (by accident), encounter." BDAG (341.2) notes that "the idea of 'coming across' or 'encountering' a book derives the sense *read*." Because the epitomizer has already used the verb ἀναγινώσκω earlier in the verse, this is also an example of stylistic variation.

ὠφέλειαν. Accusative direct object of ἐφροντίσαμεν.

2 Maccabees 2:26-32

[26]And, for us, namely those who have undertaken the toil of epitomizing, it is no easy matter but it is a work of sweat and sleeplessness, [27]just as, for the one who prepares a symposium and seeks the benefit of others, it is not easy. Nevertheless, because of the gratefulness of many, we will endure gladly the uncomfortable toil, [28]conceding the close examination about each [of the details] to the compiler, while working carefully to adhere to the guidelines of the epitome. [29]For just as the architect of a new house ought to give thought to the whole construction, while the one who undertakes to paint in encaustic and to paint living figures ought to consider only what is suitable for its decoration, so also I think concerning us. [30]To enter in and make a walk of history and make close inquiry in the matters, part by part, is fitting for the leading historian, [31]but the one who is making the paraphrase [ought to be] allowed to pursue conciseness of expression and to refuse the full presentation of narrative.

[32]From that, therefore, let us begin the narrative, while adding this to the things said already; for (it would be) silly to lengthen the material before the narrative but to cut short the narrative [itself].

In this part of the prologue the epitomizer describes the difficulty of his own task. The term κακοπάθεια is repeated (2:26, 27), underscoring the "toil" involved. Likewise, the mention of loss of sleep is found in other writers (e.g., Callimachus, *Epigr.* 27; Aristophanes, *Lys.* 27) as is the complaint of writing an extended preface that overshadows the narrative itself (e.g., Lucian of Samosata, *Hist.* 53–55). Structurally, there are three statements introduced in 2:28-31 that contrast the work of a historian with the work of an epitomizer (cf. Doran 1981, 80). Finally, the comparison between the epitomizer and "one who prepares a symposium" (2:27) appears again in the epilogue (15:37-39).

2:26 καὶ ἡμῖν μὲν τοῖς τὴν κακοπάθειαν ἐπιδεδεγμένοις τῆς ἐπιτομῆς οὐ ῥᾴδιον, ἱδρῶτος δὲ καὶ ἀγρυπνίας τὸ πρᾶγμα,

ἡμῖν. Ethical dative, indicating "the person whose feelings or viewpoint are intimately tied to the action (or state) of the verb" (Wallace, 156; Smyth §1486; *CGCG* §30.53).

μὲν . . . δὲ. Point/counterpoint set. See 2:25 on μὲν . . . δέ. As is typical in μέν/δέ constructions, the δέ material is highlighted, contrasting "an easy matter" with "a work of sweat and sleeplessness."

τοῖς . . . ἐπιδεδεγμένοις. Prf mid ptc dat masc pl ἐπιδέχομαι (attributive, modifying ἡμῖν). On the perfect, see 2:23 on δεδηλωμένα.

τὴν κακοπάθειαν. Accusative direct object of ἐπιδεδεγμένοις.

τῆς ἐπιτομῆς. Genitive of apposition ("the task *which is epitomizing*"). Verbal noun of ἐπιτέμνω.

ῥᾴδιον. Predicate adjective of an implied verb, negated by οὐ. See the use of the same adjective in 4:17 as well as the parallel term εὐχερές in 2:27, which is probably stylistic variation.

ἱδρῶτος καὶ ἀγρυπνίας. Genitive of product ("work *that produces sweat and sleeplessness*") or, more likely, quality ("work [is *one*] *of sweat and sleeplessness*"). The sense of ἀγρυπνία can be either "sleeplessness" (i.e., inability to fall asleep) or "loss of sleep" (i.e., not attempting to sleep), depending on how the genitive is understood. The word occurs only here in 2 Maccabees, but both senses are well-illustrated in Sirach. On the sense of "sleeplessness," Sir 1:30 provides an interesting parallel: "I myself too made it a most compulsory task to bring some speed and industry to the translating of this tome, meanwhile having contributed much *sleeplessness* and skill, with the aim of bringing the book to completion and to publish it" (NETS). On the sense of "loss of sleep," Sir 38:27: "So every artisan and master-artisan, who keeps going by night as by day, those who cut signets of seals, and his patience is to diversify ornamentation; he will give his heart to making a painting lifelike, and his *sleeplessness* is to complete the work" (NETS).

τὸ πρᾶγμα. Predicate nominative of an implied verb.

2:27 καθάπερ τῷ παρασκευάζοντι συμπόσιον καὶ ζητοῦντι τὴν ἑτέρων λυσιτέλειαν οὐκ εὐχερές, ὅμως διὰ τὴν τῶν πολλῶν εὐχαριστίαν ἡδέως τὴν κακοπάθειαν ὑποίσομεν,

καθάπερ. The conjunction introduces a comparative clause. The construction καθ' ἅ περ (*GE*, 999: "exactly as") is a strengthened version of καθ' ἅ ("in the way in which, as"). Robertson (967) refers to καθάπερ as "thoroughly Attic and a slight literary touch."

τῷ παρασκευάζοντι. Pres act ptc dat masc sg παρασκευάζω (substantival). Ethical dative, see 2:26 on ἡμῖν.

συμπόσιον. Accusative direct object of παρασκευάζοντι. D. Schwartz (178) notes that "[b]y alluding to a symposium, rather than simply to a meal, the author implies that although his role is as that of a caterer, the project is an important one meant to nourish the mind and the spirit." See Lucian (*Hist.* 56) for an example of a book served as a meal.

ζητοῦντι. Pres act ptc dat masc sg ζητέω (substantival). Ethical dative. Linked by καί to the article τῷ.

τὴν . . . λυσιτέλειαν. Accusative direct object of ζητοῦντι.

ἑτέρων. Objective genitive.

εὐχερές. Predicate adjective of an implied verb, negated by οὐκ.

ὅμως. Adversative particle, meaning "having said that" (*GELS*, 497) or "nevertheless" (*GE*, 1461). Here, despite the fact that epitomizing is difficult work (2:26), "*nevertheless* . . . we will gladly endure the uncomfortable toil" (NETS). Cf. also 14:18 and 15:5.

διὰ τὴν . . . εὐχαριστίαν. Cause.

τῶν πολλῶν. Subjective genitive.

ἡδέως. Adverb of manner, modifying ὑποίσομεν.

τὴν κακοπάθειαν. Accusative direct object of ὑποίσομεν.

ὑποίσομεν. Fut act ind 1 pl ὑποφέρω. The future stresses intention (cf. *CGCG* §33.43). On the use of the plural, see 2:23 on πειρασόμεθα.

2:28 τὸ μὲν διακριβοῦν περὶ ἑκάστων τῷ συγγραφεῖ παραχωρήσαντες, τὸ δὲ ἐπιπορεύεσθαι τοῖς ὑπογραμμοῖς τῆς ἐπιτομῆς διαπονοῦντες.

τὸ . . . διακριβοῦν. Pres act inf διακριβόω. The parallel constructions in 2:28 are worth considering more closely prior to offering a syntactical evaluation:

> τὸ μὲν διακριβοῦν περὶ ἑκάστων τῷ συγγραφεῖ <u>παραχωρήσαντες</u>,

> <u>conceding</u> *the close examination* about each [of the details] to the compiler,

> τὸ δὲ ἐπιπορεύεσθαι τοῖς ὑπογραμμοῖς τῆς ἐπιτομῆς <u>διαπονοῦντες</u>.

> <u>while working carefully</u> *to adhere to* the guidelines of the epitome.

Although it is possible to understand τὸ ... διακριβοῦν as complementary to παραχωρήσαντες (paralleling the second clause), the fact that διαπονέω regularly takes an infinitive complement (and παραχωρέω does not) cautions against this understanding of the syntax. Accordingly, τὸ ... διακριβοῦν is best understand as a substantive that functions as the direct object of παραχωρήσαντες.

μὲν ... δὲ. Point/counterpoint set. See 2:25 on μὲν ... δέ.

περὶ ἑκάστων. Reference. Cf. 14:9.

τῷ συγγραφεῖ. Dative indirect object of παραχωρήσαντες.

παραχωρήσαντες. Aor act ptc nom masc pl παραχωρέω (manner). The participle modifies ὑποίσομεν from 2:27, further defining the manner in which the writer endures toil. On the meaning of the verb, see *GE* (1574.1.A): "to yield, restart, recognize the authority of, acknowledge oneself inferior to" = "conceding."

τὸ ... ἐπιπορεύεσθαι. Pres mid inf ἐπιπορεύομαι (complementary). The sense of "to arrive, reach" (*GE*, 784) is maintained here, although *GELS* (278) helpfully offers the following translation: "to adhere to: + dat[ive] τοῖς ὑπογραμμοῖς τῆς ἐπιτομῆς 'the guidelines for the abridgement.'"

τοῖς ὑπογραμμοῖς. Dative of manner. The verb ἐπιπορεύομαι often occurs with the dative (*GE*, 784). Here, it describes how the epitomizer works. See *GELS* (701): "*guideline[s]* to be followed," especially with regard to a model/pattern of writing or drawing (cf. BDAG, 1036).

τῆς ἐπιτομῆς. Genitive of possession. Doran (2012, 72) notes that "an epitome possesses the characteristic of providing general descriptions, rather than giving detailed ones."

διαπονοῦντες. Pres act ptc nom masc pl διαπονέω (manner). On the syntax, see comments on παραχωρήσαντες. See *GE* (503): "to busy oneself over, strive, work carefully." Note the change of tense from the aorist παραχωρήσαντες in the preceding clause, which emphasizes the process of striving or working as opposed to the simple perfective reference to handing over the task to closer examination.

2:29 καθάπερ γὰρ τῆς καινῆς οἰκίας ἀρχιτέκτονι τῆς ὅλης καταβολῆς φροντιστέον, τῷ δὲ ἐγκαίειν καὶ ζωγραφεῖν ἐπιχειροῦντι τὰ ἐπιτήδεια πρὸς διακόσμησιν ἐξεταστέον, οὕτως δοκῶ καὶ ἐπὶ ἡμῶν.

The syntax of 2:29 is challenging because of two clauses built around verbal adjectives (φροντιστέον, ἐξεταστέον). In similar constructions elsewhere, verbal adjectives appear with a copula, which helps clarify the syntax of the clause. For example, in the Ep Jer 51, the verbal adjective γνωστέον appears with ἐστίν and the dative (τίνι):

τίνι οὖν γνωστέον ἐστὶν ὅτι οὔκ εἰσιν θεοί;

To whom, then, is it known that they are not Gods?

Although considerably simpler than the present text, this sheds light on two aspects of 2:29. First, the copula is explicit in Ep Jer 51, clarifying how the clause functions. Smyth (§944.b) notes, however, that the copula may be missing "in expressions of necessity, duty, etc.," especially with verbal adjectives (as is the case in 2:29). Second, the dative τίνι ("to whom") is functionally the agent of the clause (i.e., "*who* knows that they are not Gods?") and can be translated accordingly. This sheds light on the dative expressions (ἀρχιτέκτονι, τῷ ... ἐπιχειροῦντι) in 2:29.

καθάπερ ... οὕτως. Comparative. "Just as ... so" (cf. καθάπερ ... οὕτως καί in 6:14; 15:39; καθὼς ... οὕτως in 2:10). Doran (2012, 72) notes that "the comparison begins with two contrasting clauses, each ending with a verbal adjective that form a homoiteleuton."

γάρ. Causal, justifying the decision to condense rather than write a full history in 2:27b-28. See 1:12 on γάρ.

τῆς καινῆς οἰκίας. Objective genitive, qualifying ἀρχιτέκτονι.

ἀρχιτέκτονι. Dative of agency, supplying the subject of the verbal idea implied in φροντιστέον. Muraoka (§22wo) notes that "a dative can indicate the subject of a verb or an underlying verb where an obligation is imposed on the subject." This includes verbal adjectives ending in -τέον. Smyth (§1488) refers to this as dative of agency, noting that "regularly with verbal adjectives in -τός and -τέος, the person in whose interest an action is done, is put in the dative. The notion of agency does not belong to the dative, but it is a natural inference that the person interested is the agent" (cf. Smyth §2152; *CGCG* §37.2). On the meaning of ἀρχιτέκτων, see especially Sir 38:27.

τῆς ὅλης καταβολῆς. Genitive complement of φροντιστέον. On the genitive, see comments below. See 2:21 on the attributive structure of ὅλος.

φροντιστέον. Predicate verbal adjective of an implied verb: "one [must] *take heed*" (LEH, 653). The copula is often omitted "in expressions of necessity, duty" (Smyth §944.b; cf. *CGCG* 26.13). As a verbal adjective, φροντιστέον functions analogously with the cognate φροντίζω, which takes a genitive complement (BDAG, 1066; Smyth §2152).

τῷ ... ἐπιχειροῦντι. Pres act ptc dat masc sg ἐπιχειρέω (substantival). Dative of agency. On the function of the dative, see comments on ἀρχιτέκτονι. On the meaning of the verb, see *GE* (804): "to set about, start on, undertake [+ infinitive]," a figurative extension of "to set one's hand to."

δὲ. Development; marks a change of subject from "the architect" (ἀρχιτέκτονι) to "the one who undertakes . . ." (τῷ ἐπιχειροῦντι).

ἐγκαίειν καὶ Ζωγραφεῖν. Because ἐγκαίω and ζωγραφέω both mean "to paint," some explanation is required. They may refer, broadly, to the same thing (Abel, 313) or one may be more generic than the other (Habicht, 209). D. Schwartz (179) suggests that ζωγραφεῖν means, more specifically, "to paint animals," drawing upon evidence from Polybius, *Hist.* 12.25e7 and 12.25h.2. It is possible, and best, to recognize that ἐγκαίω "stresses color" whereas ζωγραφέω "stresses the figural quality" (Doran 2012, 72). For another comparison of historians and painters, see Plutarch, *Mor.* 346f–47a.

ἐγκαίειν. Pres act inf ἐγκαίω (complementary). On the meaning of the verb, see *GE* (582): "to paint with encaustic," which refers to applying heat to colored wax (cf. Nicklas 2011, 1382; Pliny, *Nat. Hist.* 35.39–40).

Ζωγραφεῖν. Pres act inf ζωγραφέω (complementary). On the meaning of the verb, see *GE* (895): "to paint (from life)."

τὰ ἐπιτήδεια. Accusative direct object of an implied form of ἐξετάζω, implied in the verbal adjective ἐξεταστέον. Used as a substantive, it means "what is necessary/suitable" (BDAG, 384).

πρὸς διακόσμησιν. Purpose. The noun διακόσμησις denotes "embellishment, decoration" (*GE*, 491).

ἐξεταστέον. Predicate verbal adjective of an implied verb. As a verbal adjective, ἐξεταστέον functions analogously with the cognate ἐξετάζω: "it is necessary to examine" (*GE*, 722). See comments above on φροντιστέον.

δοκῶ. Pres act ind 1st sg δοκέω. The epitomizer uses the first-person *plural* throughout the prologue, making this use of the *singular* distinct.

καὶ. Adverbial.

ἐπὶ ἡμῶν. Reference. BDAG (365.8) refers to this use of ἐπί as "a marker of perspective . . . *concerning, about.*"

2:30 τὸ μὲν ἐμβατεύειν καὶ περίπατον ποιεῖσθαι λόγων καὶ πολυπραγμονεῖν ἐν τοῖς κατὰ μέρος τῷ τῆς ἱστορίας ἀρχηγέτῃ καθήκει·

τὸ . . . ἐμβατεύειν καὶ . . . ποιεῖσθαι . . . καὶ πολυπραγμονεῖν. Compound nominative subject of καθήκει. See further comments below.

μὲν . . . δὲ. Point/counterpoint set, contrasting the writing of detailed narratives (2:30) with shortening a narrative (2:31). See 2:25 on μὲν . . . δέ. The sequence is completed in 2:31.

τὸ . . . ἐμβατεύειν. Pres act inf ἐμβατεύω (substantival). The neuter article functions to clarify that the infinitive is the first element of the compound nominative subject of καθήκει. The sense "to enter into" is common (cf. 1 Macc 12:25). Here, it is used figuratively and means "to take up a topic" (*GE*, 667).

περίπατον. Accusative direct object of ποιεῖσθαι. The sense of "walking around" (*GE*, 1637) is clear enough from the etymology. But, applied to historian's task, it refers to a digression from the main topic (LEH, 486). This meaning is clear when seen in contrast with ἐπιτρέχω ("to run over"), which is used by both Josephus (*J.W.* 1.18) and Plutarch (*Nic.* 1.1.5) to refer to summarizing written material (cf. *GE*, 800).

ποιεῖσθαι. Pres mid inf ποιέω (substantival). The second element of the compound nominative subject of καθήκει. When the middle of ποιέω is used with a verbal noun (περίπατον), this can be a periphrasis for the verb itself: περιπατέω (*GELS*, 570.II). See 1:23 on ἐποιήσαντο.

λόγων. Objective genitive (lit. "to make a walk *of history*"). *GE* (1249) notes that λόγος can refer to literary works of various genres, including history.

πολυπραγμονεῖν. Pres act inf πολυπραγμονέω (substantival). The third element of the compound nominative subject of καθήκει. On the meaning of the verb, see *GE* (1712): "to greatly busy oneself doing, be busy." Nicklas (2011, 1382) notes that πολυπραγμονέω may have the negative connotation of "being overzealous."

ἐν τοῖς κατὰ μέρος. Manner. The dative article τοῖς functions as nominalizer, converting the following PP (κατὰ μέρος) into the object of the preposition.

κατὰ μέρος. Distributive, indicating a "division of the greater whole into individual parts" (BDAG, 512.B.3; Wallace, 377).

τῷ . . . ἀρχηγέτῃ. Dative of reference. Built from ἄρχω + ἡγέομαι, the noun refers to a "leader" (*GELS*, 95).

τῆς ἱστορίας. Attributed genitive (*GELS*, 95: "leading historian"), where the "head noun, rather than the genitive, is functioning (in sense) as an attributive genitive" (Wallace, 89).

καθήκει. Pres act ind 3rd sg καθήκω (impersonal). On the meaning of the verb, see *GE* (1003): "it is appropriate, it is suitable, it is fitting, it concerns." Note the contrast between what is "fitting" (καθήκω, 2:30) for the historian and what "must be allowed" (συγχωρητέον, 2:31) for the epitomizer. On the use of the singular verb with multiple subjects, see 1:7 on ἀπέστη.

2:31 τὸ δὲ σύντομον τῆς λέξεως μεταδιώκειν καὶ τὸ ἐξεργαστικὸν τῆς πραγματείας παραιτεῖσθαι τῷ τὴν μετάφρασιν ποιουμένῳ συγχωρητέον.

μὲν ... δὲ. Point/counterpoint set. The μέν element of the set occurs in 2:30.

τὸ ... σύντομον τῆς λέξεως μεταδιώκειν καὶ τὸ ἐξεργαστικὸν τῆς πραγματείας παραιτεῖσθαι. Compound nominative subject of an implied verb.

τὸ ... σύντομον. Accusative direct object of μεταδιώκειν.

τῆς λέξεως. Genitive of reference ("[to pursue] conciseness *with reference to expression*") or, perhaps, objective genitive ("[to pursue] cutting short *words*"). MHT (3:14) note that when denoting an abstract idea, the article + adjective is usually followed by the genitive.

μεταδιώκειν. Pres act inf μεταδιώκω. The infinitival clause, τὸ ... σύντομον τῆς λέξεως μεταδιώκειν, functions as the first element of the compound nominative subject of an implied verb.

τὸ ἐξεργαστικὸν. Accusative direct object of παραιτεῖσθαι. LEH (213): "working out, full presentation."

τῆς πραγματείας. Objective genitive ("[fully present] *the narrative*").

παραιτεῖσθαι. Pres mid inf παραιτέομαι. The infinitival clause, τὸ ἐξεργαστικὸν τῆς πραγματείας παραιτεῖσθαι, functions as the second element of the compound nominative subject of an implied verb.

τῷ ... ποιουμένῳ. Pres mid ptc dat masc sg ποιέω (substantival). Dative of agency. On this function of the dative, see 2:29 on ἀρχιτέκτονι. When the middle of ποιέω is used with a verbal noun (μετάφρασιν), this can be a periphrasis for the verb itself: μεταφράζω (*GELS*, 570.II). See 1:23 on ἐποιήσαντο.

τὴν μετάφρασιν. Accusative direct object of ποιουμένῳ. The noun μετάφρασις is rare, but the related verb μεταφράζω can denote either *inter*linguitic translation (e.g., Hebrew into Greek) or *intra*linguistic translation (e.g., rewording or paraphrasing). Because the epitomizer does not make mention of difficulties that pertain to interlinguistic translation in the prologue (cf. Sir 22), it is best to understand μετάφρασις here intralinguistically (cf. Domazakis, 132–39). Thus, μετάφρασις is a virtual synonym of παράφρασις, which Theon (108P) notes in his rhetorical exercises: "Paraphrase (*paraphrasis*) consists of changing the form of expression while keeping the thoughts; it is also called metaphrase."

συγχωρητέον. Predicate verbal adjective of an implied verb: "[must be] *allowed*" (LEH, 578). The copula is often omitted "in expressions of necessity, duty" (Smyth §944.b; cf. *CGCG* §26.13). συγχωρητέον functions analogously with the cognate συγχωρέω, which governs the dative: τῷ ποιουμένῳ (BDAG, 954.2).

2:32 ἐντεῦθεν οὖν ἀρξώμεθα τῆς διηγήσεως τοῖς προειρημένοις τοσοῦτον ἐπιζεύξαντες· εὔηθες γὰρ τὸ μὲν πρὸ τῆς ἱστορίας πλεονάζειν, τὴν δὲ ἱστορίαν ἐπιτεμεῖν.

ἐντεῦθεν. Adverb, modifying ἀρξώμεθα and denoting (metaphorical) location: "thence, from that, following that" (*GE*, 704). Combined with the subjunctive verb, this signals to the reader that the prologue is about to end and, thus, that the next section is about to begin (cf. Coetzer, 38). Cf. 15:39.

οὖν. Inferential, transitioning from the preface to the main narrative/ history. See 2:15 on οὖν.

ἀρξώμεθα. Aor mid subj 1st pl ἄρχω (hortatory). The hortatory subjunctive is used when the "speaker is or speakers are suggesting to himself, herself, or themselves a course of action, whether positive or negative" (Muraoka §29ba.i; cf. Wallace, 464). The verb ἄρχω often takes the genitive case for its complement in the middle voice (cf. *GE*, 313; BDF §177; Muraoka §22p).

τῆς διηγήσεως. Genitive complement of ἀρξώμεθα.

τοῖς προειρημένοις. Prf pass ptc dat neut pl προλέγω (substantival). Dative of reference. Rather than use a simple pronoun of reference, the epitomizer uses the more usual verb with the sense of "the aforesaid." This construction is common in Greek authors such as Polybius (cf. Schmid, 3:147–48). On the use of the perfect, see 2:23 on δεδηλωμένα.

τοσοῦτον. Accusative direct object of ἐπιζεύξαντες. τοσοῦτος is demonstrative pronoun built from τόσος ("as large, as much") + οὗτος (cf. *EDG*, 1496–97).

ἐπιζεύξαντες. Aor act ptc nom masc pl ἐπιζεύγνυμι (temporal).

εὔηθες. Predicate adjective of an implied verb. Although the prefix ευ- implies a positive sense for this word, the sense of "naïve, simple, silly" (*GE*, 845) is common as well (Herodotus, *Hist.* 1.60.3; 2.45.1; Plato, *Leg.* 818b; Xenophon, *Hell.* 2.3.16).

γὰρ. Introduces the reason or ground for the epitomizer ending the preface and beginning the narrative: "*for* (it would be) foolish to lengthen the material before the narrative but to cut short the narrative (itself)." See 1:12 on γάρ.

μὲν ... δὲ. Point/counterpoint set, used to contrast the idea of lengthening the preface of the work while cutting short the narrative proper. See 2:25 on μὲν ... δέ.

τὸ. The neuter singular article functions as a nominalizer, changing the following PP (πρὸ τῆς ἱστορίας) into the accusative direct object of πλεονάζειν.

πρὸ τῆς ἱστορίας. Locative (lit. "the material *before the narrative*").

πλεονάζειν. Pres act inf πλεονάζω. The infinitival clause (τὸ . . . πρὸ τῆς ἱστορίας πλεονάζειν) is the subject of an implied verb. On the theme of keeping the preface short, see Lucian, *Hist.* 23.

τὴν . . . ἱστορίαν. Accusative direct object of ἐπιτεμεῖν.

ἐπιτεμεῖν. Fut act inf ἐπιτέμνω. The infinitival clause, τὴν . . . ἱστορίαν ἐπιτεμεῖν, is the subject of an implied verb. On the use of the future, see 2:23 on ἐπιτεμεῖν.

2 Maccabees 3:1-3

[1]While the holy city was governed in complete peace and while the laws were observed as best as possible on account of both the piety and hatred of wickedness of Onias, the high priest, [2]it also came about [that] the kings themselves honored the place and glorified the temple with the most excellent gifts [3]with the result that even Seleucus, the king of Asia, provided out of his own revenues all the expenses associated with the ministries of the sacrifices.

The narrative proper begins here. There are several linguistic features that bring cohesion to the larger narrative of 3:1-40. First, the verb (συν-) τηρέω appears in both 3:1 and 3:40, which "binds the narrative together through use of the root 'to maintain, preserve'" (Doran 2012, 89). Second, Heliodorus is welcomed (ἀποδεχθείς) by the high priest in 3:9 and Onias is welcomed (ἀποδεξάμενος) by Heliodorus in 3:35. The latter use is an unusual verbal choice for someone who is about to *depart*, but the intentional echo of the opening of the story provides the rationale for the word choice. Additionally, paronomasia occurs in multiple passages (3:15, 22, 33, 35). Multiple forms of φαίνω (3:9, 16, 24, 25, 26, 28, 30, 33, 34) and κράτος (3:22, 30, 34) appear throughout the narrative. Repetition of related forms emphasizes the heavenly appearances in the story and God's power (cf. Doran 2012, 89).

On the use of the aorist and imperfect in the narrative, see the Introduction.

3:1 Τῆς ἁγίας πόλεως κατοικουμένης μετὰ πάσης εἰρήνης καὶ τῶν νόμων ὅτι κάλλιστα συντηρουμένων διὰ τὴν Ονιου τοῦ ἀρχιερέως εὐσέβειάν τε καὶ μισοπονηρίαν,

The entirety of 3:1 forms a circumstantial frame for the main clause that begins in 3:2. The construction has "the effect of backgrounding the action of the participle, indicating that it is less important than the main verbal action" (Runge, 249; cf. *CGCG* §52.29). Although stated most clearly in 5:19-20, this establishes that the prosperity of the city is due to the faithfulness of the people (especially the leaders). For further discussion on the use of the genitive absolute, see 1:7 on βασιλεύοντος.

Τῆς ἁγίας πόλεως. Genitive subject of the participle κατοικουμένης. On the use of ἡ πόλις rather than Ιεροσολύμα, see 2:22 on τὴν πόλιν.

κατοικουμένης. Pres pass ptc gen fem sg κατοικέω (genitive absolute, temporal). While the verb often has a sense of "to live, to dwell, to inhabit" (cf. BDAG, 534), in the passive voice κατοικέω can mean "to be governed" (*GE*, 1100–1101; cf. Josephus, *Ant.* 12.139). The former sense of "inhabit" understands the reference to the people of Jerusalem (cf. D. Schwartz, 74), whereas the latter sense of "governed" understands the reference to the leadership over Jerusalem or, perhaps, more broadly the status of the city itself. On the genitive absolute, see 1:7 on βασιλεύοντος.

μετὰ πάσης εἰρήνης. Manner. The PP μετ᾽ εἰρήνης occurs 19 times in the LXX, perhaps highlighting the construction with πᾶς found here: "with/in *complete* peace." The epitomizer has an affinity for the combination μετὰ πάσης (2:22; 3:22; 5:20; 14:38; 15:1, 6, 7, 17). The notion that the city exists in "complete peace" prior to Heliodorus' arrival (3:8-9) is hyperbolic, but it sets the stage for the following events.

τῶν νόμων. Genitive subject of the participle συντηρουμένων.

ὅτι κάλλιστα. The superlative adverb is strengthened by ὅτι: "*as best as possible*" (*CGCG* §32.4; Smyth §1086; *GELS*, 511.7; Muraoka §23bf). Although LXX examples are rare, the construction is common in classical and post-classical Greek (e.g., Xenophon, *Cyr.* 7.5.82; Plato, *Symp.* 218d; Plutarch, *Sera* 2.15).

συντηρουμένων. Pres pass ptc gen masc pl συντηρέω (genitive absolute, temporal). In collocation with νόμος or νόμιμα (e.g., Ezek 18:19; Sir 32:1), the verb has the basic sense of "to observe *or* respect scrupulously" (*GE*, 2053.1; cf. *GELS*, 661.1). On the genitive absolute, see 1:7 on βασιλεύοντος.

διὰ τὴν . . . εὐσέβειάν. Cause. The noun has two acute accents because it is followed by an enclitic (τέ). When following a word with an acute accent on the antepenult, the enclitic surrenders its accent and it appears as an additional acute accent on the preceding word (Smyth §183.c).

Ονιου τοῦ ἀρχιερέως. Subjective genitive. On the identity of Onias, see esp. VanderKam (2004, 188–97) and Josephus, *Ant.* 12.156-57.

τε καὶ. The combination τὲ καί serves to unite complements, both similar and opposites (Smyth §2974), and is a closer connection than καί alone (BDF §444.2). Thus, εὐσέβειάν τε καὶ μισοπονηρίαν = "*both* (τε) the piety *and* (καί) the hatred of wickedness*.*" Cf. 3:10; 5:13; 11:20.

μισοπονηρίαν. Connected by τὲ καί to διά. The verbal form μισοπονηρέω is found elsewhere in 2 Maccabees, in reference to gentiles (4:49) and Israel's God (8:4).

3:2 συνέβαινεν καὶ αὐτοὺς τοὺς βασιλεῖς τιμᾶν τὸν τόπον καὶ τὸ ἱερὸν ἀποστολαῖς ταῖς κρατίσταις δοξάζειν,

συνέβαινεν. Impf act ind 3rd sg συμβαίνω (impersonal). This verb is commonly followed by the accusative + infinitive, as here: "it also came about [that] *the kings themselves honored*" (cf. BDAG, 956.2; BDF §408). The use of the imperfect (rather than the aorist) allows "for the painting of a static picture of what kings used to do in the good old days before our story began" (D. Schwartz, 188). Although Goldstein (200) suggests that the verb may imply that something contrary to expectation happened (e.g., the Seleucids acting piously), D. Schwartz (187) is probably correct to note that "this verb allows for the transition from the general context to the specific details which provide the background for our story: there are circumstances, something interesting 'happened' amidst them, and the story can unfold accordingly." For other uses of this verb in narrative contexts, see 4:30; 5:2, 18; 7:1; 9:2, 7; 10:5; 12:24, 34; 13:7.

καὶ. Adverb. Pleonastic, used in an expression that introduces a result clause (BDAG, 495.2.d).

αὐτοὺς. Intensive, modifying τοὺς βασιλεῖς and marking it as prominent in the discourse.

τοὺς βασιλεῖς. Accusative subject of the infinitive τιμᾶν.

τιμᾶν. Pres act inf τιμάω (indirect discourse).

τὸν τόπον. Accusative direct object of τιμᾶν. Here it refers to the temple (cf. 5:16; 6:2; 8:17), but it can also have broader reference to a location associated with a temple (cf. 13:23).

τὸ ἱερὸν. Accusative direct object of δοξάζειν.

ἀποστολαῖς ταῖς κρατίσταις. Dative of means. The noun ἀποστολή can have the meaning of "gift" or "recompense," especially in a context where gifts to a temple are implied (*GE*, 272). The adjective κρατίσταις is the superlative of κρατύς and has the sense of "most excellent" or "best" (cf. *GE*, 1173; Muraoka §37bbc). On gifts given to the Jerusalem temple by gentiles, see Cohen (1987, 412–15). Cf. Philo, *Leg.* 157, 317-19; Josephus, *J. W.* 2.412–413.

δοξάζειν. Pres act inf δοξάζω (indirect discourse).

3:3 ὥστε καὶ Σέλευκον τὸν τῆς Ἀσίας βασιλέα χορηγεῖν ἐκ τῶν ἰδίων προσόδων πάντα τὰ πρὸς τὰς λειτουργίας τῶν θυσιῶν ἐπιβάλλοντα δαπανήματα.

ὥστε. Introduces a result. This is best taken as modifying δοξάζειν from 3:2, suggesting that the many gifts offered by kings to the Jerusalem temple resulted in even Seleucus doing the same.

καὶ. Ascensive.

Σέλευκον. Accusative subject of the infinitive χορηγεῖν. On the identity of Seleucus, see 4:7, which identifies Antiochus Epiphanes IV as his successor.

τὸν . . . βασιλέα. Accusative in apposition to Σέλευκον.

τῆς Ἀσίας. Genitive of subordination (lit. "king *over Asia*"). Ἀσία was a common designation for territory of the Seleucid empire (cf. Goldstein, 201; D. Schwartz, 188).

χορηγεῖν. Pres act inf χορηγέω. Used with ὥστε to indicate a result. On the meaning of the verb, see *GE* (2368.1.D): "to supply, furnish, provide."

ἐκ τῶν ἰδίων προσόδων. Source. πρόσοδος refers to a source of "revenue" (*GELS*, 597).

πάντα . . . δαπανήματα. Accusative direct object of χορηγεῖν. In 11:31 the noun δαπάνημα refers to "necessities, supplies" (LEH, 128). The separation of the modifier from the head is an example of hyperbaton.

τὰ . . . ἐπιβάλλοντα. Pres act ptc acc neut pl ἐπιβάλλω (attributive; agreeing with πάντα). The sense of ἐπιβάλλω is "fall to, belong to" (BDAG, 367.3; *GELS*, 268), thus here, "all the expenses *associated with* the ministries of the sacrifices." The separation of the article from the participle is an example of hyperbaton where the interpositional words modify the participle.

πρὸς τὰς λειτουργίας. Association. Cf. 4:14.

τῶν θυσιῶν. Objective genitive.

2 Maccabees 3:4-8

[4]Now a certain Simon, of the tribe of Benjamin, who had been appointed captain of the temple, had a difference of opinion with the high priest about the office of the market overseer in the city. [5]And not being able to defeat Onias, he went to Apollonius son of Thraseas,

who was governor at that time of Coele-Syria and Phoenicia, ⁶and he reported that the treasury in Jerusalem was full of unspeakably great money so that the amount of excess was uncountable and [that] it did not belong to the account of the sacrifices, but [that] it is possible that these things fell under the authority of the king. ⁷When Apollonius met with the king, he explained about the money that had been reported to him. And, after selecting Heliodorus, who was in charge of the affairs, he sent [him] off, issuing commands to affect the removal of the afore-mentioned money. ⁸Immediately Heliodorus set out on the journey, ostensibly to inspect the cities of Coele-Syria and Phoenicia, but in fact to complete the purpose of the king.

3:4 Σιμων δέ τις ἐκ τῆς Βενιαμιν φυλῆς προστάτης τοῦ ἱεροῦ καθεσταμένος διηνέχθη τῷ ἀρχιερεῖ περὶ τῆς κατὰ τὴν πόλιν ἀγορανομίας·

Σιμων . . . τις. Nominative subject of διηνέχθη. The indefinite pronoun is used because the audience/reader is assumed to be unfamiliar with Simon (*GELS*, 682; Muraoka §10c). This is why he is referred to as "the previously mentioned Simon" (Ὁ . . . προειρημένος Σιμων) in 4:1 and why his background is described in 3:4. D. Schwartz (189) further suggests that τις "allows [the author] not only to indicate that this is a new character, but also to voice some disparagement, as if to say 'Our problems began because some nincompoop started a feud with such a wonderful high priest.'" For similar constructions, see 4:40; 14:3, 37.

δέ. Development, marking a change of grammatical subject from Seleucus (3:3) to "a certain Simon" in 3:4. Here D. Schwartz (189) comments on the "heavy adversative use of δέ in order to contrast a preceding idyll, even when there is no foregoing μέν." But this is probably claiming too much. It is better to understand δέ as "a procedural signal of discontinuity in the narrative" (Black, 178; cf. Runge, 31). See 1:10 on δέ.

ἐκ τῆς Βενιαμιν φυλῆς. Source/origin. Βενιαμιν is an indeclinable noun that further explains (i.e., genitive of apposition) φυλῆς. The Göttingen edition reads Βαλγεα (i.e., Bilgah) rather than Βενιαμιν, following Latin and Armenian traditions. Because Bilgah is a member of the priestly family (1 Chr 24:14; Neh 12:5) and Simon is identified as Menelaus' (a contender for the high priesthood) brother in 4:23, this reading is attractive (Habicht, 210; Doran 2012, 79; Goldstein, 201; Nicklas 2011, 1383). It is possible that Βενιαμιν emerged as a variant because φυλή is most commonly used with Israelite tribes in the LXX (cf. Grimm, 67). The implication of this textual decision is significant. If Βενιαμιν is the earliest text, then Menelaus, Simon's brother and one of 2 Maccabees' key villains, does not have a proper priestly pedigree. However, this is not only less plausible historically but it is also more difficult to explain why copyists would want to conceal this information. In addition to those cited earlier, see D. Schwartz (95–96) who prefers Βενιαμιν here.

προστάτης. Predicate nominative. The title προστάτης suggests an office of high rank within the temple (Habicht, 210; cf. Bickermann 2007, 434). In 2 Chr 24:11, the προστάτης is involved in collecting taxes for the temple and works with the high priest. This agrees with wider textual (P.Tebt 781; OGIS I, nr. 56, 73) and epigraphic evidence (see Goldstein, 201–2), where προστάτης designates a high-level temple administrator.

τοῦ ἱεροῦ. Genitive of subordination.

καθεσταμένος. Prf pass ptc nom masc sg καθίστημι (attributive). The verb, especially in the passive, can take the predicate nominative to indicate what something/someone becomes: "who had been appointed *captain*" (cf. *GE*, 1006; Wallace, 40). The choice of καθίστημι indicates that Simon was appointed (or elected) to this office rather than receiving it by heredity (cf. Goldstein, 201; Doran 2012, 81; Bickermann 2007, 434). Morphologically, because the verbal root of καθίστημι is στα, it reduplicates *sigma* to form the perfect. However, because the reduplication often dissimilates to a rough breathing in the simplex forms (*MBG* §25.6), the compound perfect forms do not have this either. Thus, στα → σεστηκα → ἕστηκα. Cf. 4:1, 50.

διηνέχθη. Aor mid ind 3rd sg διαφέρω. The main plotline of the narrative is conveyed with the aorist. On the meaning of the verb, see *GE* (516.2.B): "to differ (*in opinion*), be in disagreement, quarrel: περί τινος over s[omething]" (cf. *GELS*, 162.2). After a verb of speaking or writing, the preposition περί is expected to provide content (cf. Smyth §1693.2; LEH, 520; *GELS*, 545). On the θη- middle morphology, see 1:2 on μνησθείη. Verbs expressing conversation or quarreling often employ the middle voice because "[t]he agent (source) does something to affect the patient (endpoint); simultaneously the patient does something to affect the agent. Both participants play the part of starting point and endpoint for the energy transfer. . . . [T]he spotlight [is] on the interaction between both participants" (Aubrey, 605). Due to suppletion, the sixth principal part of (δια-) φέρω is (δια-) ἠνέχθην.

τῷ ἀρχιερεῖ. Dative complement of διηνέχθη. The dative expresses the person with whom Simon has a disagreement (*GELS*, 162.2).

περὶ τῆς . . . ἀγορανομίας. Reference. On the meaning of ἀγορανομία, see *GE* (19): "office of market overseer." See comments on διηνέχθη. D. Schwartz (190) notes that 2 Maccabees' assumption "that the high priest was involved in the affairs of the municipal officeholder, conforms well with its opening assertion [i.e., 3:1] that the high priest's merits impacted upon the city as a whole." Although the cause of disagreement between Simon and Onias (3:4) is unknown, the problems associated with fixing market prices and allowing or prohibiting goods on the market could always lead to disagreements (cf. Doran 2012, 80).

κατὰ τὴν πόλιν. Reference. On the position of the PP, see 1:1 on κατ᾽ Αἴγυπτον.

3:5 καὶ νικῆσαι τὸν Ονιαν μὴ δυνάμενος ἦλθεν πρὸς Ἀπολλώνιον Θαρσεου τὸν κατ᾽ ἐκεῖνον τὸν καιρὸν Κοίλης Συρίας καὶ Φοινίκης στρατηγὸν,

νικῆσαι. Aor act inf νικάω (complementary).

τὸν Ονιαν. Accusative direct object of νικῆσαι.

μὴ. See comment on the negation in 1:5.

δυνάμενος. Pres mid ptc nom masc sg δύναμαι (causal).

ἦλθεν. Aor act ind 3rd sg ἔρχομαι. See 2:5 on ἐλθών.

πρὸς Ἀπολλώνιον. Spatial (motion toward).

Θαρσεου. The Göttingen edition reads Θρασαίου ("Thraseas"), understanding the word as a name rather than a regional description (e.g., Tarsus). Although Abel (317) prefers Θαρσεου, Habicht (210) is correct to note that Ταρσεῖς is the epitomizer's preferred way to refer to Tarsus (e.g., 4:30). Θρασαίου is the preferred reading here, making this a genitive of relationship. Muraoka (§5cac) notes that when a personal name is followed by the father's name in the nominative, dative, or accusative, the genitive modifier is anarthrous. Cf. 3:11, Ὑρκανοῦ τοῦ Τωβιου, where the genitive is used with the article (cf. 4:21; 1 Macc 2:1). The epitomizer disambiguates the name Apollonius here in order to maintain a distinction with another Apollonius mentioned in 4:4 and 4:21.

τὸν . . . στρατηγὸν. Accusative in apposition to Ἀπολλώνιον. An example of hyperbaton, where the PP (κατ᾽ ἐκεῖνον τὸν καιρὸν) and modifiers appear between the Greek article and the substantive.

κατ᾽ ἐκεῖνον τὸν καιρὸν. Temporal. Fronting of the demonstrative "occurs mostly in temporal adjuncts" (Muraoka §34c).

Κοίλης Συρίας καὶ Φοινίκης. Genitives of subordination.

3:6 καὶ προσήγγειλεν περὶ τοῦ χρημάτων ἀμυθήτων γέμειν τὸ ἐν Ιεροσολύμοις γαζοφυλάκιον ὥστε τὸ πλῆθος τῶν διαφόρων

ἀναρίθμητον εἶναι, καὶ μὴ προσήκειν αὐτὰ πρὸς τὸν τῶν θυσιῶν λόγον, εἶναι δὲ δυνατὸν ὑπὸ τὴν τοῦ βασιλέως ἐξουσίαν πεσεῖν ταῦτα.

The syntax of 3:6 is complicated because of the five infinitives (γέμειν, εἶναι, προσήκειν, εἶναι, πεσεῖν) following the main verb (προσήγγειλεν). If εἶναι, προσήκειν, and εἶναι are construed with ὥστε, there would be three result clauses. Alternatively, if the καί that precedes μὴ προσήκειν αὐτὰ πρὸς τὸν τῶν θυσιῶν λόγον coordinates what follows with περὶ τοῦ χρημάτων ἀμυθήτων γέμειν τὸ ἐν Ιεροσολύμοις γαζοφυλάκιον, there would be three coordinate clauses, marking indirect discourse. Because the clauses constructed with προσήκειν and εἶναι (second occurrence) do not make much as sense as result clauses, it is best to connect them back to προσήγγειλεν περὶ τοῦ. . . . The clauses may be laid out as follows:

καὶ προσήγγειλεν
περὶ τοῦ χρημάτων ἀμυθήτων γέμειν τὸ ἐν Ιεροσολύμοις
        γαζοφυλάκιον
ὥστε τὸ πλῆθος τῶν διαφόρων ἀναρίθμητον εἶναι,
καὶ [περὶ τοῦ] μὴ προσήκειν αὐτὰ πρὸς τὸν τῶν θυσιῶν λόγον,
[περὶ τοῦ] εἶναι δὲ δυνατὸν ὑπὸ τὴν τοῦ βασιλέως ἐξουσίαν πεσεῖν
        ταῦτα.

προσήγγειλεν. Aor act ind 3rd sg προσαγγέλλω. On the use of a verb of speaking + περί, see 3:4 on διηνέχθη. Cf. 9:24; 10:21; 13:21.
    περὶ τοῦ χρημάτων ἀμυθήτων γέμειν τὸ ἐν Ιεροσολύμοις γαζοφυλάκιον. Reference.
    γέμειν. Pres act inf γέμω (indirect discourse). Used with περὶ τοῦ after a verb of speaking. When an articular infinitive takes a case other than the accusative for its object, it is not uncommon to position the object between the article and the infinitive (Muraoka §30abc). Bickermann (2007, 436) notes that the verb γέμω is used because coins were piled up on the ground (as opposed to being stored in jars), indicating that the temple treasury is "full."
    χρημάτων ἀμυθήτων. Genitive complement of γέμειν. Verbs of "filling" often take the genitive (*CGCG* §30.22; Smyth §1369; Wallace, 92–93, 131; Muraoka §22p). LEH (33) notes that ἀμύθητος refers to "unspeakably great [money]" (cf. *GE*, 114) and Bickermann (2007, 435–36) notes that χρήματα refers to "cash . . . rather than wealth in general" (cf. 1:14; 3:7; 4:1, 23, 27, 45; 8:25; Xenophon, *Anab.* 1.2.27; 5.2.7). On the accumulation of money in temples, see Hamilton (365–70).
    τὸ . . . γαζοφυλάκιον. Accusative subject of the infinitive γέμειν. The "treasury [in Jerusalem]" refers to the temple treasury, literally the room

where money is kept (cf. 3:12, 24, 28, 40; 4:42; 5:18; cf. Bickermann 2007, 436). Hamilton (367) notes that "Simon's function as προστάτης [cf. 3:4] provides a clue to the relation of the temple bank to the commerce of the city . . . in a role comparable to that of city banks throughout the Hellenistic world, especially in Greek cities."

ἐν Ἱεροσολύμοις. Locative.

ὥστε. Introduces a result clause, subordinate to γέμειν. The great wealth resulted in a situation where they were not able to count it.

τὸ πλῆθος. Nominative subject of εἶναι.

τῶν διαφόρων. Genitive of material or, better, reference. It is possible that διάφορον refers to "discrepancies" or "amount over, excess" in bookkeeping (Bickermann 2007, 436–39; cf. 4:28) rather than simply "ready money, cash" (*GELS*, 163; *GE*, 517; cf. 1:35). On this understanding, Simon was charging the Jews "for not spending on sacrifices all the royal budget supplied for that purpose (v. 3)" (D. Schwartz, 191; cf. Doran 2012, 81). Goldstein (204–6) rejects this interpretation and argues that the money in view is from private deposits. However, this reading must ignore the clear meaning of 3:3.

ἀναρίθμητον. Predicate adjective. On the meaning, see *GE* (151): "that cannot be counted, innumerable."

εἶναι. Pres act inf εἰμί. Used with ὥστε to indicate a result.

καὶ. The conjunction links the verb προσήκειν to περὶ τοῦ earlier in the text.

μὴ. See comment on the negation in 1:5.

προσήκειν. Pres act inf προσήκω (indirect discourse). On the meaning of the verb, see *GELS* (594): "to belong to (πρός + acc[usative])" (cf. *GE*, 1809.C).

αὐτὰ. Accusative subject of the infinitive προσήκειν. The neuter pronoun is plural, matching the sense rather than the grammatical form of its antecedent τὸ πλῆθος (cf. *CGCG* §27.11).

πρὸς τὸν . . . λόγον. Association. Cf. 1:14; 12:43 for λόγος with a similar sense. As Bickermann (2007, 438) notes, the expression ὁ τῶν θυσιῶν λόγος is "a technical term for the special account relative to the sacrifices."

τῶν θυσιῶν. Genitive of reference.

εἶναι. Pres act inf εἰμί (indirect discourse).

δὲ. Development, linking the verb προσήκειν to περὶ τοῦ earlier and marking small development in the narrative: the great wealth did not belong to the account of sacrifices, *but* [δέ] the king could still exercise authority over the funds. See 1:10 on δέ.

δυνατὸν. Predicate adjective.

ὑπὸ τήν . . . ἐξουσίαν. Subordination.

τοῦ βασιλέως. Subjective genitive.

πεσεῖν. Aor act inf πίπτω. The infinitival clause, ὑπὸ τὴν τοῦ βασιλέως ἐξουσίαν πεσεῖν ταῦτα, functions as the subject of εἶναι (BDF §393.2).

ταῦτα. Accusative subject of the infinitive πεσεῖν.

3:7 συμμείξας δὲ ὁ Ἀπολλώνιος τῷ βασιλεῖ περὶ τῶν μηνυθέντων αὐτῷ χρημάτων ἐνεφάνισεν· ὁ δὲ προχειρισάμενος Ἡλιόδωρον τὸν ἐπὶ τῶν πραγμάτων ἀπέστειλεν δοὺς ἐντολὰς τὴν τῶν προειρημένων χρημάτων ἐκκομιδὴν ποιήσασθαι.

συμμείξας. Aor act ptc nom masc sg συμμίγνυμι (temporal).

δὲ. Development, marking a change of grammatical subject to ὁ Ἀπολλώνιος. See 1:10 on δέ.

ὁ Ἀπολλώνιος. Nominative subject of ἐνεφάνισεν. The article is anaphoric, referring back to Ἀπολλώνιον in 3:5.

τῷ βασιλεῖ. Dative of association.

περὶ τῶν μηνυθέντων . . . χρημάτων. Reference. Cf. 3:6.

μηνυθέντων. Aor pass ptc gen neut pl μηνύω (attributive). LN (33.209) notes that the verb means "to provide information concerning something, with emphasis upon the fact that such information is secret or known only to a select few."

αὐτῷ. Dative indirect object of μηνυθέντων.

ἐνεφάνισεν. Aor act ind 3rd sg ἐμφανίζω. As BDAG (326.2) notes, the verb is sometimes used to provide information in communicative processes, especially in official reports to authorities: "to explain" (cf. GE, 678; Mayser II 2.267). On the use of a verb of speaking + περί, see 3:4 on διηνέχθη.

ὁ δὲ. The article functions as the nominative subject of ἀπέστειλεν and refers to the king. The use of ὁ δέ is a standard way to switch speakers/characters within a narrative where there is no explicit subject expressed elsewhere and the article functions like an anaphoric third person pronoun (cf. Muraoka §1a; Lee 2018, 35–36).

προχειρισάμενος. Aor mid ptc nom masc sg προχειρίζομαι (temporal).

Ἡλιόδωρον. Accusative direct object of προχειρισάμενος. Because the name Ἡλιόδωρος is being established in the narrative it is anarthrous (Smyth §1136; Muraoka §1b). Compare this use with the following articular uses of the name in 2:8; 3:13, 23, 31, 32, 33, 35, 37; 4:1; 5:18, where the article defines "[o]bjects already mentioned or in the mind of the speaker or writer" (Smyth §1120.b).

τὸν. The article functions as a nominalizer, changing the following PP (ἐπὶ τῶν πραγμάτων) into an accusative in apposition to Ἡλιόδωρον.

ἐπὶ τῶν πραγμάτων. Here ἐπί is a "marker of power, authority, control of or over someone or someth[ing]" (BDAG, 365.9.a; *GELS*, 263): Ἡλιόδωρον τὸν ἐπὶ τῶν πραγμάτων, "Heliodorus, who was *in charge of* the affairs."

ἀπέστειλεν. Aor act ind 3rd ἀποστέλλω.

δούς. Aor act ptc nom masc sg δίδωμι (purpose or, perhaps, manner). δίδωμι + infinitive = "to issue a command *to do* [something]" (*GELS*, 165).

ἐντολὰς. Accusative direct object of δούς.

τὴν . . . ἐκκομιδὴν. Accusative direct object of ποιήσασθαι.

τῶν προειρημένων χρημάτων. Objective genitive. Cf. 3:6. On text-critical matters related to 3:7, see Bickermann (2007, 439).

προειρημένων. Prf pass ptc gen neut pl προλέγω (attributive). Cf. 2:32; 3:28; 4:1; 6:29; 14:8.

ποιήσασθαι. Aor mid inf ποιέω (complementary). See comments on δούς above. When the middle of ποιέω is used with a verbal noun (ἐκκομιδήν), this can be a periphrasis for the verb itself: ἐκκομίζω (*GELS*, 570.II). See 1:23 on ἐποιήσαντο.

3:8 εὐθέως δὲ ὁ Ἡλιόδωρος ἐποιεῖτο τὴν πορείαν, τῇ μὲν ἐμφάσει ὡς τὰς κατὰ Κοίλην Συρίαν καὶ Φοινίκην πόλεις ἐφοδεῦσαι, τῷ πράγματι δὲ τὴν τοῦ βασιλέως πρόθεσιν ἐπιτελεῖν.

εὐθέως. Adverb of manner (cf. BDF §102.2).

δὲ. Development, marking a change of grammatical subject from Apollonius (3:7) to ὁ Ἡλιόδωρος in 3:8. See 1:10 on δέ.

ὁ Ἡλιόδωρος. Nominative subject of ἐποιεῖτο. The article is anaphoric, referring back to Ἡλιόδωρον in 3:7.

ἐποιεῖτο. Impf mid ind 3rd sg ποιέω. With the adverb εὐθέως, the imperfect verb refers to an action in process that immediately follows another action. Although some grammarians label this usage the so-called "inchoative imperfect" (e.g., Muraoka §28c.v; Wallace, 544), it is potentially misleading to claim that the imperfect stresses the beginning of an action (cf. *CGCG* §33.52). When the middle of ποιέω is used with a verbal noun (πορείαν), this can be a periphrasis for the verb itself: πορεύω (*GELS*, 570.II; BDF §310.1; BDAG, 839.2.d). See 1:23 on ἐποιήσαντο.

τὴν πορείαν. Accusative direct object of ἐποιεῖτο.

τῇ . . . ἐμφάσει. Dative of manner. The translation "ostensibly," derives from *GE* (679.A): "visible aspect, appearance, impression."

μὲν . . . δέ. Point/counterpoint set. See 2:25 on μὲν . . . δέ. As is typical in μέν/δέ constructions, the δέ material is highlighted. Here this contrasts the (false) pretense of inspecting the cities with the actuality of carrying out the king's plan.

ὡς. Purpose. Muraoka (§30bac) notes that "on very rare occasions <ὡς + inf[initive]> indicates a purpose." See 3 Macc 1:2; 4 Macc 14:1.

τὰς . . . πόλεις. Accusative direct object of ἐφοδεῦσαι.

κατὰ Κοίλην Συρίαν καὶ Φοινίκην. Locative or, more precisely, extension (see Smyth §1690). On the position of the PP, see 1:1 on κατ' Αἴγυπτον.

ἐφοδεῦσαι. Aor act inf ἐφοδεύω (purpose, see ὡς above). On the meaning of the verb, see *GE* (881): "to inspect, visit, pass in review."

τῷ πράγματι. Dative of manner.

τὴν . . . πρόθεσιν. Accusative direct object of ἐπιτελεῖν. The sense of "purpose" or "will" is intended here (cf. 3 Macc 1:22; 2:26; 5:12, 29).

τοῦ βασιλέως. Subjective genitive.

ἐπιτελεῖν. Pres act inf ἐπιτελέω (purpose, see ὡς above).

2 Maccabees 3:9-12

⁹After arriving in Jerusalem and being warmly welcomed by the high priest of the city, he communicated about the information that had been reported and he explained the reason why he was present. Then, he was inquiring whether, in truth, these things happened to be this way. ¹⁰Although the high priest indicated that there were deposits from both widows and orphans, ¹¹and also some [money] of Hyrcanus [son] of Tobias, a man found in exceedingly good standing—not as the impious Simon was falsely informing; and [that] everything [was] four hundred talents of silver and two hundred of gold; ¹²and that it would be completely impossible for those who trust in the holiness of the place and in the dignity and inviolability of the temple, which is honored throughout the world, to be treated unjustly.

For comments on the use of the imperfect indicative rather than the aorist indicative in this section, see the discussion following the translation of 3:13-29.

3:9 παραγενηθεὶς δὲ εἰς Ιεροσόλυμα καὶ φιλοφρόνως ὑπὸ τοῦ ἀρχιερέως τῆς πόλεως ἀποδεχθεὶς ἀνέθετο περὶ τοῦ γεγονότος ἐμφανισμοῦ, καὶ τίνος ἕνεκεν πάρεστιν διεσάφησεν· ἐπυνθάνετο δὲ εἰ ταῖς ἀληθείαις ταῦτα οὕτως ἔχοντα τυγχάνει.

παραγενηθεὶς. Aor mid ptc nom masc sg παραγίνομαι (temporal). The verb is often followed by εἰς + accusative of place (4:21; 5:25; 12:31;

cf. Wallace, 760.1.a). Some MSS (*L* 106) read παραγενόμενος. On the θη- middle morphology, see 1:2 on μνησθείη. Verbs expressing motion (involving a change of location or body posture) often employ the middle voice because "[t]he mover is the primary figure for the event, its energy source and energy endpoint. As an event involving internal energy, the one who induces the change is also the one who undergoes the change" (Aubrey, 598).

δὲ. Development; see 1:10 on δέ.

εἰς Ἱεροσόλυμα. Locative.

φιλοφρόνως. Adverb of manner.

ὑπὸ τοῦ ἀρχιερέως. Agency.

τῆς πόλεως. Genitive of subordination. The high priest's authority over the city is also noted in 3:1, 4; 4:2 and this is probably the reason for the redundant phrase "high priest *of the city*." A few MSS (e.g., V *L* 55 311) read καί prior to τῆς πόλεως, changing the meaning of the phrase ὑπὸ τοῦ ἀρχιερέως καὶ τῆς πόλεως: "[welcomed] by the high priest *and* by the city" (cf. 4:22). The reading with καί is probably secondary (*pace* Habicht, 211; Doran 2012, 73; Nicklas 2011, 1383) and is best understood as an attempt to smooth out the redundancy because the high priest, Onias, is definitionally also priest "of the city." The parallel with 3:35, where Heliodorus welcomes Onias (and not the city) as he departs, may also support this argument. This judgment can only be tentative because one of the most common copying mistakes is the omission of small words like καί (Royse, 183).

ἀποδεχθεὶς. Aor pass ptc nom masc sg ἀποδέχομαι (temporal). Cf. 3:35; 4:22; 13:24.

ἀνέθετο. Aor mid ind 3rd sg ἀνατίθημι. On the meaning of the verb, see BDAG (73.2): "to lay someth[ing] before someone for consideration, *communicate, refer, declare* w[ith] connotation of request for a person's opinion" (cf. *GE*, 157.2). On the use of a verb of speaking + περί, see 3:4 on διηνέχθη.

περὶ τοῦ γεγονότος ἐμφανισμοῦ. Reference.

γεγονότος. Prf act ptc gen masc sg γίνομαι (attributive).

τίνος. Genitive object of ἕνεκεν: literally, "on account of what" = "the reason why."

ἕνεκεν. Improper causal preposition with a genitive object.

πάρεστιν. Pres act ind 3rd sg πάρειμι (indirect discourse). Because πάρειμι appears in indirect discourse, the present tense must be translated using the past tense (Wallace, 457): "he was present."

διεσάφησεν. Aor act ind 3rd sg διασαφέω. On the meaning of the verb, see BDAG (236.1): "to clarify someth[ing] that is obscure, explain, lit[erally] 'make clear.'"

ἐπυνθάνετο. Impf mid ind 3rd sg πυνθάνομαι. On the meaning of the verb, see BDAG (897.1): "to seek to learn by inquiry, *inquire, ask*."

δὲ. Development; see 1:10 on δέ.

εἰ. The particle introduces the content of an indirect question after a verb of inquiry (cf. BDAG, 278.2). Cf. 14:28.

ταῖς ἀληθείαις. Dative of manner.

ταῦτα. Nominative subject of τυγχάνει. Neuter plural subjects are used commonly with a singular verb (Smyth §958). The neuter accusative demonstrative pronoun refers to "the accusation that funds from the royal budget had been accumulated rather than spent on sacrifices" (D. Schwartz, 193).

οὕτως. Adverb of manner, referring to the events described in the preceding context. The use of the linking verb ἔχω + adverb is common in classical Greek (cf. *CGCG* §26.11). See also BDAG (422.10.a) for examples of ἔχω + οὕτως.

ἔχοντα. Pres act ptc nom neut pl ἔχω (complementary). The verb ἔχω is used impersonally (cf. BDAG, 422.10.a) and describes how "the situation is."

τυγχάνει. Pres act ind 3rd sg τυγχάνω. This verb is regularly complemented by another verb, often a participle (Muraoka §31e). On the meaning of the verb, see *GELS* (690): "*to turn out* to be on examination: + [participle]." *GE* (2164.1.B) notes that τυγχάνω often appears "with [participle] [predicate] (with sign[ificance] of verb expressed by [participle] and a nuance of coincidence)." D. Schwartz (194) notes that the construction of the question ("happened to be") appears to be "especially polite, a hesitant opening for a matter unpleasant to both sides." Cf. 4:32; 9:1; Tob 5:14.

3:10 τοῦ δὲ ἀρχιερέως ὑποδείξαντος παρακαταθήκας εἶναι χηρῶν τε καὶ ὀρφανῶν,

The genitive absolute construction, τοῦ . . . ἀρχιερέως ὑποδείξαντος, forms the basis of the syntax for 3:10-12.

τοῦ . . . ἀρχιερέως. Genitive subject of the participle ὑποδείξαντος.

δὲ. Development; see 1:10 on δέ.

ὑποδείξαντος. Aor act ptc gen masc sg ὑποδείκνυμι (genitive absolute, concessive). On the genitive absolute, see 1:7 on βασιλεύοντος.

παρακαταθήκας. Predicate accusative of εἶναι. *GE* (1551) notes that παρακαταθήκη refers to a "deposit: surrendered in good faith" (cf. BDAG, 765).

εἶναι. Pres act inf εἰμί (indirect discourse with a verb of communication).

χηρῶν. Possessive genitive ("widows' [deposits]") or, possibly, objective genitive (i.e., deposits that temple authorities can give to widows and orphans, as necessary). Because temples often accumulated large amounts of money offered to the gods, temple funds were thought to be under divine protection. Hamilton (366) notes that "[t]his security factor attracted the surplus funds of states, corporations, and private individuals until custody of deposits became a regular feature of temples." Doran (2012, 82) notes that the genitive may denote either "a rhetorical ploy to suggest how heinous taking the money would be and that it will be avenged (Exod 22:22-24; Deut 10:18; Ps 68:5) or evidence of widows inheriting their husband's wealth as, for example, had Judith, who had been left gold and silver, male and female slaves, livestock and fields (Jdt 8:7; Sir 22:4)."

τε καὶ. The combination τὲ καί serves to unite complements, both similar and opposites (Smyth §2974) and is a closer connection than καί alone (BDF §444.2). See 3:1 on τε καί.

ὀρφανῶν. Possessive genitive or, possibly, objective genitive.

3:11 τινὰ δὲ καὶ Ὑρκανοῦ τοῦ Τωβίου σφόδρα ἀνδρὸς ἐν ὑπεροχῇ κειμένου — οὕτως ἦν διαβάλλων ὁ δυσσεβὴς Σιμων — , τὰ δὲ πάντα ἀργυρίου τετρακόσια τάλαντα, χρυσίου δὲ διακόσια·

τινὰ. Predicate accusative, linked by δέ to εἶναι in 3:10.

δὲ. Development; see 1:10 on δέ.

καὶ. Adverbial.

Ὑρκανοῦ. Possessive genitive or source.

τοῦ Τωβίου. Genitive of relationship. See 3:5 on Θαρσεου for comments on the use of the article. According to Josephus (*Ant.* 12.186-236), Hyrcanus is son of Joseph son of Tobias. Thus, the genitive denotes ancestry beyond a simple father-son relationship, referring to "the Tobiad" (cf. Goldstein, 207) or, as Josephus (*Ant.* 12.239) refers to them, "the descendants of Tobias" (οἱ Τωβίου παῖδες). Doran (2012, 83) rejects this reading by claiming that "the most obvious reading is that the actual father of Hyrcanus was someone called Tobias." It is not clear, though, how this reading is obvious because genitives constructed in this manner can convey relationships beyond that of father-son.

σφόδρα. Adverb of measure.

ἀνδρὸς ἐν ὑπεροχῇ κειμένου. Genitive phrase in apposition to Ὑρκανοῦ: "a man found in exceedingly good standing."

ἀνδρὸς. Genitive subject of the participle κειμένου.

ἐν ὑπεροχῇ. Locative, in a metaphorical sense.

κειμένου. Pres pass ptc gen masc sg κεῖμαι (attributive, modifying ἀνδρός).

οὕτως. Adverb of manner, modifying ἦν διαβάλλων. The Göttingen edition reads οὐχ ὡς ("not as") rather than οὕτως (cf. Doran 2012, 75; D. Schwartz, 182). R-H, following MS A, reads οὕτως: "*so* the impious Simon was falsely informing." The orthographic similarity probably led to the variants. The reading of the Göttingen edition is preferred here because it makes better sense of the literary context and is an easy copyist mistake.

ἦν διαβάλλων. Imperfect periphrastic construction, taking the person, number, and mood from ἦν; aspect, voice, and lexical form from διαβάλλων. Thus, the synthetic form would be: διαβάλλει, pres act ind 3rd sg. The *TLG* attests to about 70 uses of this form in extant Greek literature ranging from Aeschylus (6th–5th century BCE) through second century BCE. The periphrastic construction is probably motivated by pragmatic concerns, particularly the epitomizer's attempt to convey high literary style. Alternatively, it is possible that the periphrastic (rather than a finite verb) portrays an iterative event (Levinsohn 2016, 312). On motivations for periphrastic constructions, see comments in the Introduction.

ἦν. Impf act ind 3rd sg εἰμί.

διαβάλλων. Pres act ptc nom masc sg διαβάλλω (imperfect periphrastic). On the meaning of the verb, see BDAG (226): "to make a complaint about a pers[on] to a third party, *bring charges, inform* either justly or falsely" (cf. *GELS*, 148). For the false charge, see 3:4-6.

ὁ δυσσεβὴς Σιμων. Nominative subject of ἦν διαβάλλων. The word δυσσεβής (δυσ + σεβής) includes the inseparable prefix δυσ-, which "negates the good sense of a word, w[ith] notion of *hard, bad, difficult*" (BDAG, 265). In context, it contrasts with εὐσέβεια: "because of the *piety* [εὐσέβειαν] of the high priest Onias" (3:1); "the impious [δυσσεβής] Simon" (3:11). On the δυσ-compound words in 2 Maccabees, see 2:24 on δυσχέρειαν.

δὲ. Development; see 1:10 on δέ.

τὰ ... πάντα. Nominative subject of an implied verb: "everything was...."

ἀργυρίου. Genitive of material (cf. *CGCG* §30.28).

τετρακόσια τάλαντα. Predicate nominative of an implied verb. *GE* (2079) notes that in post-Homeric writers, a *talent* refers to "a commercial weight or a monetary sum that varies according to the system of measurement." For Greek numbers, see Smyth (§347).

χρυσίου. Genitive of material. It is likely that one gold talent is equivalent to ten silver talents (cf. Goldstein, 209). Thus, the amount of money estimated is about 2,400 talents of silver. See *OCD* (1572–73) for further discussion on weights and measures.

δέ. Development; see 1:10 on δέ.

διακόσια. Predicate nominative. On Greek numbers, see Smyth (§347).

3:12 ἀδικηθῆναι δὲ τοὺς πεπιστευκότας τῇ τοῦ τόπου ἁγιωσύνῃ καὶ τῇ τοῦ τετιμημένου κατὰ τὸν σύμπαντα κόσμον ἱεροῦ σεμνότητι καὶ ἀσυλίᾳ παντελῶς ἀμήχανον εἶναι.

ἀδικηθῆναι. Aor pass inf ἀδικέω (epexegetical, explaining ἀμήχανον). Thus, "it would be completely impossible [for those who trust] *to be treated unjustly*." Less likely, ἀδικηθῆναι . . . τοὺς πεπιστευκότας may function as the subject of εἶναι. MS A, which is probably secondary, reads ἀδικῆσαι (aorist active infinitive), which allows τοὺς πεπιστευκότας to be taken as the direct object of ἀδικηθῆναι: "to treat unjustly *those who trust.*"

δέ. Development; see 1:10 on δέ.

τοὺς πεπιστευκότας. Prf act ptc acc masc pl πιστεύω (substantival). Subject of the infinitive ἀδικηθῆναι.

τῇ . . . ἁγιωσύνῃ. Dative complement of πεπιστευκότας.

τοῦ τόπου. Genitive of source. As in 3:1, the τόπος and ἱερόν (below) are both used to refer to the temple.

τῇ . . . σεμνότητι καὶ ἀσυλίᾳ. Dative complements of πεπιστευκότας. Although the "inviolability" or "immunity" (ἀσυλία) of the temple would later become an official status conferred by a king, Rigsby (530–31) notes that "[i]t seems to be improbable that Jerusalem and its god . . . achieved this honor at so early a date." Accordingly, ἀσυλία is not an official proclamation, but a more general recognition on the basis of the holiness of the temple.

τοῦ τετιμημένου. Prf pass or mid ptc gen masc sg τιμάω (substantival). Genitive of identification.

κατὰ τὸν σύμπαντα κόσμον. Locative or, more precisely, extension (see Smyth §1690).

ἱεροῦ. Genitive of source, qualifying τῇ . . . σεμνότητι.

παντελῶς. Adverb of degree.

ἀμήχανον. Predicate accusative of εἶναι. On the meaning of the verb, see *GE* (109): "[to be] difficult, impossible."

εἶναι. Pres act inf εἰμί (indirect discourse with a verb of communication, modifying ὑποδείξαντος from 3:10).

2 Maccabees 3:13-23

[13]But Heliodorus, because of royal commands which he held, was saying that certainly these must be acquired for the royal treasury. [14]Having established a day, he entered in order to oversee the inspection of these [funds], and there was no small distress throughout the whole city. [15]And the priests, after prostrating themselves before the altar in their priestly vestments, were calling to heaven upon the one who had legislated about deposits, that he would keep [them] safe for those who deposited these things. [16]And seeing the countenance of the high priest was to be wounded mentally. For the face and the change of color revealed the anguish of his soul. [17]For a certain terror and trembling of body had come over the man, by which the pain lodged in his heart became evident to those watching. [18]They were still rushing out of the houses in droves to [take part in] a common supplication because the place was about to go into dishonor. [19]And, having girded up sackcloth under their breasts, women were flooding the streets. Those of the virgins who were kept inside, some were running together to the gates, others were running to walls, and others looked out through the windows. [20]And all the women, by holding up their hands to heaven, were making supplication. [21]And the confused prostration of the multitude and the anticipation of the greatly anxious high priest was pitiable. [22]So then, they were calling upon the Lord Almighty to keep the entrusted things safe with complete security for those who untrusted [them], [23]but Heliodorus went on with what had been decided.

It is somewhat unusual that the epitomizer narrates Heliodorus' actions in 3:13-23, including his entry into the temple, with 16 imperfect indicative verbs and avoids the use of the aorist indicative. It is possible, but not certain, that this is for literary effect because the epitomizer switches to the aorist to describe the "amazing appearance" (ἐπιφάνειαν μεγάλην) in 3:24 (cf. Shaw 2016, 412). Additionally, the avoidance of the aorist may be because the plotline of the narrative concerns Heliodorus' entrance into the temple, which is introduced in 3:14 and resumed in 3:24. Between these two verses, the epitomizer includes multiple reactions and responses to Heliodorus' entrance that are meant to evoke an emotional response from the reader (cf. Doran, 2012, 89). In any case, the (over-) use of the imperfect in this section is striking.

This section is also full of rhetorical embellishments. For example, Doran (1981, 49) notes paronomasia in 3:15 (παρακαταθήκης, παρακαταθεμένοις) and 3:22 (τὰ πεπιστευμένα, πεπιστευκόσιν).

3:13 ὁ δὲ Ἡλιόδωρος, δι᾽ ἃς εἶχεν βασιλικὰς ἐντολάς, πάντως ἔλεγεν εἰς τὸ βασιλικὸν ἀναλημπτέα ταῦτα εἶναι.

ὁ . . . Ἡλιόδωρος. Nominative subject of ἔλεγεν. The article is anaphoric, referring back to Ἡλιόδωρον in 3:7. The Göttingen edition reads ὁ . . . ἕτερος ("the other one," NETS), which is probably the older reading because it lacks specificity. Accordingly, some MSS (La^{BF(M)P} Sy) and R-H read Ἡλιόδωρος, making the subject of the sentence more explicit.

δὲ. Development, marking a shift of grammatical subject from Onias, the high priest, in 3:12 to Heliodorus in 3:13. See 1:10 on δέ.

δι᾽ ἃς εἶχεν βασιλικὰς ἐντολάς. The relative clause, ἃς εἶχεν, is embedded within the PP (cf. Smyth §2536). For similar constructions, see 3 Macc 3:18; 7:5, 6. Muraoka (§86dbf) notes that this construction could be rewritten as διότι εἶχε βασιλικὰς ἐντολάς.

δι᾽ . . . βασιλικάς ἐντολάς. Cause.

ἃς. Accusative direct object of εἶχεν. The relative pronoun is feminine plural, agreeing with ἐντολάς.

εἶχεν. Impf act ind 3rd sg ἔχω.

πάντως. Adverb, denoting a strong assumption ("certainly," "doubtless") within a statement (cf. BDAG, 755.1).

ἔλεγεν. Impf act ind 3rd sg. The imperfect (of a verb of speech) is used "when a reaction to a speech or command is expected" (*CGCG* §33.51).

εἰς τὸ βασιλικὸν. Locative ("[taken] *to* the βασιλικόν") or, perhaps, advantage ("[taken] *for* the βασιλικόν"). Some of the MS tradition (V *L* 58 311 La^P) reads εἰς τὴν βασιλικὴν πρόσοδον ("to/for the royal revenues"), perhaps to clarify the meaning of βασιλικόν (cf. 3:3; 4:8). On the meaning of βασιλικόν, see *GELS* (115): "royal treasury" (cf. Habicht, 212; Doran 2012, 84).

ἀναλημπτέα. Predicate verbal adjective preceding εἶναι, in agreement with ταῦτα. Alternatively, Thackeray (§15.3; cf. Muraoka §23e) notes that ἀναλημπτέα may be used as the main verb in the sentence, which is supported by MS 58, which omits εἶναι. On the meaning of ἀναλημπτέος, see *GE* (142): "that should be acquired."

ταῦτα. Accusative subject of the infinitive εἶναι. Refers to the great wealth mentioned in the prior literary context.

εἶναι. Pres act inf εἰμί (indirect discourse with a verb of communication).

3:14 ταξάμενος δὲ ἡμέραν εἰσῄει τὴν περὶ τούτων ἐπίσκεψιν
οἰκονομήσων· ἦν δὲ οὐ μικρὰ καθ᾽ ὅλην τὴν πόλιν ἀγωνία.

ταξάμενος. Aor mid ptc nom masc sg τάσσω (temporal). The collocation of τάσσω + ἡμέρα ("establish a day") is common (e.g., Polybius,
Hist. 18.10; Josephus, *Ant.* 9.136; Acts 28:23).
δὲ. Development; see 1:10 on δέ.
ἡμέραν. Accusative direct object of ταξάμενος.
εἰσῄει. Impf act ind 3rd sg εἴσειμι.
τὴν . . . ἐπίσκεψιν. Accusative direct object of οἰκονομήσων.
περὶ τούτων. Reference.
οἰκονομήσων. Fut act ptc nom masc sg οἰκονομέω (purpose). A
future circumstantial participle typically expresses purpose, conveying
the intention of the subject following the action of the main verb (cf.
CGCG §52.41; Wallace, 635; cf. Muraoka §28gia). Cf. the use of future
participles in 5:9; 10:24; 12:7.
ἦν. Impf act ind 3rd sg εἰμί.
δὲ. The conjunction δέ is used rather than καί because there is a
development in the story. Heliodorus' actions result in a great distress
throughout the city. See 1:10 on δέ.
οὐ. Muraoka (§83be) notes that "[w]hen quantifying adjectives such
as μικρός or ὀλίγος are negative, the negation is often a rhetorical device
for reinforcing the property of their respective antonym, as in Engl[ish]
not unimportant = very important, and then οὐ is selected."
μικρὰ . . . ἀγωνία. Predicate of ἦν. An example of hyperbaton, where
the modifier (μικρά) is separated from the head noun (ἀγωνία) and the
emphasis is on the "small[ness]" of the distress in a litotic statement. Additionally, PP (καθ᾽ ὅλην τὴν πόλιν) appears between the adjective and the
head. As noted above, the negation of μικρὰ ἀγωνία is an example of litotes, where "no small distress" means something like "a great distress."
καθ᾽ ὅλην τὴν πόλιν. Locative or, more precisely, extension ("*throughout* the whole city"). The adjective ὅλος typically appears in the predicate
construction, as here. On the use of ἡ πόλις rather than Ιεροσολύμα, see
2:22 on τὴν πόλιν.

3:15 οἱ δὲ ἱερεῖς πρὸ τοῦ θυσιαστηρίου ἐν ταῖς ἱερατικαῖς στολαῖς
ῥίψαντες ἑαυτοὺς ἐπεκαλοῦντο εἰς οὐρανὸν τὸν περὶ παρακαταθήκης
νομοθετήσαντα τοῖς παρακαταθεμένοις ταῦτα σῶα διαφυλάξαι.

οἱ . . . ἱερεῖς. Nominative subject of ἐπεκαλοῦντο.
δὲ. Development, marking a shift of grammatical subject from
Heliodorus in 3:14 to the priests in 3:15. See 1:10 on δέ.

πρὸ τοῦ θυσιαστηρίου. Locative.

ἐν ταῖς ἱερατικαῖς στολαῖς. State or condition. The word ἱερατικός ("pertaining to a priest," *GELS*, 338) derives from adding the -ικος ending to the noun base ἱερός. Cf. the same expression about priestly garments appears in 1 Esd 4:54; 5:44.

ῥίψαντες. Aor act ptc nom masc pl ῥίπτω (temporal).

ἑαυτούς. Accusative direct object of ῥίψαντες.

ἐπεκαλοῦντο. Impf mid ind 3rd pl ἐπικαλέω. The verb ἐπικαλέω commonly occurs with the infinitive in indirect discourse (cf. BDAG, 373.3; *CGCG* §51.32). In the middle voice, ἐπικαλέω often refers to invoking a deity in prayer (cf. *GE*, 767.2). This use of the middle corresponds to the so-called "indirect middle," which anticipates the deity's response and is, therefore, self-benefactive (Kemmer, 78–81).

εἰς οὐρανόν. Spatial. The words εἰς οὐρανόν are lacking in the Lucianic and some of the translations (*L*⁻⁵⁴² La^{LXV(P)} Sy Arm) and judged to be superfluous by Habicht (212; cf. Katz 1960, 13). However, D. Schwartz (93) correctly notes that the use of "heaven" in 3:15 anticipates the heavenly apparition in 3:25-28, 34.

τὸν . . . νομοθετήσαντα. Aor act ptc acc masc sg νομοθετέω (substantival). Subject of the infinitive διαφυλάξαι. The verb is built using νόμος + τίθημι, thus the sense "to frame laws" (*GELS*, 476.1).

περὶ παρακαταθήκης. Reference. Cf. 3:10. On the law about deposits, see Exod 22:6-14.

τοῖς παρακαταθεμένοις. Aor mid ptc dat masc pl παρακατατίθημι (substantival). Dative of advantage.

ταῦτα. Accusative direct object of παρακαταθεμένοις.

σῶα. Accusative direct object of διαφυλάξαι.

διαφυλάξαι. Aor act inf διαφυλάσσω (indirect discourse with a verb of communication).

3:16 ἦν δὲ ὁρῶντα τὴν τοῦ ἀρχιερέως ἰδέαν τιτρώσκεσθαι τὴν διάνοιαν· ἡ γὰρ ὄψις καὶ τὸ τῆς χρόας παρηλλαγμένον ἐνέφαινεν τὴν κατὰ ψυχὴν ἀγωνίαν·

ἦν . . . τιτρώσκεσθαι. The combination of εἰμί + infinitive denotes possibility (Muraoka §30bec; BDAG, 285.7). Cf. 3:21; 6:6; 14:29.

ἦν. Impf act ind 3rd sg εἰμί.

δέ. Development, marking a shift in grammatical subject from the priests (3:15) to those who see the high priest (3:16). See 1:10 on δέ.

ὁρῶντα. Pres act ptc acc masc sg ὁράω (substantival). Subject of ἦν . . . τιτρώσκεσθαι. It is possible to understand ὁρῶντα as personal ("*those who saw . . . were wounded*") or impersonal ("*to see/seeing . . . was* to be wounded") (cf. *CGCG* §36). Because the epitomizer employs lively language to evoke an emotional response from readers elsewhere in this context, it is preferable to understand ὁρῶντα in an impersonal sense here (cf. D. Schwartz, 78–79, 197).

τὴν . . . ἰδέαν. Accusative direct object of ὁρῶντα.

τοῦ ἀρχιερέως. Subjective genitive.

τιτρώσκεσθαι. Pres mid or pass inf τιτρώσκω (result). For a judgment on the voice, see discussion below under τὴν διάνοιαν. On the meaning of the verb, see *GE* (2125.2): "to [be] wound[ed]."

τὴν διάνοιαν. If the verb τιτρώσκεσθαι is middle, it is reciprocal and τὴν διάνοιαν is the accusative direct object. However, if the verb is passive, then τὴν διάνοιαν should be understood as an adverbial accusative (cf. *CGCG* 30.14): "to be wounded *with respect to the mind*" = "to be wounded *mentally*." On the basis similar collocations of τιτρώσκω + τὴν ψυχήν ("to be wounded *in the soul*"), the passive is preferred here (cf. Diodorus, *Bib.* 17.112 and Gos. Thom. 7:26). On the meaning of the term, see *GE* (499): "thought, intellectual faculty, intelligence."

ἡ . . . ὄψις καὶ τὸ . . . παρηλλαγμένον. Compound nominative subject of ἐνέφαινεν.

ἡ . . . ὄψις. Nominative subject of ἐνέφαινεν. The noun ὄψις, which is etymologically related to ὄψομαι, refers the "face" (*EDG*, 1094).

γὰρ. Introduces an explanation of preceding clause, explaining the countenance of the high priest. See 1:12 on γάρ.

τὸ . . . παρηλλαγμένον. Prf pass ptc nom neut sg παραλλάσσω (substantival). Nominative subject of ἐνέφαινεν.

τῆς χρόας. Objective genitive.

ἐνέφαινεν. Impf act ind 3rd sg ἐμφαίνω.

τὴν . . . ἀγωνίαν. Accusative direct object of ἐνέφαινεν.

κατὰ ψυχὴν. Reference.

3:17 περιεκέχυτο γὰρ περὶ τὸν ἄνδρα δέος τι καὶ φρικασμὸς σώματος, δι᾽ ὧν πρόδηλον ἐγίνετο τοῖς θεωροῦσιν τὸ κατὰ καρδίαν ἐνεστὸς ἄλγος.

περιεκέχυτο. Plprf pass ind 3rd sg περιχέω. The pluperfect is explicative, explaining the reason why the high priest's appearance changed (cf. 3:16). On the use of the pluperfect in narrative, see the Introduction.

γὰρ. Introduces the reason why the high priest's appearance changed. See 1:12 on γάρ.

περὶ τὸν ἄνδρα. Spatial.

δέος τι καὶ φρικασμὸς. Compound nominative subject of περιεκέχυτο. On the use of a singular verb with compound subjects, see 1:7 on Ἰάσων καὶ οἱ μετ᾽ αὐτοῦ. The noun δέος is commonly used in "fear clauses" (cf. *CGCG* §43.1) and appears with various "fear" terms in 2 Maccabees: φόβος (12:22), ταραχή (3:30; 13:16), τρόμος (15:23). Domazakis (166) notes that "[t]he elevated tone of the relatively infrequent δέος and the novelty of φρικασμός are . . . combined to verbally intensify one of the most emotionally charged scenes of the book." Likewise, the rare word φρικασμός is a nominalization of the verb φρικάζω ("to have chills," *GE*, 2306).

The neuter indefinite pronoun τι agrees with δέος and probably serves "to heighten the rhetorical emphasis" (BDAG, 1008.1.b.β).

σώματος. Attributed genitive.

δι᾽ ὧν. Means.

πρόδηλον. Predicate adjective preceding ἐγίνετο, in agreement with τὸ ἄλγος.

ἐγίνετο. Impf mid ind 3rd sg γίνομαι.

τοῖς θεωροῦσιν. Pres act ptc dat masc pl θεωρέω (substantival). Ethical dative, indicating that from the perspective of those looking, the high priest appeared to be in pain.

τὸ . . . ἐνεστὸς ἄλγος. Nominative subject of ἐγίνετο. τὸ ἄλγος, rather than πρόδηλον, is the grammatical subject of ἐγίνετο because it is articular (Porter 1999, 109).

ἐνεστὸς. Prf act ptc nom neut sg ἐνίστημι (attributive).

κατὰ καρδίαν. Locative.

3:18 ἔτι δὲ ἐκ τῶν οἰκιῶν ἀγεληδὸν ἐξεπήδων ἐπὶ πάνδημον ἱκετείαν διὰ τὸ μέλλειν εἰς καταφρόνησιν ἔρχεσθαι τὸν τόπον.

ἔτι. Temporal adverb. Following some MSS (V *L*⁻⁶² 311 La^LXB(M) Sy Arm), the Göttingen edition prints οἱ prior to ἔτι, supplying a grammatical subject for the verb ἐξεπήδων.

δὲ. Development. Following the explanations in 3:16-17, δέ marks the continuity to the main discourse again but also marks the shift from the priests (3:15) to the people in 3:18. See 1:10 on δέ.

ἐκ τῶν οἰκιῶν. Separation.

ἀγεληδὸν. Adverb of manner. Cf. 14:14.

ἐξεπήδων. Impf act ind 3rd pl ἐκπηδάω. On the meaning of the verb, see BDAG (307.1): "to move forward with haste, *rush* (lit. 'leap') *out.*"

ἐπὶ πάνδημον ἱκετείαν. Locative, perhaps with the additional nuance of aim ("they were rushing out *for/to* a common supplication"). Doran (2012, 76) supplies "[to] take part in" to render the English more clearly.

μέλλειν. Pres act inf μέλλω. Used with διὰ τό to denote cause (Burk, 105–6). Prior to the infinitive, MS A has the negation μή, which is almost certainly incorrect (cf. Grimm, 71).

εἰς καταφρόνησιν. Goal (cf. BDAG, 290.4.a).
ἔρχεσθαι. Pres mid inf ἔρχομαι (complementary).
τὸν τόπον. Accusative subject of the infinitive μέλλειν.

3:19 ὑπεζωσμέναι δὲ ὑπὸ τοὺς μαστοὺς αἱ γυναῖκες σάκκους κατὰ τὰς ὁδοὺς ἐπλήθυνον· αἱ δὲ κατάκλειστοι τῶν παρθένων, αἱ μὲν συνέτρεχον ἐπὶ τοὺς πυλῶνας, αἱ δὲ ἐπὶ τὰ τείχη, τινὲς δὲ διὰ τῶν θυρίδων διεξέκυπτον·

ὑπεζωσμέναι. Prf mid ptc nom fem pl ὑποζωννύω (temporal). On the meaning of the verb, *GELS* (702): "*to fasten* a piece of fabric under some part of the body."

δὲ. Development, marking a shift of grammatical subject from the people in 3:18 to the women in 3:19. See 1:10 on δέ.

ὑπὸ τοὺς μαστούς. Locative. On the use of the Greek article to indicate possession (especially of a body part), see 1:16 on τὰς κεφαλάς.

αἱ γυναῖκες. Nominative subject of ἐπλήθυνον.

σάκκους. Accusative direct object of ὑπεζωσμέναι. D. Schwartz (198) notes that sackcloth is "a sign of mourning" and "of self-humiliation intended to arouse divine sympathy." On this theme, see also 10:25.

κατὰ τὰς ὁδούς. Locative.

ἐπλήθυνον. Impf act ind 3rd pl πληθύνω. On the meaning of the verb, see *GE* (1681.1): "to make numerous, multiply, increase in number." Hence, the translation, "women *were flooding* the streets."

δὲ. Development; see 1:10 on δέ.

αἱ . . . κατάκλειστοι. Nominative subject of συνέτρεχον in a left-dislocation. Literally, "enclosed, shut up" (*GE*, 1055).

τῶν παρθένων. Partitive genitive. Preventing virgins from public appearance is a common theme in Jewish literature (cf. 3 Macc 1:18; 4 Macc 18:7; Sir 42:11; Philo, *Flacc.* 89).

αἱ. Nominative subject of συνέτρεχον. The article is a functional equivalent to the third person personal pronoun. Muraoka (§1a) notes that the "original demonstrative or deictic value of the article is retained only when it is enclitically followed by μέν or δέ. These two particles may occur . . . in a disjunctive, contrastive expression" (cf. Wallace, 211–12).

μὲν . . . δὲ . . . δὲ. Correlative, introducing a series: "some . . . others . . . [some] others." On the anticipatory sense of μέν, see 2:25 on μὲν . . . δὲ . . . δέ.

συνέτρεχον. Impf act ind 3rd pl συντρέχω.

ἐπὶ τοὺς πυλῶνας. Locative, marking "movement to or contact [with] a goal" (BDAG, 363.4).

ἐπὶ τὰ τείχη. Locative.

τινὲς. Nominative subject of διεξέκυπτον.
διὰ τῶν θυρίδων. Locative.
διεξέκυπτον. Impf act ind 3rd pl διεκκύπτω.

3:20 πᾶσαι δὲ προτείνουσαι τὰς χεῖρας εἰς τὸν οὐρανὸν ἐποιοῦντο τὴν λιτανείαν·

πᾶσαι. Nominative subject of ἐποιοῦντο, agreeing with αἱ γυναῖκες in 3:19.
δὲ. Development; see 1:10 on δέ.
προτείνουσαι. Pres act ptc nom fem pl προτείνω (manner).
τὰς χεῖρας. Accusative direct object of προτείνουσαι. On the use of the Greek article to indicate possession (especially of a body part), see 1:16 on τὰς κεφαλάς.
εἰς τὸν οὐρανὸν. Spatial.
ἐποιοῦντο. Impf mid ind 3rd pl ποιέω. When the middle of ποιέω is used with a verbal noun (λιτανείαν), this can be a periphrasis for the verb itself: λιτανεύω (*GELS*, 570.II; BDF §310.1; BDAG, 839.2.d). See 1:23 on ἐποιήσαντο.
τὴν λιτανείαν. Accusative direct object of ἐποιοῦντο.

3:21 ἐλεεῖν δ᾽ ἦν τὴν τοῦ πλήθους παμμιγῆ πρόπτωσιν τήν τε τοῦ μεγάλως ἀγωνιῶντος ἀρχιερέως προσδοκίαν.

ἐλεεῖν ... ἦν. The combination of εἰμί + infinitive denotes ability, possibility, or permission (Muraoka §30bec; BDAG, 285.7). Cf. 3:16; 6:6; 14:29.
ἐλεεῖν. Pres act inf ἐλεέω (substantival). Subject of ἦν.
δ᾽. Development, marking a shift of grammatical subject and logical development in the storyline. See 1:10 on δέ.
ἦν. Impf act ind 3rd sg εἰμί.
τὴν ... παμμιγῆ πρόπτωσιν. Accusative subject of the infinitive ἐλεεῖν ... ἦν. In 13:12 πρόπτωσις clearly refers to "prostration as an act of supplication" (D. Schwartz, 199). D. Schwartz suggests that πρόπτωσις may be used metaphorically, referring to supplication more generally. Doran (2012, 85) notes that παμμιγῆ (accusative) should agree with πλήθους (genitive) rather than πρόπτωσιν (accusative), and is thus an example of hypallage: literally, "of the *diverse* multitude" rather than "the *diverse* prostration." Many other scholars understand παμμιγῆ similarly (cf. D. Schwartz, 199; Goldstein, 195). But, Smyth (§3027) notes that hypallage is "almost always confined to poetry." It is better to understand παμμιγῆ in the sense of "confused" (cf. *GE*, 1528): "the *confused* prostration." Thus, the

text does not imply the crowd was diverse/mixed (*pace* Doran), but that those coming out to pray were doing so in a chaotic or confused way.

τοῦ πλήθους. Subjective genitive. Refers to "a great number, multitude, crowd" (*GE*, 1681). In reference to people, πλῆθος is used both negatively (e.g., 2:21; 14:1, 41; 15:21) and positively (e.g., 4:5; 9:2; 11:16) in 2 Maccabees.

τήν . . . προσδοκίαν. Accusative subject of the infinitive ἐλεεῖν . . . ἦν. On the meaning of the verb, see *GELS* (593): "what one anticipates: anxiously."

τε. The enclitic particle follows the word(s) that it joins together, here τὴν παμμιγῆ πρόπτωσιν and τήν προσδοκίαν. Used alone, τέ is a "marker of connection between coordinate nonsequential items" (BDAG, 993.2).

τοῦ . . . ἀγωνιῶντος ἀρχιερέως. Subjective genitive.

ἀγωνιῶντος. Pres act ptc gen masc sg ἀγωνιάω (attributive).

μεγάλως. Adverb of manner.

3:22 οἱ μὲν οὖν ἐπεκαλοῦντο τὸν παγκρατῆ κύριον τὰ πεπιστευμένα τοῖς πεπιστευκόσιν σῶα διαφυλάσσειν μετὰ πάσης ἀσφαλείας.

οἱ μὲν. When the article is combined with μέν (or δέ), there is typically a contrast between a person or group, often indicating a topic shift (cf. *CGCG* §28.27-28).

οἱ. Nominative subject of ἐπεκαλοῦντο.

μὲν . . . δὲ. Point/counterpoint set. The set is completed in 3:23. See 2:26 on μὲν . . . δέ.

οὖν. Resumptive, marking a high-level boundary in the discourse. See 2:16 on οὖν.

ἐπεκαλοῦντο. Impf mid ind 3rd pl ἐπικαλέω. On the use of the middle voice to invoke a deity in prayer, see 3:15 on ἐπεκαλοῦντο.

τὸν παγκρατῆ κύριον. Accusative direct object of ἐπεκαλοῦντο.

τὰ πεπιστευμένα. Prf pass ptc acc neut pl πιστεύω (substantival). Direct object of διαφυλάσσειν.

τοῖς πεπιστευκόσιν. Prf act ptc dat masc pl πιστεύω (substantival). Dative of advantage.

σῶα. Accusative direct object of τὰ πεπιστευμένα.

διαφυλάσσειν. Pres act inf διαφυλάσσω (indirect discourse).

μετὰ πάσης ἀσφαλείας. Manner.

3:23 ὁ δὲ Ἡλιόδωρος τὸ διεγνωσμένον ἐπετέλει.

ὁ . . . Ἡλιόδωρος. Nominative subject of ἐπετέλει. The article is anaphoric, referring back to Ἡλιόδωρον in 3:7.

μὲν . . . δὲ. The set begins in 3:22.

τὸ διεγνωσμένον. Prf pass ptc acc neut sg διαγινώσκω (substantival). Direct object of ἐπετέλει.

ἐπετέλει. Impf act ind 3rd sg ἐπιτελέω. For other uses of ἐπιτελέω, see 3:8, 23; 12:8; 14:29; 15:5.

2 Maccabees 3:24-28

[24]And when he was already present there with his bodyguards at the treasury, the Master of spirits and of all power made a great appearance, with the result that all those who were bold enough to accompany [him], because they were astounded by the power of God, fell into faintness and fear. [25]For a certain horse appeared to them, having a frightful rider and being adorned with beautiful armor. And galloping furiously, it forcefully shook its front hooves at Heliodorus. And the one who sat upon [the horse] appeared, having on a suit of golden armor. [26]Then, two other young men appeared to him, [they were] exceptional in strength, most beautiful with respect to their appearance, distinguished with respect to their garments, who also while standing on each side were flogging him continually, throwing many blows at him. [27]And suddenly after he fell to the ground and was compassed with great darkness, after they picked [him] up and put [him] on a stretcher, [28]the one who entered just now with a great retinue and all [his] bodyguard into the previously mentioned treasury, they carried off [him], having rendered him helpless, recognizing clearly the sovereignty of God.

Several aspects of 3:24-28 have suggested to some scholars that multiple epiphanic traditions have been blended together here. First, the introduction of "two other young men" (3:26) is abrupt and, in light of other traditions where two angels appear (e.g., 3 Macc 6:18), it is possible that an earlier version of the story had these men/angels appear earlier in the story. While we certainly cannot discount that the epitomizer's use of sources accounts for some of unique aspects his narrative, here it is also possible that the shortening of the narrative may explain the abruptness. Second, the use of the pluperfect (ἔρριπτο) in 3:29 to describe Heliodorus as "laid out" is unusual because in 3:28 he was carried away by his bodyguards. For further discussion, see 3:29 on ἔρριπτο.

3:24 αὐτόθι δὲ αὐτοῦ σὺν τοῖς δορυφόροις κατὰ τὸ γαζοφυλάκιον ἤδη παρόντος ὁ τῶν πνευμάτων καὶ πάσης ἐξουσίας δυνάστης ἐπιφάνειαν μεγάλην ἐποίησεν ὥστε πάντας τοὺς κατατολμήσαντας συνελθεῖν καταπλαγέντας τὴν τοῦ θεοῦ δύναμιν εἰς ἔκλυσιν καὶ δειλίαν τραπῆναι·

αὐτόθι. Adverb of place.

δὲ. Development; see 1:10 on δέ.

αὐτοῦ. Genitive subject of the participle παρόντος.

σὺν τοῖς δορυφόροις. Association. In the LXX, δορυφόρος (δόρυ + φέρω, lit. "spear-carrier") appears only in 2 and 4 Maccabees (e.g., 4 Macc 5:2; 6:1; etc.). On the use of the article like a pronoun, see 1:16 on τὰς κεφαλάς.

κατὰ τὸ γαζοφυλάκιον. Locative.

ἤδη. Temporal adverb.

παρόντος. Pres act ptc gen masc sg πάρειμι (genitive absolute, temporal). On the genitive absolute, see 1:7 on βασιλεύοντος.

ὁ . . . δυνάστης. Nominative subject of ἐποίησεν. The separation of the article from the noun is an example of hyperbaton where the interpositional words modify it. The epitomizer uses δυνάστης ("master, sovereign, chief, governor" *GE*, 558) to refer to God multiple times (3:24, 12:25, 28; 15:3, 4, 29), in effect placing God in opposition to earthly rulers.

τῶν πνευμάτων καὶ πάσης ἐξουσίας. Genitives of subordination. The unfamiliarity of the expression "Master *of spirits*" (cf. 14:46) may have led some copyists (cf. MSS V *L* 731⁻⁶²) to change τῶν πνευμάτων to (τῶν) πατέρων ("the Master of *the fathers*"). Although a less common expression, the preferred reading is τῶν πνευμάτων, which makes good sense of the description of angels in the following context (cf. Doran 2012, 212; D. Schwartz, 201).

ἐπιφάνειαν μεγάλην. Accusative direct object of ἐποίησεν.

ἐποίησεν. Aor act ind 3rd sg ποιέω.

ὥστε. Introduces a result clause, modifying ἐποίησεν.

πάντας τοὺς κατατολμήσαντας. Accusative subject of the infinitive συνελθεῖν.

τοὺς κατατολμήσαντας. Aor act ptc acc masc pl κατατολμάω (substantival). This compound form of τολμάω ("to show boldness") has a similar meaning: "to be very daring" (*GE*, 1087). Cf. 5:15.

συνελθεῖν. Aor act inf συνέρχομαι. The infinitive clause, πάντας τοὺς κατατολμήσαντας συνελθεῖν, functions as the subject of τραπῆναι.

καταπλαγέντας. Aor pass ptc acc masc pl καταπλήσσω (cause). The participle is in the accusative case because it agrees with the accusative subject of the infinitive.

τὴν ... δύναμιν. Accusative of respect, with καταπλαγέντας. Reference to "spirits" and powers earlier in the verse should not led one to interpret the singular δύναμιν as a reference to angelic beings. For that, one would expect the plural (cf. Grimm, 73).

τοῦ θεοῦ. Genitive of source ("the power derived from God") or producer ("the power that God produces"). θεός is articular in accordance with Apollonius' Canon, where "both the head noun and the genitive noun normally have or lack the article" (Wallace, 239).

εἰς ἔκλυσιν καὶ δειλίαν. Spatial. On εἰς, see BDAG (290.4.b): "of change from one state to another w[ith] verbs of changing." The noun ἔκλυσις has the sense "loss of physical strength . . . + δειλία 'fear'" (*GELS*, 212).

τραπῆναι. Aor pass inf τρέπω. Used with ὥστε to indicate a result. On the meaning of the verb, see *GELS* (686): "to fall involuntarily into a certain state." The collocation of τρέπω + εἰς is common (cf. Jdt 15:3; 2 Macc 8:5; 12:42; 3 Macc 1:27; 5:16, 36; 4 Macc 1:12; Sir 37:2; 39:27).

3:25 ὤφθη γάρ τις ἵππος αὐτοῖς φοβερὸν ἔχων τὸν ἐπιβάτην καὶ καλλίστῃ σαγῇ διακεκοσμημένος, φερόμενος δὲ ῥύδην ἐνέσεισεν τῷ Ἡλιοδώρῳ τὰς ἐμπροσθίους ὁπλάς· ὁ δὲ ἐπικαθήμενος ἐφαίνετο χρυσῆν πανοπλίαν ἔχων.

ὤφθη. Aor pass ind 3rd sg ὁράω. On the morphology, see 2:8 on ὀφθήσεται.

γάρ. Introduces an explanation of the "amazing manifestation" (ἐπιφάνειαν μεγάλην) from 3:24.

τις ἵππος. Nominative subject of ὤφθη. It is possible, as Levinsohn (2000, 134) notes, that τις is used because a major figure in the narrative is being introduced.

αὐτοῖς. Dative indirect object of ὤφθη. D. Schwartz (201) notes that "careful phrasing leaves open the possibility that only Heliodorus and his men, but no others, saw the horse." Cf. 3:26, 33. This ambiguity sets the stage for 4:1, where Simon claims that the attack was staged.

φοβερὸν ... τὸν ἐπιβάτην. Accusative direct object of ἔχων. The adjective φοβερός refers to something "capable of instilling a sense of dread and fear" (*GELS*, 718; cf. Prov 12:25). An example of hyperbaton where the modifier (φοβερόν) precedes the head (τὸν ἐπιβάτην), both of which surround the participle ἔχων. The effect is that "frightful[ness]" of the rider is emphasized in the construction.

ἔχων. Pres act ptc nom masc sg ἔχω (attributive, modifying ἵππος).

καλλίστῃ σαγῇ. Dative complement of διακεκοσμημένος. The noun σαγή refers to a "harness" of a horse and, by extension, to the battle equipment or "armor" the horse wears (*GE*, 1890). Cf. with the term πανοπλία ("full set of weapons," *GE*, 1535) at the end of 3:25.

διακεκοσμημένος. Prf pass ptc nom masc sg διακοσμέω (attributive, modifying ἵππος). Cf. the use of διακόσμησις in 2:29.

φερόμενος. Pres mid ptc nom masc sg φέρω (means).

δὲ. Development; see 1:10 on δέ.

ῥύδην. Adverb of manner.

ἐνέσεισεν. Aor act ind 3rd sg ἐνσείω. On the meaning of the verb, see *GELS* (240): "to cause to move swiftly and forcefully: + acc[usative] and dat[ive] (aim)."

τῷ Ἡλιοδώρῳ. Dative indirect object of ἐνέσεισεν. The article is anaphoric, referring back to Ἡλιόδωρον in 3:7.

τὰς ἐμπροσθίους ὁπλάς. Accusative direct object of ἐνέσεισεν.

ὁ . . . ἐπικαθήμενος. Pres mid ptc nom masc sg ἐπικάθημαι (substantival). Subject of ἐφαίνετο.

δὲ. Development, marking a change of subject from τις ἵππος ("a certain horse") to ὁ ἐπικαθήμενος ("the one sitting"). See 1:10 on δέ.

ἐφαίνετο. Impf mid ind 3rd sg φαίνω.

χρυσῆν πανοπλίαν. Accusative direct object of ἔχων. Cf. this description of the rider's "golden armor" with the adornment of the horse mentioned earlier in 3:25.

ἔχων. Pres act ptc nom masc sg ἔχω (attributive, modifying ὁ ἐπικαθήμενος).

3:26 ἕτεροι δὲ δύο προσεφάνησαν αὐτῷ νεανίαι τῇ ῥώμῃ μὲν ἐκπρεπεῖς, κάλλιστοι δὲ τὴν δόξαν, διαπρεπεῖς δὲ τὴν περιβολήν, οἳ καὶ περιστάντες ἐξ ἑκατέρου μέρους ἐμαστίγουν αὐτὸν ἀδιαλείπτως πολλὰς ἐπιρριπτοῦντες αὐτῷ πληγάς.

ἕτεροι . . . δύο . . . νεανίαι. Nominative subject of προσεφάνησαν.

δὲ. Development, marking a change of subject from ὁ ἐπικαθήμενος (3:25) to the two young men in 3:26. See 1:10 on δέ.

προσεφάνησαν. Aor pass ind 3rd pl προσφαίνομαι. On the meaning of the verb, see *GE* (1831): "to appear in addition."

αὐτῷ. Dative indirect object of προσεφάνησαν.

τῇ ῥώμῃ. Dative of reference, with an implied verb.

μὲν ... δὲ ... δὲ. Correlative, introducing a series. On the anticipatory sense of μέν, see 2:25.

ἐκπρεπεῖς. Predicate adjective of an implied verb. See Muraoka (§94da) on noun clauses without the copula.

κάλλιστοι. Predicate adjective of an implied verb.

τὴν δόξαν. Accusative of respect, with an implied verb. On the sense of δόξα as "appearance," see 15:13.

διαπρεπεῖς. Predicate adjective of an implied verb.

τὴν περιβολήν. Accusative of respect, with an implied verb.

οἵ. Nominative subject of ἐμαστίγουν. The antecedent of the relative pronoun is the young men mentioned at the beginning of 3:26.

καὶ. Adverbial.

περιστάντες. Aor act ptc nom masc pl περιΐστημι (temporal).

ἐξ ἑκατέρου μέρους. Position. See *GELS* (202.10): "with nouns ... indicating a position relative to a given point of reference."

ἐμαστίγουν. Impf act ind 3 pl μαστιγόω. On the meaning of the verb, see *GE* (1285.1): "to whip, flog, scourge."

αὐτὸν. Accusative direct object of ἐμαστίγουν.

ἀδιαλείπτως. Adverb of frequency.

πολλὰς ... πληγάς. Accusative direct object of ἐπιρριπτοῦντες. An example of hyperbaton, where the modifier precedes the head.

ἐπιρριπτοῦντες. Pres act ptc nom masc pl ἐπιρριπτέω (manner).

αὐτῷ. Dative indirect object of ἐπιρριπτοῦντες.

3:27 ἄφνω δὲ πεσόντα πρὸς τὴν γῆν καὶ πολλῷ σκότει περιχυθέντα συναρπάσαντες καὶ εἰς φορεῖον ἐνθέντες,

The four participles in 3:27 each modify ἔφερον in 3:28. Thus, 3:27 is a circumstantial frame for understanding the main action of 3:28. Moreover, the switch from accusative singular participles (πεσόντα, περιχυθέντα) to nominative plural participles (περιχυθέντα, συναρπάσαντες) indicates the actions of Heliodorus and the two men are being described in 3:27.

ἄφνω. Adverb, denoting something that "suddenly, unexpectedly" happens (*GE*, 358). In particular, it is not the appearance of the horse and rider but Heliodorus' sudden fall that is emphasized.

δὲ. Development, marking a development in the narrative. The subject from 3:26 remains the same, indicating that it is the two young men that carry off Heliodorus. See 1:10 on δέ.

πεσόντα. Aor act ptc acc masc sg πίπτω (temporal). The participle is accusative singular because it refers to Heliodorus (i.e., τὸν ... εἰσελθόντα) in 3:28. Although Culy (441) maintains that "[a]dverbial participles will always be nominative, except in genitive absolute constructions or when they modify an infinitive," this analysis is not convincing. As Runge (261) notes about accusative circumstantial participles, "the case of the participle matches the reference to the participant in the main clause."

πρὸς τὴν γῆν. Spatial.

πολλῷ σκότει. Dative of manner.

περιχυθέντα. Aor pass ptc acc masc sg περιχέω (temporal). On the meaning of the verb, see *GE* (1652.3): "to crowd *or* flock around."

συναρπάσαντες. Aor act ptc nom masc pl συναρπάζω (temporal). On the meaning of the verb, see *GE* (2026): "to take away, seize, snatch."

εἰς φορεῖον. Locative.

ἐνθέντες. Aor act ptc nom masc pl ἐντίθημι (temporal).

3:28 τὸν ἄρτι μετὰ πολλῆς παραδρομῆς καὶ πάσης δορυφορίας εἰς τὸ προειρημένον εἰσελθόντα γαζοφυλάκιον ἔφερον ἀβοήθητον ἑαυτῷ καθεστῶτα φανερῶς τὴν τοῦ θεοῦ δυναστείαν ἐπεγνωκότες.

τὸν . . . εἰσελθόντα. Aor act ptc acc masc sg εἰσέρχομαι (substantival). Direct object of ἔφερον: "they carried *the who entered*." In classical Greek it is not uncommon to use a compound verb with the same preposition (εἰς) repeated in the clause. As Smyth (§1549) notes, "[w]hen the idea of place is emphatic, the preposition may be repeated" (cf. Robertson, 559). The separation of the article from the adjective is an example of hyperbaton where the interpositional words modify τὸν εἰσελθόντα.

ἄρτι. Temporal adverb. BDAG (136.1): "ref[erring] to the immediate past, *just (now)*."

μετὰ πολλῆς παραδρομῆς καὶ πάσης δορυφορίας. Accompaniment. Cf. δορυφόρος in 3:24.

εἰς τὸ προειρημένον . . . γαζοφυλάκιον. Spatial. For the "previously mentioned treasury," see 3:6 and 3:24.

τὸ προειρημένον. Prf pass ptc acc neut sg προλέγω (attributive).

ἔφερον. Impf act ind 3rd pl φέρω.

ἀβοήθητον. Accusative complement/predicate of καθεστῶτα.

ἑαυτῷ. Dative complement of καθεστῶτα. Following some MSS (98-107), the Göttingen edition reads αὐτόν rather than ἑαυτῷ ("as one who had become powerless to help *himself*"). This would convert the structure into an object-complement double accusative construction.

καθεστῶτα. Prf act ptc acc masc sg καθίστημι (temporal or, perhaps, causal). LEH (296) notes that καθίστημι + dative and predicate = "*to make, to render so and so*." Grimm (74) notes that here καθίστημι functions similarly to εἶναι. The perfect (stative verbal aspect) describes the state of the Heliodorus.

φανερῶς. Adverb form of φανερός: "openly, manifestly, clearly" (*GE* 2253.E).

τὴν . . . δυναστείαν. Accusative direct object of ἐπεγνωκότες.

τοῦ θεοῦ. Subjective genitive.

ἐπεγνωκότες. Prf act ptc nom masc pl ἐπιγινώσκω (causal). The Göttingen edition reads the accusative singular ἐπεγνωκότα rather than the nominative plural ἐπεγνωκότες, converting the participle into a reference to Heliodorus ("[because Heliodorus] recognized the sovereignty of God") rather than the two young men (cf. Habicht, 213; Doran 2012, 77). However, if the reading of R-H is maintained, then the participle refers to the knowledge of the two young men.

2 Maccabees 3:29-34

[29]And he, because of the divine action, was speechless, and being deprived of all hope and healing, he lay there, [30]but they were praising the Lord, the one who treated marvelously his own place. And the temple, although it was full of fear and tumult a little earlier, because the Lord Almighty appeared, it filled up with joy and gladness. [31]Quickly some of Heliodorus' friends were begging Onias to call upon the Most High even to grant life to the one lying down breathing his very last [breath]. [32]Then, the high priest, having become suspicious whether the king might have the opinion that some wrong doing was carried out concerning Heliodorus by the Jews, offered a sacrifice on behalf of the healing of the man. [33]Now, while the high priest was making atonement, the same young men appeared again to Heliodorus, being dressed in the same clothing and they stood and said, "Be very grateful to Onias the high priest, for because of him the Lord has granted life to you. [34]Now you, who have been flogged by heaven, proclaim to all the majestic power of God." And after saying these things, they became invisible.

The epitomizer employs the imperfect (2:30, 31), pluperfect (2:29, 30), and the aorist (2:32, 33, 34) to tell this section of the story. The pluperfect in 2:29 is particularly challenging (see comments below). The plotline of the story, as expected, is conveyed with the aorist: the high priest sacrificed (3:32), the young men appeared again (3:33), they spoke (3:33), and they disappeared (3:34).

3:29 καὶ ὁ μὲν διὰ τὴν θείαν ἐνέργειαν ἄφωνος καὶ πάσης ἐστερημένος ἐλπίδος καὶ σωτηρίας ἔρριπτο,

ὁ μὲν. See 3:22 on οἱ μέν.

ὁ. The article functions as the nominative subject of an implied verb.

μὲν . . . δὲ. Point/counterpoint set, setting up a contrast between Heliodorus' silence (3:29) and the crowd's praise (3:30). The set is completed in 3:30. See 2:26 on μὲν . . . δέ.

διὰ τὴν θείαν ἐνέργειαν. Cause.

ἄφωνος. Predicate adjective of an implied verb.

πάσης . . . ἐλπίδος καὶ σωτηρίας. Genitive complement of στερέω, used to denote the thing deprived. The collocation of στερέω + σωτηρία is common in wider Greek literature (e.g., Thucydides, *Hist.* 7.71.3). The separation of the modifier from the head is an example of hyperbaton where, perhaps, the modifier is emphasized.

ἐστερημένος. Prf pass ptc nom masc sg στερέω (causal or, less likely, manner). On the meaning of the verb, see *GE* (1959.2): "to be deprived, robbed, stripped." The sense of "deprived" fits the context best, where Heliodorus is injured and unable to receive help. Cf. the use of the same verb in 13:10.

ἔρριπτο. Plprf act ind 3rd sg ῥίπτω. The switch from the imperfect (ἔφερον in 3:28) to the pluperfect (ἔρριπτο in 3:29) is awkward and multiple explanations have been offered by scholars. A source critical approach is endorsed by Bickermann (2007, 447–48), Habicht (172–73), and Goldstein (213), who each argue that the mismatch results from multiple traditions being fused together—although these scholars do not agree on the nature of the source(s). Against the source critical approach, Doran argues that the entire narrative of 3:24-34 is tightly knit together and, more importantly, that 3:29 and 3:30 are linked closely with the μέν/δέ construction. Thus, Doran (2012, 86) concludes that the statement that Heliodorus is "laid out" remains a true description of the man as he is laid out (on a stretcher) and carried away. This argument carries little force because ἔρριπτο (3:29) echoes the earlier phrase ἐπιρριπτοῦντες αὐτῷ πληγάς (3:26), suggesting a relationship between the flogging and the fall (cf. Doran 1981, 20–21). Moreover, there are better linguistic choices to describe Heliodorus "laid out" on a stretcher (e.g., ἔκειτο).

While the source critical theories of Bickermann, Habicht, and Goldstein are not implausible, the typical narrative function of the pluperfect suggests an alternative explanation. Because the pluperfect often functions to explicate reasons for actions and events, this basic function should be acknowledged here (cf. *CGCG* §33.50; Campbell, 237). This generally aligns with D. Schwartz's (203) explanation for ἔρριπτο, where he states that "having completed the details about Heliodorus the author is reverting to a more general view of what happened."

3:30 οἱ δὲ τὸν κύριον εὐλόγουν τὸν παραδοξάζοντα τὸν ἑαυτοῦ τόπον, καὶ τὸ μικρῷ πρότερον δέους καὶ ταραχῆς γέμον ἱερὸν τοῦ παντοκράτορος ἐπιφανέντος κυρίου χαρᾶς καὶ εὐφροσύνης ἐπεπλήρωτο.

οἱ δὲ. See 3:22 on οἱ μέν.

οἱ. Nominative subject of εὐλόγουν, probably referring to the people at the temple.

μὲν . . . δὲ. See 3:29.

τὸν κύριον. Accusative direct object of εὐλόγουν.

εὐλόγουν. Impf act ind 3rd pl εὐλογέω. The collocation of εὐλογέω + κύριος, common in the LXX, indicates that the people were verbally saying words of praise.

τὸν παραδοξάζοντα. Pres act ptc acc masc sg παραδοξάζω (attributive, modifying τὸν κύριον). The verb παραδοξάζω is a neologism of the Greek Pentateuch, with three significant uses in LXX Exodus. God *treated* the Israelites *differently* than the Egyptians by protecting them from the various plagues (8:22; 9:4; 11:7). Because פלה is a byform of פלא (cf. *DCH* 6:689–90), it is likely that the LXX Exodus translator confused פלא ("wonder," *DCH* 6:686) for פלה ("to be wonderful," *DCH* 6:683), producing the form παραδοξάζω. Cf. Exod 8:22; 9:4; 11:7; Wis 19:5 for descriptions of God "acting marvelously" on behalf of Israel. See Domazakis (296–99).

τὸν . . . τόπον. Accusative direct object of τὸν παραδοξάζοντα.

ἑαυτοῦ. Possessive genitive.

τὸ . . . ἱερὸν. Nominative subject of ἐπεπλήρωτο. The separation of the article from the head is an example of hyperbaton where the entire clause is framed.

μικρῷ. Dative of measure, used with the adverb (πρότερον) to express "the degree to which one entity differs from another" (*CGCG* 30.54).

πρότερον. Temporal adverb, helping establish that "a little earlier" the temple was full of fear.

δέους καὶ ταραχῆς. Genitive complements of γέμον. Verbs of filling often take the genitive (Smyth §1369; Wallace, 131, 92–93; Muraoka §22p).

γέμον. Pres act ptc nom neut sg γέμω (concessive). The verb γέμω refers to a "state rather than a procedure" of fullness or "being full" (BDAG, 191; cf. *GE*, 421).

τοῦ παντοκράτορος ... κυρίου. Genitive subject of the participle
ἐπιφανέντος.

ἐπιφανέντος. Aor pass ptc gen masc sg ἐπιφαίνω (genitive absolute,
causal). On the genitive absolute, see 1:7 on βασιλεύοντος.

χαρᾶς καὶ εὐφροσύνης. Genitive complement of ἐπεπλήρωτο. See
above on filling verbs.

ἐπεπλήρωτο. Plprf pass ind 3rd sg πληρόω.

3:31 ταχὺ δέ τινες τῶν τοῦ Ἡλιοδώρου συνήθων ἠξίουν τὸν Ονιαν
ἐπικαλέσασθαι τὸν ὕψιστον καὶ τὸ ζῆν χαρίσασθαι τῷ παντελῶς ἐν
ἐσχάτῃ πνοῇ κειμένῳ.

ταχὺ. Temporal adverb, used to denote either the *pacing* of an activity ("quickly") or the (short) *span of time* before an activity ("soon" or
"quickly") (BDAG, 993.2). Here, ταχύ refers to the short span of time
between Heliodorus receiving injuries (3:26-28) and his companions
asking Onias to pray for his healing.

δέ. Development; see 1:10 on δέ.

τινες. Nominative subject of ἠξίουν.

τῶν ... συνήθων. Partitive genitive. The word means "friend, confi-
dant" (*GE*, 2043).

τοῦ Ἡλιοδώρου. Genitive of relationship. The article is anaphoric,
referring back to Ἡλιόδωρον in 3:7.

ἠξίουν. Impf act ind 3rd pl ἀξιόω. Although more commonly used to
make requests to God (cf. 5:4; 8:14, 29; 10:4, 16; 12:42), when the verb
ἀξιόω is used of someone making a request of their enemy, it is fitting to
translate as "beg." See 2:8 on ἠξίωσεν.

τὸν Ονιαν. Accusative subject of the infinitive ἐπικαλέσασθαι.

ἐπικαλέσασθαι. Aor mid inf ἐπικαλέω (indirect discourse). On
the use of the middle voice to invoke a deity in prayer, see 3:15 on
ἐπεκαλοῦντο.

Heliodorus' men beg the high priest to call upon God by means of
prayer. Yet, as 3:32 indicates, Onias offers a sacrifice. This underscores
that "one of the ways to pray is to bring a sacrifice" (D. Schwartz, 203).
On this, see Philo (*Spec. Laws* 1.195) who says that "if anyone cares
to examine closely the motives which led men of the earliest times to
resort to sacrifices as a medium of prayer and thanksgiving, he will find
that two hold the highest place. One is the rendering of honour to God
for the sake of Him only and with no other motive, a thing both necessary and excellent. The other is the signal benefit which the worshipper
receives, and this is twofold, on one side directed to obtaining a share in
blessings, on the other to release from evils." See also Sanders (77–80).

τὸν ὕψιστον. Accusative direct object of ἐπικαλέσασθαι. Bickermann (2007, 456) notes that this epithet was used for the God of Jerusalem in official Greek documents. Thus, the epithet "Most High" is an appropriate designation for Israel's God in the diaspora because, rhetorically, it leaves open the possibility that other gods exist. It is used by both Jews (e.g., Jdt 13:18; Sir 4:10) and non-Jews (e.g., 1 Esd 2:2; Dan 4:2; Josephus, *Ant.* 16.163; Acts 16:17).

καὶ. Ascensive: "even" (Robertson, 1181).

τὸ ζῆν. Pres act inf ζάω (substantival). The infinitive functions as the direct object of χαρίσασθαι.

χαρίσασθαι. Aor mid inf χαρίζομαι (purpose).

τῷ . . . κειμένῳ. Pres pass ptc dat masc sg κεῖμαι (substantival). Indirect object of χαρίσασθαι.

παντελῶς. Adverb of manner. *GELS* (522): with ἐν ἐσχάτῃ πνοῇ, "breathing the very last."

ἐν ἐσχάτῃ πνοῇ. Temporal, indicating a precise point in time (cf. *GELS*, 231).

3:32 ὕποπτος δὲ γενόμενος ὁ ἀρχιερεὺς μήποτε διάλημψιν ὁ βασιλεὺς σχῇ κακουργίαν τινὰ περὶ τὸν Ἡλιόδωρον ὑπὸ τῶν Ἰουδαίων συντετελέσθαι προσήγαγεν θυσίαν ὑπὲρ τῆς τοῦ ἀνδρὸς σωτηρίας.

ὕποπτος. Predicate adjective of γενόμενος.

δὲ. Development, marking a change of subject from τινες in 3:31 to the high priest in 3:32. See 1:10 on δέ.

γενόμενος. Aor mid ptc nom masc sg γίνομαι (temporal or, possibly, causal).

ὁ ἀρχιερεὺς. Nominative subject of προσήγαγεν.

μήποτε. Used with the subjunctive, introducing an indirect question. It has the sense of "whether, perhaps" (BDAG, 648.3).

διάλημψιν. Accusative direct object of σχῇ. This refers to a "judgement, opinion" (LEH, 140).

ὁ βασιλεὺς. Nominative subject of σχῇ.

σχῇ. Aor act subj 3rd sg ἔχω.

κακουργίαν τινὰ. Accusative subject of the infinitive συντετελέσθαι. On the meaning of κακουργία (κακός + ἔργον), see *GE* (1018): "wrong doing."

περὶ τὸν Ἡλιόδωρον. Reference. The article is anaphoric, referring back to Ἡλιόδωρον in 3:7.

ὑπὸ τῶν Ἰουδαίων. Agency. On the translation "Jews," see 1:1 on Ἰουδαίοις.

συντετελέσθαι. Prf pass inf συντελέω (indirect discourse). While it is possible that συντετελέσθαι is adnominal, explaining διάλημψιν, it is better understood as complementing διάλημψιν ὁ βασιλεὺς σχῇ (Muraoka §30bda): "the king might have the opinion . . . that some wrong doing *was carried out*."

προσήγαγεν. Aor act ind 3rd sg προσάγω.

θυσίαν. Accusative direct object of προσήγαγεν.

ὑπὲρ τῆς . . . σωτηρίας. Representation ("he offered a sacrifice *on behalf of the healing*"). This contrasts with 3:29, where Helidorus was "deprived of all hope and *healing* [σωτηρίας]."

τοῦ ἀνδρὸς. Objective genitive.

3:33 ποιουμένου δὲ τοῦ ἀρχιερέως τὸν ἱλασμὸν οἱ αὐτοὶ νεανίαι πάλιν ἐφάνησαν τῷ Ἡλιοδώρῳ ἐν ταῖς αὐταῖς ἐσθήσεσιν ἐστολισμένοι καὶ στάντες εἶπον Πολλὰς Ονια τῷ ἀρχιερεῖ χάριτας ἔχε, διὰ γὰρ αὐτόν σοι κεχάρισται τὸ ζῆν ὁ κύριος·

ποιουμένου. Pres mid ptc gen masc sg ποιέω (genitive absolute, temporal). When the middle of ποιέω is used with a verbal noun (ἱλασμόν), this can be a periphrasis for the verb itself: ἱλάσκομαι (*GELS*, 570.II). See 1:23 on ἐποιήσαντο. On the genitive absolute, see 1:7 on βασιλεύοντος.

δὲ. Development; see 1:10 on δέ.

τοῦ ἀρχιερέως. Genitive subject of the participle ποιουμένου.

τὸν ἱλασμὸν. Accusative direct object of ποιουμένου. The high priest makes expiation (ἱλασμός) for Heliodorus, a sacrifice on behalf of his sins.

οἱ αὐτοὶ νεανίαι. Nominative subject of ἐφάνησαν. The adjective αὐτοί is in attributive position and is an identical adjective (lit. "the *same* young men").

πάλιν. Adverb modifying ἐφάνησαν. BDAG (753.4) refers to "the repetition in the same (or similar) manner, *again, once more, anew* of someth[ing] a pers[on] has already done." Cf. 3:26.

ἐφάνησαν. Aor pass ind 3rd pl φαίνω.

τῷ Ἡλιοδώρῳ. Dative indirect object of ἐφάνησαν. The article is anaphoric, referring back to Ἡλιόδωρον in 3:7. Only Heliodorus is said to witness the appearance. Cf. 3:25.

ἐν ταῖς αὐταῖς ἐσθήσεσιν. Manner. Marker of state or condition (BDAG, 327.2.a). On the identical adjective, see above. On the unusual morphology of ἐσθήσεσιν, BDAG (396) notes that "[t]he dat[ive] pl[ural] form ἐσθήσεσι, which is not unanimously attested . . . , does not come from a word ἔσθησις, for which there is no reliable evidence in the sing[ular], nor in the pl[ural] except for the dative (s[ee] LSJ), but belongs to ἐσθής; it is the result of an attempt to make the dat[ive] ending more conspicuous by doubling it."

ἐστολισμένοι. Prf pass ptc nom masc pl στολίζω (attributive, modifying οἱ αὐτοὶ νεανίαι).

στάντες. Aor act ptc nom masc pl ἵστημι (attendant circumstance).

εἶπον. Aor act ind 3rd pl εἶπον.

Πολλὰς ... χάριτας. Accusative direct object of ἔχε. The separation of the modifier from the head is an example of hyperbaton where the modifier is emphasized. The words of the young men who speak to Heliodorus are an example of paronomasia (χάριτας, κεχάρισται).

Ονια τῷ ἀρχιερεῖ. Dative of advantage.

ἔχε. Pres act impv 2nd sg ἔχω. The collocation of ἔχω + χαρίς is common and here means something like "to give thanks."

διὰ ... αὐτόν. Cause.

γὰρ. The explanatory particle introduces the grounds for the preceding assertion about having much gratitude. See 1:12 on γάρ.

σοι. Dative indirect object of κεχάρισται.

κεχάρισται. Prf mid ind 3rd sg χαρίζομαι.

τὸ ζῆν. Pres act inf ζάω (substantival). Direct object of κεχάρισται.

ὁ κύριος. Nominative subject of κεχάρισται.

3:34 σὺ δὲ ἐξ οὐρανοῦ μεμαστιγωμένος διάγγελλε πᾶσι τὸ μεγαλεῖον τοῦ θεοῦ κράτος. ταῦτα δὲ εἰπόντες ἀφανεῖς ἐγένοντο.

σὺ. Nominative subject of διάγγελλε.

δὲ. Development; see 1:10 on δέ.

ἐξ οὐρανοῦ. Source/origin ("[flogging] from heaven") or cause ("[flogging] *caused by* heaven"). It is possible that οὐρανός is a substitute for ὁ θεός (cf. *GELS*, 514).

μεμαστιγωμένος. Prf pass ptc nom masc sg μαστιγόω (attributive, modifying σύ). Refers to the flogging mentioned in 3:26.

διάγγελλε. Pres act impv 2nd sg διαγγέλλω.

πᾶσι. Dative indirect object of διάγγελλε.

τὸ μεγαλεῖον ... κράτος. Accusative direct object of διάγγελλε.

τοῦ θεοῦ. Genitive of source or, more likely, subjective genitive.

ταῦτα. Accusative direct object of εἰπόντες.

δὲ. Development; see 1:10 on δέ.

εἰπόντες. Aor act ptc nom masc pl εἶπον (temporal).

ἀφανεῖς. Predicate adjective in agreement with the implied subject of ἐγένοντο.

ἐγένοντο. Aor mid ind 3rd pl γίνομαι.

2 Maccabees 3:35-40

³⁵Then Heliodorus, after offering a sacrifice to the Lord, and vowing great vows to the one who saved his life, and acknowledging Onias, moved military camp to the king. ³⁶And he was bearing witness to the works of the supreme God to all, which he had seen with his eyes. ³⁷But when the king asked Heliodorus what sort of person might be suitable to be sent once more to Jerusalem, he said, ³⁸"If you have any enemy or plotter of things, send him there, and after he has been flogged, you shall welcome him back, if he should even come through safely, because there is truly some divine power around the place. ³⁹For the very one who has a celestial dwelling is the overseer and helper of that place, and he destroys by striking those who come on the basis of evil intent." ⁴⁰The story concerning Heliodorus and the preservation of the treasury turned out thusly.

3:35 ὁ δὲ Ἡλιόδωρος θυσίαν ἀνενέγκας τῷ κυρίῳ καὶ εὐχὰς μεγίστας εὐξάμενος τῷ τὸ ζῆν περιποιήσαντι καὶ τὸν Ονιαν ἀποδεξάμενος ἀνεστρατοπέδευσεν πρὸς τὸν βασιλέα.

ὁ . . . Ἡλιόδωρος. Nominative subject of ἀνεστρατοπέδευσεν. The article is anaphoric, referring back to Ἡλιόδωρον in 3:7.

δὲ. Development, marking a change of subject from "the young men" (οἱ νεανίαι) in 3:33-34 to Heliodorus in 3:35. See 1:10 on δέ.

θυσίαν. Accusative direct object of ἀνενέγκας.

ἀνενέγκας. Aor act ptc nom masc sg ἀναφέρω (temporal). See 1:18 on ἀνήνεγκεν.

τῷ κυρίῳ. Dative indirect object of ἀνενέγκας.

εὐχὰς μεγίστας. Accusative direct object of εὐξάμενος. The noun εὐχή often appears as the cognate object of εὔχομαι (cf. Gen 28:20; Lev 27:2; Num 6:2; Deut 23:22; Judg 11:30; etc.).

εὐξάμενος. Aor mid ptc nom masc sg εὔχομαι (temporal). The description of Heliodorus' actions is an example of paronomasia (εὐχὰς, εὐξάμενος).

τῷ . . . περιποιήσαντι. Aor act ptc dat masc sg περιποιέω (substantival). Indirect object of εὐξάμενος. On the meaning of the verb, see *GE* (1639): "to make it so that one survives, make escape, save."

τὸ ζῆν. Pres act inf ζάω (substantival). Direct object of περιποιήσαντι. The object infinitive can be either articular or anarthrous (Robertson, 1058–59).

τὸν Ονιαν. Accusative direct object of ἀποδεξάμενος.

ἀποδεξάμενος. Aor mid ptc nom masc sg ἀποδέχομαι (temporal). A "greeting" verb is an unusual choice for this part of the story, but it is probably used intentionally to echo the opening of the story when Heliodorus was welcomed (ἀποδεχθείς) by the high priest of the city (3:9).

ἀνεστρατοπέδευσεν. Aor act ind 3rd sg ἀναστρατοπεδεύω. On the meaning of the verb, see *GELS* (45): "to move military camp."

πρὸς τὸν βασιλέα. Spatial (motion toward).

3:36 ἐξεμαρτύρει δὲ πᾶσιν ἅπερ ἦν ὑπ᾽ ὄψιν τεθεαμένος ἔργα τοῦ μεγίστου θεοῦ.

ἐξεμαρτύρει. Impf act ind 3rd sg ἐκμαρτυρέω.

δὲ. Development; see 1:10 on δέ.

πᾶσιν. Dative indirect object of ἐξεμαρτύρει.

ἅπερ. Accusative direct object of ἦν . . . τεθεαμένος. The relative pronoun agrees with ἔργα. On this word, Muraoka (§86d) notes that "ἔργα [is] an explanatory expansion or complement . . . of the object ἅπερ rather than as a delayed antecedent."

ἦν . . . τεθεαμένος. Pluperfect periphrastic construction, taking the person, number, and mood from ἦν; aspect, voice, and lexical form from τεθεαμένος. Thus, the synthetic form would be τεθέαται, prf mid ind 3rd sg. The *TLG* attests to 348 uses of this form in extant Greek literature, but none of these uses appears in the window of time close to the writing of 2 Maccabees. The periphrastic construction is probably motivated by pragmatic concerns, particularly the epitomizer's attempt to convey high literary style. Moreover, Levinsohn (2016, 324) argues that copular perfects "portray states that result from completed events as ongoing." On motivations for periphrastic constructions, see comments in the Introduction.

ἦν. Impf act ind 3rd sg εἰμί.

ὑπ᾽ ὄψιν. Means. Porter (1999, 45) notes that "no elements may intervene between the auxiliary verb and the participle [in a periphrastic construction] except for those which complete or directly modify the participle."

τεθεαμένος. Prf mid ptc nom masc sg θεάομαι (pluperfect periphrastic).

ἔργα. Accusative direct object of ἐξεμαρτύρει.

τοῦ μεγίστου θεοῦ. Genitive of production.

3:37 τοῦ δὲ βασιλέως ἐπερωτήσαντος τὸν Ἡλιόδωρον ποῖός τις εἴη ἐπιτήδειος ἔτι ἅπαξ διαπεμφθῆναι εἰς Ἱεροσόλυμα, ἔφησεν,

τοῦ . . . βασιλέως. Genitive subject of the participle ἐπερωτήσαντος.

δὲ. Development, marking a change of subject from Heliodorus (3:35-36) to the king (3:37). See 1:10 on δέ.

ἐπερωτήσαντος. Aor act ptc gen masc sg ἐπερωτάω (genitive absolute, temporal). On the genitive absolute, see 1:7 on βασιλεύοντος.

τὸν Ἡλιόδωρον. Accusative direct object of ἐπερωτήσαντος. The article is anaphoric, referring back to Ἡλιόδωρον in 3:7.

ποῖός τις. Nominative subject of εἴη. The interrogative pronoun ποῖός is qualitative and commonly appears in direct and indirect questions (BDAG, 843.1.a.β).

εἴη. Pres act opt 3rd sg εἰμί. Although the indicative is normally used to ask an indirect question, after a secondary tense the optative is typical if not expected (CGCG §42.7–8; Muraoka §29dc.iii; MHT 3:130–31).

ἐπιτήδειος. Predicate adjective of εἴη.

ἔτι ἅπαξ. An idiom (lit. "yet once") for "once more" (GE, 226). Cf. Gen 18:32; Judg 6:39; Hag 2:6.

διαπεμφθῆναι. Aor pass inf διαπέμπω (epexegetical to ἐπιτήδειος).

εἰς Ἰεροσόλυμα. Locative, indicating motion toward ("to Jerusalem").

ἔφησεν. Aor act ind 3rd sg φημί.

3:38 Εἴ τινα ἔχεις πολέμιον ἢ πραγμάτων ἐπίβουλον, πέμψον αὐτὸν ἐκεῖ, καὶ μεμαστιγωμένον αὐτὸν προσδέξῃ, ἐάνπερ καὶ διασωθῇ, διὰ τὸ περὶ τὸν τόπον ἀληθῶς εἶναί τινα θεοῦ δύναμιν·

Εἴ. Introduces a first-class conditional clause (Smyth §2298), which uses εἰ + present indicative in the protasis. The first-class conditional introduces neutral conditions where the writer or speaker "gives no indication of the likelihood of the realization of the action in the protasis" (CGCG §49.4). Thus, the reality of the protasis is assumed for the sake of argument. The particle εἰ has the acute accent because τινα, an enclitic, loses its accent to the preceding word (Smyth §181–82).

τινα ... πολέμιον. Accusative direct object of ἔχεις. The indefinite pronoun is used because the individual in view is "unknown or irrelevant" (CGCG §29.38). The separation of the modifier from the head is an example of hyperbaton where the modifier is emphasized.

ἔχεις. Pres act ind 2nd sg ἔχω. After direct discourse has been introduced (cf. ἔφησεν in 3:37), a switch to the present tense is expected in narrative (cf. Campbell, 76).

ἤ. The disjunctive particle denotes an alternative to what precedes (i.e., "or"), but not a mutually exclusive one.

πραγμάτων. Objective genitive. See 1:33 on τὸ πρᾶγμα.

ἐπίβουλον. Accusative direct object of ἔχεις.

πέμψον. Aor act impv 2nd sg πέμπω.

αὐτὸν. Accusative direct object of πέμψον.

ἐκεῖ. Adverb of place.

μεμαστιγωμένον. Prf pass ptc acc masc sg μαστιγόω (temporal). The participle is accusative because it agrees with αὐτόν. On circumstantial participles in oblique cases, see 3:27 on πεσόντα.

αὐτὸν. Accusative direct object of προσδέξῃ.

προσδέξῃ. Fut mid ind 2nd sg προσδέχομαι.

ἐάνπερ. The construction ἐάν + περ (GE, 577: "if indeed, if however") is part of a third-class conditional clause (Smyth §2323), using ἐάν + subjunctive in the protasis. As a prospective conditional, in which a future verb is expected in the apodosis (cf. προσδέξῃ), the clause "presents the fulfillment of the condition as very well possible/likely" (CGCG §49.6).

καὶ. Ascensive.

διασωθῇ. Aor pass subj 3rd sg διασῴζω. Subjunctive used with ἐάνπερ.

περὶ τὸν τόπον. Spatial.

ἀληθῶς. Adverb, denoting emphasis.

εἶναί. Pres act inf εἰμί. Used with διὰ τό to denote cause. The neuter article τό indicates the case of εἶναι (Burk, 27–46). The verb has two accents, the circumflex and acute, because it is followed by an enclitic (τινα). When following a word with a circumflex on the penult, the enclitic surrenders its accent, and it appears as an additional acute accent on the preceding word (Smyth §183.c).

τινα . . . δύναμιν. Predicate of εἶναί.

θεοῦ. Attributive genitive (τινα θεοῦ δύναμιν = "some *divine* power") or qualitative (Muraoka §5aa).

3:39 αὐτὸς γὰρ ὁ τὴν κατοικίαν ἐπουράνιον ἔχων ἐπόπτης ἐστὶν καὶ βοηθὸς ἐκείνου τοῦ τόπου καὶ τοὺς παραγινομένους ἐπὶ κακώσει τύπτων ἀπολλύει.

αὐτὸς. Either the nominative subject of ἐστίν ("he, the one who has a heaven dwelling, is . . .") or, more likely, an intensive modifier of ὁ . . . ἔχων ("the *very* one who has a heavenly dwelling is . . .").

γὰρ. Causal conjunction, explaining the source of the divine power mentioned in 3:38. See 1:12 on γάρ.

ὁ . . . ἔχων. Pres act ptc nom masc sg ἔχω (substantival). Subject of ἐστίν. For an alternative understanding of the syntax, see comments on αὐτός.

τὴν κατοικίαν ἐπουράνιον. Accusative direct object of ἔχων. The adjective ἐπουράνιος (ἐπί + οὐρανός) refers to a "celestial" location (cf. Homer, Il. 6.129; Od. 17.484).

ἐπόπτης. Predicate nominative of ἐστίν.

ἐστὶν. Pres act ind 3rd sg εἰμί.

βοηθὸς. Predicate nominative of ἐστίν.

ἐκείνου τοῦ τόπου. Objective genitive.

τοὺς παραγινομένους. Pres mid ptc acc masc pl παραγίνομαι (substantival). Direct object of ἀπολλύει.

ἐπὶ κακώσει. Cause.

τύπτων. Pres act ptc nom masc sg τύπτω (manner).

ἀπολλύει. Pres act ind 3rd sg ἀπόλλυμι.

3:40 καὶ τὰ μὲν κατὰ Ἡλιόδωρον καὶ τὴν τοῦ γαζοφυλακίου τήρησιν οὕτως ἐχώρησεν.

τὰ. The article functions as a nominalizer, changing the PP (κατὰ Ἡλιόδωρον) into the nominative subject of ἐχώρησεν. "*The things* concerning [κατά] . . ." refers to "*the story* concerning [κατά] . . ." (cf. BDAG, 689.2.h.α; Muraoka §6a.i). See 2:19 on τά.

μὲν . . . δὲ. Transitional. While the use of μέν in a statement summarizing 3:1-39 appears unusual, the corresponding particle δέ is found at the beginning of a new section in 4:1. Goldstein (215) notes that 3:40 "closes the unit on Heliodorus but contains the Greek particle [μέν] to let the reader know that there will be more to come" (cf. D. Schwartz, 205). For other uses of μέν/δέ to connect events, see 7:42–8:1; 10:9-10; 15:24-25. See also the Introduction for brief discussion of transitional μέν/δέ.

κατὰ Ἡλιόδωρον καὶ τὴν . . . τήρησιν. Reference.

τοῦ γαζοφυλακίου. Objective genitive. See 3:6 on τὸ . . . γαζοφυλάκιον.

οὕτως. Adverb, used to denote "conclusive or recapitulary force" (*GE*, 1508). All of 3:40 functions as a concluding summary of 3:1-39.

ἐχώρησεν. Aor act ind 3rd sg χωρέω. On the meaning of the verb, see *GELS* (739): "*to turn out* in a certain way at the end." For similar summarizing uses of χωρέω, see 13:26; 15:37.

2 Maccabees 4:1-6

[1]But the aforementioned Simon, the one who became an informer about the money and against the native land, was speaking evil of Onias, [saying] both that it was he who had incited Heliodorus and supervised the maker of evils. [2]And he dared to say [that] the benefactor of the city and the guardian of the same people and a zealot for the laws [was] a plotter against the interests of the state. [3]When the hostility progressed to such

an extent that even murders were carried out by a certain one of those approved by Simon, ⁴Onias—seeing the difficulty of the dispute and [that] Apollonius [son] of Menestheus, the governor of Coele-Syria and Phoenicia, was encouraging the wickedness of Simon—⁵went to the king, not being an accuser of the fellow-citizens but paying attention to the welfare for all the multitude, both public and private. ⁶For he saw [that] without royal concern, to find peace was still impossible for the government and [that] Simon would not end his folly.

The peace initially described in 2 Maccabees 3 has been dismantled. Thus, the major themes of defending the fatherland (πατρίς, 5:8, 9, 15; 8:21, 33; 13:3, 11, 14; 14:18) and the ancestral laws (πάτριοι νόμοι, 6:1; 7:2, 37) begin in 4:1. Moreover, several linguistic features bring cohesion to the narrative. For example, several terms that appear in 4:1-6 are taken up at the conclusion of 2 Maccabees 4, including the use of καθίστημι to describe both Onias (4:1) and Menelaus (4:50), the theme of being a "plotter" (ἐπίβουλος), either "against the interests of the state" (4:2) or "against . . . fellow citizens" (4:50), and the description of both Simon (4:4) and Menelaus (4:47, 50) as "wicked" (κακία).

The opening verses of chapter four employ imperfect verbs (ἐκακολόγει, ἐτόλμα), setting up the descriptive background to the main plotline of the narrative that begins in 4:5.

4:1 Ὁ δὲ προειρημένος Σιμων ὁ τῶν χρημάτων καὶ τῆς πατρίδος ἐνδείκτης γεγονὼς ἐκακολόγει τὸν Ονιαν, ὡς αὐτός τε εἴη τὸν Ἡλιόδωρον ἐπισεσεικὼς καὶ τῶν κακῶν δημιουργὸς καθεστηκώς,

Ὁ . . . προειρημένος Σιμων. Nominative subject of ἐκακολόγει. Previously, 3:4 referred to Simon as "a certain Simon" (Σιμων . . . τις), indicating that he is (presumed to be) unfamiliar to readers/hearers of this text.

προειρημένος. Prf mid ptc nom masc sg προεῖπον (attributive, modifying Σιμων).

μὲν . . . δὲ. See 3:40.

ὁ . . . γεγονὼς. Prf act ptc nom masc sg γίνομαι (attributive, modifying Σιμων). Several MSS (19-62 46-52) have the aorist middle participle γενόμενος rather than γεγονώς, which is more common and expected in this construction. The separation of the article from the adjective is an example of hyperbaton where most of the interpositional words modify the participle.

τῶν χρημάτων καὶ τῆς πατρίδος. Genitives of reference. The negative connotation of ἐνδείκτης suggests that τῆς πατρίδος should be rendered "*against* the native land."

ἐνδείκτης. Predicate of ὁ γεγονώς. This rare word may mean either "denouncer, accuser" or "one who informs" (*GE*, 687).

ἐκακολόγει. Impf act ind 3rd sg κακολογέω. On the meaning of the verb, see BDAG (500): "speak evil of, revile, insult."

τὸν Ονιαν. Accusative direct object of ἐκακολόγει.

ὡς. Introduces a clausal complement with an implied verb of speaking (cf. BDAG, 1105.5) (cf. MS 236, which repeats the verb, ἐκακολόγειτο). Indirectly reported speech "is normally introduced with subordinating conjunctions such as ὅτι, διότι, or ὡς" (Muraoka §79a). See similar uses in 2:4; 7:17.

αὐτός. Nominative subject of εἴη. MS A reads οὗτος ("this one"), which may be a mistake due to graphic similarity.

τε ... καὶ. Correlative construction: "both . . . and." See 1:14 on τε ... καί.

εἴη ... ἐπισεσεικώς. Perfect periphrastic construction, taking the person, number, and mood from εἴη; aspect, voice, and lexical form from ἐπισεσεικώς. Thus, the synthetic form would be: ἐπισεσείκοι, prf act opt 3rd sg. There are no uses of the perfect optative of ἐπισείω attested in the *TLG*, suggesting here the periphrasis is due to preferred morphology. Smyth (§694) notes that "[t]he perfect optative is commonly formed periphrastically by the perfect active participle and εἴην, εἴης, εἴη, etc." Shaw (2016, 413) notes that "since Greek lacks a past optative form for εἰμί . . . the sense is pluperfect here." On motivations for periphrastic constructions, see comments in the Introduction.

εἴη. Pres act opt 3rd sg εἰμί. After a secondary tense verb (ἐκακολόγει), the optative is used in a content clause to indicate an indirect question, the so-called "oblique optative" (Muraoka §29dc. iv; §80b; cf. Wallace, 483).

τὸν Ἡλιόδωρον. Accusative direct object of εἴη ... ἐπισεσεικώς. Although intervening between the auxiliary verb and the participle, Porter (1999, 45) notes that elements that "complete or directly modify the participle" in a periphrastic construction may appear in this position (cf. Muraoka §31fj).

ἐπισεσεικώς. Prf act ptc nom masc sg ἐπισείω (perfect periphrastic). The meaning of ἐπισείω here is debated because the verb can have several senses: "to shake," "to push, incite," or "to make an attack" (*GE*, 787). However, *GE* is correct that the latter meaning is "dubious" because the verb should then occur with a substantive in the dative case to mark who is threatened or attacked. Doran (2012, 92) rightly notes that ἐπισείω + accusative usually means "to incite, stir up" (cf. Goldstein, 220; Judg 1:14; 1 Kgdms 26:19; 2 Kgdms 24:1; 1 Chr 21:1).

καὶ. The conjunction that links καθεστηκώς to εἴη, creating another periphrastic construction.

τῶν κακῶν. Objective genitive, qualifying δημιουργός.

δημιουργὸς. Predicate nominative of καθεστηκώς. *GE* (1006) notes that the verb may take a predicate nominative. The expression "maker of evils" is found in Greek tragedy (e.g., Euripides, *Fr.* 1059). D. Schwartz (214) notes an interesting parallel in Xenophon (*Hell.* 6.4.7): "but some say all these things (i.e., miraculous portents) had been engineered."

[εἴη] . . . καθεστηκώς. Perfect periphrastic construction, taking the person, number, and mood from εἴη; aspect, voice, and lexical form from καθεστηκώς. Thus, the synthetic form would be: καθειστήκοι, prf act opt 3rd sg. Motivations for periphrastics are discussed earlier, in 1:6 at ἐσμεν προσευχόμενοι. The synthetic form is attested 71 times in the *TLG*, but none occur with a reasonable window of time close to the writing of 2 Maccabees. See above on the use of periphrasis for the perfect optative.

καθεστηκώς. Prf act ptc nom masc sg καθίστημι (perfect periphrastic). The meaning of καθίστημι here is "to assign someone to a position of authority" (BDAG, 492.2; cf. D. Schwartz, 214). On the morphology, see 3:4 on καθεσταμένος.

4:2 καὶ τὸν εὐεργέτην τῆς πόλεως καὶ τὸν κηδεμόνα τῶν ὁμοεθνῶν καὶ ζηλωτὴν τῶν νόμων ἐπίβουλον τῶν πραγμάτων ἐτόλμα λέγειν.

τὸν εὐεργέτην . . . καὶ τὸν κηδεμόνα . . . καὶ ζηλωτὴν. Compound accusative subjects of an implied infinitive copula. On the ellipsis of the infinitive copula, see BDF (§127) and Smyth (§945). The infinitive signals indirect discourse.

τὸν εὐεργέτην. The first element of the compound accusative subject of an implied infinitive copula. Εὐεργέτης refers to "benefactor as a title of princes and other honored pers[ons], esp[ecially] those recognized for their civic contributions" (BDAG, 405).

τῆς πόλεως. Objective genitive, qualifying τὸν εὐεργέτην.

τὸν κηδεμόνα. The second element of the compound accusative subject of an implied infinitive copula. The rare term κηδεμόνα denotes a "protector" or "guardian" of the nation (cf. P.Oxy. 41.13, 26). Doran (2012, 92) notes a parallel where a certain Tarkondimotus is celebrated as "the benefactor and protector of the people" (τὸν εὐεργέτη[ν] καὶ κηδεμόνα τοῦ δήμου, OGIS 752).

τῶν ὁμοεθνῶν. Objective genitive, qualifying τὸν κηδεμόνα. The adjective is used as a substantive. Built from ὁμός + ἔθνος, the compound word means "belonging to the same people" (*EDG*, 377). The more simplex form, ἐθνῶν, appears in some MSS (52* 106) but is secondary.

ζηλωτὴν. The third element of the compound accusative subject of an implied infinitive copula. BDAG (427.1.a.β) notes that this refers to "one who is earnestly committed to a side or cause, enthusiast, adherent, loyalist." For an earlier description of Onias' zeal for the law, see 3:1.

τῶν νόμων. Objective genitive, qualifying ζηλωτήν.

ἐπίβουλον. Predicate accusative of an implied infinitive copula.

τῶν πραγμάτων. Objective genitive, qualifying ἐπίβουλον. See *GE* (1731): "government, power, supremacy" or "government in power, established regime." See also the description of Alcimus in 14:26 as a "conspirator against his kingdom" (τὸν . . . ἐπίβουλον τῆς βασιλείας, NETS).

ἐτόλμα. Impf act ind 3rd sg τολμάω. The verb often appears with the infinitive as its complement (cf. *GE*, 2129.1.A).

λέγειν. Pres act inf λέγω (complementary).

4:3 τῆς δὲ ἔχθρας ἐπὶ τοσοῦτον προβαινούσης ὥστε καὶ διά τινος τῶν ὑπὸ τοῦ Σιμωνος δεδοκιμασμένων φόνους συντελεῖσθαι,

τῆς . . . ἔχθρας. Genitive subject of the participle προβαινούσης.

δὲ. Development; see 1:10 on δέ.

ἐπὶ τοσοῦτον. Direction. See BDAG (1012.3.b): "so great/strong, to such extent," followed by the genitive and ὥστε (cf. 3 Macc 2:26; 3:1). See also 2:32 on τοσοῦτον.

προβαινούσης. Pres act ptc gen fem sg προβαίνω (genitive absolute, temporal). On the genitive absolute, see 1:7 on βασιλεύοντος.

ὥστε. Descriptive, explanatory (epexegetical). See especially *GELS* (750.4).

καὶ. Ascensive.

διά τινος. Agency.

τῶν . . . δεδοκιμασμένων. Prf pass ptc gen masc pl δοκιμάζω (substantival). Partitive genitive. Here the verb δοκιμάζω denotes "to scrutinize for fitness to hold office and approve" (Goldstein, 222). The separation of the article from the head is an example of hyperbaton where the interpositional words modify the participle.

ὑπὸ τοῦ Σιμωνος. Agency.

φόνους. Accusative subject of the infinitive συντελεῖσθαι. On the meaning of the term, see *GE* (2299): "homicide, killing, murder."

συντελεῖσθαι. Pres pass inf συντελέω. Used with ὥστε to explain the preceding clause (Muraoka §30bcb). On the meaning of συντελέω, see 3:32 on συντετελέσθαι.

4:4 συνορῶν ὁ Ονιας τὸ χαλεπὸν τῆς φιλονεικίας καὶ Ἀπολλώνιον Μενεσθέως τὸν Κοίλης Συρίας καὶ Φοινίκης στρατηγὸν συναύξοντα τὴν κακίαν τοῦ Σιμωνος,

Rather than asyndeton, several traditions supply a conjunction that links 4:4 to 4:3: inferential—οὖν (L⁻⁶²), הַצִּיל (Sy); concessive—*autem* (Laˣ); conjunctive—*etiam* (Laᴮᶠ). However, because 4:3 lacks an indicative verb in a main clause, it is preferable to take 4:3 as a circumstantial clause (note the genitive absolute construction) that sets up the main clause in 4:5. The grammatical subject, ὁ Ονιας, is introduced in 4:4.

συνορῶν. Pres act ptc nom masc sg συνοράω (temporal or, perhaps, causal). The participle has two accusative direct objects that modify it (τὸ χαλεπὸν, Ἀπολλώνιον).

ὁ Ονιας. Nominative subject of διεκομίσθη in 4:5.

τὸ χαλεπὸν. Accusative direct object of συνορῶν.

τῆς φιλονεικίας. Attributed genitive ("difficult *dispute*") or genitive of apposition, qualifying τὸ χαλεπόν. φιλονεικία is rare in the Greek of the LXX, but an illuminating parallel is found in Josephus (*J.W.* 7.431): "In all this, however, Onias was not actuated by honest motives; his aim was rather to *rival* (φιλονεικία) the Jews at Jerusalem, against whom he harboured resentment for his exile, and he hoped by erecting this temple to attract the multitude away from them to it" (LCL). Both here in 4:4 and in Josephus, the sense of φιλονεικία is that of "rivalry, dispute, quarrel" (*GE*, 2282).

Ἀπολλώνιον. Accusative direct object of συνορῶν. This Apollonius is the successor of Apollonius son of Thraseas, mentioned in 3:5.

Μενεσθέως. Genitive of relationship. Several MSS read a form of μαίνομαι ("to rage, be mad, be delirious") rather than the proper name (cf. 4:21; 5:24): μαίνεσθαι ὡς τόν (V q⁻¹³⁰ ³⁷⁰ 771 Laⱽ), μαίνεσθαι τόν (L 46-52 58 311). This reading is clearly secondary, but probably reflects a scribal tendency to portray Apollonius negatively (cf. D. Schwartz, 265).

τὸν . . . στρατηγὸν. Accusative in apposition to Ἀπολλώνιον.

Κοίλης Συρίας καὶ Φοινίκης. Genitives of subordination ("governor *over Coele-Syria and Phoeniciea*").

συναύξοντα. Pres act ptc acc masc sg συναύξω (indirect discourse). Following a verb of perception (συνορῶν), the accusative participle indicates indirect discourse and it agrees with Ἀπολλώνιον (cf. *CGCG* §52.18; Wallace, 645–46). The participle is present because the action, as it is perceived, is ongoing. On the meaning of the verb, see *GE* (2027.1): "to contribute to the increasing" = "to encourage."

τὴν κακίαν. Accusative direct object of συναύξοντα.

τοῦ Σίμωνος. Subjective genitive, qualifying τὴν κακίαν.

4:5 πρὸς τὸν βασιλέα διεκομίσθη οὐ γινόμενος τῶν πολιτῶν κατήγορος, τὸ δὲ σύμφορον κοινῇ καὶ κατ᾽ ἰδίαν παντὶ τῷ πλήθει σκοπῶν·

πρὸς τὸν βασιλέα. The PP functions like the dative case (τῷ βασιλεῖ), making πρὸς τὸν βασιλέα the indirect object of διεκομίσθη (cf. Smyth §1702; §3003). Cf. 9:27. The Göttingen edition reads ὡς rather than πρός (cf. MSS A L 311). The rarity of ὡς as a preposition in Koine Greek easily explains the substitution for πρός (cf. BDF §203; Muraoka §26d).

διεκομίσθη. Aor mid ind 3rd sg διακομίζω. Although θε- (or θη-) is typically understood to mark passive morphology, it is actually a dual-voice form and here it is middle (see Aubrey, 563–625; Caragounis, 153). Verbs of motion (e.g., ἀφικνέομαι, ἔρχομαι, πορεύομαι, etc.) often use middle-voice morphology (cf. N. Miller, 423–30). The verb means "to transport" (*GE*, 491) and in this specific context it denotes Onias taking himself to the king to make an appeal. Cf. 9:29.

οὐ. Here and several other times (e.g., 4:6, 34; 5:6, 15, 17; 8:11; 9:22; 14:6) a participle is negated by οὐ rather than μή. This pattern is consistent with classical Greek, where negation occurs as οὐ when the participle states a fact and μή when it states a condition (Smyth §2728).

γινόμενος. Pres mid ptc nom masc sg γίνομαι (purpose).

τῶν πολιτῶν. Objective genitive, modifying κατήγορος. πολῖται ("fellow citizens") is the standard way the epitomizer refers to Jews (4:50; 5:6, 8, 23; 9:19; 14:8; cf. D. Schwartz, 6-7).

κατήγορος. Predicate nominative. See *GE* (1099): "accuser."

τὸ ... σύμφορον. Accusative direct object of σκοπῶν.

δὲ. After the negation, the conjunction means "rather" (cf. BDAG, 213.4.c).

κοινῇ καὶ κατ᾽ ἰδίαν. This adverbial expression is a common idiom: "both public and private" (BDAG, 551.1.c; cf. 9:26; Josephus, *Ant.* 4.310; Polybius, *Hist.* 39.6.3). Cf. 9:26.

παντὶ τῷ πλήθει. Dative of person affected with σκοπῶν (BDAG, 197.4.b).

σκοπῶν. Pres act ptc nom masc sg σκοπέω (purpose). The verb is a figurative extension of the more basic meaning of σκοπέω, "to pay attention to, take care of" (*GE*, 1930.1.B).

4:6 ἑώρα γὰρ ἄνευ βασιλικῆς προνοίας ἀδύνατον εἶναι τυχεῖν εἰρήνης ἔτι τὰ πράγματα καὶ τὸν Σιμωνα παῦλαν οὐ λημψόμενον τῆς ἀνοίας.

ἑώρα. Impf act ind 3rd sg ὁράω. Here the verb denotes "to come to the conclusion through observation" + infinitive clause and participial clause (*GELS*, 503).

γὰρ. Introduces the reason why Onias went to the king (4:4-5). See 1:12 on γάρ.

ἄνευ βασιλικῆς προνοίας. The preposition (plus the genitive) marks the "absence of" something (*GELS*, 50). The king's "concern" or "attention" (προνοίας) is contrasted with Simon's "folly" (τῆς ἀνοίας).

ἀδύνατον. Predicate accusative of εἶναι.

εἶναι. Pres act inf εἰμί (indirect discourse).

τυχεῖν. Aor act inf τυγχάνω. The infinitival clause, τυχεῖν εἰρήνης, functions as the subject of εἶναι (cf. Muraoka §69f). BDAG (1019.1) notes that τυγχάνω often appears with the genitive of what one finds or meets: "to find *peace*."

εἰρήνης. Genitive complement of τυχεῖν. MS 74 has the accusative form: εἰρήνην.

ἔτι. Temporal adverb.

τὰ πράγματα. Accusative subject of the infinitive τυχεῖν. See 4:2 on τῶν πραγμάτων.

τὸν Σιμωνα. Accusative subject of λημψόμενον. The participle takes its own subject in an oblique case (cf. Muraoka §70a).

παῦλαν. Accusative direct object of λημψόμενον.

οὐ. On the negation οὐ with a participle, see 4:5 on οὐ. Further, Smyth (§2729) notes that "οὐ is used with a supplementary participle (in indirect discourse) in agreement with a noun (or pronoun, expressed or unexpressed) depending on a verb of *knowing, showing, perceiving*, etc."

λημψόμενον. Fut mid ptc acc masc sg λαμβάνω (indirect discourse). Literally, "not receiving [an end of folly]." The future participle conveys the notion of futurity. When the middle of λαμβάνω is used with a verbal noun (παῦλαν), this can be a periphrasis for the verb itself: παυσόμενον (BDAG, 584.10.c): "Simon *would not end* his folly."

τῆς ἀνοίας. Objective genitive, qualifying παῦλαν.

2 Maccabees 4:7-17

[7]But, after Seleucus died and Antiochus, the one also called Epiphanes, received the kingdom, Jason, the brother of Onias, obtained by corruption the high priesthood, [8]promising to the king by a petition three hundred and sixty talents of silver and eighty talents from some other income.

⁹In addition to these things, he promised also to sign over one hundred and fifty if it would be permitted by his authority to put together a gymnasium and training center for him and to register those from Antioch in Jerusalem. ¹⁰And after the king consented and [Jason] grasped the office, he turned his fellow countrymen immediately to the Greek character. ¹¹And the royal benevolence established for the Jews by John—the father of Eupolemus, who served as the ambassador for friendship and military alliance with the Romans—setting [that] aside, and destroying the lawful polity, he was innovating unlawful customs. ¹²For he gladly set up a gymnasium under the very acropolis and led around the best of the young men subjugating them under a petasus hat. ¹³There was a certain height of Hellenization and an occasion of the adoption of strange customs because of the surpassing wickedness of Jason, who [was] impious and not [really] a high priest ¹⁴with the result that with regard to the ministry at the altar the priests were no longer eager. Rather, despising the temple and neglecting the sacrifices, they hastened to partake of the unlawful distribution in the wrestling school after the signal of the gong, ¹⁵and holding the paternal honor as nothing and regarding the Greek opinions as excellent. ¹⁶For this reason a dangerous circumstance seized them, and they were envying the customs of them and they desired to assimilate completely those who were enemies and avengers. ¹⁷For to live an ungodly life in regard to the divine laws [is] no easy thing. Certainly, the following events will demonstrate these things.

The mention of building a "gymnasium and training center" and registering "those from Antioch in Jerusalem" (4:9) is no mere rehearsal of events. As 4:16 states, "for this reason a dangerous circumstance seized them."

4:7 Μεταλλάξαντος δὲ τὸν βίον Σελεύκου καὶ παραλαβόντος τὴν βασιλείαν Ἀντιόχου τοῦ προσαγορευθέντος Ἐπιφανοῦς ὑπενόθευσεν Ἰάσων ὁ ἀδελφὸς Ονιου τὴν ἀρχιερωσύνην,

Μεταλλάξαντος. Aor act ptc gen masc sg μεταλλάσσω (genitive absolute, temporal). The collocation of μεταλλάσσω + βίον is an idiom: "to change life" = "to die" (LEH, 396). Goldstein (226) notes that the idiom arose "in connection with heroes, who were worshipped after their deaths and could not be said to have died but rather 'passed' or 'changed' to another existence" (cf. Habicht, 215; Doran 2012, 95). On the genitive absolute, see 1:7 on βασιλεύοντος.

δὲ. Development; see 1:10 on δέ.

τὸν βίον. Accusative direct object of Μεταλλάξαντος.

Σελεύκου. Genitive subject of the participle Μεταλλάξαντος. For details of Seleucus' death, see Appian (*Syr.* 45).

παραλαβόντος. Aor act ptc gen masc sg παραλαμβάνω (genitive absolute, temporal). On the genitive absolute, see 1:7 on βασιλεύοντος.

τὴν βασιλείαν. Accusative direct object of παραλαβόντος.

Ἀντιόχου τοῦ προσαγορευθέντος Ἐπιφανοῦς. See Muraoka (§31ca) on formulas for indicating a nickname.

Ἀντιόχου. Genitive subject of the participle παραλαβόντος.

τοῦ προσαγορευθέντος. Aor pass ptc gen masc sg προσαγορεύω (attributive, modifying Ἀντιόχου). The verb means "to ... designate (*with a certain name*)" (*GE*, 1789).

Ἐπιφανοῦς. Sometimes classified as a predicate genitive, this is actually the genitive complement in an object-complement construction (cf. Muraoka §71a). This construction often occurs with a passive verb where "A is called B." On the name Epiphanes and the wordplay with ἐπιφανεία, see 2:20 on πρὸς Ἀντίοχον τὸν Ἐπιφανῆ.

ὑπενόθευσεν. Aor act ind 3rd sg ὑπονοθεύω. According to the *TLG*, the earliest attested occurrence of ὑπονοθεύω, and the only compound formed from νοθεύω (*EDG*, 1022–23), is found in 2 Maccabees. Domazakis (163–64) provides foundational analysis of the word, highlighting the closest literary (e.g., Diodorus Siculus, *Lib. Hist.* 6.5.1) and epigraphic evidence (*Mylasa* 133.2) to 2 Maccabees. The epigraphic evidence is suggestive: "by corruption to obtain [ὑπονοθεύειν] additional acquisitions on behalf of the public treasury and to procure the ruin of some persons for the meager common benefit of the city." The inscription describes the "fraudulent methods by which the Mylasan tax-gatherers obtained property on behalf of the state treasury" (Domazakis, 163). Thus, the sense of "obtain by corruption" (cf. *GE*, 2227) or "usurp through fraud" would best fit this context where Jason is purchasing the high priesthood with money (cf. 4:8-9).

Ἰάσων. Nominative subject of ὑπενόθευσεν. As noted by Josephus, Jason was also called Ιησοῦς (*Ant.* 12.238). The fact that 2 Maccabees refers to him only by a Greek name underscores Jason's alignment within the growing Hellenistic movement (cf. Hengel, 277–83; Doran 2012, 96).

ὁ ἀδελφὸς. Nominative in apposition with Ἰάσων.

Ονιου. Genitive of relationship.

τὴν ἀρχιερωσύνην. Accusative direct object of ὑπενόθευσεν.

4:8 ἐπαγγειλάμενος τῷ βασιλεῖ δι' ἐντεύξεως ἀργυρίου τάλαντα ἑξήκοντα πρὸς τοῖς τριακοσίοις καὶ προσόδου τινὸς ἄλλης τάλαντα ὀγδοήκοντα.

ἐπαγγειλάμενος. Aor mid ptc nom masc sg ἐπαγγέλλομαι (means). The participle follows the main verb ὑπενόθευσεν (4:7) and explains it: "Jason obtained by corruption the high priesthood *promising* [money]." Less likely, the participle could denote the cause of the corruption, but both the position of the participle (after the main verb) and the tense (aorist) make this less likely (cf. Wallace, 631). The verb is inherently middle because a promise implies a relationship between the subject and the recipient.

τῷ βασιλεῖ. Dative indirect object of ἐπαγγειλάμενος.

δι' ἐντεύξεως. Means. BDAG (339.1) notes that ἔντευξις is a technical term that denotes "a formal request put to a high official or official body, *petition, request*" (cf. *GELS*, 241).

ἀργυρίου. Genitive of material (cf. *CGCG* §30.28).

τάλαντα ἑξήκοντα πρὸς τοῖς τριακοσίοις. Accusative direct object of ἐπαγγειλάμενος. On the meaning of talent, see 3:11.

ἑξήκοντα πρὸς τοῖς τριακοσίοις. Πρός is additive. Luraghi (285) notes that the additive notion of πρός "is based on the idea of physical addition: if an entity is located by another entity, the former can be conceived as added to the later" (cf. *GELS*, 589; BDAG, 873.2.b). Thus, "sixty *in addition to* three-hundred" = "three hundred and sixty." See similar uses in 4:9; 5:21, 24; 8:22; 9:17, 25; 10:31; 11:11; 12:2, 20; 14:4. Some later MSS (*L*) read ἑξακοσίοις ("six hundred") rather than τριακοσίοις, reflecting the need to adjust the numbers for inflation (cf. Goldstein, 227). See Smyth (§347) on numbers.

καὶ. The conjunction that links a second direct object to ἐπαγγειλάμενος.

προσόδου τινός ἄλλης. Genitive of source (lit. "[eighty talents] from some other income"). Whereas the regular revenue was probably from the temple tribute (Goldstein, 227), it is not clear from where this income derives. On the meaning of πρόσοδος, see 3:3 on ἐκ τῶν ἰδίων προσόδων.

τάλαντα ὀγδοήκοντα. Accusative direct object of ἐπαγγειλάμενος.

4:9 πρὸς δὲ τούτοις ὑπισχνεῖτο καὶ ἕτερα διαγράφειν πεντήκοντα πρὸς τοῖς ἑκατόν, ἐὰν ἐπιχωρηθῇ διὰ τῆς ἐξουσίας αὐτοῦ γυμνάσιον καὶ ἐφηβεῖον αὐτῷ συστήσασθαι καὶ τοὺς ἐν Ιεροσολύμοις Ἀντιοχεῖς ἀναγράψαι.

πρὸς . . . τούτοις. Adverbial, modifying ὑπισχνεῖτο: "in addition to *these things*" (BDAG, 583.2.b). See similar uses in 5:23; 9:17, 25; 12:2; 14:4.

δὲ. Development; see 1:10 on δέ.

ὑπισχνεῖτο. Impf mid ind 3rd sg ὑπισχνέομαι. On the use of the middle for verbs of praying, promising, or petitioning, see 4:8 on ἐπαγγειλάμενος.

καὶ. Adverbial.

ἕτερα . . . πεντήκοντα πρὸς τοῖς ἑκατόν. Accusative direct object of διαγράφειν.

πεντήκοντα πρὸς τοῖς ἑκατόν. Πρός is additive. This refers to "fifty *in addition* to one hundred" = "one hundred and fifty." See 4:8 on ἑξήκοντα πρὸς τοῖς τριακοσίοις. See Smyth (§347) on numbers.

διαγράφειν. Pres act inf διαγράφω (complementary). *GE* (483) translates διαγράφω as "to pay," but D. Schwartz (218–19) rightly suggests that "to sign over" is better suited. Some MSS (*L*) have the aorist διαγράψαι.

ἐὰν. Introduces a third-class conditional clause (Smyth §2323), which uses ἐάν + subjunctive in the protasis. The third-class conditional introduces prospective conditions where the writer or speaker "presents fulfillment of the condition as very well possible/likely" (*CGCG* §49.6; cf. Porter 1999, 262).

ἐπιχωρηθῇ. Aor pass subj 3rd sg ἐπιχωρέω (impersonal). Subjunctive used with ἐάν. The Göttingen edition reads ἐπιχορηγηθῇ ("he supplied, furnished"), which is the more difficult reading (cf. Doran 2012, 94). The reading printed in R-H is well-attested (*q*[71]), as are several similar variants: ἀποχωρήθη (71), συγχωρήθη (*L* 46-52 55 58 311), ἐπισυγχωρήθη (771). The orthographic similarities may have contributed to the confusion of the forms ἐπιχωρέω and ἐπιχοργέω. R-H's reading is preferred.

διὰ τῆς ἐξουσίας. Agency.

αὐτοῦ. Subjective genitive, referring to the king (4:8). Doran (2012, 97) notes that many commentators understand Jason as the antecedent of the pronoun. However, the very act of building a *gymnasium* likely required official permission, making it all but certain that the pronoun refers to the king.

γυμνάσιον καὶ ἐφηβεῖον. Accusative direct objects of συστήσασθαι. This is one of the earliest references to a *gymnasium* in Syria and Palestine (cf. 1 Macc 1:14-15; Josephus, *Ant.* 12.251). Based on the text of 2 Maccabees, it is difficult to know the extent of the gymnasium's architecture. However, reference to the "wrestling yard" (παλαίστρα) in 4:14 gives some indication of the structure (cf. Hengel, 70–71). The latter term, ἐφηβεῖον, denotes part of the gymnasium used by young men for exercise and was a common Greek educational institution that helped to ensure political rights to its graduates, and was also associated with military training (Habicht, 216; cf. *GE*, 878).

αὐτῷ. Dative of advantage. It is possible that the antecedent of the pronoun is Jerusalem ("to put together . . . *for it*"). But epigraphic evidence suggests that αὐτῷ refers to the king: "for him." Gymnasiums were often named for individuals, especially kings (Doran 2012, 97).

συστήσασθαι. Aor mid inf συνίστημι (complementary). On the meaning of the verb, see *GELS* (658): "*to put together* a group for an action."

τοὺς ἐν Ἱεροσολύμοις Ἀντιοχεῖς ἀναγράψαι. It is possible to take the article τούς with Ἀντιοχεῖς ("the Antiochenes in Jerusalem") or as a nominalizer of ἐν Ἱεροσολύμοις ("those in Jerusalem as Antiochenes"). The former option understands ἐν Ἱεροσολύμοις as denoting location, specifying where the group called "the Antiochenes" is located. The latter option understands Ἀντιοχεῖς as a predicate accusative, which is a construction attested elsewhere with ἀναγράψαι (SIG³ 108.29-30; 126.2-4; 193.21-22). This understanding does not restrict who in Jerusalem is an Antiochene. On balance, this expression refers not to the granting of Antiochene citizenship, but to the conversion of Jerusalem into a Greek *polis* called "Antioch in Jerusalem" (cf. Dommershausen, 124; Bolyki, 131–39). For fuller discussion, see D. Schwartz (530–32), Parente (3–38), Habicht (216), Doran (2012, 98–101), and especially, Kennell (10–24).

τοὺς . . . Ἀντιοχεῖς. Accusative direct object of ἀναγράψαι.

ἐν Ἱεροσολύμοις. Locative. See 1:1 on ἐν Ἱεροσολύμοις.

ἀναγράψαι. Aor act inf ἀναγράφω (complementary). Based on epigraphic parallels, Kennell (15–16) argues that ἀναγράφω may denote "the recording of new citizens' names on a stele erected in a prominent place." Thus, "to inscribe" the names of Hellenizers in Jerusalem serves as a public registry (cf. *GELS*, 38). Codex V reads ἀναγορεῦσαι: "to declare publicly [those from Antioch in Jerusalem]."

4:10 ἐπινεύσαντος δὲ τοῦ βασιλέως καὶ τῆς ἀρχῆς κρατήσας εὐθέως πρὸς τὸν Ἑλληνικὸν χαρακτῆρα τοὺς ὁμοφύλους μετέστησε.

ἐπινεύσαντος. Aor act ptc gen masc sg ἐπινεύω (genitive absolute, temporal). ἐπινεύω means "to give consent (by a nod)" (BDAG, 376). Due to Homeric (e.g., *Il.* 15.72) and epigraphic parallels, Kennell (17) suggests that ἐπινεύω is a technical term that means "to give royal assent." Further, Kennell (17) notes that "[w]ith the appropriately epic overtones of divinity which [ἐπινεύω] implied, officials in the chancelleries of the Seleucids and their successors enhanced the dignity of their sovereigns." See further discussion of νεύω in *EDG* (1011). Cf. the same term in 11:15 and 14:20. On the genitive absolute, see 1:7 on βασιλεύοντος.

δὲ. Development; see 1:10 on δέ.

τοῦ βασιλέως. Genitive subject of the participle ἐπινεύσαντος, referring to Antiochus from 4:7.

τῆς ἀρχῆς. Genitive complement of κρατήσας. Following BDAG (138.7), this denotes "the sphere of one's official activity, *rule, office.*"

κρατήσας. Aor act ptc nom masc sg κρατέω (temporal). Jason (4:7) is the subject of the participle. Verbs of touching often take the genitive case for a complement, as here (BDF §170; Wallace, 131).

εὐθέως. Temporal adverb, modifying μετέστησε. Fronted for emphasis.

πρὸς τὸν Ἑλληνικὸν χαρακτῆρα. Direction/spatial, used figuratively. The noun χαρακτήρ is used elsewhere in the Greek of the LXX to denote scars caused by leprosy (Lev 13:28) and family resemblance of a child and his/her parents (4 Macc 15:4). BDAG (1077.3) notes χαρακτήρ refers to a "characteristic trait or manner, *distinctive mark.*"

τοὺς ὁμοφύλους. Accusative direct object of μετέστησε. Used as a substantive, the term ὁμόφυλος (ὁμός "common," φῦλον "tribe") denotes "of the same race" or "descent, of the same stock" (*GE*, 1459). "Fellow countrymen" captures the sense well (cf. NETS).

μετέστησε. Aor act ind 3rd sg μεθίστημι. As a figurative extension of the meaning "changing location" (cf. 11:23), here μεθίστημι means "to bring to a different point of view, *turn away, mislead*" (BDAG, 625.2). *GE* (1296) provides examples where a "political situation" (τὰ πράγματα) is changed (cf. 1 Macc 8:13). Doran (2012, 103) rightly notes that LXX uses also show that μεθίστημι can have covenantal resonances (e.g., Judg 10:16; 4 Kgdms 17:23; Isa 54:10; Dan 11:31), bringing out "the covenant-breaking resonances of what Jason is doing."

4:11 καὶ τὰ κείμενα τοῖς Ιουδαίοις φιλάνθρωπα βασιλικὰ διὰ Ιωάννου τοῦ πατρὸς Εὐπολέμου τοῦ ποιησαμένου τὴν πρεσβείαν ὑπὲρ φιλίας καὶ συμμαχίας πρὸς τοὺς Ῥωμαίους παρώσας καὶ τὰς μὲν νομίμους καταλύων πολιτείας παρανόμους ἐθισμοὺς ἐκαίνιζεν.

τὰ κείμενα. Pres pass ptc acc neut pl κεῖμαι (attributive, modifying φιλάνθρωπα βασιλικὰ). *GE* (1108) discusses several meanings for κεῖμαι, including "to be set up or arranged or offered, *of prizes, contests, etc.*"

τοῖς Ιουδαίοις. Dative of advantage. See 1:1 on Τοῖς ἀδελφοῖς τοῖς . . . Ιουδαίοις.

φιλάνθρωπα βασιλικὰ. Accusative direct object of παρώσας. φιλάνθρωπα is a standard description of a king's benevolent action toward his subjects (Doran 2012, 103). The adjective is used as a substantive.

διὰ Ιωάννου. Agency.

τοῦ πατρὸς. Genitive in simple apposition to Ιωάννου.

Εὐπολέμου. Genitive of relationship.

τοῦ ποιησαμένου. Aor mid ptc gen masc sg ποιέω (attributive, modifying Εὐπολέμου or, less likely, Ιωάννου). While it is possible to construe τοῦ ποιησαμένου with Ιωάννου, making John the one who served as ambassador, this is less likely than the alternative because of parallel appositional constructions elsewhere in 2 Maccabees (e.g., 4:2; 13:2). Doran (2012, 104) is correct that "[s]ince the participial phrase comes immediately after Eupolemos, the normal reading would be that Eupolemos governs the participial phrase." This means that Eupolemus is associated with the mission to Rome, an interpretation that has the added advantage of agreeing with 1 Macc 8:17. When the middle of ποιέω is used with a verbal noun (πρεσβείαν), this can be a periphrasis for the verb itself: πρεσβεύω (GELS, 570.II). See 1:23 on ἐποιήσαντο.

τὴν πρεσβείαν. Accusative direct object of ποιησαμένου.

ὑπὲρ φιλίας καὶ συμμαχίας. Reference or, perhaps, advantage. Following the periphrasis of ποιέω + πρεσβείαν, ὑπέρ denotes acting in some entity's interest (BDAG, 1030.A.1.a.β). συμμαχία denotes a "military alliance" (GE, 2001).

πρὸς τοὺς Ῥωμαίους. Relationship (BDAG, 874.3.c).

παρώσας. Aor act ptc nom masc sg παρωθέω (temporal). On the meaning of the verb, see GELS (537): "to set aside and ignore." In some MSS, an alternate verb appears in an indicative form, perhaps to ease the complicated syntax: παρώσατο (q⁻⁹⁸ L⁻¹⁹ 46-52 58 311) or ἀπώσατο (98 19).

τὰς . . . νομίμους . . . πολιτείας. Accusative direct object of καταλύων. The ungrammatical use of the masculine adjective (νομίμους) to modify a feminine noun (πολιτείας) resulted in MS A changing the adjective to νόμιμας. Doran (2012, 105) notes that the mismatch occurs in order to emphasize the contrast between "lawful" and "lawless" (παρανόμους, which is masculine) in 4:11. The pairing/contrasting of the feminine and masculine occurs elsewhere in Greek literature (e.g., Isocrates, Ad Nic. 22; Aristotle, Mund. 400b24; Josephus, Ant. 11.76).

More difficult, perhaps, is translating πολιτεία in this context. GELS (476) glosses the entire phrase as "lawful ways of life," but this loses the civic nuance of πολιτεία (cf. D. Schwartz, 222; pace Goldstein, 229). What may be said with more certainty is that τὰς νομίμους πολιτείας stands in contrast to παρανόμους ἐθισμούς, which helps explain the plural πολιτείας.

μὲν. Anticipatory, underscoring the contrast between νομίμους ("lawful") with παρανόμους ("unlawful"). Although μέν is often correlated with δέ (or καί, ἀλλά, etc.), μέν can also correlate with asyndeton (cf. Mayser II 2:164.4). Such uses of μέν are "preparatory" (cf.

Denniston, 380), meaning that the corresponding clause is not stated but implied. Here μέν appears without an accompanying particle (e.g., δέ, καί, etc.). See 2:25 on μὲν . . . δὲ . . . δέ.

καταλύων. Pres act ptc nom masc sg καταλύω (means).

παρανόμους ἐθισμοὺς. Accusative direct object of ἐκαίνιζεν. *GELS* (530) suggests "inclined to transgress the (divine) law."

ἐκαίνιζεν. Impf act ind 3rd sg καινίζω. The sense of "to do s[omething] new" or "to innovate" (*GE*, 1010) is surely a negative description in light of parallel accounts in Josephus (e.g., *Ant.* 7.362; 15.178; 20.216-18).

4:12 ἀσμένως γὰρ ὑπ᾽ αὐτὴν τὴν ἀκρόπολιν γυμνάσιον καθίδρυσεν καὶ τοὺς κρατίστους τῶν ἐφήβων ὑποτάσσων ὑπὸ πέτασον ἤγαγεν.

ἀσμένως. Adverb of manner, modifying καθίδρυσεν and denoting the "joy" that Jason felt setting up a gymnasium.

γὰρ. Explanatory, elaborating with specific details about the "unlawful customs" that were established in 4:11. See 1:12 on γάρ.

ὑπ᾽ αὐτὴν τὴν ἀκρόπολιν. Locative. Both the intensive ("the acropolis *itself*") or identifying ("the *very* acropolis") uses of αὐτός are possible in predicate structure (Smyth §1206b; 1210a), but *GELS* (104) notes that when αὐτός "precedes an articular noun phrase . . . [it] emphasizes the identity." On the possible location of the gymnasium, Bar-Kochva (445–65) suggests it was constructed below the southeastern hill of Jerusalem. However, the ἀκρόπολις probably refers to the Seleucid castle built by Antiochus Epiphanes (Nicklas 2011, 1386; Dommershausen, 124) and was also a term used by Strabo (*Geogr.* 16.2.37) to denote Jerusalem's temple.

γυμνάσιον. Accusative direct object of καθίδρυσεν.

καθίδρυσεν. Aor act ind 3rd sg καθιδρύω.

τοὺς κρατίστους τῶν ἐφήβων ὑποτάσσων ὑπὸ πέτασον ἤγαγεν. Although LEH (490) suggests the translation, "he made the noblest of the young men wear the petasus," the military overtones of training in the gymnasium suggests that the phrase τοὺς κρατίστους τῶν ἐφήβων be rendered as "the strongest of the young men." That is, the phrase does not denote the aristocratic nobility of the gymnasium, but rather the strong young men enlisted as Jason's enforcers (Kennell, 21–22). Based on parallels with Herodotus (*Hist.* 1.59) and Plutarch (*Ag. Cleom.* 7.8; 17.2), Kennell (22) further notes that building up a personal security team "was a defining characteristic of the budding tyrant."

τοὺς κρατίστους. Accusative direct object of ἤγαγεν.

τῶν ἐφήβων. Partitive genitive. Refers to a "male adolescent 18 years of age or older" (*GELS*, 308).

ὑποτάσσων. Pres act ptc nom masc sg ὑποτάσσω (means). The verb ὑποτάσσω denotes "to place under the authority and rule of" = "making them wear a petasus hat" (*GELS*, 706). Kennell (21–22) argues that the verb has military overtones, denoting that Jason is "drawing up" strong young men as recruits. It is also possible that the choice of verb was for the sake of word-play: ὑποτάσσων ὑπὸ πέτασον. This similarity resulted in Codex V omitting ὑποτάσσων due to *homoiarchton*.

ὑπὸ πέτασον. Locative or, possibly, subordination. The collocation of ὑποτάσσω + ὑπὸ has the sense of "to be subject *under* [*something*]" (BDAG, 1042.1). πέτασος refers to "a head covering with a large brim, used for shelter from the sun during gymnastic exercises" (*GE*, 1656). Even though most Greeks exercised naked, there is some evidence that Jews might have remained partially clothed (cf. Thucydides, *Hist*. 1.6). Second Maccabees does not clarify this point (cf. 1 Macc 1:14-15; Josephus, *Ant*. 12.241), but if young Jewish men were exercising naked, the warning of Jub. 3:31 would surely apply: "they should cover their shame and should not uncover themselves as the gentiles uncover themselves." However, due to the impractical nature of the *petasus* hat, it is possible that the entire clause is a euphemism for Jason making the youth perform gymnastic exercises: "subjugating them under a *petasus* hat" = "to perform the exercises" (cf. Nicklas 2011, 1386; Dommershausen, 124; D. Schwartz, 224).

ἤγαγεν. Aor act ind 3rd sg ἄγω.

4:13 ἦν δ᾿ οὕτως ἀκμή τις Ἑλληνισμοῦ καὶ πρόσβασις ἀλλοφυλισμοῦ διὰ τὴν τοῦ ἀσεβοῦς καὶ οὐκ ἀρχιερέως Ἰάσωνος ὑπερβάλλουσαν ἀναγνείαν.

ἦν. Impf act ind 3rd sg εἰμί. This is the so-called existential use of εἰμί, where the verb occurs with only a grammatical subject and has the basic sense of "exist" (*CGCG* §26.10).

δ᾿. Development, marking a change of subject from Antiochus to an impersonal subject in 4:13. See 1:10 on δέ.

οὕτως. Adverb, denoting "a relatively high degree" (BDAG, 742.3).

ἀκμή τις . . . καὶ πρόσβασις. Nominative subjects of ἦν. τις is used to moderate an expression "that is too definite" (BDAG, 1008.1.b.β; Smyth §1268). See 1:7 on ἀκμή.

Ἑλληνισμοῦ. Partitive genitive. In contrast with Ἰουδαϊσμός (2:21; 8:1; 14:38), here the epitomizer uses Ἑλληνισμός, which refers to the adoption of Greek customs by non-Greeks (i.e., Jews). The heroes of 2 Maccabees are characterized as those who reject Ἑλληνισμός. Hengel (2) translates ἀκμή τις Ἑλληνισμοῦ as "a climax of Hellenizing tendencies," but this is probably too definite. See discussion in Mason (2016, 179–80).

ἀλλοφυλισμοῦ. Genitive of apposition. See *GE* (95): "adoption of strange customs." In context, the particular sense is adopting non-Jewish customs. For the epitomizer, ἀλλοφυλισμός denotes an "activity that in the author's view threatens the survival of the *ethnos*" (Mason 2016, 180). This is vividly demonstrated in 6:24, where Eleazar refuses "to foreignize" (εἰς ἀλλοφυλισμόν) by eating pork.

διὰ τὴν . . . ὑπερβάλλουσαν ἀναγνείαν. Cause. The separation of the article from the noun is an example of hyperbaton where the interpositional words modify the head.

ὑπερβάλλουσαν. Pres act ptc acc fem sg ὑπερβάλλω (attributive).

Ἰάσωνος. Subjective genitive, qualifying ἀναγνείαν.

τοῦ ἀσεβοῦς καὶ οὐκ ἀρχιερέως. Genitives in apposition to Ἰάσωνος. Muraoka (§83i) notes that the underlying syntactical structure is "a negative equational clause <something is not A>."

4:14 ὥστε μηκέτι περὶ τὰς τοῦ θυσιαστηρίου λειτουργίας προθύμους εἶναι τοὺς ἱερεῖς, ἀλλὰ τοῦ μὲν νεὼ καταφρονοῦντες καὶ τῶν θυσιῶν ἀμελοῦντες ἔσπευδον μετέχειν τῆς ἐν παλαίστρῃ παρανόμου χορηγίας μετὰ τὴν τοῦ δίσκου πρόσκλησιν,

ὥστε. Result. Related back to the main clause in 4:13.

μηκέτι . . . ἀλλὰ. The correlative pair organizes a negative-positive construction in which the focal element of the negative clause (περὶ τὰς τοῦ θυσιαστηρίου λειτουργίας προθύμους εἶναι τοὺς ἱερεῖς) serves to emphasize the focal element of the positive clause (τοῦ μὲν νεὼ καταφρονοῦντες).

περὶ τὰς . . . λειτουργίας. Reference. See discussion of the contrast between λειτουργία and χορηγία below.

τοῦ θυσιαστηρίου. Genitive of place (i.e., "ministry *at the altar*") or, less likely, production (i.e., "ministry *produced by the altar*").

προθύμους. Predicate adjective preceding εἶναι, in agreement with τοὺς ἱερεῖς. *GE* (1765) suggests "eager, good-spirited" as possible translations. The situation envisioned is that certain priests, who each had a share in the responsibilities of the temple cult, were not eager to do this work.

εἶναι. Pres act inf εἰμί. Used with ὥστε to indicate a result.

τοὺς ἱερεῖς. Accusative subject of the infinitive εἶναι.

τοῦ . . . νεὼ. Genitive complement of καταφρονοῦντες. Verbs of emotion are often complemented by genitives (cf. Wallace, 131).

Alternatively, Muraoka (§22oa) labels this a genitive of cause, expressing admiration, accusation, or contempt. The noun νεώς is an Attic form (cf. 6:2; 8:2; 9:16; 10:3, 5; 13:23; 14:33, 35; 15:18, 33).

μὲν . . . καὶ. The slight contrast implied in μέν/δέ is evaded by pairing μέν with a particle that denotes addition (Denniston, 374). Because μέν signals "anticipation of a related sentence that follows" (Runge, 75), the καί signals that new information is added.

καταφρονοῦντες. Pres act ptc nom masc pl καταφρονέω (manner).

τῶν θυσιῶν. Genitive complement of ἀμελοῦντες.

ἀμελοῦντες. Pres act ptc nom masc pl ἀμελέω (manner). *GELS* (32) notes that ἀμελέω takes the genitive to indicate the person or thing one neglects.

ἔσπευδον. Impf act ind 3rd pl σπεύδω. Used with the infinitive (μετέχειν) to "define a mode of action indicated by the second [verb]" (Muraoka §64).

μετέχειν. Pres act inf μετέχω (complementary). This verb is used with the genitive to indicate "the thing *in* or *of* something" (BDAG, 642.1). Kennell (18–19) notes that μετέχω "is the proper verb to describe members of a gymnasium, who were eligible to partake of its amenities and any distributions which open-handed magistrates might furnish."

τῆς . . . παρανόμου χορηγίας. Genitive after a verb of sharing (μετέχειν). Doran (2012, 106) notes the contrast between χορηγία and λειτουργία, which can both have the sense of "expenses." However, because λειτουργία refers to "the ministry [at the altar]" in 4:14, χορηγία denotes general actions or practices, particularly, a "distribution." The distribution in reference here is anointing oil (Habicht, 218; Doran 2012, 106). Cf. 5:10, 27. The separation of the article from the head is an example of hyperbaton. The placement of the PP between the article and its head clarifies that the PP modifies the NP.

ἐν παλαίστρῃ. Locative. See *GE* (1523): "palaistra, *training ground for wrestling.*" This is the only structure of the gymnasium mentioned explicitly in 2 Maccabees. Doran (2012, 102) notes that this "was usually a court surrounded by a colonnaded porch with rooms leading off it." However, Kennell (23) quite plausibly suggests that the lack of literary and archeological evidence is because Jerusalem's παλαίστρα may have been converted from a large, existing structure.

μετὰ τὴν . . . πρόσκλησιν. Temporal.

τοῦ δίσκου. Genitive of apposition. This probably denotes a "gong (a slightly convex metallic disk that gives a loud, resonant tone when struck)" (LEH, 157; cf. Nicklas 2011, 1387) rather than "a disc thrown by athletes" (*pace GELS*, 172). The "signal of the gong" indicates that the gymnasium is open (cf. Doran 2012, 106; Kennell, 18).

4:15 καὶ τὰς μὲν πατρῴους τιμὰς ἐν οὐδενὶ τιθέμενοι, τὰς δὲ Ἑλληνικὰς δόξας καλλίστας ἡγούμενοι.

μὲν . . . δὲ. Point/counterpoint set. See 2:25 on μὲν . . . δέ.

τὰς . . . πατρῴους τιμὰς. Accusative direct object of τιθέμενοι. The contrast between τιμή ("honor") and δόξα ("opinion") highlights the epitomizer's positive perspective toward Jewish tradition (cf. Doran 2012, 106).

ἐν οὐδενὶ. Manner.

τιθέμενοι. Pres mid ptc nom masc pl τίθημι (manner).

τὰς . . . Ἑλληνικὰς δόξας. Accusative direct object of ἡγούμενοι in an object-complement double accusative construction.

καλλίστας. Complement in object-complement double accusative construction. Kennell (19) notes that καλλίστας "had a specific application in honorific decrees passed by assemblies of citizens or denizens of the gymnasium" (cf. *MAMA* 8.484; 8.474).

ἡγούμενοι. Pres mid ptc nom masc pl ἡγέομαι (manner).

4:16 ὧν καὶ χάριν περιέσχεν αὐτοὺς χαλεπὴ περίστασις, καὶ ὧν ἐζήλουν τὰς ἀγωγὰς καὶ καθ᾽ ἅπαν ἤθελον ἐξομοιοῦσθαι, τούτους πολεμίους καὶ τιμωρητὰς ἔσχον·

Here begins a digression that spans from 4:16-17. In this short departure from the main narrative, the epitomizer explains the cause of suffering for the Jews under Antiochus' rule. Whereas Onias was characterized as a "zealot for the laws" (ζηλωτὴν τῶν νόμων, 4:2), the young priests were "envying the customs [of the Greeks]" (ὧν ἐζήλουν τὰς ἀγωγάς, 4:16). This depiction of the assimilation to Greek customs and the rejection of Jewish tradition and law, using the ζηλ- root, is striking. Moreover, the ironic result of attaining "a certain height of Hellenization" (4:13) is that the Greeks became their enemies (4:16). For more comments on digressions, see the Introduction.

ὧν . . . χάριν. Cause. The accusative of χάρις is used as a preposition (cf. BDAG, 1078; BDF §160). It typically follows the word it modifies (cf. Jdt 8:19; 1 Macc 12:45; 13:4; 3 Macc 5:41; Sir 32:2; 34:12) and it takes the genitive case. The neuter relative pronoun has a conceptual referent (Wallace, 333–34) and refers to the preceding context where Jews in Jerusalem loved the Greek way of life.

περιέσχεν. Aor act ind 3rd sg περιέχω. On the meaning of the verb, see BDAG (800.2): "to take hold of completely" = "to seize."

αὐτοὺς. Accusative direct object of περιέσχεν.

χαλεπὴ περίστασις. Nominative subject of περιέσχεν.

ὧν. Subjective genitive, qualifying τὰς ἀγωγὰς.

ἐζήλουν. Impf act ind 3rd pl ζηλόω.

τὰς ἀγωγὰς. Accusative direct object of ἐζήλουν.

καθ᾽ ἅπαν. Reference: "in every respect" = "completely." Cf. 15:30.

ἤθελον. Aor act ind 3rd pl θέλλω.

ἐξομοιοῦσθαι. Pres mid inf ἐξομοιόω (complementary). On the meaning of the verb, see *GELS* (254): "to imitate and become alike."

τούτους. Accusative direct object of ἔσχον in an object-complement double accusative construction.

πολεμίους καὶ τιμωρητὰς. Complements in an object-complement double accusative construction. The rare term τιμωρητής ("avenger") is probably a neologism that combines the stem of τιμωρός ("avenging") with the suffix of κολαστής ("punisher") or ἐκδικητής ("avenger, punisher") (Domazakis, 159–63).

ἔσχον. Aor act ind 3rd pl ἔχω.

4:17 ἀσεβεῖν γὰρ εἰς τοὺς θείους νόμους οὐ ῥᾴδιον, ἀλλὰ ταῦτα ὁ ἀκόλουθος καιρὸς δηλώσει.

ἀσεβεῖν. Prf act inf ἀσεβέω. The infinitive clause, ἀσεβεῖν . . . εἰς τοὺς θείους νόμους, functions as the subject of an implied copula (see BDF §393.2). Cf. the description of Jason in 4:13: τοῦ ἀσεβοῦς.

γὰρ. Introduces an explanation of the preceding clause, explaining why calamity seized those who embraced Hellenization. See 1:12 on γάρ.

εἰς τοὺς θείους νόμους. Reference.

οὐ. The negation works with the first clause in 4:17 and is not coordinate with ἀλλά in the second clause: "to live an ungodly life . . . [is] *no* easy thing."

ῥᾴδιον. Stands in predicate position to the subject infinitive as a substantive. See *GELS* (611): "*easy* of execution."

ἀλλὰ. Transitional, denoting that "the preceding is to be regarded as a settled matter" (BDAG, 45.3).

ταῦτα. Accusative direct object of δηλώσει.

ὁ ἀκόλουθος καιρὸς. Nominative subject of δηλώσει. See *GELS* (21): "the subsequent course of events" = "the following events."

δηλώσει. Fut act ind 3rd sg δηλόω. The future stresses intention (cf. *CGCG* §33.43).

2 Maccabees 4:18-22

[18]Now when the quinquennial contest was being celebrated in Tyre and the king was present, [19]the vile Jason sent envoys as if from Jerusalem,

Antiochenes carrying three hundred drachmas of silver for the sacrifice to Hercules. And those carrying it requested not to use [it] for sacrifice because that was not appropriate but to expend [it] for another cost. [20]So then, these things were allotted for the sacrifice to Heracles because of the sender but [they were actually allotted] for the outfitting of the triremes because of the carrier's decision. [21]When Apollonius [son] of Menestheus was sent to Egypt on account of the coronation of King Philometor, having learned that he had become hostile toward his government, Antiochus was giving thought to his own safety. Therefore, after coming to Joppa he went to Jerusalem. [22]And being welcomed magnificently by Jason and the city, he was received with torch-bearers and shouts. So then, he encamped in Phoenicia.

4:18 Ἀγομένου δὲ πενταετηρικοῦ ἀγῶνος ἐν Τύρῳ καὶ τοῦ βασιλέως παρόντος,

The entirety of 4:18 forms a circumstantial frame for the main clause that begins in 4:19. On this construction, see the Introduction comments at 3:1.

Ἀγομένου. Pres pass ptc gen masc sg ἄγω (genitive absolute, temporal). Here the verb means something like "to celebrate" because it is paired with a formal athletic contest. On the meaning of ἄγω, see 1:9 on ἄγητε. On the genitive absolute, see 1:7 on βασιλεύοντος.

δὲ. Development; see 1:10 on δέ.

πενταετηρικοῦ ἀγῶνος. Genitive subject of the participle Ἀγομένου. The adjective πενταετηρικός is an example of "Greek 'inclusive' counting, which counted the first and the last year in a sequence" (D. Schwartz, 226). Thus, "quinquennial" = "coming every fourth year" (e.g., the Olympic games). The noun ἀγών refers to a "contest in sports" (*GELS*, 9). Cf. 10:28; 14:18, 43.

ἐν Τύρῳ. Locative.

τοῦ βασιλέως. Genitive subject of the participle παρόντος.

παρόντος. Pres act ptc gen masc sg πάρειμι (genitive absolute, temporal). On the genitive absolute, see 1:7 on βασιλεύοντος.

4:19 ἀπέστειλεν Ἰάσων ὁ μιαρὸς θεωροὺς ὡς ἀπὸ Ἱεροσολύμων Ἀντιοχεῖς ὄντας παρακομίζοντας ἀργυρίου δραχμὰς τριακοσίας εἰς τὴν τοῦ Ἡρακλέους θυσίαν, ἃς καὶ ἠξίωσαν οἱ παρακομίζοντες μὴ χρῆσθαι εἰς θυσίαν διὰ τὸ μὴ καθήκειν, εἰς ἑτέραν δὲ καταθέσθαι δαπάνην.

ἀπέστειλεν. Aor act ind 3rd sg ἀποστέλλω.

Ἰάσων ὁ μιαρὸς. Nominative subject of ἀπέστειλεν. The Göttingen edition reads ὁ μιερός rather than ὁ μιαρός, which is a spelling
variation that does not affect the meaning. This description of Jason
as "polluted" links him with the negative evaluation of Antiochus IV
(5:6; 7:34; 9:13) and Nikanor (15:32). Although language of pollution
often denotes ritual impurity (e.g., Jdt 10:13), in 2 Maccabees μιαρός/
μιερός always denotes moral impurity. This sense is particularly clear
in 7:34: "O impious and most *impure* of all men" (ὦ ἀνόσιε καὶ πάντων
ἀνθρώπων μιαρώτατε).

θεωροὺς. Accusative direct object of ἀπέστειλεν. See *GE* (941):
"envoy, ambassador."

ὡς. Used with a PP (ἀπὸ Ἱεροσολύμων) to express intention (*GE*,
2427.II.H.B).

ἀπὸ Ἱεροσολύμων. Separation or, perhaps, source, marking the point
of departure (cf. BDAG, 105.3.a.β).

Ἀντιοχεῖς. Predicate accusative of ὄντας.

ὄντας. Pres act ptc acc masc pl εἰμί (attributive, modifying θεωρούς).

παρακομίζοντας. Pres act ptc acc masc pl παρακομίζω (attributive,
modifying Ἀντιοχεῖς).

ἀργυρίου. Genitive of material (cf. *CGCG* 30.28).

δραχμὰς τριακοσίας. Accusative direct object of παρακομίζοντας.
Citing epigraphic sources (SIG 398.44–45; 402.30; OGIS 319.20), Goldstein (233) observes that sacrifices could cost between 100–500 drachmas each. Due to inflation, the number "three hundred" was updated to
"thirty-three hundred" (e.g., δραχμὰς τριακοσίας τρισχίλιας) in some
later MSS (*L* Sy 728 311). For Greek numbers, see Smyth (§347).

εἰς τὴν . . . θυσίαν. Purpose.

τοῦ Ἡρακλέους. Genitive of destination/purpose. The god Heracles
is associated with the chief god of Tyre (D. Schwartz, 227).

ἄς. Accusative direct object of οἱ παρακομίζοντες. The feminine
plural relative pronoun refers to δραχμὰς τριακοσίας ("three hundred
drachmas").

ἠξίωσαν. Aor act ind 3rd pl ἀξιόω. In 2 Maccabees ἀξιόω most often
has the sense of "to ask" or "to implore" (cf. 3:31; 5:4; 7:28; 8:14, 29; 9:26;
10:4, 16, 26; 11:17, 24; 12:11, 24, 42).

οἱ παρακομίζοντες. Pres act ptc nom masc pl παρακομίζω (substantival). Subject of ἠξίωσαν.

μὴ χρῆσθαι. Pres mid inf χράω (indirect discourse). Cf. 6:4, 21; 14:31
for other uses of χράω in similar contexts. Note the present infinitive
is used here and the aorist infinitive is used at the end of the verse.
The selection of these different tenses is intentional because each has a

different aspectual significance. The present (imperfective verbal aspect) indicates the habitual or general nature of the action.

εἰς θυσίαν. Purpose.

μὴ καθήκειν. Pres act inf καθήκω. Used with διὰ τό to denote cause (see Burk, 105–6).

εἰς ἑτέραν . . . δαπάνην. Purpose. Although δαπάνη is used only here in 2 Maccabees, it appears multiple times in 1 Maccabees to denote a "cost" or "expenditure" in connection with the temple (e.g., 1 Macc 3:30; 10:39, 44, 45).

δέ. Development; see 1:10 on δέ.

καταθέσθαι. Aor mid inf κατατίθημι (indirect discourse). Note that the previous infinitive was present, not aorist.

4:20 ἔπεσε μὲν οὖν ταῦτα διὰ μὲν τὸν ἀποστείλαντα εἰς τὴν τοῦ Ἡρακλέους θυσίαν, ἕνεκεν δὲ τῶν παρακομιζόντων εἰς τὰς τῶν τριηρέων κατασκευάς.

ἔπεσε. Aor act ind 3rd sg πίπτω. On the meaning of the verb, see *GELS* (558): "to be allotted."

μὲν οὖν. Transitional, marking a "more to-the-point, relevant text segment" (*CGCG* §59.73). As individual particles, οὖν marks a transition to a new subject and μέν anticipates an antithesis ("so then, therefore," cf. Smyth §2901c). Although some scholars speak of an solitary, emphatic μέν (cf. Denniston, 359–68), this function was falling out in classical Greek (Fresch 2017b, 277–78). Thus, it is best to take this μέν in coordination with the following μέν/δέ construction. Finally, on the assumption that οὖν modifies the following μέν/δέ construction, the transition occurs in multiple stages: "these things were allotted for the sacrifice to Heracles *but* [they were actually allotted] for the outfitting of the triremes." See especially Brookins and Longenecker (135), Thrall (34–35), and Denniston (470–81). The Göttingen edition reads δέ rather than μέν οὖν, which denotes only a development (e.g., shift of grammatical subject) in the narrative.

ταῦτα. Nominative subject of ἔπεσε. Neuter plural subjects often take singular verbs (Smyth §959). The antecedent of the demonstrative is the drachmas mentioned in 4:19.

διὰ . . . τὸν ἀποστείλαντα. Cause or, less likely, agency (cf. BDAG, 225.B.2.d).

τὸν ἀποστείλαντα. Aor act ptc acc masc sg ἀποστέλλω (substantival).

μὲν . . . δέ. Point/counterpoint set, setting up a contrast between Jason's intention and the carrier's intention. See 2:26 on μέν . . . δέ.

εἰς τὴν . . . θυσίαν. Purpose, modifying ἀποστείλαντα rather than ἔπεσε.

τοῦ Ἡρακλέους. Genitive of destination/purpose.

ἕνεκεν . . . τῶν παρακομιζόντων. Improper causal preposition with a genitive object (BDAG, 334.1).

τῶν παρακομιζόντων. Pres act ptc gen masc pl παρακομίζω (substantival).

εἰς τὰς . . . κατασκευάς. Purpose, modifying παρακομιζόντων rather than ἔπεσε.

τῶν τριηρέων. Objective genitive. The *trireme* refers to a "long, sleek, light ship, . . . [that] was rowed by 170 oarsmen and staffed by 30 marines, archers, and sailors (with a helmsman) to make a total ship's crew of 200. It was equipped with a bronze ram on the prow to punch a hole in enemy ships or smash through their oars. There are still some questions about the interior arrangement, but most historians of ancient naval warfare believe that the 'three' in triêrês refers to three banks of oars manned by one oarsman each and staggered one on top of the other" (Bugh, 275).

4:21 Ἀποσταλέντος δὲ εἰς Αἴγυπτον Ἀπολλωνίου τοῦ Μενεσθέως διὰ τὰ πρωτοκλίσια τοῦ Φιλομήτορος βασιλέως μεταλαβὼν Ἀντίοχος ἀλλότριον αὐτὸν τῶν αὐτοῦ γεγονέναι πραγμάτων τῆς καθ᾽ αὑτὸν ἀσφαλείας ἐφρόντιζεν· ὅθεν εἰς Ιοππην παραγενόμενος κατήντησεν εἰς Ιεροσόλυμα.

Ἀποσταλέντος. Aor pass ptc gen masc sg ἀποστέλλω (genitive absolute, temporal). On the genitive absolute, see 1:7 on βασιλεύοντος.

δὲ. Development; see 1:10 on δέ.

εἰς Αἴγυπτον. Locative.

Ἀπολλωνίου. Genitive subject of the participle Ἀποσταλέντος. This Apollonius was first mentioned in 4:4.

τοῦ Μενεσθέως. Genitive of relationship.

διὰ τὰ πρωτοκλίσια. Cause. The MS tradition has multiple options, probably because there is no ceremony known as πρωτοκλίσια in Ptolemaic Egypt (cf. Goldstein, 234). Habicht (219) is correct to affirm that πρωτοκλίσια is best. On the meaning of πρωτοκλίσια (lit. "first reclining" from πρωτο + κλιν-), the noun probably describes Philometer's coronation as the time when he first occupied his seat of authority as king (cf. D. Schwartz, 229). Thus, "festival for the proclamation, of a king" (*GE*, 1848).

τοῦ Φιλομήτορος βασιλέως. Objective genitive. βασιλέως is in simple apposition to τοῦ Φιλομήτορος.

μεταλαβὼν. Aor act ptc nom masc sg μεταλαμβάνω (temporal). Cf. the verb in 11:6; 12:8; 12:5, 21; 13:23; 15:1.

Ἀντίοχος. Nominative subject of ἐφρόντιζεν.

ἀλλότριον. Predicate accusative of γεγονέναι, in agreement with αὐτόν. See *GELS* (28): "unfavorably disposed." Cf. 14:26 for the same phrase.

αὐτὸν. Accusative subject of the infinitive γεγονέναι.

τῶν . . . πραγμάτων. Objective genitive, qualifying ἀλλότριον.

αὐτοῦ. Genitive of subordination.

γεγονέναι. Prf act inf γίνομαι (indirect discourse).

τῆς . . . ἀσφαλείας. Genitive complement of ἐφρόντιζεν. As a figurative extension, ἀσφάλεια denotes "safety" (*GE*, 326).

καθ᾽ αὑτὸν. Reference.

ἐφρόντιζεν. Impf act ind 3rd sg φροντίζω. Verbs of perception often take the genitive case (Wallace, 131; BDAG, 1066). The verb denotes "to think of, worry about, care about, be anxious about" (*GE*, 2309).

ὅθεν. Relative adverb (ὅ -θεν), used as an inferential conjunction (cf. *GE*, 1428.B). Cf. 4:36, 46; 5:11; 10:13; 12:45; 14:7.

εἰς Ιοππην. Locative.

παραγενόμενος. Aor mid ptc nom masc sg παραγίνομαι (temporal).

κατήντησεν. Aor act ind 3rd sg καταντάω. On the meaning of the verb, see BDAG (523.1): "to get to a geographical destination, come (to), arrive (at), reach, w[ith] εἰς and acc[usative] of place."

εἰς Ιεροσόλυμα. Locative.

4:22 μεγαλομερῶς δὲ ὑπὸ τοῦ Ἰάσωνος καὶ τῆς πόλεως ἀποδεχθεὶς μετὰ δᾳδουχίας καὶ βοῶν εἰσεδέχθη, εἶθ᾽ οὕτως εἰς τὴν Φοινίκην κατεστρατοπέδευσεν.

μεγαλομερῶς. Adverb of manner, modifying εἰσεδέχθη.

δὲ. Development; see 1:10 on δέ.

ὑπὸ τοῦ Ἰάσωνος καὶ τῆς πόλεως. Agency.

ἀποδεχθεὶς. Aor pass ptc nom masc sg ἀποδέχομαι (means). Cf. the description of welcome in 3:9.

μετὰ δᾳδουχίας καὶ βοῶν. Manner. Processions with torches and shouting "were common in Hellenistic monarchies" (Goldstein, 235).

εἰσεδέχθη. Aor pass ind 3rd sg εἰσδέχομαι.

εἶθ᾽ οὕτως. Adverbial expression of time. But, as D. Schwartz (230) notes it implies cause as well. Εἶτα is a "a transition word to mark an addition to someth[ing] just stated" (BDAG, 295.2). Cf. 15:13 and Wis 17:15 for the same expression.

εἰς τὴν Φοινίκην. Locative. On the use (or lack) of the article with geographic names, see 1:1 on κατ᾽ Αἴγυπτον.

κατεστρατοπέδευσεν. Aor act ind 3rd sg καταστρατοπεδεύω. Apparently, the reason that Antiochus encamped in Phoenicia was either because of the distraction caused by the celebratory welcome or, less likely, that he found no evidence of pro-Ptolemaic sympathy (cf. D. Schwartz, 230).

2 Maccabees 4:23-29

[23]Now after a three-year period, Jason sent Menelaus, the brother of the aforementioned Simon, to carry the money to the king and to complete the records for necessary state affairs. [24]But he, after being presented to the king and honoring him with the appearance of authority, secured for himself the high priesthood, surpassing Jason by three hundred talents of silver. [25]After receiving the royal commands, he arrived bearing nothing worthy of the high priesthood but having the anger of a cruel tyrant and the impulses of a wild animal. [26]And Jason, the one who undermined his own brother, was undermined by another [person] and was forced to flee into the countryside of Ammon. [27]Now Menelaus took the office, but he paid regularly nothing of the promised money to the king [28]even though Sostratus, the commander of the acropolis, was making demands, for the [job of] collection of the discrepancies was [given] to that one. For this reason the two were summoned by the king. [29]And Menelaus left behind Lysimachus, his own brother, as the substitute in the high priesthood, and Sostratus [left behind] Crates as substitute over the Cyprians.

The plotline of the narrative is carried forward with the aorist indicative in this section. In 4:26-27 present and pluperfect verbs appear in order to set up the story that Menelaus and Sostratos "were summoned" (4:28) by the king.

4:23 Μετὰ δὲ τριετῆ χρόνον ἀπέστειλεν Ἰάσων Μενέλαον τὸν τοῦ προσημαινομένου Σίμωνος ἀδελφὸν παρακομίζοντα τὰ χρήματα τῷ βασιλεῖ καὶ περὶ πραγμάτων ἀναγκαίων ὑπομνηματισμοὺς τελέσοντα.

Μετὰ . . . τριετῆ χρόνον. Temporal (lit. "after a three-year period"). However, the identical phrase in 14:1 must be understood inclusively (i.e., "in the third year") because of the information in 13:1 and 14:4. In summary, this expression is not precise, especially because it is not clear whether the count of years begins after Jason's appointment or Antiochus' visit to Jerusalem (cf. D. Schwartz, 230–31).

δὲ. Development; see 1:10 on δέ.

ἀπέστειλεν. Aor act ind 3rd sg ἀποστέλλω.

Ἰάσων. Nominative subject of ἀπέστειλεν.

Μενέλαον. Accusative direct object of ἀπέστειλεν. Because the name Μενέλαος is being established in the narrative it is anarthrous (Smyth §1136; Muraoka §1b). Compare this use with the following articular uses of the name (4:27, 29, 32, 34, 43, 45, 47, 50; 5:5, 15), where the article defines "[o]bjects already mentioned or in the mind of the speaker or writer" (Smyth §1120.b).

τὸν . . . ἀδελφὸν. Accusative in apposition to Μενέλαον.

τοῦ προσημαινομένου Σίμωνος. Genitive of relationship. Simon was last mentioned in 4:1-6.

προσημαινομένου. Pres pass ptc gen masc sg προσημαίνω (attributive). In the passive προσημαίνω is virtually synonymous with προλέγω (cf. GE, 1810). Cf. uses of προλέγω in 2:32; 3:7, 28; 4:1; 6:29; 14:8.

παρακομίζοντα. Pres act ptc acc masc sg παρακομίζω (purpose). The participle is accusative because it agrees with Μενέλαον. It is possible to understand the παρακομίζοντα in apposition to Μενέλαον ("Menelaus . . . who carried money to the king"). However, the telic sense of the present participle is suggested by four factors. First, the participle follows the main verb (ἀπέστειλεν), which is characteristic of telic participles (Wallace, 636). Second, participles following a verb of sending are often telic (Smyth §2065). Third, the present participle is parallel with the future participle τελέσοντα, which must be understood telically (Wallace, 635). Fourth, the rarity of the future form of παρακομίζω (only 2 uses attested in the TLG) suggests that the epitomizer employed the present as a replacement form. On circumstantial participles in oblique cases, see 3:27 on πεσόντα.

τὰ χρήματα. Accusative direct object of παρακομίζοντα. This refers to the money promised in 4:8-9.

τῷ βασιλεῖ. Dative indirect object of παρακομίζοντα.

περὶ πραγμάτων ἀναγκαίων. Reference.

ὑπομνηματισμοὺς. Accusative direct object of τελέσοντα. Finding the reading of R-H and Göttingen too difficult, Habicht (220) prefers the reading of MSS V 542: χρηματισμους ("negotiations, decrees"). This would suggest that Menelaus went back to Antiochus and completed "negotiations." But the reading printed in the Göttingen edition and R-H is better, assuming with D. Schwartz (231) that "[t]he nature of [the records] did not, evidently, interest our author, who likes to give us the impression that he knows more than he tells and thus avoids wasting our time." On the meaning of ὑπομνηματισμός, see 2:13 on ἐν τοῖς ὑπομνηματισμοῖς.

τελέσοντα. Fut act ptc acc masc sg τελέω (purpose). Future participles almost always denote purpose (cf. Muraoka §28gia).

**4:24 ὁ δὲ συσταθεὶς τῷ βασιλεῖ καὶ δοξάσας αὐτὸν τῷ προσώπῳ τῆς
ἐξουσίας εἰς ἑαυτὸν κατήντησεν τὴν ἀρχιερωσύνην ὑπερβαλὼν τὸν
Ἰάσωνα τάλαντα ἀργυρίου τριακόσια.**

ὁ δὲ. The article functions as the nominative subject of κατήντησεν
and refers to Menelaus. See 3:7 on ὁ δέ.

συσταθεὶς. Aor pass ptc nom masc sg συνίστημι (temporal). On the
meaning of the verb, see BDAG (972.2): "to bring together as friends
or in a trusting relationship by commending/recommending, *present,
introduce/recommend someone to someone else.*"

τῷ βασιλεῖ. Dative indirect object συσταθείς.

δοξάσας. Aor act ptc nom masc sg δοξάζω (temporal). It is tempting to take this participle as an example of attendant circumstance with
κατήντησεν (i.e., "honored . . . and secured"), but the καί that precedes
it suggests it should be construed similarly to συσταθείς.

αὐτὸν. Accusative direct object of δοξάσας. If αὐτόν is understood
as a third person pronoun (i.e., "praising *him*") the referent could be the
king, Philometor (4:21, 24). Less likely, if it is understood as a reflexive
pronoun (i.e., "praising *himself*") then the referent would be Menelaus
(4:23). Later traditions of 2 Maccabees clearly reflect his ambiguity.
Latin versions have Menelaus extolling the king whereas Syriac versions
opt for the reflexive understanding (cf. Goldstein, 236).

τῷ προσώπῳ. Dative of manner.

τῆς ἐξουσίας. Genitive of identification (BDAG, 888.4), qualifying
τῷ προσώπῳ.

εἰς ἑαυτὸν. Advantage.

κατήντησεν. Aor act ind 3rd sg καταντάω. While καταντάω is typically intransitive (cf. 4:21, 44; 6:14) and has a meaning like "to arrive,
reach" (*GE*, 1067), here the transitive use means something like "to
obtain" (*GE*, 1067).

τὴν ἀρχιερωσύνην. Accusative direct object of κατήντησεν.

ὑπερβαλών. Aor act ptc nom masc sg ὑπερβάλλω (manner). From
the basic sense of ὑπερβάλλω as "to throw beyond, overshoot, outstrip,
pass, surpass" (*GE*, 2197) derives the specific connotation of "outbid" in
this context.

τὸν Ἰάσωνα. Accusative direct object of ὑπερβαλών.·

τάλαντα . . . τριακόσια. Accusative of measure. Although Muraoka
(§60b) translates this clause as "outbidding Jason *with* 300 talents of silver," this language might imply that Menelaus paid *only* 300 talents of

silver. But, based on 4:7-8, this cannot be the case. Jason paid 360 talents of silver plus another 80 talents. So, for Menelaus to "outbid" Jason, he would need to pay *more* than Jason. Accordingly, the translation "surpassing Jason *by* three hundred talents of silver" (cf. NETS) is preferred.

ἀργυρίου. Genitive of material (cf. *CGCG* §30.28).

4:25 λαβὼν δὲ τὰς βασιλικὰς ἐντολὰς παρεγένετο τῆς μὲν ἀρχιερωσύνης οὐδὲν ἄξιον φέρων, θυμοὺς δὲ ὠμοῦ τυράννου καὶ θηρὸς βαρβάρου ὀργὰς ἔχων.

λαβὼν. Aor act ptc nom masc sg λαμβάνω (temporal).

δὲ. Development; see 1:10 on δέ.

τὰς βασιλικὰς ἐντολὰς. Accusative direct object of λαβὼν. Cf. 3:13 for a similar expression about "royal commands."

παρεγένετο. Aor mid ind 3rd sg παραγίνομαι.

μὲν . . . δὲ. Point/counterpoint set. See 2:26 on μὲν . . . δέ.

τῆς . . . ἀρχιερωσύνης. Genitive complement of ἄξιον.

οὐδὲν ἄξιον. Accusative direct object of φέρων.

φέρων. Pres act ptc nom masc sg φέρω (manner).

θυμοὺς. Accusative direct object of φέρων. Rather than the singular, the plural is used because the sense is "categorical" or "general" (Wallace, 403; Smyth §1000–1012).

ὠμοῦ τυράννου. Subjective genitive, qualifying θυμούς. D. Schwartz (232) notes that τύραννος is used as "a pejorative term for a lone ruler." Cf. 7:27.

θηρὸς βαρβάρου. Subjective genitive, qualifying ὀργάς.

ὀργὰς. Accusative direct object of ἔχων. *GELS* (504) notes that ὀργή carries "no moral connotation." On the plural, see comments earlier on θυμούς.

ἔχων. Pres act ptc nom masc sg ἔχω (manner).

4:26 καὶ ὁ μὲν Ἰάσων ὁ τὸν ἴδιον ἀδελφὸν ὑπονοθεύσας ὑπονοθευθεὶς ὑφ᾽ ἑτέρου φυγὰς εἰς τὴν Ἀμμανῖτιν χώραν συνήλαστο.

ὁ . . . Ἰάσων. Nominative subject of συνήλαστο.

μὲν . . . δὲ. Point/counterpoint set. See 2:26 on μὲν . . . δέ. The set is completed in 4:27, connecting the actions of Jason and Menelaus more closely.

ὁ . . . ὑπονοθεύσας. Aor act ptc nom masc sg ὑπονοθεύω (attributive, modifying ὁ . . . Ἰάσων). On the meaning of the verb, see 4:7 on ὑπενόθευσεν. The separation of the article from the participle is an example of hyperbaton.

τὸν ἴδιον ἀδελφὸν. Accusative direct object of ὁ ὑπονοθεύσας.

ὑπονοθευθεὶς. Aor pass ptc nom masc sg ὑπονοθεύω (attendant circumstance). The use of ὑπονοθεύσας ὑπονοθευθεὶς is an example of paronomasia, highlighting the justice of Jason's exodus and resonating with the larger theme of "just deserts" (cf. Doran 1981, 92–94).

ὑφ᾽ ἑτέρου. Agency.

φυγὰς. Adverbial accusative of manner, modifying συνήλαστο.

εἰς τὴν Ἀμμανῖτιν χώραν. Locative. See 1:1 on ἐν τῇ χώρᾳ.

συνήλαστο. Plprf mid or pass ind 3rd sg συνελαύνω. Although the verb may be middle, the passive form is suggested by use of a passive participle that modifies this verb. On the meaning of the verb, see *GELS* (655): "*to force to move away* into an undesirable situation." *EDG* (401–2) notes that in the perfect, (συν-)ἐλαύνω is sometimes formed by -ασμαι, which would account for the *sigma* present in this form. Technically the morphology is "a secondary formation" related to ἐλαστρέω. Cf. the same verb in 4:42; 5:5.

4:27 ὁ δὲ Μενέλαος τῆς μὲν ἀρχῆς ἐκράτει, τῶν δὲ ἐπηγγελμένων τῷ βασιλεῖ χρημάτων οὐδὲν εὐτάκτει·

ὁ ... Μενέλαος. Nominative subject of ἐκράτει. Having established the subject, Μενέλαος, in 4:23, the subsequent references in 2 Maccabees 4–5 are articular, indicating anaphoric use of the article.

μὲν ... δὲ. See 4:26.

τῆς ... ἀρχῆς. Genitive complement of ἐκράτει.

μὲν ... δὲ. Point/counterpoint set. The epitomizer constructs this set within another μὲν ... δέ set that spans from 4:26 to 4:27. See 2:26 on μὲν ... δέ.

ἐκράτει. Impf act ind 3rd sg κρατέω. Verbs of touching often take the genitive case for the direct object, as here (BDF §170; Wallace, 131). Doran (2012, 115) notes the similar sounding verbs (ἐκράτει, εὐτάκτει) is an example of parachesis.

τῶν ... ἐπηγγελμένων ... χρημάτων. Partitive genitive, modifying οὐδέν.

ἐπηγγελμένων. Prf pass ptc gen neut pl ἐπαγγέλλομαι (attributive).

τῷ βασιλεῖ. Dative indirect object of ἐπηγγελμένων.

οὐδὲν. Accusative direct object of εὐτάκτει.

εὐτάκτει. Impf act ind 3rd sg εὐτακτέω. On the meaning of the verb, see *GE* (869): "to pay regularly."

4:28 ποιουμένου δὲ τὴν ἀπαίτησιν Σωστράτου τοῦ τῆς ἀκροπόλεως ἐπάρχου, πρὸς τοῦτον γὰρ ἦν ἡ τῶν διαφόρων πρᾶξις· δι᾽ ἣν αἰτίαν οἱ δύο ὑπὸ τοῦ βασιλέως προσεκλήθησαν,

ποιουμένου δὲ τὴν ἀπαίτησιν Σωστράτου τοῦ τῆς ἀκροπόλεως ἐπάρχου. As punctuated in Göttingen and R-H, the clause that begins 4:28 is ungrammatical. Several solutions have been proposed for this problem, including changing the particle δέ to δή (Katz 1960, 13) or deleting δέ altogether (Habicht, 220). The simplest (and best) solution is to re-punctuate the text, reading the genitive absolute clause in relation to 4:27 rather than 4:28 (cf. Doran 2012, 112; Coetzer, 68).

ποιουμένου. Pres mid ptc gen masc sg ποιέω (genitive absolute; temporal or, better, concessive). When the middle of ποιέω is used with a verbal noun (ἀπαίτησιν), this can be a periphrasis for the verb itself: ἀπαιτέω (*GELS*, 570.II). See 1:23 on ἐποιήσαντο. On the genitive absolute, see 1:7 on βασιλεύοντος.

δὲ. Development, see 1:10 on δέ.

τὴν ἀπαίτησιν. Accusative direct object of ποιουμένου.

Σωστράτου. Genitive subject of the participle ποιουμένου.

τοῦ . . . ἐπάρχου. Genitive in apposition to Σωστράτου.

τῆς ἀκροπόλεως. Genitive of subordination ("commander *over the acropolis*").

πρὸς τοῦτον. The PP provides the functional equivalent of an indirect object of ἦν. However, *GELS* (591.III.17) suggests that here πρός "marks an entity to which [something] properly belongs: 'the collection of monies was up to him.'"

γὰρ. Explanatory, providing an explanation for why Sostratus was making demands. See 1:12 on γάρ.

ἦν. Impf act ind 3rd sg εἰμί. See *GELS* (193): "to belong to, be had by."

ἡ . . . πρᾶξις. Nominative subject of ἦν. *GE* (1734) notes the use of this term to denote the "collection, levy" of payments, tribute, fines, etc.

τῶν διαφόρων. Genitive of apposition. As noted in 1:35, διάφορα was used by Hellenistic authors to refer to "a large sum of money" (*GE*, 517). Here it likely that the sense of διάφορα from 3:6 is more likely: "the job of [collecting] the discrepancies" (ἡ τῶν διαφόρων πρᾶξις).

δι᾽ ἣν αἰτίαν. Cause. This is an internally headed relative clause, wherein the noun that the relative clause modifies (αἰτίαν) appears within the relative clause. BDAG (31.1) notes that αἰτία refers to "that which is responsible for a condition, *cause, reason*." See 4:35, 42, 49; 8:26 for an identical phrase.

οἱ δύο. Nominative subject of προσεκλήθησαν.

ὑπὸ τοῦ βασιλέως. Agency.

προσεκλήθησαν. Aor pass ind 3rd pl προσκαλέομαι. On the meaning of the verb, see *GELS* (595): "to summon (for an interview)."

4:29 καὶ ὁ μὲν Μενέλαος ἀπέλιπεν τῆς ἀρχιερωσύνης διάδοχον Λυσίμαχον τὸν ἑαυτοῦ ἀδελφόν, Σώστρατος δὲ Κράτητα τὸν ἐπὶ τῶν Κυπρίων.

ὁ . . . Μενέλαος. Nominative subject of ἀπέλιπεν. On the article, see 4:27.

μὲν . . . δὲ. Point/counterpoint set. See 2:25 on μὲν . . . δέ.

ἀπέλιπεν. Aor act ind 3rd sg ἀπολείπω. *GELS* (78) notes that the verb denotes "not taking along with one and to take care of matters during one's temporary absence." Cf. 13:23.

τῆς ἀρχιερωσύνης. Genitive of apposition, qualifying διάδοχον.

διάδοχον. Complement in an object-complement double accusative construction. The meaning of διάδοχος is "substitute," in the sense of someone who "stands in for Menelaus in his absence" (D. Schwartz, 233; cf. Goldstein, 237; *GE*, 485.A). For example, Josephus (*Ant.* 12.237-38) recounts that Onias' brother Jesus was supposed to replace Onias when he died rather than Onias' infant son.

Λυσίμαχον. Accusative direct object of ἀπέλιπεν in an object-complement double accusative construction.

τὸν . . . ἀδελφόν. Accusative in apposition to Λυσίμαχον.

ἑαυτοῦ. Genitive of relationship.

Σώστρατος. Nominative subject of an implied form of ἀπέλιπεν.

Κράτητα. Accusative direct object of an implied form of ἀπέλιπεν in an object-complement double accusative construction.

τὸν. The article agrees with διάδοχον and resumes it. Complement in an object-complement double accusative construction.

ἐπὶ τῶν Κυπρίων. Subordination. According to BDAG (365.9), ἐπί can function as a "marker of power, authority, control of or over someone or someth[ing]."

2 Maccabees 4:30-38

[30]Now as these things were going on, it came about that the Tarsians and Mallotians revolted because they had been given as a gift to Antiochus, the concubine of the king. [31]Therefore, the king went quickly in order to settle the matters and he left Andronicus, one from those seated in honor, as a substitute. [32]But Menelaus, thinking that he had seized an opportune moment, stole some golden vessels from those of

the temple and gave [them] to Andronicus. And he happened to sell others to both Tyre and the surrounding cities. ³³Recognizing also these things fully, Onias disputed [them], having withdrawn to an inviolable place at Daphne, which is situated near Antioch. ³⁴Therefore Menelaus, taking Andronicus aside, encouraged [him] to subdue Onias. So he, after approaching Onias and persuading [him] with deception and greeting [him] warmly with oaths, giving [him] his right hand—even though he remained suspicious—he convinced [him] to come out of the sanctuary, and immediately he imprisoned [him], having no respect for what is just. ³⁵For this reason, not only the Jews but also many from other nations were indignant and angry because of the unjust murder of the man. ³⁶After the king returned from the regions around Cilicia, the Jews throughout the city—the Greeks also shared in the hatred of evil—appealed [to the king] concerning the unreasonable murder of Onias. ³⁷Therefore Antiochus, who was deeply disturbed and moved to compassion and weeping because of the moderation and good conduct of those who died, ³⁸and burning with rage, stripping off the purple robe of Andronicus and rending his undergarments, he was leading [him] through the whole city to the very spot where he acted impiously toward Onias. There he killed the murderer, the Lord repaid him a worthy punishment.

4:30 Τοιούτων δὲ συνεστηκότων συνέβη Ταρσεῖς καὶ Μαλλώτας στασιάζειν διὰ τὸ Ἀντιοχίδι τῇ παλλακῇ τοῦ βασιλέως ἐν δωρεᾷ δεδόσθαι.

Τοιούτων. Genitive subject of the participle συνεστηκότων.

δὲ. Development; see 1:10 on δέ.

συνεστηκότων. Prf act ptc gen neut pl συνίστημι (genitive absolute, temporal). On the meaning of the verb, see *GELS* (658.II.7; cf. *GE*, 2046.2.A): "to come into existence" = "as these things were going on." On the genitive absolute, see 1:7 on βασιλεύοντος.

συνέβη. Aor act ind 3rd sg συμβαίνω. See 3:2 on συνέβαινεν.

Ταρσεῖς καὶ Μαλλώτας. Accusative subjects of the infinitive στασιάζειν. The proper nouns denote "[people] of Tarsus" and "[people] of Mallos" (*GE*, 2084, 1277), thus the translation "Tarsians and Mallotians" (cf. D. Schwartz, 234).

στασιάζειν. Pres act inf στασιάζω (indirect discourse). See *GE* (1952): "*in politics* to form a party *or* faction, be at odds, *or* in conflict, fight, rebel, *in the state, in the city.*"

Ἀντιοχίδι. Dative indirect object of δεδόσθαι. On royal concubines in general, see Strabo, *Geog.* 13.4.3 and Josephus, *Ag. Ap.* 2.55.

τῇ παλλακῇ. Dative in apposition to Ἀντιοχίδι.

τοῦ βασιλέως. Possessive genitive.

ἐν δωρεᾷ. Manner. The PP functions "as an auxiliary in periphrasis for adverbs" (BDAG, 330.11).

δεδόσθαι. Prf pass inf δίδωμι. The preposition διὰ τό + infinitive is used to indicate cause. The neuter article τό indicates the case of βεβρῶσθαι (Burk 27–46). The separation between διὰ τό and δεδόσθαι is an example of hyperbaton. The Göttingen edition prints διδόσθαι rather than δεδόσθαι (V L⁻⁵³⁴ 46-52 55 Tht.), which is difficult to distinguish in English.

4:31 θᾶττον οὖν ὁ βασιλεὺς ἦκεν καταστεῖλαι τὰ πράγματα καταλιπὼν τὸν διαδεχόμενον Ἀνδρόνικον τῶν ἐν ἀξιώματι κειμένων.

θᾶττον. Comparative adverb of ταχύς, modifying ἦκεν and denoting time.

οὖν. Resumptive, continuing the main narrative begun in 4:30. See 2:15 on οὖν.

ὁ βασιλεὺς. Nominative subject of ἦκεν.

ἦκεν. Impf act ind 3rd sg ἥκω.

καταστεῖλαι. Aor act inf καταστέλλω (purpose).

τὰ πράγματα. Accusative direct object of καταστεῖλαι. See 1:33 on τὸ πρᾶγμα.

καταλιπὼν. Aor act ptc nom masc sg καταλείπω (attendant circumstance).

τὸν διαδεχόμενον. Pres mid ptc acc masc sg διαδέχομαι (substantival). Complement in an object-complement double accusative construction. On the meaning of the verb, see the discussion of the cognate term διάδοχον in 4:29.

Ἀνδρόνικον. Accusative direct object of καταλιπών in an object-complement double accusative construction. Because the name Ἀνδρόνικος is being established in the narrative it is anarthrous (Smyth §1136; Muraoka §1b). Compare this use with the following articular uses of the name (4:32, 34, 38), where the article defines "[o]bjects already mentioned or in the mind of the speaker or writer" (Smyth §1120.b).

τῶν . . . κειμένων. Pres mid ptc gen masc pl κεῖμαι (substantival). Partitive genitive. Verbs expressing state or condition are typically middle (N. Miller, 430). The separation of the article from the participle is an example of hyperbaton. The placement of the PP between the article and its head clarifies that the PP modifies the participle.

ἐν ἀξιώματι. Locative.

4:32 νομίσας δὲ ὁ Μενέλαος εἰληφέναι καιρὸν εὐφυῆ χρυσώματά τινα τῶν τοῦ ἱεροῦ νοσφισάμενος ἐχαρίσατο τῷ Ἀνδρονίκῳ καὶ ἕτερα ἐτύγχανεν πεπρακὼς εἴς τε Τύρον καὶ τὰς κύκλῳ πόλεις.

νομίσας. Aor act ptc nom masc sg νομίζω (temporal or, perhaps, causal).

δὲ. Development; see 1:10 on δέ.

ὁ Μενέλαος. Nominative subject of ἐχαρίσατο. On the article, see 4:27.

εἰληφέναι. Prf act inf λαμβάνω (indirect discourse). The phrase εἰληφέναι καιρὸν εὐφυῆ serves as the object of νομίσας. Morphologically, because λαμβάνω begins with *lamda*, it undergoes vocalic reduplication (ει) rather than consonantal reduplication in the perfect. *MBG* (§31.2d) suggests the following explanation of the perfect stem: λαβ → ειλαβ → ειληβ → εἴληφα.

καιρὸν εὐφυῆ. Accusative direct object of εἰληφέναι. An "(opportune) moment" (*GELS*, 307).

χρυσώματά τινα. Accusative direct object of νοσφισάμενος. The noun χρυσώματα has a second acute accent because τινα, an enclitic, loses its accent to the preceding word (Smyth §181–82).

τῶν. The article resumes χρύσωμα without repeating it. Genitive of separation.

τοῦ ἱεροῦ. Possessive genitive.

νοσφισάμενος. Aor mid ptc nom masc sg νοσφίζω (attendant circumstance). On the meaning of the verb, see *GE* (1406.2): "to set aside for oneself, appropriate, steal."

ἐχαρίσατο. Aor mid ind 3rd sg χαρίζομαι.

τῷ Ἀνδρονίκῳ. Dative indirect object of ἐχαρίσατο. On the article, see 4:31 on Ἀνδρόνικον.

ἕτερα. Accusative direct object of πεπρακώς. The adjective is neuter because it agrees with χρυσώματα, indicating that Menelaus took "other [vessels]" from the temple.

ἐτύγχανεν. Impf act ind 3rd sg τυγχάνω. This verb is regularly complemented by another verb, often a participle (Muraoka §31e; *CGCG* §52.8).

πεπρακώς. Prf act ptc nom masc sg πιπράσκω (complementary).

εἴς τε Τύρον καὶ τὰς κύκλῳ πόλεις. Spatial. The preposition εἰς appears here with the accent because τέ, an enclitic particle, loses its accent to the preceding word (Smyth §181–82).

τε . . . καὶ. Correlative construction: "both . . . and." τε . . . καί connects words more closely than καί alone: "*both* Tyre *and* the surrounding cities" (BDF §444.2; BDAG, 933.2.c).

τὰς κύκλῳ πόλεις. The adverb is used like an attributive adjective (Muraoka §24b).

4:33 ἃ καὶ σαφῶς ἐπεγνωκὼς ὁ Ονιας ἀπήλεγχεν ἀποκεχωρηκὼς εἰς ἄσυλον τόπον ἐπὶ Δάφνης τῆς πρὸς Ἀντιόχειαν κειμένης.

ἃ. Accusative direct object of ἐπεγνωκώς. The relative pronoun should be rendered as a demonstrative ("these things") and points backward in 4:32.

καὶ. Adverbial.

σαφῶς. Adverb of degree, portraying the conscientiousness of Onias (cf. Grimm, 92).

ἐπεγνωκὼς. Prf act ptc nom masc sg ἐπιγινώσκω (temporal).

ὁ Ονιας. Nominative subject of ἀπήλεγχεν. Onias has not been mentioned since 4:7, which may suggest that some of the source material available to the epitomizer was lost (cf. D. Schwartz, 236).

ἀπήλεγχεν. Impf act ind 3rd sg ἀπελέγχω.

ἀποκεχωρηκὼς. Prf act ptc nom masc sg ἀποχωρέω (temporal). On the meaning of the verb, see BDAG (125): "to move away from a point, go away."

εἰς ἄσυλον τόπον. Spatial. The unusual reference to "an inviolable place" suggests the discomfort of stating that Onias went to a pagan temple (of Apollo). D. Schwartz (236) notes that "the author [of 2 Maccabees] did not want to pass up using the story, because the juicy combination of asylum violation and murder was too good to refuse." GE (324) notes that εἰς ἄσυλον τόπον = "refuge, sanctuary."

ἐπὶ Δάφνης. Locative. According to Strabo (Geog. 16.2.6), there was a famous temple of Apollo at Daphne and this is likely the place of refuge.

τῆς . . . κειμένης. Pres mid ptc gen fem sg κεῖμαι (substantival). Genitive of apposition.

πρὸς Ἀντιόχειαν. Spatial, denoting close proximity (BDAG, 875.3.g; GELS, 591.III.14).

4:34 ὅθεν ὁ Μενέλαος λαβὼν ἰδίᾳ τὸν Ἀνδρόνικον παρεκάλει χειρώσασθαι τὸν Ονιαν· ὁ δὲ παραγενόμενος ἐπὶ τὸν Ονιαν καὶ πεισθεὶς ἐπὶ δόλῳ καὶ δεξιασθεὶς μεθ᾽ ὅρκων δοὺς δεξιάν, καίπερ ἐν ὑποψίᾳ κείμενος, ἔπεισεν ἐκ τοῦ ἀσύλου προελθεῖν, ὃν καὶ παρα-χρῆμα παρέκλεισεν οὐκ αἰδεσθεὶς τὸ δίκαιον.

ὅθεν. Introduces an inferential clause. Cf. 4:21.

ὁ Μενέλαος. Nominative subject of παρεκάλει. On the article, see 4:27.

λαβὼν ἰδίᾳ τὸν Ἀνδρόνικον. An idiomatic expression: "taking Andronicus aside."

λαβών. Aor act ptc nom masc sg λαμβάνω (temporal).

ἰδίᾳ. Adverb of ἴδιος, referring to "by oneself." See 4:5.

τὸν Ἀνδρόνικον. Accusative direct object of λαβών. On the article, see 4:31 on Ἀνδρόνικον.

παρεκάλει. Impf act ind 3rd sg παρακαλέω.

χειρώσασθαι. Aor mid inf χειρόω (indirect discourse). On the meaning of the verb, see *GE* (2352): "to subdue, bring into one's power, master, conquer." Here NETS translates as "to kill," which is probably a correct contextual inference. The epitomizer uses multiple euphemisms for killing in this chapter: χειρόω (4:36), παρακλείω (4:34), ἀποκοσμέω (4:38).

τὸν Ονιαν. Accusative direct object of χειρώσασθαι.

ὁ δὲ. The article functions as the nominative subject of ἔπεισεν and refers to Andronicus. See 3:7 on ὁ δέ.

παραγενόμενος. Aor mid ptc nom masc sg παραγίνομαι (temporal). See 3:9 on παραγενηθείς. For an alternative understanding of the sentence, see Habicht (221), who assumes the entire sentence is corrupt.

ἐπὶ τὸν Ονιαν. Locative.

πεισθείς. Aor pass ptc nom masc sg πείθω (manner). The regularity of the collocation πείθω + ἐπί (e.g., 7:40; 1 Macc 10:71; 10:77; etc.) is strong evidence that the sense of "trust in," or "be confident in" is implied here. A possible translation of the collocation would be "trusting in [his] guile" = "persuading [him] with guile" (cf. Goldstein, 240).

ἐπὶ δόλῳ. Cause or, following the previous note, locative: where πείθω + dative (person or thing) denotes what someone depends on or trusts in (BDAG, 792.2.a).

δεξιασθείς. Aor pass ptc nom masc sg δεξιάζω (manner). The meaning of δεξιάζω is clarified by the expression δίδωμι δεξιάν: "to greet with the right hand" (*GELS*, 143). The various textual variants listed in the Göttingen edition are probably due to the rarity of this word. According to the *TLG*, this is only extant use of δεξιάζω.

μεθ᾽ ὅρκων. Manner. It is possible to take ὅρκων as a "categorical plural" (cf. MHT 3:25-26) and render it in the singular: "with an oath" (Zeitlin and Tedesche, 139).

δούς. Aor act ptc nom masc sg δίδωμι (manner).

δεξιάν. Accusative direct object of δούς. Used as a substantive for "*right* hand," denoting a "pledge" (*GE*, 466). In expressions of "giving the *right* [hand]," the word χείρ is often omitted (cf. MHT 3:17). BDAG (217.1.b) notes that "The pl[ural] δεξιαί is used in Hom[er] of pledges given in good faith with the right hand" (cf. *Il.* 2.341; 4.159).

καίπερ. Concessive conjunction, clarifying or marking the concessive force of the participle (BDF §425.1; Muraoka §31dg; §72i.viii).

ἐν ὑποψίᾳ. Locative, in a metaphorical sense. This rare term refers to "suspicion" (*GE*, 2240).

κείμενος. Pres pass ptc nom masc sg κεῖμαι (concessive). See καίπερ above.

ἔπεισεν. Aor act ind 3rd sg πείθω.

ἐκ τοῦ ἀσύλου. Separation. Compare with εἰς ἄσυλον τόπον in 4:34.

προελθεῖν. Aor act inf προέρχομαι (complementary).

ὅν. Accusative direct object of παρέκλεισεν.

παραχρῆμα. Adverb, with the sense of "on the spot, forthwith" (*GELS*, 532). Cf. 4:38; 5:18; 7:4; 10:22; 11:36.

παρέκλεισεν. Aor act ind 3rd sg παρακλείω. Strictly speaking, παρακλείω means "to shut up, imprison" (*GE*, 1552). However, in context it seems clear that death is implied, suggesting that παρακλείω is a euphemism. Thus, some Latin versions of 2 Maccabees translate the verb with *peremit* (from *perimō*, "to take away entirely, destroy"). See discussion in Habicht (221) and Goldstein (240).

οὐκ. On the negation οὐ with a participle, see 4:5 on οὐ.

αἰδεσθείς. Aor pass ptc nom masc sg αἰδέομαι (manner or, perhaps, causal).

τὸ δίκαιον. Accusative direct object of αἰδεσθείς.

4:35 δι᾽ ἣν αἰτίαν οὐ μόνον Ἰουδαῖοι, πολλοὶ δὲ καὶ τῶν ἄλλων ἐθνῶν ἐδείναζον καὶ ἐδυσφόρουν ἐπὶ τῷ τοῦ ἀνδρὸς ἀδίκῳ φόνῳ.

δι᾽ ἣν αἰτίαν. Cause. See 4:28 on δι᾽ ἣν αἰτίαν.

οὐ μόνον ... δὲ καί. "Not only ... but also." The expression is less severe than the more common οὐ μόνον ... ἀλλὰ καί.

Ἰουδαῖοι. Nominative subject of an implied ἐδείναζον. In the οὐ μόνον ... δὲ καί construction, ellipsis of the verb is common.

πολλοί. Nominative subject of ἐδείναζον.

τῶν ἄλλων ἐθνῶν. Partitive genitive. It is significant that gentiles joined with Jews in outrage over this event.

ἐδείναζον. Impf act ind 3rd pl δεινάζω. The rare verb δεινάζω is probably derived from δεινός (lit. "dreadful") and, following the Old Latin versions of 2 Maccabees, is rendered something like "to be indignant" (Latin: *indignor*).

ἐδυσφόρουν. Impf act ind 3rd pl δυσφορέω.

ἐπὶ τῷ ... ἀδίκῳ φόνῳ. Cause.

τοῦ ἀνδρὸς. Objective genitive.

4:36 τοῦ δὲ βασιλέως ἐπανελθόντος ἀπὸ τῶν κατὰ Κιλικίαν τόπων ἐνετύγχανον οἱ κατὰ πόλιν Ιουδαῖοι συμμισοπονηρούντων καὶ τῶν Ἑλλήνων ὑπὲρ τοῦ παρὰ λόγον τὸν Ονιαν ἀπεκτονῆσθαι.

τοῦ . . . βασιλέως. Genitive subject of the participle ἐπανελθόντος.

δὲ. Development, marking a change of grammatical subject from 4:35. See 1:10 on δέ.

ἐπανελθόντος. Aor act ptc gen masc sg ἐπανέρχομαι (genitive absolute, temporal). On the genitive absolute, see 1:7 on βασιλεύοντος.

ἀπὸ τῶν . . . τόπων. Separation.

κατὰ Κιλικίαν. Locative.

ἐνετύγχανον. Impf act ind 3rd pl ἐντυγχάνω. On the meaning of the verb, see BDAG (341.1.a): "approach or appeal to someone."

οἱ . . . Ιουδαῖοι. Nominative subject of ἐνετύγχανον. On the meaning of Ιουδαίος, see 1:1 on Τοῖς ἀδελφοῖς τοῖς . . . Ιουδαίοις.

κατὰ πόλιν. Locative ("*in* the city") or, more precisely, extension ("*throughout* the city"; see Smyth §1690). On the syntax of the PP, see 1:1 on κατ᾽ Αἴγυπτον.

συμμισοπονηρούντων. Pres act ptc gen masc pl συμμισοπονηρέω (genitive absolute, temporal). On the meaning of the verb, see *GE* (2003): "to share in execrating" = "[the Greeks also] shared in the hatred of evil." D. Schwartz (238) observes that hatred of evil is a repeated theme in 2 Maccabees (cf. 3:1; 4:49; 8:4). On the genitive absolute, see 1:7 on βασιλεύοντος.

καὶ. Adverbial.

τῶν Ἑλλήνων. Genitive subject of the participle συμμισοπονηρούντων. See BDAG (318.2.a): "in the broader sense, all persons who came under the influence of Greek, as distinguished from Israel's culture."

ὑπὲρ τοῦ παρὰ λόγον τὸν Ονιαν ἀπεκτονῆσθαι. Reference.

ἀπεκτονῆσθαι. Aor mid inf ἀποκτείνω (indirect discourse). Used with ὑπὲρ τοῦ after a verb of speaking. When an articular infinitive takes a case other than the accusative for its object, it is not uncommon to sandwich the object between the article and the infinitive (Muraoka §30abc).

παρὰ λόγον. Opposition. *GELS* (434) notes that λόγος here denotes "reasonable expectation based on calculation and consideration." Polybius (*Hist.* 2.38.5) contrasts κατὰ λόγον with παρὰ λόγον, suggesting that παρὰ λόγον means "unreasonable." Thus, D. Schwartz (238) notes that "the murder violates not only 'justice' (δίκη) but also logic (λόγος)."

τὸν Ονιαν. Accusative direct object of ἀπεκτονῆσθαι.

4:37 ψυχικῶς οὖν ὁ Ἀντίοχος ἐπιλυπηθεὶς καὶ τραπεὶς ἐπὶ ἔλεος καὶ δακρύσας διὰ τὴν τοῦ μετηλλαχότος σωφροσύνην καὶ πολλὴν εὐταξίαν,

ψυχικῶς. Adverb of manner.

οὖν. Inferential. See 2:15 on οὖν.

ὁ Ἀντίοχος. Nominative subject of ἠσέβησεν (4:38) and, therefore, of all the nominative singular participles in 4:37 (ἐπιλυπηθείς, τραπείς, δακρύσας).

ἐπιλυπηθεὶς. Aor pass ptc nom masc sg ἐπιλυπέω (attributive, modifying ὁ Ἀντίοχος). Domazakis (179) notes that "ἐπιλυπέω has the emotive sense that the simplex λυπέω commonly bears." On the meaning of the verb, see *GE* (776): "to be disturbed."

τραπεὶς. Aor pass ptc nom masc sg τρέπω (attributive, modifying ὁ Ἀντίοχος).

ἐπὶ ἔλεος. Spatial.

δακρύσας. Aor act ptc nom masc sg δακρύω (attributive, modifying ὁ Ἀντίοχος).

διὰ τὴν . . . σωφροσύνην καὶ πολλὴν εὐταξίαν. Cause. The adjective πολύς denotes "large, strong, powerful . . . *of value or esteem*" (*GE*, 1713). Goldstein (241) notes that "'[u]pright character' . . . and 'orderly life' . . . are cardinal virtues for a citizen or subject of a Greek state."

τοῦ μετηλλαχότος. Prf act ptc gen masc sg μεταλλάσσω (substantival). Subjective genitive, qualifying πολλὴν εὐταξίαν. On the meaning of μεταλλάσσω, see 4:7 on μεταλλάξαντος.

4:38 καὶ πυρωθεὶς τοῖς θυμοῖς παραχρῆμα τὴν τοῦ Ἀνδρονίκου πορφύραν περιελόμενος καὶ τοὺς χιτῶνας περιρρήξας περιαγαγὼν καθ᾽ ὅλην τὴν πόλιν ἐπ᾽ αὐτὸν τὸν τόπον, οὗπερ τὸν Ονιαν ἠσέβησεν, ἐκεῖ τὸν μιαιφόνον ἀπεκόσμησεν τοῦ κυρίου τὴν ἀξίαν αὐτῷ κόλασιν ἀποδόντος.

πυρωθεὶς. Aor pass ptc nom masc sg πυρόω (manner or, perhaps, causal). It is best to take πυρωθείς with περιελόμενος and περιρρήξας.

τοῖς θυμοῖς. Dative of manner. The plural indicates either a large quantity or wide range of emotions (Muraoka §21b).

παραχρῆμα. Temporal adverb.

τὴν . . . πορφύραν. Accusative direct object of περιελόμενος. Denotes a "robe made of purple fabric . . . worn by dignitaries" (*GELS*, 579). The action of removing his clothing effectively strips of his rank and prepares him to be executed (cf. Goldstein, 241).

τοῦ Ἀνδρονίκου. Possessive genitive. On the article, see 4:31 on Ἀνδρόνικον.

περιελόμενος. Aor mid ptc nom masc sg περιαιρέω (temporal, in relation to περιαγαγών).

τοὺς χιτῶνας. Accusative direct object of περιρρήξας. Denotes "a garment worn next to the skin" = "undergarments" (BDAG, 1085).

περιρρήξας. Aor act ptc nom masc sg περιρρήγνυμι (temporal, in relation to περιαγαγών).

περιαγαγών. Aor act ptc nom masc sg περιάγω (attendant circumstance).

καθ᾽ ὅλην τὴν πόλιν. Extension. On the use of ἡ πόλις rather than Ἱεροσόλυμα, see 2:22 on τὴν πόλιν.

ἐπ᾽ αὐτὸν τὸν τόπον. Locative. The use of αὐτός is identifying.

οὗπερ. Adverb of place: "to the very spot where" (GELS, 513). A common theme throughout 2 Maccabees is that enemies die in a way that corresponds to their persecution of the Jews (cf. 4:42; 8:33; 13:6-8). Thus, here, Andronicus dies "in the very spot where" he killed Onias.

τὸν Ονιαν. Accusative of reference.

ἠσέβησεν. Aor act ind 3rd sg ἀσεβέω.

ἐκεῖ. Adverb of place.

τὸν μιαιφόνον. Accusative direct object of ἀπεκόσμησεν. Adjective used as a substantive. Cf. 12:6.

ἀπεκόσμησεν. Aor act ind 3rd sg ἀποκοσμέω. On the meaning of the verb, see GE (254): "to eliminate from the world, kill." The word is not well-attested prior to 2 Maccabees, but the basic sense in context is clear because of the direct object.

τοῦ κυρίου. Genitive subject of the participle ἀποδόντος. The epitomizer assumes that "kings of this world are only tools" used by God (D. Schwartz, 239).

τὴν ἀξίαν... κόλασιν. Accusative direct object of ἀποδόντος. The meaning of ἄξιος is "worthy" in the sense of "accurately corresponding, comparable" (GELS, 61.1). In context, Andronicus' "worthy punishment" refers to his death which is only fitting because he himself killed (cf. 4:34).

αὐτῷ. Dative indirect object of ἀποδόντος.

ἀποδόντος. Aor act ptc gen masc sg ἀποδίδωμι (genitive absolute; result or, perhaps, epexegetical). Less typically, the genitive absolute construction follows the main verb (cf. 4:39; 7:4; Gen 23:10; 48:7; Exod 19:9; Job 6:17). Because participles that denote result typically follow the main verb (Wallace, 637), this may explain why the genitive participle follows ἀπεκόσμησεν. On the genitive absolute, see 1:7 on βασιλεύοντος.

2 Maccabees 4:39-42

[39]Now because many sacrilegious acts were committed against the city by Lysimachus with the knowledge of Menelaus and because the news spread outside, a multitude gathered together against Lysimachus, because many gold vessels had already been carried off [from the temple]. [40]When the crowds were becoming excited and filled with rage, Lysimahcus armed about three thousand [men] and began an unjust attack. A certain Auranus led the way, although he was advancing in years and no less [advancing] in folly. [41]But, knowing also about the attack of Lysimachus, some took up stones, some blocks of wood, and some out of the ashes at hand, and they were throwing [them] in utter confusion at those around Lysimachus. [42]For this reason, they wounded many of them and they even killed some. They forced everyone to flee and they killed the temple robber himself near the treasury.

4:39 Γενομένων δὲ πολλῶν ἱεροσυλημάτων κατὰ τὴν πόλιν ὑπὸ τοῦ Λυσιμάχου μετὰ τῆς τοῦ Μενελάου γνώμης καὶ διαδοθείσης ἔξω τῆς φήμης ἐπισυνήχθη τὸ πλῆθος ἐπὶ τὸν Λυσίμαχον χρυσωμάτων ἤδη πολλῶν διενηνεγμένων.

Γενομένων. Aor mid ptc gen neut pl γίνομαι (genitive absolute; temporal or, perhaps, causal). Muraoka (§31hc) notes that 4:39 is an example of "multiple independent gen[itive] abs[olute] constructions dependent on one principle verb." On the genitive absolute, see 1:7 on βασιλεύοντος.

δὲ. Development; see 1:10 on δέ.

πολλῶν ἱεροσυλημάτων. Genitive subject of the participle Γενομένων. According to BDAG (471.2), ἱεροσυλέω means "to commit irreverent acts, commit sacrilege."

κατὰ τὴν πόλιν. Opposition. On the use of ἡ πόλις rather than Ἱεροσολύμα, see 2:22 on τὴν πόλιν.

ὑπὸ τοῦ Λυσιμάχου. Agency.

μετὰ τῆς . . . γνώμης. Association. *GELS* (452) notes the preposition may denote "*accompanied by*, indicating a trait, or an accompanying action which characterizes an action." Literally, "with the knowledge [of Menelaus]."

τοῦ Μενελάου. Subjective genitive.

διαδοθείσης. Aor pass ptc gen fem sg διαδίδωμι (genitive absolute; temporal or, perhaps, causal). See above on multiple genitive absolute constructions dependent on the same main verb. On the meaning of the verb, *GE* (485.2) suggests "to be propagated, spread," as a typical translation for the spread of rumors or news. On the genitive absolute, see 1:7 on βασιλεύοντος.

ἔξω. Adverb of place. After reference to the "city" (i.e., Jerusalem), ἔξω clearly refers to the countryside. See 1:1 on ἐν τῇ χώρᾳ.

τῆς φήμης. Genitive subject of the participle διαδοθείσης.

ἐπισυνήχθη. Aor pass ind 3rd sg ἐπισυνάγω.

τὸ πλῆθος. Nominative subject of ἐπισυνήχθη.

ἐπὶ τὸν Λυσίμαχον. Opposition.

χρυσωμάτων... πολλῶν. Genitive subject of the participle διενηνεγμένων.

ἤδη. Temporal adverb.

διενηνεγμένων. Prf pass ptc gen neut pl διαφέρω (genitive absolute, causal). The genitive absolute follows the main verb; see 4:38 on ἀποδόντος. D. Schwartz (240): "[t]he author is careful to make us understand that the situation was so bad that even law-abiding subjects of the crown could no longer be expected to retrain themselves." On the meaning of the verb, see 1:18 on ἀνήνεγκεν. See above on multiple genitive absolute constructions dependent on the same main verb. On the genitive absolute, see 1:7 on βασιλεύοντος.

4:40 ἐπεγειρομένων δὲ τῶν ὄχλων καὶ ταῖς ὀργαῖς διεμπιπλαμένων καθοπλίσας ὁ Λυσίμαχος πρὸς τρισχιλίους κατήρξατο χειρῶν ἀδίκων προηγησαμένου τινὸς Αυρανου προβεβηκότος τὴν ἡλικίαν, οὐδὲν δὲ ἧττον καὶ τὴν ἄνοιαν·

ἐπεγειρομένων. Pres mid ptc gen masc pl ἐπεγείρω (genitive absolute; temporal or, perhaps, causal). On the meaning of the verb, see *GELS* (261): "fig[urative], to arouse, awaken an emotion, sentiment." The verb occurs in the middle because it describes the emotional state of the crowd (cf. N. Miller, 428–29). On the genitive absolute, see 1:7 on βασιλεύοντος.

δὲ. Development; see 1:10 on δέ.

τῶν ὄχλων. Genitive subject of the participle ἐπεγειρομένων. Compared to πλῆθος, ὄχλος is a more neutral term and here it denotes the general populace of Jerusalem. See discussion in 3:21 on τοῦ πλήθους.

ταῖς ὀργαῖς. Dative of content (Wallace, 170; Muraoka §55b).

διεμπιπλαμένων. Pres mid ptc gen masc pl διεμπίμπλημι (genitive absolute; temporal or, perhaps, causal). This rare term means "to fill up, gorge" (*GE*, 524). On the genitive absolute, see 1:7 on βασιλεύοντος.

καθοπλίσας. Aor act ptc nom masc sg καθοπλίζω (attendant circumstance). A more intensive form of ὁπλίζω ("to get someth[ing] ready," or

"equip w[ith] someth[ing]," used frequently to describe military prepa-
rations) (BDAG, 716). Cf. the use of the verb in 15:11.

ὁ Λυσίμαχος. Nominative subject of κατήρξατο.

πρὸς τρισχιλίους. Refers to an approximate number: "*about* three
thousand" (*GELS*, 591.III.15). See Smyth (§347) on numbers.

κατήρξατο. Aor mid ind 3rd sg κατάρχω.

χειρῶν ἀδίκων. Genitive complement of κατήρξατο. Literally, "unjust
hands," which refers to "acts of violence" (*GE*, 2349.4.B). This sense use
of χείρ (cf. Homer, *Od.* 20.267; Aeschylus, *Eum.* 260) is clarified by the
description of Lysimachus' attack in 4:41. On (κατ-)ἄρχω with the genitive, see 2:32 on ἀρξώμεθα.

προηγησαμένου. Aor mid ptc gen masc sg προηγέομαι (genitive
absolute, means). On the meaning of the verb, see *GE* (1763): "to
guide, take the lead, go ahead." On the genitive absolute, see 1:7 on
βασιλεύοντος.

τινὸς Αὐρανου. Genitive subject of the participle προηγησαμένου.
See 3:4 on Σιμων . . . τις. Noting the possible Hasmonaean derivation
of this name, Goldstein (242) suggests that perhaps the epitomizer "is
suggesting that a kinsman of the Hasmonaeans was an ardent supporter
of Lysimachus."

προβεβηκότος. Prf act ptc gen masc sg προβαίνω (concessive).

τὴν ἡλικίαν. Accusative direct object of προβεβηκότος. See *GELS*
(319): "advanced in age."

οὐδὲν. Accusative of respect.

δὲ. Development; see 1:10 on δέ.

ἧττον. Nominative subject of implied form of προβαίνω. On the
morphology, 2 Maccabees uses the Attic form, which uses the ττ rather
than σσ (cf. BDF §34.1; Doran 1981, 26–27).

καὶ. Adverbial.

τὴν ἄνοιαν. Accusative direct object of implied form of προβαίνω.

4:41 συνιδόντες δὲ καὶ τὴν ἐπίθεσιν τοῦ Λυσιμάχου συναρπάσαντες οἱ
μὲν πέτρους, οἱ δὲ ξύλων πάχη, τινὲς δὲ ἐκ τῆς παρακειμένης σποδοῦ
δρασσόμενοι φύρδην ἐνετίνασσον εἰς τοὺς περὶ τὸν Λυσίμαχον·

συνιδόντες. Aor act ptc nom masc pl συνοράω (temporal or, less
likely, causal).

δὲ. Development; see 1:10 on δέ.

καὶ. Adverbial.

τὴν ἐπίθεσιν. Accusative direct object of συνιδόντες. See *GELS*
(272): "military assault."

τοῦ Λυσιμάχου. Subjective genitive.

συναρπάσαντες. Aor act ptc nom masc pl συναρπάζω (attendant circumstance). The participle has two accusative direct objects that modify it (πέτρους, πάχη).

οἱ... οἱ... τινὲς. Nominative subjects of ἐνετίνασσον: "some . . . some . . . others."

μὲν... δὲ... δὲ. Correlative, introducing a series: "some . . . others . . . [some] others." On the anticipatory sense of μέν, see 2:25.

πέτρους. Accusative direct object of συναρπάσαντες. On the use of stones as a weapon, see 1:16.

ξύλων. Genitive of material.

πάχη. Accusative direct object of συναρπάσαντες.

τινὲς. Unusual for τίς because of its "light communicative load" (Muraoka §9a), the plural τινές appears in the initial position of the clause (cf. 3:19).

ἐκ τῆς παρακειμένης σποδοῦ. Source ("*out of* the ashes at hand"), separation ("*away from* the ashes at hand"), or partitive. The choice to translate "ashes" rather than "dust" is supported by 13:8, which clearly uses σποδός for "ashes." The mention of "wood" and "ashes" may suggest that these were from the altar. If this is correct, the epitomizer's point is that the very implements of the temple were utilized to defend the temple. This underscores Menelaus' negative portrayal in 2 Maccabees and coheres with the description Menelaus' death in 13:8: "he had committed many sins against the altar whose fire and ashes were holy" (NETS) (cf. D. Schwartz, 241–42). Alternatively, Goldstein (242) suggests that the "unarmed mob had to improvise weapons from street rubbish."

παρακειμένης. Pres mid ptc gen fem sg παράκειμαι (attributive). Verbs of sitting are usually middle (N. Miller, 430).

δρασσόμενοι. Pres mid ptc nom masc pl δράσσομαι (attendant circumstance).

φύρδην. Adverb: "in utter confusion" (*GELS*, 724).

ἐνετίνασσον. Impf act ind 3rd pl ἐντινάσσω. Cf. the verb in 11:11. The imperfect (imperfective verbal aspect) portrays the event as incomplete or unfolding.

εἰς τοὺς περὶ τὸν Λυσίμαχον. Spatial.

τοὺς. The article functions as a nominalizer, changing the PP (περὶ τὸν Λυσίμαχον) into a substantive that functions as the object of a preposition.

περὶ τὸν Λυσίμαχον. Association. See 1:13 on περὶ αὐτόν.

4:42 δι' ἣν αἰτίαν πολλοὺς μὲν αὐτῶν τραυματίας ἐποίησαν, τινὰς δὲ καὶ κατέβαλον, πάντας δὲ εἰς φυγὴν συνήλασαν, αὐτὸν δὲ τὸν ἱερόσυλον παρὰ τὸ γαζοφυλάκιον ἐχειρώσαντο.

δι' ἣν αἰτίαν. Cause. See 4:28 on δι' ἣν αἰτίαν.

πολλοὺς . . . τραυματίας. Accusative direct object of ἐποίησαν.

μὲν . . . δὲ. Point/counterpoint set. See 2:25 on μὲν . . . δέ.

αὐτῶν. Partitive ("many *of them*") or objective genitive.

ἐποίησαν. Aor act ind 3rd pl ποιέω. Like the use of ποιέω in the middle, here the active form is used with a verbal noun (τραυματίας) as a periphrasis for the verb itself: τραυματίζω (*GELS*, 570.II). See 1:23 on ἐποιήσαντο.

τινὰς. Accusative direct object of κατέβαλον.

καὶ. The conjunction marks "incremental addition" (Muraoka §78a): "*even* killed some." Cf. Neh 13:5; 2 Ezra 6:5.

κατέβαλον. Aor act ind 3rd pl καταβάλλω. From the literal sense, "to cast downwards," derives the sense "to kill" (*GE*, 1043.1.C).

πάντας. Accusative direct object of συνήλασαν.

δὲ. Development; see 1:10 on δέ.

εἰς φυγὴν. Spatial.

συνήλασαν. Aor act ind 3rd pl συνελαύνω. On the meaning of the verb, see 4:26 on συνήλαστο.

αὐτὸν . . . τὸν ἱερόσυλον. Accusative direct object of ἐχειρώσαντο. Refers to a "temple robber" (BDAG, 471.1; *GELS*, 339). The pronoun αὐτός is intensive: "himself."

δὲ. Development; see 1:10 on δέ.

παρὰ τὸ γαζοφυλάκιον. Locative. See 3:6 on the meaning of γαζοφυλάκιον.

ἐχειρώσαντο. Aor act ind 3rd pl χειρόω.

2 Maccabees 4:43-50

[43]About these things, a charge was brought against Menelaus. [44]When the king arrived in Tyre, three men who were sent by the senate presented the case before him. [45]But even though he was already forsaken, Menelaus promised quite a sum of money to Ptolemy [son] of Dorymenes in order to persuade the king. [46]Therefore, Ptolemy, taking [him] aside into a certain peristyle as if for refreshing, changed the king's mind. [47]And the one who caused all the wickedness, Menelaus, he acquitted of the accusations. But those miserable people who, even if they were speaking with Scythopolis, these innocent ones he sentenced to death. [48]Therefore, those who spoke on behalf of the city and the populace and the

sacred vessels quickly endured the unjust punishment. [49]For this reason even the Tyrians, hating the wickedness, supplied impressively for their funeral. [50]But Menelaus, because of the greediness of those in power, remained in office, growing in wickedness, having become the chief plotter against his fellow-citizens.

4:43 περὶ δὲ τούτων ἐνέστη κρίσις πρὸς τὸν Μενέλαον.

περὶ ... τούτων. Reference. The demonstrative pronoun has a conceptual antecedent (Wallace, 333): "these things" refers to "these events" mentioned in 4:39-42.

δὲ. Development; see 1:10 on δέ.

ἐνέστη. Aor act ind 3rd sg ἐνίστημι.

κρίσις. Nominative subject of ἐνέστη. On the legal language in this passage, see also δικαιολογίαν in 4:44.

πρὸς τὸν Μενέλαον. Opposition. On the article, see 4:27.

4:44 καταντήσαντος δὲ τοῦ βασιλέως εἰς Τύρον ἐπ᾽ αὐτοῦ τὴν δικαιολογίαν ἐποιήσαντο οἱ πεμφθέντες τρεῖς ἄνδρες ὑπὸ τῆς γερουσίας.

καταντήσαντος. Aor act ptc gen masc sg καταντάω (genitive absolute, temporal). On the genitive absolute, see 1:7 on βασιλεύοντος.

δὲ. Development; see 1:10 on δέ.

τοῦ βασιλέως. Genitive subject of the participle καταντήσαντος.

εἰς Τύρον. Spatial.

ἐπ᾽ αὐτοῦ. Spatial.

τὴν δικαιολογίαν. Accusative direct object of ἐποιήσαντο. See *GE* (529): "judiciary discourse, defense, justification" = "the case."

ἐποιήσαντο. Aor mid ind 3rd pl ποιέω. When the middle of ποιέω is used with a verbal noun (δικαιολογίαν), this can be a periphrasis for the verb itself: ἐδικαιολογήσαντο (*GELS*, 570.II). See 1:23 on ἐποιήσαντο.

οἱ πεμφθέντες. Aor pass ptc nom masc pl πέμπω (attributive, modifying τρεῖς ἄνδρες).

τρεῖς ἄνδρες. Nominative subject of ἐποιήσαντο.

ὑπὸ τῆς γερουσίας. Agency. On the meaning of γερουσία, see 1:10 on ἡ γερουσία καὶ Ἰουδας.

4:45 ἤδη δὲ λελειμμένος ὁ Μενέλαος ἐπηγγείλατο χρήματα ἱκανὰ τῷ Πτολεμαίῳ Δορυμένους πρὸς τὸ πεῖσαι τὸν βασιλέα.

ἤδη. Temporal adverb, modifying either λελειμμένος ("*already* as good as beaten," NETS) or ἐπηγγείλατο ("he *already* promised").

δὲ. Development, marking a change of subject from the three men (4:44) to Menelaus in 4:45. See 1:10 on δέ.

λελειμμένος. Prf pass ptc nom masc sg λείπω (concessive). In context the verb denotes that Menelaus is all but defeated: "forsaken" (*GELS*, 428.1; cf. *GE*, 1222.3.A).

ὁ Μενέλαος. Nominative subject of ἐπηγγείλατο. On the article, see 4:27.

ἐπηγγείλατο. Aor mid ind 3rd sg ἐπαγγέλλομαι.

χρήματα ἱκανά. Accusative direct object of ἐπηγγείλατο. The adjective ἱκανός denotes something "considerable in quantity" = "quite a sum of money" (*GELS*, 339).

τῷ Πτολεμαίῳ. Dative indirect object of ἐπηγγείλατο. D. Schwartz (243) notes that even though this is the first (and only) mention of "Ptolemy son of Dorymenes," the epitomizer does not introduce him with some of the standard formulas he used elsewhere (e.g., 3:4; 4:40; 10:11; 14:3; etc.). According to D. Schwartz, this is due to "careless abridging."

Δορυμένους. Genitive of relationship.

πεῖσαι. Aor act inf πείθω. Used with πρὸς τό to denote purpose (see Burk, 107–9). Here, as 7:26, persuasion implies a payment of money.

τὸν βασιλέα. Accusative direct object of πεῖσαι.

4:46 ὅθεν ἀπολαβὼν ὁ Πτολεμαῖος εἴς τι περίστυλον ὡς ἀναψύξοντα τὸν βασιλέα μετέθηκεν,

ὅθεν. Inferential. See 4:21, 34; 5:11; 10:13; 12:45; 14:7.

ἀπολαβών. Aor act ptc nom masc sg ἀπολαμβάνω (means).

ὁ Πτολεμαῖος. Nominative subject of μετέθηκεν.

εἴς τι περίστυλον. Spatial. A *peristyle* (περί + στῦλος) refers to a structure with columns that enclose it. The preposition εἰς appears here with the accent because τί, an indefinite pronoun, loses its accent to the preceding word (Smyth §181–82).

ὡς. Purpose. See 1:14 on ὡς with a future participle.

ἀναψύξοντα. Fut act ptc acc masc sg ἀναψύχω (purpose). The participle is in the accusative because it agrees with τὸν βασιλέα. Literally, "to lift his spirit," but the expression means to "to get fresh air." D. Schwartz (244) notes the irony of the expression: "Ptolemy took the king aside as if in order to 'elevate' (ἀνά) his spirit/soul, but in fact mislead him into the debasement of condemning the innocent and acquitting the guilty."

τὸν βασιλέα. Accusative direct object of μετέθηκεν.

μετέθηκεν. Aor act ind 3rd sg μετατίθημι. The collocation of μετατίθημι + τὸν βασιλέα (cf. 3 Kgdms 20:25) means "to change (the nature of) the king's mind" (cf. *GELS*, 455).

4:47 καὶ τὸν μὲν τῆς ὅλης κακίας αἴτιον Μενέλαον ἀπέλυσεν τῶν κατηγορημένων, τοῖς δὲ ταλαιπώροις, οἵτινες, εἰ καὶ ἐπὶ Σκυθῶν ἔλεγον, ἀπελύθησαν ἀκατάγνωστοι, τούτοις θάνατον ἐπέκρινεν.

τὸν . . . αἴτιον. Accusative in apposition to Μενέλαον. See BDAG (31.1): "one who is *the cause, source*."

μὲν . . . δὲ. Point/counterpoint set. See 2:25 on μὲν . . . δέ.

τῆς ὅλης κακίας. Objective genitive. On the attributive structure of ὅλος, see 2:21.

Μενέλαον. Accusative direct object of ἀπέλυσεν.

ἀπέλυσεν. Aor act ind 3rd sg ἀπολύω. The legal context suggests that the verb should be translated as "to release" = "to acquit" (*GE*, 259.1.A).

τῶν κατηγορημένων. Prf pass ptc gen masc pl κατηγορέω (substantival). Genitive of reference.

τοῖς . . . ταλαιπώροις. Dative of disadvantage. The adjective (used as a substantive) serves as the topic of what follows and is resumed by the pronoun οἵτινες. Muraoka (§84b) notes that "[a] fronted constituent can be in a case other than nominative and resumed subsequently in the same case."

οἵτινες. Nominative subject of ἔλεγον, pointing back to its antecedent, τοῖς . . . ταλαιπώροις. The indefinite relative is used like a regular relative pronoun.

εἰ καὶ. The combination of εἰ καί marks a concessive idea: "even if" (cf. *GE*, 596.II.B). On the diachronic development of this expression, see Caragounis (294–97).

εἰ. Introduces a second-class conditional clause (Smyth §2302), using εἰ + imperfect indicative in the protasis. The second-class conditional introduces a counterfactual condition where the writer or speaker "considers the fulfillment of a present or past condition impossible or no longer possible" (*CGCG* §49.10). While ἄν is expected in the apodosis, Muraoka (§89ba) notes that "[i]n a few cases the particle ἄν is missing" (cf. Wallace, 694). This understanding is further confirmed by the addition of ἄν after ἀπελύθησαν in some of the MS tradition (e.g., *q* 19-93 55 58). Cf. 5:18.

ἐπὶ Σκυθῶν. Locative.

ἔλεγον. Impf act ind 3rd pl λέγω.

ἀπελύθησαν. Aor pass ind 3rd pl ἀπολύω.

ἀκατάγνωστοι. Nominative subject of ἀπελύθησαν. See BDAG (35): "pert[aining] to not being considered blameworthy, *not condemned*."

τούτοις. Dative indirect object of ἐπέκρινεν. Resumes οἵτινες.

θάνατον. Accusative direct object of ἐπέκρινεν.

ἐπέκρινεν. Aor act ind 3rd sg ἐπικρίνω.

4:48 ταχέως οὖν τὴν ἄδικον ζημίαν ὑπέσχον οἱ περὶ πόλεως καὶ δήμων καὶ τῶν ἱερῶν σκευῶν προηγορήσαντες.

ταχέως. Temporal adverb.

οὖν. Inferential, introducing a conclusion drawn from 4:17: since those who were innocent were sentenced to death, they are receiving an unjust penalty. See 2:15 on οὖν.

τὴν ἄδικον ζημίαν. Accusative direct object of ὑπέσχον.

ὑπέσχον. Aor act ind 3rd pl ὑπέχω.

οἱ . . . προηγορήσαντες. Aor act ptc nom masc pl προηγορέω (substantival). Subject of ὑπέσχον. On the meaning of the verb, see *GE* (1763): "to speak for, in defense of."

περὶ πόλεως καὶ δήμων καὶ τῶν ἱερῶν σκευῶν. Reference. Two text critical issues are relevant. Many MSS (*q* 542 46-52 58 106 771) read ὑπέρ rather than περί because the sense of representation or advantage is clear: "*on behalf of, for the sake of*" (cf. Wallace, 383). περί is the preferred reading because it clarifies the meaning of the text. The noun δήμων also appears in the singular, δήμου, in several MSS (V *L*-542 La Sy). Although many commentators prefer the plural (Goldstein, 243), the singular finds a good parallel in 15:14 and is preferred here. On δῆμος, see BDAG (223.2): "in a Hellenistic city, a convocation of citizens called together for the purpose of transacting official business, *popular assembly*." See D. Schwartz (245) and especially Habicht (224) for further discussion of the difference between δῆμος and λαός.

On the use of ἡ πόλις rather than Ιεροσόλυμα, see 2:22 on τὴν πόλιν.

4:49 δι᾽ ἣν αἰτίαν καὶ Τύριοι μισοπονηρήσαντες τὰ πρὸς τὴν κηδείαν αὐτῶν μεγαλοπρεπῶς ἐχορήγησαν.

δι᾽ ἣν αἰτίαν. Cause. See 4:28 on δι᾽ ἣν αἰτίαν.

καὶ. Ascensive.

Τύριοι. Nominative subject of ἐχορήγησαν. Doran (2012, 120) notes that "[t]he article is lacking before Tyrians, and so not the Tyrians as a whole but some Tyrians are meant."

μισοπονηρήσαντες. Aor act ptc nom masc pl μισοπονηρέω (concessive).

τὰ. The neuter article functions as a nominalizer, changing the PP (πρὸς τὴν κηδείαν) into the accusative direct object of ἐχορήγησαν.

πρὸς τὴν κηδείαν. Purpose. *GE* (1121) lists two different, seemingly divergent senses for κηδεία: "kinship, *hence also* union, alliance" and "funeral, funeral honors, burial." But, *EDG* (684) observes that the related term κῆδος has the primary sense of "care, mourning, funeral rites."

αὐτῶν. Subjective genitive.

μεγαλοπρεπῶς. Adverb of manner.

ἐχορήγησαν. Aor act ind 3rd pl χορηγέω. See 3:3 on χορηγεῖν.

4:50 ὁ δὲ Μενέλαος διὰ τὰς τῶν κρατούντων πλεονεξίας ἔμενεν ἐπὶ τῇ ἀρχῇ ἐπιφυόμενος τῇ κακίᾳ μέγας τῶν πολιτῶν ἐπίβουλος καθεστώς.

ὁ . . . Μενέλαος. Nominative subject of ἔμενεν. On the article, see 4:27.

δὲ. Development, marking a change of subject from the Tyrians to Menelaus. See 1:10 on δέ.

διὰ τὰς . . . πλεονεξίας. Cause.

τῶν κρατούντων. Pres act ptc gen masc pl κρατέω (substantival). Subjective genitive, identifying those who are being greedy.

ἔμενεν. Impf act ind 3rd sg μένω.

ἐπὶ τῇ ἀρχῇ. Locative. See BDAG (138.7): "in office."

ἐπιφυόμενος. Pres mid ptc nom masc sg ἐπιφύω (result). On the meaning of the verb, see GE (803): "to grow . . . be generated, arise," often with the dative. The result of Menelaus remaining in office is that he grew in wickedness.

τῇ κακίᾳ. Dative complement of ἐπιφυόμενος.

μέγας . . . ἐπίβουλος. Predicate nominative of καθεστώς. GE (1006) notes that the verb may take a predicate nominative (cf. 3:28; 4:1; 14:5).

τῶν πολιτῶν. Objective genitive. See 4:5 on τῶν πολιτῶν.

καθεστώς. Prf act ptc nom masc sg καθίστημι (cause). LEH (296) notes that καθίστημι + dative and predicate = "*to make, to render so and so*." On the morphology, see 3:4 on καθεσταμένος.

2 Maccabees 5:1-10

[1]Now about this time, Antiochus set out on a second attack into Egypt. [2]Then it came about that, throughout the entire city for almost forty days, cavalry appeared running through the air, having golden vestments, being fully armed in units with spears and drawn knives, [3]and troops of horses drawn up for battle. And there were attacks and counterattacks from each [side], and brandishing of shields, and a surplus of spears, and hurling of arrows, and the brilliance of golden adornment and manifold breastplates. [4]Therefore, everyone was praying that the appearance was for the good. [5]Now when a false report arose that Antiochus had lost his life, Jason took not less than a thousand men and unexpectedly accomplished an assault against the city. When the ones upon

the wall were forced back and finally the city was taken, Menelaus fled into the acropolis. ⁶And Jason was mercilessly slaughtering his fellow citizens, not realizing [that] good fortune against kinsmen is the greatest misfortune. Rather, he was imagining to set up trophies from enemies and not from the same people. ⁷He did not grasp the office. But, in the end, receiving shame from the plot, he came again as a fugitive into [the countryside] of Ammon. ⁸Finally, he met a miserable end, accused before Aretas, the ruler of the Arabs, fleeing from city to city, pursued by everyone, hated as a rebel against the laws and detested as the executioner of his country and compatriots, he was driven into Egypt. ⁹And the one who banished many [people] from the fatherland perished in exile, after having embarked for the Lacedaemonians seeking protection on account of kinship [ties]. ¹⁰And the one who threw out a multitude of the unburied [corpses] was unlamented, and he had neither any kind of funeral nor an ancestral tomb.

Whereas 2 Maccabees 3 ended with a μέν . . . δέ construction, linking the end of the narrative in chapter 3 to the storyline of chapter 4 (see 3:40 on μέν . . . δέ), it is noteworthy that 2 Maccabees 4 ends without this construction. As D. Schwartz (249) suggests, the effect of this choice is that readers will assume that "[t]he wicked Menelaus is here to stay." As promised in 2:21, this passage describes the second "appearance" (ἐπιφάνεια) from heaven (the first was in 3:24-26). Rhetorically, there are patterns of suspense and relief, as noted by Coetzer (258). In 5:2-4, divine "appearances" may be understood as good or bad (suspense). In 5:5, Menelaus flees the scene (relief). In 5:6, Jason kills his fellow Jews (suspense). In 5:7-9, Jason flees and ultimately dies (relief). In the following pericope, 5:11-16, Antiochus attacks Jerusalem itself (suspense). Following Coetzer (258–59), 5:1-10 is coherent because it skillfully shows that the various events were "engineered by God."

5:1 Περὶ δὲ τὸν καιρὸν τοῦτον τὴν δευτέραν ἔφοδον ὁ Ἀντίοχος εἰς Αἴγυπτον ἐστείλατο.

Περὶ δὲ τὸν καιρὸν τοῦτον. Temporal, denoting a general sense of time (*GELS*, 546). The demonstrative pronoun commonly occurs in predicate position. D. Schwartz (251) helpfully notes that "[t]ransitional phrases such as this one allow authors to impart some appearance of continuity to narratives which have in fact skipped to new places and themes." Cf. 6:1; 9:1; 11:1.
τὴν δευτέραν ἔφοδον. Adverbial accusative. Technically, this is a cognate accusative expression that modifies the intransitive ἐστείλατο.

The cognate accusative can be related in lexical origin or, as here, meaning (cf. *CGCG* §30.12). The meaning of ἔφοδος (preferred over ἄφοδον in MS A) is much debated. The sense of "assault, raid" (*GE*, 882.3.C) is well-established in 2 Maccabees (8:12; 12:21; 13:26; 14:15; 15:8). But, the problem with this sense in 5:1 is the reference to a "*second attack*" when 2 Maccabees has not mentioned a *first* one. This may suggest either that the more generic sense of "approach" is understood for ἔφοδος in 5:1 or, more preferably, that the epitomizer has offered only a condensed account of several attacks (cf. Doran 2012, 125; Habicht, 224). The former view is significantly weakened upon consideration of other uses of ἔφοδος in 2 Maccabees, each of which has the more hostile sense of "assault" (8:12; 12:21; 13:26; 14:15; 15:8). Thus, it may be preferable to understand this reference to a "second assault" as an (accidental?) inclusion left over from the epitomizing process. For a helpful summary of the details, including comparison with the attacks described in 1 Maccabees and Josephus, see D. Schwartz (533–36) or Coetzer (252–53).

ὁ Ἀντίοχος. Nominative subject of ἐστείλατο.

εἰς Αἴγυπτον. Direction ("*into* Egypt") or, perhaps, disadvantage ("*against* Egypt").

ἐστείλατο. Aor mid ind 3rd sg στέλλω. Used intransitively in the middle voice with the cognate accusative, στέλλω means "to set out, depart, go" (*GE*, 1957.2.A). The aorist stem of στέλλω is different due to a stem vowel shift: ε → ει (*MBG*, 301; cf. Smyth §121).

5:2 συνέβη δὲ καθ' ὅλην τὴν πόλιν σχεδὸν ἐφ' ἡμέρας τεσσαράκοντα φαίνεσθαι διὰ τῶν ἀέρων τρέχοντας ἱππεῖς διαχρύσους στολὰς ἔχοντας καὶ λόγχας σπειρηδὸν ἐξωπλισμένους καὶ μαχαιρῶν σπασμούς,

On the textual location of καὶ μαχαιρῶν σπασμούς, see the opening comment in 5:3.

συνέβη. Aor act ind 3rd sg συμβαίνω. Commonly followed by accusative + infinitive, as here: φαίνεσθαι ... τρέχοντας ἱππεῖς "[it came about that] ... cavalry appeared running" (cf. BDAG, 956.2). On the use of συμβαίνω at key transitions from general context to specific details, see 3:2 on συνέβαινεν.

δὲ. Development; see 1:10 on δέ.

καθ' ὅλην τὴν πόλιν. Locative, denoting extension ("*throughout* the whole city"). Although Egypt (4:21; 5:1) and Tyre (4:18, 32, 44) were more recently mentioned, the epitomizer is back to talking about Jerusalem. On the use of ἡ πόλις rather than Ιεροσόλυμα, see 2:22 on τὴν πόλιν.

σχεδόν. The adverb is used like an attributive adjective (cf. Muraoka §24b), modifying ἐφ᾽ ἡμέρας τεσσαράκοντα: "for *almost* forty days."

ἐφ᾽ ἡμέρας τεσσαράκοντα. Temporal: "over a period of . . ." (Wallace, 376).

φαίνεσθαι. Pres mid inf φαίνω (indirect discourse).

διὰ τῶν ἀέρων. Locative. The PP could modify either φαίνεσθαι or τρέχοντας. However, the latter is preferable because it would be more natural to construct the former with ἐν (cf. Num 23:3; 2 Kgdms 11:27; 1 Macc 4:50). The noun is plural in much of the MS tradition (cf. τοῦ ἀέρος in *L* ⁻⁵⁴² 311 La^{BP} Sy), as is typical for a "plural of expanse" (Muraoka §21g).

τρέχοντας. Pres act ptc acc masc pl τρέχω (attributive, modifying ἱππεῖς).

ἱππεῖς. Accusative subject of the infinitive φαίνεσθαι.

διαχρύσους στολὰς. Accusative direct object of ἔχοντας.

ἔχοντας. Pres act ptc acc masc pl ἔχω (attributive, modifying ἱππεῖς).

λόγχας. Accusative of respect, qualifying ἐξωπλισμένους. As in Sophocles, Euripides, and Pindar, λόγχη may refer to "troops of armed spearsmen" (cf. Goldstein, 247; *GE*, 1251). A good number of MSS (64*-236-728-19-62-93 La^{-VP}), however, read λόχους referring to "an armed band, body of troops" (LSJ, 1063.3). It is difficult to decide which reading is better. However, on balance, λόχους may be preferable because 5:2 would then only be referring to the military units rather than weapons used by those units (cf. D. Schwartz, 252; Habicht, 224–25).

σπειρηδόν. Adverb of manner, describing the arming the soldiers "in companies." Σπειρηδόν is used only here and 12:2 in the LXX. The term is found in Polybius to describe a Roman tactical unit (Goldstein, 248), perhaps of 256 men (*Hist.* 5.5.9). However, *GELS* (630) numbers the groups as "60 or 120 troops."

ἐξωπλισμένους. Prf mid ptc acc masc pl ἐξοπλίζω (attributive, modifying ἱππεῖς). On the meaning of the verb, see *GE* (728.2): "to arm oneself, be armed."

μαχαιρῶν. Objective genitive, modifying σπασμούς. Although μάχαιρα can denote a "sword," the sense of "knife" is more likely because the epitomizer uses other words for "sword" (cf. 15:15) (cf. D. Schwartz, 252). On the possible sacrificial overtones of the word in the LXX and Second Temple Jewish literature, see especially Fredriksen (312–25).

σπασμούς. Accusative direct object of ἐξωπλισμένους. A verbal noun from σπάω (cf. *GELS*, 629). As in Plutarch (*Oth.* 17.1), here it refers to "a sword/knife drawn from its sheath."

5:3 καὶ ἵλας ἵππων διατεταγμένας καὶ προσβολὰς γινομένας καὶ καταδρομὰς ἑκατέρων καὶ ἀσπίδων κινήσεις καὶ καμάκων πλήθη καὶ βελῶν βολὰς καὶ χρυσέων κόσμων ἐκλάμψεις καὶ παντοίους θωρακισμούς.

The Göttingen edition moves καὶ μαχαιρῶν σπασμούς to the beginning of 5:3, which is inconsequential due to the lack of punctuation, spacing, chapter numbers, or verse numbers in the text when it was written. However, the Göttingen edition does note a significant variant, relocating these words after πλήθη. Many scholars follow this judgment, reasoning that "[t]his restores order: first the [military] units, then their movements, then their weapons" (D. Schwartz, 252; cf. Habicht, 225; Doran 2012, 122).

The use of nouns rather than full clauses expresses vividness (cf. Goldstein, 247).

ἵλας. Accusative subject of an implied form of φαίνεσθαι (cf. 5:2): "[there appeared] troops. . . ."

ἵππων. Genitive of material, qualifying ἵλας.

διατεταγμένας. Prf mid ptc acc fem pl διατάσσω (attributive, modifying ἵλας). On the morphology of the verb, τάσσω is built from the root *ταγ (cf. *MBG* §26.1–3).

προσβολὰς . . . καὶ καταδρομὰς. Accusative complement of γινομένας.

γινομένας. Pres mid ptc acc fem pl γίνομαι (indirect discourse).

ἑκατέρων. Genitive of separation, modifying προσβολὰς . . . καὶ καταδρομάς. See *GE* (622): "each of two, the one and the other."

ἀσπίδων. Objective genitive, modifying κινήσεις.

κινήσεις. Accusative complement of an implied form of γίνομαι. See *GE* (1130): "movement, shifting" = "brandishing [of shields]."

καμάκων. Genitive of apposition.

πλήθη. Accusative complement of an implied form of γίνομαι. See *GE* (1681): "excessive quantity, surplus."

βελῶν. Objective genitive, modifying βολάς.

βολὰς. Accusative complement of an implied form of γίνομαι. See *GELS* (120): "[a]ct of hurling [arrows]."

χρυσέων κόσμων. Objective genitive, qualifying ἐκλάμψεις. See *GELS* (409): "ornaments . . . of golden." Cf. διαχρύσους στολὰς in 5:2.

ἐκλάμψεις. Accusative complement of an implied form of γίνομαι. See *GE* (635): "brilliance, radiance."

παντοίους θωρακισμούς. Accusative complement of an implied form of γίνομαι. *GE* (958) notes that θωρακισμός denotes a "state of being armed with a breastplate."

5:4 διὸ πάντες ἠξίουν ἐπ᾽ ἀγαθῷ τὴν ἐπιφάνειαν γεγενῆσθαι.

διὸ. Inferential conjunction, introducing "an expository or hortatory thesis that is inferred from what has already been stated" (Levinsohn 2014, 329). This meaning is likely related to the etymology of διό = δι᾽ ὅ ("for which reason") (BDAG, 250). The reason why everyone was praying (5:4): because of the divine manifestations (5:2-3).

πάντες. Nominative subject of ἠξίουν.

ἠξίουν. Impf act ind 3rd pl ἀξιόω. For the use of ἀξιόω for prayer, see 3:20; 8:14, 29; 10:4, 16, 26; 12:42. The imperfect verb (imperfective verbal aspect) suggests habitual practice.

ἐπ᾽ ἀγαθῷ. Used with γίνομαι, the preposition ἐπί is prefixed to the predicate ἀγαθῷ (cf. Muraoka §61bb; *GE*, 429–30). On the use of ἀγαθός in reference to a "*good* omen," see *GE* (6). Portents were typically ambiguous, so the hope that the apparition might be "for the good" is a reasonable wish.

τὴν ἐπιφάνειαν. Accusative subject of the infinitive γεγενῆσθαι. See 2:21 on τὰς . . . ἐπιφανείας.

γεγενῆσθαι. Prf mid inf γίνομαι (indirect discourse). Some MSS (V *q* L⁻⁵⁴² 55 58) have the aorist γενέσθαι, which may be a correction (either accidental or intentional) to the more common aorist infinitive.

5:5 γενομένης δὲ λαλιᾶς ψευδοῦς ὡς μετηλλαχότος Ἀντιόχου τὸν βίον παραλαβὼν ὁ Ἰάσων οὐκ ἐλάττους τῶν χιλίων αἰφνιδίως ἐπὶ τὴν πόλιν συνετελέσατο ἐπίθεσιν· τῶν δὲ ἐπὶ τῷ τείχει συνελασθέντων καὶ τέλος ἤδη καταλαμβανομένης τῆς πόλεως ὁ Μενέλαος εἰς τὴν ἀκρόπολιν ἐφυγάδευσεν.

γενομένης. Aor mid ptc gen fem sg γίνομαι (genitive absolute, temporal). On the genitive absolute, see 1:7 on βασιλεύοντος.

δὲ. Development; see 1:10 on δέ.

λαλιᾶς ψευδοῦς. Genitive subject of the participle γενομένης.

ὡς. Introduces either the content of the "false report" (λαλιᾶς ψευδοῦς) or, perhaps, a cause (cf. *GE*, 2425.II.D). Muraoka (§31hd) notes that "[w]hen a message contained in a gen[itive] abs[olute] clause is not meant as factually true, or as the speaker's or writer's own opinion, but as a subjective formulation of a pretext or ground for a certain action or a rumor, ὡς is prefixed."

μετηλλαχότος. Prf act ptc gen masc sg μεταλλάσσω (genitive absolute, indirect discourse). On the meaning of μεταλλάσσω + βίον, see 4:7 on Μεταλλάξαντος. On the genitive absolute, see 1:7 on βασιλεύοντος.

Ἀντιόχου. Genitive subject of the participle μετηλλαχότος.

τὸν βίον. Accusative direct object of μετηλλαχότος.

παραλαβών. Aor act ptc nom masc sg παραλαμβάνω (attendant circumstance).

ὁ Ἰάσων. Nominative subject of συνετελέσατο.

ἐλάττους. Accusative direct object of παραλαβών. The adjective ἐλάττους functions as the comparative of μικρός and the collocation οὐκ + ἐλάσσων = "not less than" (BDAG, 313.1; *GELS*, 221). On the Attic morphology, see 4:40 on ἧττον. Cf. 8:9; 10:18; 12:4, 10.

τῶν χιλίων. Partitive genitive, following the comparative adjective ἐλάττους. But, also see Muraoka (§77bc), who suggests genitive of measure.

αἰφνιδίως. Adverb of manner. See *GE* (61): "unexpectedly."

ἐπὶ τὴν πόλιν. Opposition (cf. LN 90.34). On the use of ἡ πόλις rather than Ιεροσολύμα, see 2:22 on τὴν πόλιν.

συνετελέσατο. Aor mid ind 3rd sg συντελέω.

ἐπίθεσιν. Accusative direct object of συνετελέσατο. See *GELS* (272): "military *assault*." *Pace* Goldstein (254), who thinks that "coup" would better translate the term on the basis of parallel expressions in the Hebrew Bible (cf. 2 Chr 25:27; Gen 27:35; etc.).

τῶν. The article functions as a nominalizer, changing the PP (ἐπὶ τῷ τείχει) into the genitive subject of the participle συνελασθέντων.

δὲ. Development, marking a change of subject from Jason to "the ones upon the wall." See 1:10 on δέ.

ἐπὶ τῷ τείχει. Locative.

συνελασθέντων. Aor pass ptc gen masc pl συνελαύνω (genitive absolute, temporal). On the genitive absolute, see 1:7 on βασιλεύοντος.

τέλος ἤδη. Adverbial. τέλος is used in various adverbial expressions, especially without the article: "finally, at last" (cf. Muraoka §22xg; Mayser II 2.327–30; BDAG, 998.2.b). Cf. 13:16.

καταλαμβανομένης. Pres pass ptc gen fem sg καταλαμβάνω (genitive absolute, causal). On the genitive absolute, see 1:7 on βασιλεύοντος.

τῆς πόλεως. Genitive subject of the participle καταλαμβανομένης.

ὁ Μενέλαος. Nominative subject of ἐφυγάδευσεν.

εἰς τὴν ἀκρόπολιν. Spatial. On the possible location of the acropolis, see 4:12 on ὑπ᾽ αὐτὴν τὴν ἀκρόπολιν.

ἐφυγάδευσεν. Aor act ind 3rd sg φυγαδεύω. On the meaning of the verb, see *GELS* (721): "to flee from danger or misery."

5:6 ὁ δὲ Ἰάσων ἐποιεῖτο σφαγὰς τῶν πολιτῶν τῶν ἰδίων ἀφειδῶς οὐ συννοῶν τὴν εἰς τοὺς συγγενεῖς εὐημερίαν δυσημερίαν εἶναι τὴν μεγίστην, δοκῶν δὲ πολεμίων καὶ οὐχ ὁμοεθνῶν τρόπαια καταβάλλεσθαι.

Doran (2012, 127) notes that the description of Jason's opponents is increasingly specific and heightens the emotion: πολῖται ("citizens"), συγγενεῖς ("kinsfolk"), and ὁμοέθνοι ("same race").

ὁ . . . Ἰάσων. Nominative subject of ἐποιεῖτο.

δὲ. Development, marking a change of subject to Jason. See 1:10 on δέ.

ἐποιεῖτο. Impf mid ind 3rd sg ποιέω. When the middle of ποιέω is used with a verbal noun (σφαγάς), this can be a periphrasis for the verb itself: σφάζω (GELS, 570.II). See 1:23 on ἐποιήσαντο. The imperfect verb utilizes imperfective aspect, portraying the action as unfolding and, in this case, repeating.

σφαγὰς. Accusative direct object of ἐποιεῖτο.

τῶν πολιτῶν τῶν ἰδίων. Objective genitive, qualifying σφαγάς.

ἀφειδῶς. Adverb of manner.

οὐ. On the negation οὐ with a participle, see 4:5 on οὐ.

συννοῶν. Pres act ptc nom masc sg συννοέω (causal).

τὴν . . . εὐημερίαν. Accusative subject of the infinitive εἶναι. The word εὐημερία (lit. "good day" or "good luck") is often used to denote a military victory (Doran 2012, 127; Habicht, 225).

εἰς τοὺς συγγενεῖς. Disadvantage.

δυσημερίαν . . . τὴν μεγίστην. Predicate accusative. The word δυσημερίαν (lit. "bad day" or "bad luck") includes the inseparable prefix δυσ-, which "negates the good sense of a word, w[ith] notion of hard, bad, difficult" (BDAG, 265). In context, it contrasts with τὴν εὐημερίαν. On the δυσ-compound words in 2 Maccabees, see 2:24 on δυσχέρειαν.

εἶναι. Pres act inf εἰμί (indirect discourse with a verb of cognition).

δοκῶν. Pres act ptc nom masc sg δοκέω (causal).

δὲ. Development; see 1:10 on δέ. Here, after the negation, δέ means "rather."

πολεμίων. Genitive of subordination.

οὐχ. Negative particle that normally occurs with indicative verbs is used here in an elliptical clause negating an implied participle (δοκῶν). On the negation οὐ with a participle, see 4:5 on οὐ.

ὁμοεθνῶν. Genitive of subordination. On the meaning of this word, see 4:2 on τῶν ὁμοεθνῶν.

τρόπαια. Accusative direct object of καταβάλλεσθαι. "Trophies" or "monuments" were often set up "for having put the enemy to flight" (GE, 2157; e.g., Euripides, Phoen. 570–77; Her. 786; Thucydides, Hist. 2.92.4; Aeschylus, Sept. 277; etc.).

καταβάλλεσθαι. Pres mid inf καταβάλλω (complementary). The middle voice is common in constructions implying self-interest (N. Miller, 429).

5:7 τῆς μὲν ἀρχῆς οὐκ ἐκράτησεν, τὸ δὲ τέλος τῆς ἐπιβουλῆς αἰσχύνην λαβὼν φυγὰς πάλιν εἰς τὴν Ἀμμανῖτιν ἀπῆλθεν.

τῆς . . . ἀρχῆς. Genitive complement of ἐκράτησεν (Wallace, 131; BDF §169–78). On the meaning of ἀρχή, see 4:10 on τῆς ἀρχῆς. Specifically, the office in view is that of the high priesthood (cf. 4:2, 19-20, 27, 50). Goldstein (254) notes the untranslatable wordplay of ἀρχῆς and τέλος, which can both mean "office" and one refers to "beginning" and the other "end."

μὲν . . . δὲ. Point/counterpoint set. See 2:25 on μὲν . . . δέ.

οὐκ ἐκράτησεν. Aor act ind 3rd sg κρατέω.

τὸ . . . τέλος. Adverbial accusative: "in the end" (Muraoka §22xg; cf. BDAG, 998.2.b.α). See 5:5 on τέλος ἤδη.

τῆς ἐπιβουλῆς. Genitive of cause, qualifying αἰσχύνην.

αἰσχύνην. Accusative direct object of λαβών.

λαβὼν. Aor act ptc nom masc sg λαμβάνω (attendant circumstance or, perhaps, causal).

φυγὰς. Adverbial accusative of manner, modifying ἀπῆλθεν.

πάλιν. Adverb.

εἰς τὴν Ἀμμανῖτιν. Locative. Cf. the fuller expression εἰς τὴν Ἀμμανῖτιν χώραν in 4:26. Words such as χωρά are frequently omitted because they can be inferred easily from context (MHT 3:16–17).

ἀπῆλθεν. Aor act ind 3rd sg ἀπέρχομαι. The Göttingen edition reads παρῆλθεν (MS A *q*) rather than ἀπῆλθεν (MS V 452) or ἀπῄει (MS *L*⁻⁵⁴²). Nicklas (2011, 1390) notes that the Greek is difficult to distinguish in translation. However, following Goldstein (255), it is likely that "the scribes of the simpler reading probably altered the reading of A and *q* because they failed to grasp its elegant irony: the defeated fugitive *succeeded* in slipping back through to his starting point."

5:8 πέρας οὖν κακῆς καταστροφῆς ἔτυχεν. ἐγκληθεὶς πρὸς Ἀρέταν τὸν τῶν Ἀράβων τύραννον πόλιν ἐκ πόλεως φεύγων διωκόμενος ὑπὸ πάντων στυγούμενος ὡς τῶν νόμων ἀποστάτης καὶ βδελυσσόμενος ὡς πατρίδος καὶ πολιτῶν δήμιος εἰς Αἴγυπτον ἐξεβράσθη,

πέρας. The accusative noun πέρας is used as an adverb to mark something that is additional in a series: "finally, in conclusion, further(more)" (BDAG, 797.3; cf. Muraoka §22xg).

οὖν. Resumptive, taking up the main narrative line from 5:6. See 2:15 on οὖν.

κακῆς καταστροφῆς. Genitive complement of ἔτυχεν. The Göttingen edition reads ἀναστροφῆς ("mode of life," *GE*, 156.C) rather than καταστροφῆς, which would require taking πέρας as the accusative direct object of ἔτυχεν, with κακῆς ἀναστροφῆς as a genitive modifier: "he met the end of his bad way of life." However, τυγχάνω appears with the genitive in the Greek of this period and this reading is probably secondary (cf. Goldstein, 255). Supporting this view is the fact that πέρας οὖν is a standard adverbial expression, suggesting that readers would not be likely to construe πέρας as an accusative noun. Goldstein (255) suggests that the secondary reading may have arisen because scribes wanted to contrast Jason's bad way of life (5:8) with the description of Eleazar's "excellent way of life" (καλλίστης ἀναστροφῆς) in 6:23. This is possible, even if ultimately not knowable.

ἔτυχεν. Aor act ind 3rd sg τυγχάνω. The verb τυγχάνω is used with the genitive "of person or thing that one meets" (BDAG, 1019.1).

ἐγκληθεὶς. Aor pass ptc nom masc sg ἐγκαλέω (means). The Göttingen edition reads ἐγκλεισθείς (cf. La Sy Arm) rather than ἐγκληθείς. The reading in R-H (and followed by many interpreters) is conjectural, but because of the orthographic similarity between the words, because of the common interchange of η and ει (Caragounis, 536), and because the collocation of ἐγκλειθείς + πρός ("to imprison to") makes very little sense, the reading in R-H is preferred.

πρὸς Ἀρέταν. Spatial.

τὸν . . . τύραννον. Accusative in apposition to Ἀρέταν. On the meaning of τύραννος, see 4:25 on ὠμοῦ τυράννου.

τῶν Ἀράβων. Genitive of subordination.

πόλιν. Accusative direct object of φεύγων.

ἐκ πόλεως. Muraoka (§21j): "A substantive may be repeated to indicate *recurrence*." Cf. similar constructions in Gen 39:10; 2 Chron 30:10; 4 Kgdms 9:2. *GELS* (202) notes that ἐκ "indicates close succession or proximity, with a noun repeated (the first noun in the acc[usative])."

φεύγων. Pres act ptc nom masc sg φεύγω (means).

διωκόμενος. Pres pass ptc nom masc sg διώκω (means or, perhaps, concessive). If concessive, the idea is that Jason successfully fled from city to city, "*even though* he was pursued by everyone."

ὑπὸ πάντων. Agency.

στυγούμενος. Pres pass ptc nom masc sg στυγέω (means or, perhaps, concessive).

ὡς. Introduces a comparative clause, involving ellipsis: "hated by everyone *as* a rebel (is hated)."

τῶν νόμων. Objective genitive.

ἀποστάτης. Nominative subject of an implied form of στυγέω. See *GELS* (83): "one who renounces one's allegiance . . . religious apostate."

βδελυσσόμενος. Pres pass ptc nom masc sg βδελύσσω (means).

ὡς. Introduces a comparative clause, involving ellipsis: "detested *as* the executioner (is detested)."

πατρίδος καὶ πολιτῶν. Objective genitives.

δήμιος. Nominative subject of an implied form of βδελύσσω. See *GELS* (147): "public executioner."

εἰς Αἴγυπτον. Spatial.

ἐξεβράσθη. Aor pass ind 3rd sg ἐκβράζω. Cf. the same verb in 1:12.

5:9 καὶ ὁ συχνοὺς τῆς πατρίδος ἀποξενώσας ἐπὶ ξένης ἀπώλετο πρὸς Λακεδαιμονίους ἀναχθεὶς ὡς διὰ τὴν συγγένειαν τευξόμενος σκέπης.

ὁ . . . ἀποξενώσας. Aor act ptc nom masc sg ἀποξενόω (substantival). Subject of ἀπώλετο. On the meaning of the verb, see *GELS* (80): "to expel to a foreign land."

συχνοὺς. Accusative direct object of ἀποξενώσας. See *GE* (2062): in the plural, usually "many." Adjective used as a substantive.

τῆς πατρίδος. Genitive of separation.

ἐπὶ ξένης. Temporal.

ἀπώλετο. Aor mid ind 3rd sg ἀπόλλυμι. The description of Jason's death is an example of paronomasia (ἀποξενώσας ἐπὶ ξένης ἀπώλετο).

πρὸς Λακεδαιμονίους. Spatial. This means "to Sparta" (Nicklas 2011, 1390).

ἀναχθεὶς. Aor mid ptc nom masc sg ἀνάγω (temporal). Although θε- (or θη-) is typically understood to mark passive morphology, it is actually a dual-voice form and here it is middle (see Aubrey, 563–625; Caragounis, 153). Verbs of motion (e.g., ἀφικνέομαι, ἔρχομαι, πορεύομαι, etc.) often use middle-voice morphology (cf. N. Miller, 423–30). See *GE* (132.2.A): "to put out to sea, set sail, embark."

ὡς. Used with a PP (διὰ τὴν συγγένειαν) to express intention (*GE*, 2427.II.H.B).

διὰ τὴν συγγένειαν. Cause.

τευξόμενος. Fut mid ptc nom masc sg τυγχάνω (purpose). "[S]ince purpose is accomplished *as a result* of the action of the main verb . . . [t]he future adverbial participle *always* belongs [in this category]" (Wallace, 635; Muraoka §28gia). See 5:8 on ἔτυχεν.

σκέπης. Genitive complement of τευξόμενος.

5:10 καὶ ὁ πλῆθος ἀτάφων ἐκρίψας ἀπένθητος ἐγενήθη καὶ κηδείας οὐδ᾽ ἡστινοσοῦν οὔτε πατρῴου τάφου μετέσχεν.

ὁ . . . ἐκρίψας. Aor act ptc nom masc sg ἐκρίπτω (substantival). Nominative subject of ἐγενήθη.

πλῆθος. Accusative direct object of ἐκρίψας.

ἀτάφων. Partitive genitive, qualifying πλῆθος. The contrast between the Tyrians paying for funerals (4:49) and Jason tossing corpses away without burial (5:10; cf. 9:15) portrays Jason as "the worst [of] villains" (D. Schwartz, 257).

ἀπένθητος. Predicate adjective.

ἐγενήθη. Aor pass ind 3rd sg γίνομαι.

κηδείας. Genitive after a verb of sharing (μετέσχεν). On the meaning of κηδεία, see 4:49 on πρὸς τὴν κηδείαν.

οὐδ᾽ . . . οὔτε. Negative correlative construction: "Neither . . . nor" (BDF §445.1).

ἡστινοσοῦν. The indefinite relative pronoun is an attributive modifier of κηδείας: "*of any kind of* funeral" (*GELS*, 510; *GE*, 1495).

πατρῴου τάφου. Genitive after a verb of sharing (μετέσχεν). Cf. 4:14; 5:27.

μετέσχεν. Aor act ind 3rd sg μετέχω. On the meaning of the verb, see *GE* (1332.1): "to take part, participate" = "he had."

2 Maccabees 5:11-16

[11]When [news] came to the king concerning what had happened, he thought that Judea was in revolt. Therefore, raging like a beast in spirit, he broke camp from Egypt and took the city at spear-point. [12]And he ordered his soldiers to cut down mercilessly those whom they ran into and to slaughter those who went into houses. [13]And there was destruction of young and old, [there was] disappearance of both young men and women as well as children, [there was] slaughter of both virgins and infants. [14]And in all of three days, eighty thousand [people] were destroyed, forty thousand [were killed] by the use of hands and no fewer were sold than those who were killed. [15]But, not being content with these things, he was bold enough to enter into the most holy temple of the whole world, having as a guide Menelaus, who became a traitor both of the laws and of country [16]and taking the sacred vessels with his polluted hands and with profane hands making off with all of the things offered by other kings for the increase and glory and honor of the place.

The variety of expression in this passage is characteristic of the epitomizer's style (cf. D. Schwartz, 68–71). In 5:13 the epitomizer employs
three words (ἀναίρεσις, ἀφανισμός, and σφαγαί) to refer to the act of
killing. In 5:16 the epitomizer uses parallel expressions to refer to "polluted" (ταῖς μιαραῖς χερσίν) and "profane" (ταῖς βεβήλοις χερσίν) hands.
For additional discussion of the variety of expression in 2 Maccabees,
see especially Doran (1981, 42–45).

**5:11 Προσπεσόντων δὲ τῷ βασιλεῖ περὶ τῶν γεγονότων διέλαβεν
ἀποστατεῖν τὴν Ιουδαίαν· ὅθεν ἀναζεύξας ἐξ Αἰγύπτου τεθηριωμένος
τῇ ψυχῇ ἔλαβεν τὴν μὲν πόλιν δοριάλωτον,**

Προσπεσόντων. Aor act ptc gen neut pl προσπίπτω (genitive absolute, temporal). Used impersonally. On the meaning of the verb, see
GELS (598.3): "to come one's way, arrive." Cf. the same verb in 8:12; 9:3;
10:26; 13:1; 14:1, 28. On the genitive absolute, see 1:7 on βασιλεύοντος.

δὲ. Development; see 1:10 on δέ.

τῷ βασιλεῖ. Dative complement of Προσπεσόντων.

περὶ τῶν γεγονότων. Reference.

τῶν γεγονότων. Prf act ptc gen neut pl γίνομαι (substantival): "the
things that came about" = "what had happened."

διέλαβεν. Aor act ind 3rd sg διαλαμβάνω. On the meaning of the
verb, see *GE* (493.C): "to distinguish (*with the mind*), take a side, decide."
Cf. διάλημψις in 3:32, which refers to a "judgment" (*GE*, 495). It is significant that the conflict between the Jews and the king is based upon what
Antiochus mistakenly "thought" (cf. D. Schwartz, 257).

ἀποστατεῖν. Pres act inf ἀποστατέω (indirect discourse).

τὴν Ιουδαίαν. Accusative subject of the infinitive ἀποστατεῖν.

ὅθεν. Introduces an inferential clause. Cf. 4:21, 34, 46.

ἀναζεύξας. Aor act ptc nom masc sg ἀναζεύγνυμι (attendant
circumstance).

ἐξ Αἰγύπτου. Separation. Because geographic names definitionally refer to unique entities, the presence (or absence) of the article is
not predictable. Muraoka (§5cb) notes that within a PP, Αἴγυπτος
is almost always anarthrous (e.g., 1:1, 10; 4:21; 5:1, 8; 9:29; 3 Macc
2:25; 3:20).

τεθηριωμένος. Prf mid ptc nom masc sg θηριόομαι (manner). Cf.
the description of Menelaus in 4:26.

τῇ ψυχῇ. Dative of respect.

ἔλαβεν. Aor act ind 3rd sg λαμβάνω.

τὴν ... πόλιν. Accusative direct object of ἔλαβεν.

μὲν . . . καί. The slight contrast implied in μέν/δέ is evaded by pairing μέν with a particle that denotes addition (Denniston, 374). Because μέν signals "anticipation of a related sentence that follows" (Runge, 75), the καί signals that new information is added. The sequence is completed in 5:12.

δοριάλωτον. If δοριάλωτον is understood as a substantive (i.e., "[someone taken] captive"), then it would be the complement of ἔλαβεν in an object-complement double accusative construction. However, the parallel expression in 10:24, including the collocation of λαμβάνω + δοριάλωτος, suggests that an adverbial accusative construction is more plausible here. Literally, "captured with the spear" (GE, 549). Goldstein (257) notes that "persons or cities captured through combat were completely at the mercy of the conqueror. . . . Such a city was said to be 'spear-won,' [δοριάλωτος], or captured 'by force.'" The point, of course, is that Antiochus is treating the people as war combatants when, in fact, they are not (cf. 1 Macc 1:20).

5:12 καὶ ἐκέλευσεν τοῖς στρατιώταις κόπτειν ἀφειδῶς τοὺς ἐμπίπτοντας καὶ τοὺς εἰς τὰς οἰκίας ἀναβαίνοντας κατασφάζειν.

μὲν . . . καί. See 5:11.

ἐκέλευσεν. Aor act ind 3rd sg κελεύω. Used with the present infinitive, rarely (BDF §338.2).

τοῖς στρατιώταις. Dative indirect object of ἐκέλευσεν.

κόπτειν. Pres act inf κόπτω (indirect discourse).

ἀφειδῶς. Adverb of manner. Cf. 5:6.

τοὺς ἐμπίπτοντας. Pres act ptc acc masc pl ἐμπίπτω (substantival). Direct object of κόπτειν. On the meaning of the verb, see GELS (228): "[to cut down] those whom they run into." Cf. 10:17, 35.

τοὺς . . . ἀναβαίνοντας. Pres act ptc acc masc pl ἀναβαίνω (substantival). Direct object of κατασφάζειν.

εἰς τὰς οἰκίας. Spatial.

κατασφάζειν. Pres act inf κατασφάζω (indirect discourse).

5:13 ἐγίνετο δὲ νέων καὶ πρεσβυτέρων ἀναίρεσις, ἀνήβων τε καὶ γυναικῶν καὶ τέκνων ἀφανισμός, παρθένων τε καὶ νηπίων σφαγαί.

ἐγίνετο. Impf mid ind 3rd sg γίνομαι. The verb forms the basis for the rest of 5:13 and has predicate nominatives that modify it (ἀναίρεσις, ἀφανισμός, and σφαγαί), appearing in the final part of each clause.

δέ. Development; see 1:10 on δέ.

νέων καὶ πρεσβυτέρων. Objective genitives, modifying ἀναίρεσις. Both adjectives are used as substantives.

ἀναίρεσις. Predicate nominative, agreeing with the implied singular subject of ἐγίνετο. See *GE* (136): "destruction."

ἀνήβων. Objective genitive. The Göttingen edition lacks ἀνήβων τε καί (cf. MS A *l*), perhaps due to dittography with ἀναίρεσις.

τε καὶ. The combination τὲ καί serves to unite complements, both similar and opposites (Smyth §2974) and is a closer connection than καί alone (BDF §444.2). Additionally, τε signals that something is first in an enumeration (cf. *CGCG* §59.37). Thus, ἀνήβων τε καὶ γυναικῶν καὶ τέκνων ἀφανισμός = "*both* (τε) the disappearance of young men *and* (καί) women *as well as* children." Cf. 3:1, 10; 5:13; 11:20.

γυναικῶν. Objective genitive.

τέκνων. Objective genitive.

ἀφανισμός. Predicate nominative, agreeing with the implied singular subject of an implied ἐγίνετο. *GE* (352) glosses "disappearance," which should be understood as a euphemism for killing (e.g., "annihilation, extermination").

παρθένων. Objective genitive.

νηπίων. Objective genitive.

σφαγαί. Predicate nominative, agreeing with the implied singular subject of an implied ἐγίνετο. Cf. 5:6.

5:14 ὀκτὼ δὲ μυριάδες ἐν ταῖς πάσαις ἡμέραις τρισὶν κατεφθάρησαν, τέσσαρες μὲν ἐν χειρῶν νομαῖς, οὐχ ἧττον δὲ τῶν ἐσφαγμένων ἐπράθησαν.

ὀκτὼ . . . μυριάδες. Nominative subject of κατεφθάρησαν. This number is probably exaggerated, on which see Broshi (5–14). The exaggeration is part of the epitomizer's strategy to vilify Antiochus and gain sympathy from readers (Coetzer, 255).

δὲ. Development; see 1:10 on δέ.

ἐν ταῖς πάσαις ἡμέραις τρισὶν. Temporal. *GELS* (538.II.f) notes that sometimes an articular πᾶς is used "w[ith] a num[eral] to indicate a precise quantity." Literally, "in all of three days" (Doran 2012, 123).

κατεφθάρησαν. Aor pass ind 3rd pl καταφθείρω. On the meaning of the verb, see *GE* (1089): "to be destroyed."

τέσσαρες. Nominative subject of an implied κατεφθάρησαν.

μὲν . . . δὲ. Point/counterpoint set. See 2:25 on μὲν . . . δέ.

ἐν χειρῶν νομαῖς. Instrumental. The idiom νομή + χείρ (in the genitive) means "by the use of hands." Thus, *GE* (1402.D) suggests "*use* by force in battle" and *GELS* (475) suggests "hand-to-hand fight."

ἧττον. Nominative subject of ἐπράθησαν, negated by οὐχ. On the Attic morphology, see 4:40 on ἧττον.

τῶν ἐσφαγμένων. Prf pass ptc gen masc pl σφάζω (substantival).
Genitive of comparison.

ἐπράθησαν. Aor pass ind 3rd pl πιπράσκω.

5:15 οὐκ ἀρκεσθεὶς δὲ τούτοις κατετόλμησεν εἰς τὸ πάσης τῆς γῆς ἁγιώτατον ἱερὸν εἰσελθεῖν ὁδηγὸν ἔχων τὸν Μενέλαον τὸν καὶ τῶν νόμων καὶ τῆς πατρίδος προδότην γεγονότα,

οὐκ ἀρκεσθεὶς. Aor pass ptc nom masc sg ἀρκέω (causal). The passive voice of the verb has the sense of "to content oneself, be satisfied"
(*GE*, 298) and takes a dative complement.

δὲ. Development; see 1:10 on δέ.

τούτοις. Dative complement of ἀρκεσθεὶς. The neuter demonstrative
pronoun has a conceptual antecedent, referring to the preceding phrase
(Wallace, 333).

κατετόλμησεν. Aor act ind 3rd sg κατατολμάω. Cf. 3:24, where those
who were "*bold enough* to accompany (Heliodorus)" are described with
the same verb.

εἰς τὸ . . . ἁγιώτατον ἱερὸν. Locative. The adjective ἁγιώτατον is the
superlative form of ἅγιος ("most holy temple").

πάσης τῆς γῆς. Partitive genitive.

εἰσελθεῖν. Aor act inf εἰσέρχομαι (complementary). On the εισ-
compound verb + εἰς, see 3:28 on τὸν . . . εἰσελθόντα.

ὁδηγὸν. Complement in an object-complement double accusative
construction. See BDAG (690.1): "one who leads the way in reaching a
desired destination, guide, leader."

ἔχων. Pres act ptc nom masc sg ἔχω (means).

τὸν Μενέλαον. Accusative direct object of ἔχων in an object-
complement double accusative construction. The fact that Menelaus
guides Antiochus into the temple, a place where gentiles are forbidden
to enter, underscores his wickedness.

τὸν . . . γεγονότα. Prf act ptc acc masc sg γίνομαι (attributive, modifying τὸν Μενέλαον). The separation of the article from the participle
is an example of hyperbaton where the interpositional words modify the
participle.

καὶ . . . καὶ. Correlative construction: "both . . . and" (BDF §444.3;
BDAG, 495.1.f).

τῶν νόμων . . . τῆς πατρίδος. Objective genitives ("[a traitor] of the
laws and of country"). Cf. the similar description of Jason in 5:8-9.

προδότην. Accusative direct object of τὸν γεγονότα. Xenophon
(*Hell.* 1.7.22) also notes that temple robbery makes one a "traitor."

5:16 καὶ ταῖς μιαραῖς χερσὶν τὰ ἱερὰ σκεύη λαμβάνων καὶ τὰ ὑπ᾽ ἄλλων βασιλέων ἀνατεθέντα πρὸς αὔξησιν καὶ δόξαν τοῦ τόπου καὶ τιμὴν ταῖς βεβήλοις χερσὶν συσσύρων.

For an excellent discussion of the text critical problems in 5:16, see Goldstein (258–60). Below, I discuss only those most pertinent.

ταῖς μιαραῖς χερσίν. Dative of instrument. Hayes (51) argues that Antiochus' "profane" or "polluted" hands denotes a moral impurity rather than simply his gentile identity. On the ritual impurity of gentiles (categorically "sinners"), see Jdt 10:13. The Göttingen edition reads ταῖς μιεραῖς. On the variation between ὁ μιερός and ὁ μιαρός, see 4:19 on Ἰάσων ὁ μιαρός.

τὰ ἱερὰ σκεύη. Accusative direct object of λαμβάνων. This is a surprisingly bare description of Antiochus' plunder from the temple (cf. 1 Macc 1:21-23; Josephus, *Ant.* 12.249). D. Schwartz (260) suggests that this is "an eloquent example of what does and does not interest our diasporan author."

λαμβάνων. Pres act ptc nom masc sg λαμβάνω (result or, perhaps, purpose). Although it is tempting to translate this participle as attendant circumstance, because the participle follows the verb it modifies (κατετόλμησεν, 5:15) and is present tense, it is best to take it as a result (or purpose) of Antiochus entering the temple. The verb ἐδεδίδου (*L* 311 Sy) was probably added to the end of 5:16 to complement λαμβάνων (*pace* Goldstein, 259).

τὰ . . . ἀνατεθέντα. Aor pass ptc acc neut pl ἀνατίθημι (substantival). Direct object of συσσύρων (lit. "the things offered"). It is surprising that the epitomizer describes these gifts by diasporan kings to the temple in more detail than "the sacred vessels" (τὰ ἱερὰ σκεύη). This probably shows that the epitomizer cares deeply about approval of Judaism by others (cf. 3:2).

ὑπ᾽ ἄλλων βασιλέων. Agency.

πρὸς αὔξησιν καὶ δόξαν . . . καὶ τιμήν. Purpose. Αὔξησις refers to "increase in prestige: of temple" (*GELS*, 103).

τοῦ τόπου. Genitive of source.

ταῖς βεβήλοις χερσίν. Dative of instrument. *GELS* (116) notes that βεβήλοις often has a "pejorative connotation." See comments on ταῖς μιαραῖς χερσίν above.

συσσύρων. Pres act ptc nom masc sg συσσύρω (result or, perhaps, purpose). On the meaning of the verb, see *GELS* (663): "to make off with all of: + acc[usative]."

2 Maccabees 5:17-20

[17]And Antiochus was elated in spirit, not seeing that, because of the sins of those who lived in the city, the Sovereign was angered briefly. Therefore, there came about neglect concerning the place. [18]Now if it had not happened that there were many sins, just as Heliodorus, the one who had been sent by king Seleucus for the investigation of the treasury, this one, immediately upon advancing [into the temple], would have been flogged and diverted from [his] audacity. [19]But [the Lord did not choose] the nation because of the place. Rather, he chose the place because of the nation. [20]Therefore, even the place itself, having shared in the misfortunes that came upon the nation, afterward shared in the benefits. And what had been abandoned in the wrath of the Almighty was restored again with all glory by the reconciliation of the Almighty.

Here begins a digression that spans from 5:17-20. In this short departure from the main narrative, the epitomizer reflects on what has happened and concludes that sin results in suffering (cf. 4:16-17). As the rest of the work makes clear, such suffering is not meant to destroy, but edify (cf. 6:12; 7:33). Moreover, God, and not Antiochus, is in charge of Jerusalem's destiny. The epitomizer communicates this clearly by noting that Antiochus "was elated" and "did not perceive" (5:17). The point is that readers of the text should not be similarly misled (Coetzer, 256). For more on digressions, see the Introduction.

5:17 καὶ ἐμετεωρίζετο τὴν διάνοιαν ὁ Ἀντίοχος οὐ συνορῶν ὅτι διὰ τὰς ἁμαρτίας τῶν τὴν πόλιν οἰκούντων ἀπώργισται βραχέως ὁ δεσπότης, διὸ γέγονεν περὶ τὸν τόπον παρόρασις.

ἐμετεωρίζετο. Impf mid ind 3rd sg μετεωρίζομαι. The theme of Antiochus' elation appears also in 5:21; 7:34; 9:8. The imperfect verb (imperfective verbal aspect) suggests habitual or regular practice.

τὴν διάνοιαν. Accusative of respect, with ἐμετεωρίζετο.

ὁ Ἀντίοχος. Nominative subject of ἐμετεωρίζετο.

οὐ. On the negation οὐ with a participle, see 4:5 on οὐ.

συνορῶν. Pres act ptc nom masc sg συνοράω (result).

ὅτι. Introduces a content clause that is the clausal complement (indirect discourse) of συνορῶν.

διὰ τὰς ἁμαρτίας τῶν τὴν πόλιν οἰκούντων. Cause. D. Schwartz (261) notes that the idea that God's anger is kindled "because of the sins" is "a major theological premise of the book" (cf. 4:16-17; 6:14-16; 7:32).

τῶν . . . οἰκούντων. Pres act ptc gen masc pl οἰκέω (substantival). Subjective genitive.

τὴν πόλιν. Accusative direct object of τῶν οἰκούντων. On the use of ἡ πόλις rather than Ἱεροσόλυμα, see 2:22 on τὴν πόλιν.

ἀπώργισται. Prf mid ind 3rd sg ἀποργίζομαι. On the meaning of the verb, see GE (266): "to become angry." D. Schwartz (262) notes that "we are still in the time of God's anger, and God turns *away* (thus allowing Antiochus free rein)." This contrasts with the use of ἐπώργισται in 7:33, where God is still angry but is pursuing reconciliation.

βραχέως. Temporal adverb.

ὁ δεσπότης. Nominative subject of ἀπώργισται. This epithet emphasizes God's ability and power to defend Jerusalem, even if God lacks the will do so in a specific situation. Cf. other uses of the epithet in 5:20; 6:14; 9:13; 15:22.

διό. Inferential conjunction, introducing "an expository or hortatory thesis that is inferred from what has already been stated" (Levinsohn 2014, 329). See 5:4 on διό.

γέγονεν. Prf act ind 3rd sg γίνομαι.

περὶ τὸν τόπον. Reference. Unlike in some other instances in 2 Maccabees, where τόπος refers to the temple (e.g., 3:2, 12, 18), here it refers more generally to the city of Jerusalem, as is indicated by the reference to "the sins of those who lived in the city" (τὰς ἁμαρτίας τῶν τὴν πόλιν οἰκούντων) earlier in 5:17 (*pace* BDAG, 1011.1.b).

παρόρασις. Predicate nominative. GE (1589) suggests "neglect, negligence, lack of care," thus, "because this place had been abandoned." God's anger results in the exceptional situation that God neglects his people (cf. 3:39).

5:18 εἰ δὲ μὴ συνέβη προσενέχεσθαι πολλοῖς ἁμαρτήμασιν, καθάπερ ἦν ὁ Ἡλιόδωρος ὁ πεμφθεὶς ὑπὸ Σελεύκου τοῦ βασιλέως ἐπὶ τὴν ἐπίσκεψιν τοῦ γαζοφυλακίου, οὗτος προαχθεὶς παραχρῆμα μαστιγωθεὶς ἀνετράπη τοῦ θράσους.

εἰ. Introduces a second-class conditional clause (Smyth §2302), using εἰ + aorist indicative in the protasis. The second-class conditional introduces a counterfactual condition where the writer or speaker "considers the fulfillment of a present or past condition impossible or no longer possible" (CGCG §49.10). While ἄν is expected in the apodosis, Muraoka (§89ba) notes that "[i]n a few cases the particle ἄν is missing" (cf. Wallace, 694). This understanding is further confirmed by the addition of ἄν after ἁμαρτήμασιν in some of the MS tradition (L⁻⁵⁴² 311 Sy). Cf. 4:47.

δὲ. Development; see 1:10 on δέ.

μὴ συνέβη. Aor act ind 3rd sg συμβαίνω. The Göttingen edition prints the imperfect form συνέβαινε (following most MSS), but R-H follows MS A. The imperfect form, which is probably best, captures the sense of the action better (cf. Doran 2012, 123). On this construction, see 3:2 on συνέβαινεν.

προσενέχεσθαι. Pres mid inf προσενέχομαι (indirect discourse). The Göttingen edition reads προενέχεσθαι, although Nicklas (2011, 1391) notes there is no significant difference in meaning.

πολλοῖς ἁμαρτήμασιν. Dative complement of προσενέχεσθαι.

καθάπερ. The conjunction introduces a comparative clause. On the function, see 2:27.

ἦν. Impf act ind 3rd sg εἰμί.

ὁ Ἡλιόδωρος. Nominative subject of ἦν.

ὁ πεμφθεὶς. Aor pass ptc nom masc sg πέμπω (attributive, modifying ὁ Ἡλιόδωρος).

ὑπὸ Σελεύκου τοῦ βασιλέως. Agency.

ἐπὶ τὴν ἐπίσκεψιν. Goal. ἐπί can denote "extension toward a goal, usually implying reaching the goal" (LN 84.17; cf. BDAG, 364.4.b; *GE*, 752.II.C.g). On the use of ἐπίσκεψις for the "investigation" of a crime, see *GE* (788).

τοῦ γαζοφυλακίου. Objective genitive. On the meaning "treasury," see 3:6 on τὸ . . . γαζοφυλάκιον.

οὗτος. Nominative subject of ἀνετράπη. Although only a few MSS (V 58) read καί prior to this substantive, many consider it "indispensable" to the phrase (Habicht, 227; cf. Doran 2012, 123). The omission of small words like καί is one of the most common accidental copyist mistakes (cf. Royse, 183).

προαχθεὶς. Aor pass ptc nom masc sg προάγω (attendant circumstance).

παραχρῆμα. Adverb. On the sense of this adverb, see 4:34 on παραχρῆμα.

μαστιγωθεὶς. Aor pass ptc nom masc sg μαστιγόω (attendant circumstance).

ἀνετράπη. Aor pass ind 3rd sg ἀνατρέπω. On the meaning of the verb, see *GE* (158): "to be diverted," with the genitive (cf. *GELS*, 47).

τοῦ θράσους. Genitive complement of ἀνετράπη.

5:19 ἀλλ' οὐ διὰ τὸν τόπον τὸ ἔθνος, ἀλλὰ διὰ τὸ ἔθνος τὸν τόπον ὁ κύριος ἐξελέξατο.

Note the elegant reversal of two key terms (τόπος, ἔθνος) in this verse. The subject and verb are delayed until the end of the clause in order to maintain the symmetry.

ἀλλ'. Marker of contrast, introducing a correction of a mistaken expectation. The description of the nation's sins in 5:17-18 might lead to the conclusion that God's favor toward the Jews was only because of the place (διὰ τὸν τόπον). But, the epitomizer corrects this misunderstanding by clearly stating that the Lord chose the place because of the people (διὰ τὸ ἔθνος).

οὐ ... ἀλλά. A point/counterpoint set (Runge, 92–100). According to Heckert (23), following a negated statement (with οὐ or μή) the particle ἀλλά "introduces a correction of the expectation created by the first conjunct; an incorrect expectation is cancelled and a proper expectation is put in its place." Ellipsis of the verb is common in constructions of this type (cf. BDF §479.1).

διὰ τὸν τόπον. Cause.

τὸ ἔθνος. Accusative direct object of an implied ἐξελέξατο. In contrast with the plural uses of ἔθνος in 2 Maccabees, which always refer to gentile nations (1:27; 4:35; 6:4, 14; 8:5, 9, 16; 10:4; 11:3; 12:13; 13:11; 14:14-15; 15:8, 10), the singular uses of ἔθνος refer to Israel (5:19, 20; 6:31; 7:37; 10:8; 11:25, 27; 14:34).

διὰ τὸ ἔθνος. Cause.

τὸν τόπον. Accusative direct object of ἐξελέξατο.

ὁ κύριος. Nominative subject of ἐξελέξατο.

ἐξελέξατο. Aor mid ind 3rd sg ἐκλέγομαι.

5:20 διόπερ καὶ αὐτὸς ὁ τόπος συμμετασχὼν τῶν τοῦ ἔθνους δυσπετημάτων γενομένων ὕστερον εὐεργετημάτων ἐκοινώνησεν, καὶ ὁ καταλειφθεὶς ἐν τῇ τοῦ παντοκράτορος ὀργῇ πάλιν ἐν τῇ τοῦ μεγάλου δεσπότου καταλλαγῇ μετὰ πάσης δόξης ἐπανωρθώθη.

διόπερ. Inferential conjunction introducing a logical conclusion (cf. *GELS*, 171). The addition of -περ adds force to the conjunction διό. Here, concluding the digression (5:17-20): the temple does not ensure God's protection of the place, but also God does not forget the temple.

καὶ. Ascensive.

αὐτὸς. Intensive adjective modifying ὁ τόπος.

αὐτὸς ὁ τόπος. Nominative subject of ἐκοινώνησεν.

συμμετασχών. Aor act ptc nom masc sg συμμετέχω (temporal or, perhaps, concessive). *GELS* (647): "to have a share of experiencing together." After a verb of sharing, the genitive case is expected (cf. BDF §182).

τῶν . . . δυσπετημάτων. Genitive after a verb of sharing. Domazakis (127–29) notes that δυσπέτημα was probably coined by the epitomizer. On the meaning of the prefix δυσ-, see 3:11 on ὁ δυσσεβὴς Σιμων. Note the homoiteleuton with εὐεργετημάτων.

τοῦ ἔθνους. Predicate genitive.

γενομένων. Aor mid ptc gen neut pl γίνομαι (attributive, modifying τῶν . . . δυσπετημάτων).

ὕστερον. Temporal adverb: "thereafter, afterwards" (*GELS*, 707.II). Cf. 6:15.

εὐεργετημάτων. Genitive complement of ἐκοινώνησεν.

ἐκοινώνησεν. Aor act ind 3rd sg κοινωνέω.

ὁ καταλειφθεὶς. Aor pass ptc nom masc sg καταλείπω (substantival). Subject of ἐπανωρθώθη. Note the alliteration with καταλλαγῇ.

ἐν τῇ . . . ὀργῇ. Instrumental or, better, cause.

τοῦ παντοκράτορος. Genitive of source (indicating a judgment) or, perhaps, subjective genitive (indicating an action). See 1:25 on δίκαιος καὶ παντοκράτωρ καὶ αἰώνιος.

πάλιν. Adverb.

ἐν τῇ . . . καταλλαγῇ. Cause. Echoes and contrasts with ἐν τῇ . . . ὀργῇ earlier in the clause.

τοῦ μεγάλου δεσπότου. Objective genitive.

μετὰ πάσης δόξης. Manner. Cf. discussion in 3:1 on μετὰ πάσης εἰρήνης.

ἐπανωρθώθη. Aor pass ind 3rd sg ἐπανορθόω.

2 Maccabees 5:21-27

[21]Then Antiochus carried off eighteen hundred talents from the temple and departed quickly into Antioch, supposing in his arrogance to make the land navigable and the sea passable because of the elation of [his] heart. [22]He also left officials to afflict the people. In Jerusalem, [he left] Philip, who was of Phyrgian descent, but had a more barbarous character than the one who appointed [him]. [23]And in Gerizim, [he left] Andronicus and, in addition to them, Menelaus, who worse than the others was exalting himself over the citizens, having intense hate toward the Jewish citizens. [24]And he sent the Mysarch Apollonius with an army [of] about twenty-two thousand, commanding [him] to slaughter all

those in adulthood and to sell the women and the youth. [25]Now this one, upon arriving in Jerusalem, pretended to be peaceful and waited until the holy day of the Sabbath. And finding the Jews resting, he ordered military maneuvers for those under him. [26]And he stabbed all the ones who came upon the spectacle and he rushed into the city with his armed men and killed a great multitude [of people]. [27]But Judas, the one also [called] Maccabeus, being about the tenth [person], and he withdrew into the wilderness and he lived in the mountains with his companions. And they continued living on grassy food in order not to share in the defilement.

In the final section of 2 Maccabees 5, the epitomizer portrays Antiochus as "a divine pretender," possibly drawing upon both Jewish and Greco-Roman traditions in his characterization of Antiochus (Wheaton, 255). The most obvious parallel from Jewish Scripture comes from LXX Job 9:8, where it is Israel's God "who alone stretched out the sky and walks on the sea as on dry ground" (NETS). Likewise, in Hellenistic tradition the vanity of the Persian king Xerxes is depicted in that he desires to build a walkway across the water (cf. Herodotus, *Hist.* 7.22-24, 33-36; Aeschylus, *Pers.* 745-50). Goldstein (260–61) is correct to conclude that, in this depiction of Antiochus, the epitomizer employed traditional imagery from both Jewish and Greco-Roman tradition in order to display the arrogance of Antiochus.

5:21 Ὁ γοῦν Ἀντίοχος ὀκτακόσια πρὸς τοῖς χιλίοις ἀπενεγκάμενος ἐκ τοῦ ἱεροῦ τάλαντα θᾶττον εἰς τὴν Ἀντιόχειαν ἐχωρίσθη οἰόμενος ἀπὸ τῆς ὑπερηφανίας τὴν μὲν γῆν πλωτὴν καὶ τὸ πέλαγος πορευτὸν θέσθαι διὰ τὸν μετεωρισμὸν τῆς καρδίας.

Ὁ ... Ἀντίοχος. Nominative subject of ἐχωρίσθη.

γοῦν. Following the digression (5:17-20), the post-positive γοῦν (γε + οὖν) signals a return to the main plotline of the narrative (cf. Grimm, 104). See *GELS* (136.1): "introduces a new phase in a chain of connected events."

ὀκτακόσια πρὸς τοῖς χιλίοις ... τάλαντα. Accusative direct object of ἀπενεγκάμενος. On the meaning of τάλαντον, see 3:11.

ὀκτακόσια πρὸς τοῖς χιλίοις. πρός is additive. Thus, "eight hundred *in addition to* one thousand" = "eighteen hundred." Some later MSS adjusted this number for inflation: ἐννακισχιλίοις ("nine thousand," MS 58) or τρισχιλίοις ("three thousand," MSS 46-52). On this construction, see 4:8 on ἑξήκοντα πρὸς τοῖς τριακοσίοις. See Smyth (§347) on numbers.

ἀπενεγκάμενος. Aor mid ptc nom masc sg ἀποφέρω (attendant circumstance). See 1:18 on ἀνήνεγκεν.

ἐκ τοῦ ἱεροῦ. Separation.

θᾶττον. Temporal adverb.

εἰς τὴν Ἀντιόχειαν. Spatial.

ἐχωρίσθη. Aor pass ind 3rd sg χωρίζω.

οἰόμενος. Pres mid ptc nom masc sg οἴομαι (manner). On the meaning of the verb, see *GELS* (490): "to assume as probable though not absolutely certain" + infinitive. Cf. 7:24.

ἀπὸ τῆς ὑπερηφανίας. Cause. See *GELS* (698): "arrogance, pride." This expression is parallel with διὰ τὸν μετεωρισμὸν τῆς καρδίας later in 5:23.

τὴν μὲν γῆν πλωτὴν καὶ τὸ πέλαγος πορευτὸν. The adjective πλωτός denotes "navigable" sea (cf. *GELS*, 567). Likewise, the adjective πορευτός denotes "suitable for traveling (by land)" (*GE*, 1722). However, the epitomizer applies these adjectives to the opposite entities. Rather than "navigable sea" and "passable land," he speaks of "navigable land" and "passable sea." The point is that Antiochus' self-delusion leads him to think he can do impossible (or miraculous) things. This ironic description is one of the clearest examples of the epitomizer drawing upon a Greek literary theme or antecedent. In particular, Antiochus' actions mirror the arrogance of Xerxes, who wanted to dig a massive canal through the city of Athos as well as build a bridge over the Hellespont. According to Herodotus (*Hist.* 7.22-24, 33-36), "Xerxes gave command for this digging out of pride, because he would display his power and leave memorials of it; for they might very easily have drawn their ships across the isthmus; yet he bade them dig a canal from sea to sea, wide enough to float two triremes rowed abreast" (here, 7.24, LCL). For similar descriptions of Antiochus' delusion, see 9:8, 10. See 7:19 and 9:12 as well.

τὴν . . . γῆν. Accusative direct object of an implied verb (θέσθαι) in an object-complement double accusative construction.

μὲν . . . καὶ. The slight contrast implied in μέν/δέ is evaded by pairing μέν with a particle that denotes addition (Denniston, 374). Because μέν signals "anticipation of a related sentence that follows" (Runge, 75), the καί signals that new information is added. Several MSS (*L*⁻⁵⁴² 311 La^VBDP) read τὸ δὲ πέλαγος, creating the μέν/δέ construction.

πλωτὴν. Accusative complement of an implied verb (θέσθαι) in an object-complement double accusative construction.

τὸ πέλαγος. Accusative direct object of θέσθαι in an object-complement double accusative construction.

πορευτὸν. Accusative complement of θέσθαι in an object-complement double accusative construction.

θέσθαι. Aor mid inf τίθημι (indirect discourse). On the meaning of the verb, see *GELS* (679.II.4): "to cause to become," used with a double accusative construction.

διὰ τὸν μετεωρισμὸν. Cause. This figurative expression (of arrogance) is parallel with ἀπὸ τῆς ὑπερηφανίας earlier in 5:23. Noting the similarity with the parallel expression, Habicht (227) suggests these words are a marginal notation that entered the body of the text.

τῆς καρδίας. Objective genitive.

5:22 κατέλιπεν δὲ καὶ ἐπιστάτας τοῦ κακοῦν τὸ γένος, ἐν μὲν Ἱεροσολύμοις Φίλιππον, τὸ μὲν γένος Φρύγα, τὸν δὲ τρόπον βαρβαρώτερον ἔχοντα τοῦ καταστήσαντος,

κατέλιπεν. Aor act ind 3rd sg καταλείπω.

δὲ. Development; see 1:10 on δέ.

καὶ. Adverbial.

ἐπιστάτας. Accusative direct object of κατέλιπεν. Denotes a "city governor" or "official" (D. Schwartz, 263; Habicht, 227).

τοῦ κακοῦν. Pres act inf κακόω (purpose). Burk (63) notes that purpose may seem an unusual feature of the genitive + infinitive construction. However, Smyth (§1408) rightly notes that the purpose (which emphasizes the *end* of an action) and cause (which emphasizes the *beginning* of an action) are conceptually similar. Thus, the normal ablatival sense of the genitive case may explain the development of the construction τοῦ + infinitive to denote purpose (see Burk, 63–67). Doran (2012, 132) draws attention to Exod 1:11 where Pharaoh "set over them *overseers* [ἐπιστάτας] of tasks *in order to afflict* [ἵνα κακώσωσιν] them in the tasks" (NETS).

τὸ γένος. Accusative direct object of κακοῦν.

ἐν ... Ἱεροσολύμοις. Locative.

μὲν ... μὲν ... δὲ. Point/counterpoint set. The particle μέν is repeated to refer to a previous clause (cf. *GE*, 1310.2.F). The placement of μέν between the preposition and its object is not uncommon for an enclitic particle. See 2:26 on μέν ... δέ.

Φίλιππον. Accusative direct object of an implied form of καταλείπω. Because the name Φίλιππος is being established in the narrative it is anarthrous (Smyth §1136; Muraoka §1b). Compare this use with the following articular uses of the name in 6:11; 8:8; 13:23, where the article defines "[o]bjects already mentioned or in the mind of the speaker or writer" (Smyth §1120.b).

τὸ ... γένος Φρύγα. Accusative in apposition to Φίλιππον. γένος appears "with name of a people to denote nationality" (BDAG, 194.3).

τὸν ... τρόπον βαρβαρώτερον. Accusative direct object of ἔχοντα.

ἔχοντα. Pres act ptc acc masc sg ἔχω (attributive, modifying Φίλιππον). On the idiomatic usage of ἔχω + an adverbial expression of manner, see 1:24 on ἔχουσα.

τοῦ καταστήσαντος. Aor act ptc gen masc sg καθίστημι (substantival). Comparison, using the genitive. On the basic sense here, see 3:4 on καθεσταμένος.

5:23 ἐν δὲ Γαριζιν Ἀνδρόνικον, πρὸς δὲ τούτοις Μενέλαον, ὃς χείριστα τῶν ἄλλων ὑπερήρετο τοῖς πολίταις, ἀπεχθῆ δὲ πρὸς τοὺς πολίτας Ἰουδαίους ἔχων διάθεσιν.

There is some debate over whether ἀπεχθῆ δὲ πρὸς τοὺς πολίτας Ἰουδαίους ἔχων διάθεσιν belongs with 5:23 (cf. D. Schwartz, 264–65) or should be linked to 5:24 (cf. Habicht, 227–28; Goldstein, 261; Doran 2012, 124). In the latter case, the words are used to motivate Antiochus' sending of Apollonius. In the former case, the words describe Menelaus. Following D. Schwartz (265): "[b]ut to begin now to explain Antiochus' behavior toward the Jews seems late and superfluous, and it appears that it is rather Menelaus who is new here and the intended object of the author's denigration." Accordingly, the punctuation of R-H and the Göttingen edition is followed.

ἐν ... Γαριζιν. Locative. The Göttingen edition reads Αργαριζιν, which is combination of the full toponym: הר גרזים ("Mount Gerizim").

δὲ. Development; see 1:10 on δέ.

Ἀνδρόνικον. Accusative direct object of an implied κατέλιπεν, see 5:22.

πρὸς ... τούτοις. Adverbial: "in addition to *these/them.*" See 4:9 on πρὸς ... τούτοις.

δὲ. Development; see 1:10 on δέ.

Μενέλαον. Accusative direct object of an implied κατέλιπεν, see 5:22.

ὃς. Nominative subject of ὑπερήρετο.

χείριστα. Accusative direct object of ὑπερήρετο.

τῶν ἄλλων. Genitive of comparison with χείριστα.

ὑπερήρετο. Impf mid ind 3rd sg ὑπεραίρω. Doran (2012, 132) notes that in the middle, ὑπεραίρω denotes "to exalt oneself, to lord over." The use of the dative complement is exceptional with the middle, but may follow the pattern of the active (cf. Demosthenes, *Cor.* 18.220).

τοῖς πολίταις. Dative complement of ὑπερήρετο.

ἀπεχθῆ ... διάθεσιν. Accusative direct object of ἔχων. The separation of the modifier from the head is an example of hyperbaton where the modifier (ἀπεχθῆ) is emphasized.

δὲ. Development; see 1:10 on δέ.

πρὸς τοὺς πολίτας Ἰουδαίους. Opposition.

ἔχων. Pres act ptc nom masc sg ἔχω (causal). Because of protentional ambiguity, some MSS (*L*⁻⁵⁴² Sy Tht) read ἔχων ὁ Ἀντίοχος here, supplying the understood grammatical subject for 5:23-24. For additional discussion of text critical issues caused by this ambiguity, see Goldstein (261–63).

5:24 ἔπεμψεν δὲ τὸν Μυσάρχην Ἀπολλώνιον μετὰ στρατεύματος, δισμυρίους δὲ πρὸς τοῖς δισχιλίοις, προστάξας τοὺς ἐν ἡλικίᾳ πάντας κατασφάξαι, τὰς δὲ γυναῖκας καὶ τοὺς νεωτέρους πωλεῖν.

ἔπεμψεν. Aor act ind 3rd sg πέμπω.

δὲ. Development; see 1:10 on δέ. Following from the ambiguities mentioned in 5:23, some MSS omit this particle.

τὸν Μυσάρχην. Accusative in apposition to Ἀπολλώνιον. The designation of Apollonius as "the Mysarch" identifies him as "a commander of mercenaries from Mysia in Asia Minor" (Doran 2012, 132; cf. Goldstein, 265). D. Schwartz (265) notes a possible play on words given that μύσος (cf. 6:19, 25) means "abomination."

Ἀπολλώνιον. Accusative direct object of ἔπεμψεν.

μετὰ στρατεύματος. Association.

δισμυρίους ... πρὸς τοῖς δισχιλίοις. Πρός is additive. Here, "twenty thousand *in addition to* two-thousand" = "twenty-two thousand." See 4:8 on ἑξήκοντα πρὸς τοῖς τριακοσίοις. This number is probably inflated. The awkwardness of the syntax resulted in several MSS (*L*⁻⁵⁴² 56 311 771) altering δισμυρίους to δισμυρίων so that it can modify στρατεύματος: "an army *of twenty-two thousand.*" As read in R-H and the Göttingen edition, this would be an example of the accusative of respect (cf. Smyth §1601b).

δὲ. Development; see 1:10 on δέ.

προστάξας. Aor act ptc nom masc sg προστάσσω (manner).

τοὺς ... πάντας. Accusative direct object of κατασφάξαι.

ἐν ἡλικίᾳ. Temporal. The idiom "in the height" = "adult men" (*GELS*, 319.2). Cf. 4:40; 5:24; 6:18, 23-24; 7:27; 15:30.

κατασφάξαι. Aor act inf κατασφάζω (indirect discourse).

τὰς ... γυναῖκας καὶ τοὺς νεωτέρους. Accusative direct objects of πωλεῖν. BDAG (669.3.b.β) notes that the comparative form of νέος is often used as a substantive with little or no comparative force.

δὲ. Development; see 1:10 on δέ.

πωλεῖν. Pres act inf πωλέω (indirect discourse).

5:25 οὗτος δὲ παραγενόμενος εἰς Ιεροσόλυμα καὶ τὸν εἰρηνικὸν ὑποκριθεὶς ἐπέσχεν ἕως τῆς ἁγίας ἡμέρας τοῦ σαββάτου καὶ λαβὼν ἀργοῦντας τοὺς Ιουδαίους τοῖς ὑφ᾽ ἑαυτὸν ἐξοπλισίαν παρήγγειλεν,

οὗτος. Nominative subject of ἐπέσχεν.

δὲ. Development; see 1:10 on δέ.

παραγενόμενος. Aor mid ptc nom masc sg παραγίνομαι (temporal).

εἰς Ιεροσόλυμα. Spatial (motion toward).

τὸν εἰρηνικὸν. Predicate accusative of an implied infinitive copula. Some MSS (L^{-542} 311) read εἶναι after ὑποκριθεὶς: "pretending [to be] peaceful."

ὑποκριθεὶς. Aor mid ptc nom masc sg ὑποκρίνω (attendant circumstance). *GE* (2223) suggests a figurative sense: "to feign, fake, imitate." Verbs of self-involvement are typically middle (N. Miller, 428). For an example of ὑποκρίνω with a complementary infinitive, see 4 Macc 6:15.

ἐπέσχεν. Aor act ind 3rd sg ἐπέχω. On the meaning of the verb, see *GELS* (263): "to wait without proceeding to next action." The strategy of waiting until Sabbath to attack Jews is well-documented in other sources (e.g., Josephus, *Ag. Ap.* 1.209-11; *Ant.* 12.5-6; 1 Macc 2:29-38).

ἕως τῆς ἁγίας ἡμέρας. Although ἕως is a temporal conjunction (BDAG, 422.1-2), it often functions as a preposition followed by the genitive (BDAG, 423.3). The PP conveys duration of time.

τοῦ σαββάτου. Genitive of apposition. There is some variation between the singular (5:25; 8:26, 27, 28; 12:38) and the plural (15:3) of σάββατον in 2 Maccabees, although there is no discernable difference in meaning.

λαβὼν. Aor act ptc nom masc sg λαμβάνω (temporal or, perhaps, causal).

ἀργοῦντας τοὺς Ιουδαίους. Accusative direct object of λαβών.

ἀργοῦντας. Pres act ptc acc masc pl ἀργέω (attributive). On the meaning of the verb, see *GELS* (89): "to rest from work."

τοῖς. The dative article functions as a nominalizer, changing the following PP (ὑφ᾽ ἑαυτόν) into the indirect object of παρήγγειλεν.

ὑφ᾽ ἑαυτὸν. Subordination.

ἐξοπλισίαν. Accusative direct object of παρήγγειλεν. Doran (2012, 132) suggests that ἐξοπλισίαν "resonates with the use of ἐξωπλισμένους" in the vision of 5:2, perhaps suggesting that the vision has been fulfilled (cf. D. Schwartz, 266–67).

παρήγγειλεν. Aor act ind 3rd sg παραγγέλλω.

5:26 καὶ τοὺς ἐξελθόντας πάντας ἐπὶ τὴν θεωρίαν συνεξεκέντησεν καὶ εἰς τὴν πόλιν σὺν τοῖς ὅπλοις εἰσδραμὼν ἱκανὰ κατέστρωσεν πλήθη.

τοὺς ἐξελθόντας πάντας. Accusative direct object of συνεξεκέντησεν.
τοὺς ἐξελθόντας. Aor act ptc acc masc pl ἐξέρχομαι (substantival).
ἐπὶ τὴν θεωρίαν. Locative. Denotes "s[omething] unusual which is visually observed" (*GELS*, 329).
συνεξεκέντησεν. Aor act ind 3rd sg συνεκκεντέω. On the meaning of the verb, see *GE* (2033): "to pierce."
εἰς τὴν πόλιν. Locative.
σὺν τοῖς ὅπλοις. Association. By figurative extension, the plural of ὅπλον is used to refer to "soldiers" or, better, "armed soldiers" (*GE*, 1471). This is common for neuter nouns, which can be used to refer to humans in a generic sense (cf. Muraoka §22ee).
εἰσδραμών. Aor act ptc nom masc sg εἰστρέχω (attendant circumstance). On the εἰσ-compound verb + εἰς, see 3:28 on τὸν . . . εἰσελθόντα.
ἱκανὰ . . . πλήθη. Accusative direct object of κατέστρωσεν.
κατέστρωσεν. Aor act ind 3rd sg καταστρώννυμι.

5:27 Ιουδας δὲ ὁ καὶ Μακκαβαῖος δέκατός που γενηθεὶς καὶ ἀναχωρήσας εἰς τὴν ἔρημον θηρίων τρόπον ἐν τοῖς ὄρεσιν διέζη σὺν τοῖς μετ᾽ αὐτοῦ, καὶ τὴν χορτώδη τροφὴν σιτούμενοι διετέλουν πρὸς τὸ μὴ μετασχεῖν τοῦ μολυσμοῦ.

Ιουδας. Nominative subject of διέζη.
δὲ. Development; see 1:10 on δέ.
ὁ καὶ Μακκαβαῖος. Nominative NP in apposition to Ιουδας. The article ὁ functions as a nominalizer in an idiomatic expression (lit. "the also Maccabeus"), which is functionally equivalent to ὁ καλούμενος καὶ Μακκαβαῖος (cf. 10:12). *NewDocs* (1:89–96) notes the following constructions are common for double names: (1) A ὁ / ἡ καί B; and (2) A ἐπικαλούμενος B. See 8:1; 10:12; and esp. Acts 13:8: Σαῦλος δέ, ὁ καὶ Παῦλος ("now Saul, who is also called Paul"). On the name Μακκαβαῖος, see 2:19 on κατὰ τὸν Ιουδαν τὸν Μακκαβαῖον.
δέκατός. Predicate nominative. The ordinal has two acute accents because it is followed by an enclitic (που). When following a word with an acute on the antepenult, the enclitic surrenders its accent, and it appears as an additional acute accent on the preceding word (Smyth §183.c). It is possible that this is the earliest extant reference to the concept of a ten-member quorum for Jewish communities (cf. Flusser, 518).
που. The enclitic adverb is a "marker of numerical approximation" (BDAG, 857.2; *GELS*, 580.2).

γενηθεὶς. Aor pass ptc nom masc sg γίνομαι (attributive, modifying Ιουδας).

ἀναχωρήσας. Aor act ptc nom masc sg ἀναχωρέω (attendant circumstance). The collocation of ἀναχωρέω + εἰς is common (BDAG, 75.1.b) and has the sense of "to withdraw [to somewhere]" (*GE*, 162.A).

εἰς τὴν ἔρημον. Locative. The adjective ἔρημος is used as a substantive to denote "an uninhabited region or locality, desert, grassland, wilderness (in contrast to cultivated and inhabited country)" (BDAG, 392.2). In Jewish thinking, the wilderness was (Isa 52:11-12) and would remain (1QS 9.19-20; *Mart. Isa.* 2:8) a place apart from the corruption of sinful society where God's people (a remnant) would remain until the land was purified.

The Göttingen edition lacks this reading and has only ἐν τοῖς ὄρεσιν in its place. D. Schwartz (267–68) suggests that εἰς τὴν ἔρημον may have been a gloss explaining ὄρος. Nevertheless, the reading is reasonably secure in the MS tradition (V *L*⁻⁵⁴² 55 58 LA Sy Arm Lucif).

θηρίων τρόπον. Comparison. This post-positioned preposition is always preceded by the genitive (cf. Muraoka §42c). Cf. 8:35; 10:6; 3 Macc 4:9; 4 Macc 11:10; Job 4:9. τρόπος is used commonly with animals (BDAG, 1017.1).

ἐν τοῖς ὄρεσιν. Locative.

διέζη. Impf act ind 3rd sg διαζάω.

σὺν τοῖς μετ᾽ αὐτοῦ. Association.

τοῖς. The article functions as a nominalizer, changing the PP (μετ᾽ αὐτοῦ) into a substantive.

μετ᾽ αὐτοῦ. Association.

τὴν χορτώδη τροφὴν. Accusative direct object of σιτούμενοι. Literally, "grassy food." Stemberger (215–16) notes that "the refusal [to eat] pagan food and drink is connected with situations of crisis, Israel on the way to exile or already in a hostile foreign land or attacked by foreign forces (the Seleucids desecrating the temple and forcing the Jews to abandon their religion). . . . Food laws could certainly help to establish social barriers between Jews and non-Jews." For other examples of avoiding eating pagan food, see Josephus (*War* 2.143; *Life* 14).

σιτούμενοι. Pres mid ptc nom masc pl σιτέομαι (complementary). On the meaning of the verb, see *GELS* (621): "to live on s[omething] . . . as food."

διετέλουν. Impf act ind 3rd pl διατελέω. Used with the participle σιτούμενοι to "denote the state in which one remains" (BDAG, 238).

μετασχεῖν. Aor act inf μετέχω. Used with πρὸς τὸ [μή] to denote purpose.

τοῦ μολυσμοῦ. Genitive after a verb of sharing (μετασχεῖν). Verbal noun of μολύνω. On the pollution of the temple, see 6:2. The cleansing of the polluted temple happens in 10:3.

2 Maccabees 6:1-11

¹Now after not much time, the king dispatched Geron the Athenian to compel the Jews to change from the ancestral laws and no longer to conduct life by the laws of God ²and both to defile the temple in Jerusalem and to name it [the temple] of Zeus Olympios and [to name] the [temple] in Gerizim, just as those who inhabited the place happened [to be hospitable], [the temple] of Zeus Xenios. ³And the intensification of evil was dangerous and difficult in every way. ⁴For indeed the temple was becoming filled with debauchery and reveling by the gentiles, who were carousing with prostitutes and who had intercourse in the sacred precincts with women, but, moreover, bringing inside things that are not proper. ⁵And the altar was filled with unlawful things that were forbidden by the laws. ⁶And one could not keep the sabbath, nor observe ancestral feasts, nor, put simply, confess to being a Jew. ⁷And with bitter force, on the monthly celebration of the birth of the king, they were brought for the [consumption of] sacrifices. And when the feast of Dionysius came, they were compelled, having ivy, to make processionals for Dionysus. ⁸Then a decree went forth into the neighboring Greek cities, at Ptolemy's suggestion, to observe the same customs toward the Jews and to [compel them to] eat pagan sacrifices ⁹and to cut down those who did not choose to go over to Greek customs. Therefore, one could see the misery that was present. ¹⁰For two women were brought in because they circumcised their children. And, after hanging the infants from their breasts and parading them publicly around the city, they threw [them] down from the city wall. ¹¹And others who gathered together nearby in caves in order to celebrate the seventh day secretly, being betrayed to Philip, were burned together because their piety kept them from defending themselves, in conformity with the glory of the sacred day.

Disaster finally strikes in 6:1-11, including the defilement of the temple (6:2-5), prohibition of practicing Jewish law (6:1, 6), and idolatrous worship of Dionysus (6:7). Yet, the description of disaster is brief, leaving attention on the expanded martyrdom accounts that follow in 6:18-31 and 7:1-42. D. Schwartz (273) helpfully notes that the key theme of chapter 6 is "that suffering for one's religion is a positive and useful thing."

Although the aorist carries the plotline of the narrative (6:1, 8, 10, 11), a number of imperfect indicative verbs in 6:2-7 help describe the background or, perhaps, the results of the king compelling Jews to depart from the law.

6:1 Μετ' οὐ πολὺν δὲ χρόνον ἐξαπέστειλεν ὁ βασιλεὺς γέροντα Ἀθηναῖον ἀναγκάζειν τοὺς Ιουδαίους μεταβαίνειν ἀπὸ τῶν πατρίων νόμων καὶ τοῖς τοῦ θεοῦ νόμοις μὴ πολιτεύεσθαι,

Μετ' οὐ πολὺν . . . χρόνον. Temporal. Here μετά is used as a "marker of time after another point of time, *after*" (BDAG, 637.B.2). Cf. 5:1. The imprecise chronology is typical for the epitomizer (cf. D. Schwartz, 274). If the chronology of 1 Maccabees is followed, the year would be 167 BCE (cf. 1 Macc 1:20, 29).

δὲ. Development; see 1:10 on δέ. As a postpositive, δέ typically appears as the second word in a clause. However, in order not to break up a PP, sometimes δέ appears as the second constituent, treating the core of the PP as a unit (cf. BDF §475.2).

ἐξαπέστειλεν. Aor act ind 3rd sg ἐξαποστέλλω. *GE* (715.1) notes the sense "to dispatch, send." On the basis of parallel uses in 14:12 and 14:27, D. Schwartz (274–75) argues that ἐξαποστέλλω (rather than plain ἀποστέλλω) should be understood as "an indication of intensification and urgency."

ὁ βασιλεὺς. Nominative subject of ἐξαπέστειλεν.

γέροντα Ἀθηναῖον. Accusative direct object of ἐξαπέστειλεν. The noun Ἀθηναῖον is either an attributive modifier or in apposition to γέροντα. It is either a title or a proper name, thus: "the Athenian *elder*" (Bartlett, 261), "an Athenian *senator*" (NETS), or "*Geron* the Athenian" (Wilhelm, 20–22; Katz 1960, 14; Habicht, 229; Goldstein, 270; D. Schwartz, 275; Doran 2012, 133; Nicklas 2011, 1392). It may denote an elderly man between the ages of 60 and 80 years old. Yet, because "age played an important role in the selection of pers[ons] for special social and political functions," some render γέρων as "senator" (BDAG, 195).

Based on the style of 2 Maccabees, Goldstein (271) argues that "Geron the Athenian" is the best translation because: (1) titles are always articular in the Greek of 2 Maccabees, except for in predicate nominative (e.g., 15:12) and double accusative constructions (e.g., 14:13); (2) if Ἀθηναῖον is attributive, then a named enemy would be expected because this was the epitomizer's standard practice elsewhere (e.g., 3:7; 4:23; etc.). Cf. Katz (1960, 14).

ἀναγκάζειν. Pres act inf ἀναγκάζω (purpose).

τοὺς Ιουδαίους. Accusative subject of the infinitive μεταβαίνειν.

μεταβαίνειν. Pres act inf μεταβαίνω (indirect discourse). On the meaning of the verb, see *GE* (1321.A): "to change place *or* position."

ἀπὸ τῶν πατρίων νόμων. Separation. The epitomizer may be evoking a dual meaning of πάτριοι νόμοι, which in Hellenistic Greek literature was a common phrase "referring to Hellenistic cultural tradition" but in a Jewish context would "refer to Israelite ancestral law" (Simkovich, 300).

τοῖς . . . νόμοις. Dative of instrument. The "laws [of God]" refers to Torah.

τοῦ θεοῦ. Genitive of source. The genitive noun is articular because of Apollonius' Canon; see 3:24 on τοῦ θεοῦ.

μὴ. See comment on the negation in 1:5.

πολιτεύεσθαι. Pres mid inf πολιτεύομαι (indirect discourse). The choice of this verb "serves to compare religious life to life according to a municipal code" (D. Schwartz, 275). On the meaning of the verb, see also BDAG (846.3): "to conduct one's life, *live, lead one's life*." Cf. the use of the same verb in 11:25.

6:2 μολῦναι δὲ καὶ τὸν ἐν Ἱεροσολύμοις νεὼ καὶ προσονομάσαι Διὸς Ὀλυμπίου καὶ τὸν ἐν Γαριζιν, καθὼς ἐτύγχανον οἱ τὸν τόπον οἰκοῦντες, Διὸς Ξενίου.

μολῦναι. Aor act inf μολύνω (indirect discourse, modifying ἀναγκάζειν in 6:1). On the meaning of the verb, see *GE* (1358.1): "to stain, befoul, defile."

δὲ. Development; see 1:10 on δέ.

καὶ . . . καὶ. Likely correlative: "both . . . and." But it is possible that the first καί is adverbial: "*also* to pollute" (NETS).

τὸν . . . νεὼ. Accusative direct object of μολῦναι. See 4:14 on τοῦ . . . νεώ.

ἐν Ἱεροσολύμοις. Locative. On the attributive position of the PP, see 1:1 on κατ᾽ Αἴγυπτον.

προσονομάσαι. Aor act inf προσονομάζω (indirect discourse, modifying ἀναγκάζειν in 6:1). On the meaning of the verb, see *GE* (1820.1): "to call, denominate" = "to name."

Διὸς Ὀλυμπίου. Possessive genitive ("Zeus Olympios' [place]") or, less likely, source ("[the place dependent upon] Zeus Olympios"). Ζεύς, the main god in the Greek pantheon, is inflected as Διός in the genitive case.

τὸν. Accusative direct object of ἐπισυνήγαγεν. The article resumes νεώ without repeating it.

ἐν Γαριζιν. Locative. The Göttingen edition reads Αργαριζιν, which is combination of two Hebrew words of the full toponym: הר גרזים ("Mount Gerizim"). Cf. 5:23.

καθὼς ἐτύγχανον οἱ τὸν τόπον οἰκοῦντες. Either "just as those who inhabit the place *happen* [to be]" (cf. Doran 2012, 124; NETS) or, reading ἐνετύγχανον for ἐτύγχανον, "just as those who inhabit the place *requested*" (cf. D. Schwartz, 276). See further comments on ἐτύγχανον below.

καθὼς. Introduces a clause of comparison.

ἐτύγχανον. Impf act ind 3rd pl τυγχάνω. It is tempting to harmonize 2 Maccabees with a parallel account in Josephus, *Ant.* 12.258-61:

> To King Antiochus Theos Epiphanes, a memorial from the Sidonians in Shechem. Our forefathers because of certain droughts in their country, and following a certain ancient superstition, made it a custom to observe the day which is called the Sabbath by the Jews, and they erected a temple without a name on the mountain called Garizein, and there offered the appropriate sacrifices. . . . [W]e are distinct from them [the Jews] both in race and in customs, and *we ask that* [προσαγορευθῆναι] the temple without a name be known as that of Zeus Hellenios. (LCL, *emphasis added*)

Based on this parallel, many follow an emendation suggested by Niese (519) and read ἐνετύγχανον: "they were petitioning" (cf. D. Schwartz, 276; Habicht, 229; Zeitlin and Tedesche, 153). The emendation ἐνετύγχανον is minimal and could easily be explained by orthography or harmonization within the context of 2 Maccabees (cf. 6:12). There are two key problems with this understanding. First, it portrays Antiochus positively (i.e., he honors the Samaritan's request) when the larger context suggests that Antiochus' actions are coercive and unwelcome (cf. Doran 2012, 134; D. Schwartz, 538–39). Second, the words betray an anti-Samaritan bias, where the name change of the Samaritan temple to "Zeus Xenios" is "as the residents of the place requested." Such a perspective finds little favor in 2 Maccabees (cf. 5:22-23; *pace* Dexinger, 130) and, for this reason, D. Schwartz argues that καθὼς ἐνετύγχανον οἱ τὸν τόπον οἰκοῦντες must be "an addition to the basic text of [2 Maccabees]." Thus, emending the text creates a problem that D. Schwartz solves by positing that a later writer added to the text.

The printed text of R-H and Göttingen suggests that the temple at Gerizim was given a new name (Διὸς Ξενίου) that corresponds to the people who lived there: i.e., the Samaritans "happen to be [hospitable]."

This understanding requires no textual emendation, and is an example of brachylogy, where the adjective ξένιοι should be supplied from the near context (Doran 2012, 124).

οἱ ... οἰκοῦντες. Pres act ptc nom masc pl οἰκέω (substantival). Subject of ἐτύγχανον.

τὸν τόπον. Accusative direct object of οἱ οἰκοῦντες. On the use of τόπος to refer to a temple, see 3:2 on τὸν τόπον.

Διὸς Ξενίου. Possessive genitive ("Zeus Xenios' [place]") or, less likely, source ("[the place dependent upon] Zeus Xenios"). This was a common epithet for Zeus (*OCD*, 1589), emphasizing his *hospitality* (e.g., Homer, *Il.* 13.625; Aeschylus, *Ag.* 61–62, 374; Plato, *Leg.* 12.953e; Plutarch, *Amat.* 20). It may have been attractive to Jews (or Samaritans) as well because of biblical descriptions of hospitality (e.g., Gen 14:18-20; Deut 10:18; Ps 146:9). Goldstein (274) also suggests that Διὸς Ξενίου "reflects a punning translation" of Γαριζιν because an alternative form of Zeus' name was Ζήν in Greek poetry (cf. *GE*, 891, for multiple forms of Zeus' name).

6:3 χαλεπὴ δὲ καὶ τοῖς ὅλοις ἦν δυσχερὴς ἡ ἐπίτασις τῆς κακίας.

χαλεπὴ. Predicate adjective, meaning "dangerous" (*GELS*, 727.3). Cf. 4:16.

δὲ. Development; see 1:10 on δέ.

τοῖς ὅλοις. Dative of manner or action. Either masculine (i.e., "for everyone") or, better, taken as a neuter plural that functions as a substantive: "in *every way*" (cf. BDAG, 704.3). However, see *GELS* (494.e), which suggests that τοῖς ὅλοις = ὅλως.

ἦν. Impf act ind 3rd sg εἰμί. The verb has two predicates, linked by καί.

δυσχερὴς. Predicate adjective, meaning "difficult to handle and bear" (*GELS*, 181). Cf. the only other LXX examples in 9:7, 24; 14:45.

ἡ ἐπίτασις. Nominative subject of ἦν. See *GELS* (283): "intensified involvement: + gen[itive]." Cf. the similar construction in 5:22: ἐπιστάτας τοῦ κακοῦν. The article marks ἐπίτασις as the grammatical subject rather than the predicate (cf. Wallace, 42–46).

τῆς κακίας. Genitive of apposition ("[the intensification] of evil") or, perhaps, objective genitive ("[to intensify] evil").

6:4 τὸ μὲν γὰρ ἱερὸν ἀσωτίας καὶ κώμων ὑπὸ τῶν ἐθνῶν ἐπεπληροῦτο ῥᾳθυμούντων μεθ᾽ ἑταιρῶν καὶ ἐν τοῖς ἱεροῖς περιβόλοις γυναιξὶ πλησιαζόντων, ἔτι δὲ τὰ μὴ καθήκοντα ἔνδον εἰσφερόντων.

τὸ ... ἱερὸν. Nominative subject of ἐπεπληροῦτο.

μὲν γάρ . . . δέ. Point/counterpoint. See 2:25 on μὲν . . . δέ. Used with γάρ (which introduces an explanation), the construction means: "for indeed . . . but" (BDAG, 629.1.a.α).

ἀσωτίας καὶ κώμων. Genitive complements of ἐπεπλήρωτο. Verbs of "filling" often take the genitive (Smyth §1369; Wallace, 131, 92–93). ἀσωτία (as opposed to σώζω) "gener[ally] denotes 'wastefulness' . . . esp[ecially] exhibited in convivial gatherings" (BDAG, 148). In the LXX, κῶμος appears only here and in Wis 14:23, both having the negative sense of "excessive feasting" (BDAG, 580).

ὑπὸ τῶν ἐθνῶν. Agency.

ἐπεπληροῦτο. Impf pass ind 3rd sg ἐπιπληρόω.

ῥᾳθυμούντων. Pres act ptc gen neut pl ῥᾳθυμέω (attributive, modifying τῶν ἐθνῶν). Because the participle is genitive and neuter, it is best to understand it as attributive: "[the gentiles] who were carousing." Alternatively, Muraoka (§31df) suggests this is a circumstantial participle in an oblique case. On the nature of the cult, see D. Schwartz (276–77) and Doran (2012, 135).

μεθ᾽ ἑταιρῶν. Association. Abel (361) offers an alternative, but less likely, reading with a different accent, ἑταίρων ("companions"), seeking to avoid an obvious repetition in context: "*with prostitutes* and had intercourse with women."

ἐν τοῖς ἱεροῖς περιβόλοις. Locative.

γυναιξί. Dative of association.

πλησιαζόντων. Pres act ptc gen neut pl πλησιάζω (attributive, modifying τῶν ἐθνῶν).

ἔτι. Adverb, used "pert[aining] to number . . . *that which is added to what is already at hand*" (BDAG, 400.2.b).

τὰ μὴ καθήκοντα. Pres act ptc acc neut pl καθήκω (substantival). Object of εἰσφερόντων. On the meaning of the verb, see BDAG (491): "to be appropriate, *come/reach to, be proper/fitting*." This terse expression "lets us imagine [the author] knows the details but spares us as part of his 'epitomizing'" (D. Schwartz, 277). Cf. the similar expression in 4:19.

ἔνδον. Adverb of place. See *GELS* (235): "into a space inside."

εἰσφερόντων. Pres act ptc gen neut pl εἰσφέρω (attributive, modifying τῶν ἐθνῶν).

6:5 τὸ δὲ θυσιαστήριον τοῖς ἀποδιεσταλμένοις ἀπὸ τῶν νόμων ἀθεμίτοις ἐπεπλήρωτο.

τὸ . . . θυσιαστήριον. Nominative subject of ἐπεπλήρωτο.

δέ. Development; see 1:10 on δέ.

τοῖς ἀποδιεσταλμένοις . . . ἀθεμίτοις. Dative of content (Wallace, 170–71). Verbs of "filling" sometimes take the dative (cf. Muraoka §22wla). On ἀθέμιτος, see BDAG (24): "refers primarily not to what is forbidden by ordinance but to violation of tradition or common recognition of what is seemly or proper." Cf. 7:1; 10:34.

ἀποδιεσταλμένοις. Prf pass ptc dat neut pl ἀποδιαστέλλω (attributive).

ἀπὸ τῶν νόμων. Agency.

ἐπεπλήρωτο. Plprf pass ind 3rd sg πληρόω. The pluperfect is explicative, further explaining the improper actions and objects in the temple (cf. 6:4). On the use of the pluperfect in narrative, see the Introduction.

6:6 ἦν δ᾽ οὔτε σαββατίζειν οὔτε πατρῴους ἑορτὰς διαφυλάττειν οὔτε ἁπλῶς Ἰουδαῖον ὁμολογεῖν εἶναι,

ἦν. Impf act ind 3rd sg εἰμί (impersonal).

δ᾽. Development; see 1:10 on δέ.

οὔτε . . . οὔτε . . . οὔτε. Coordinating conjunctions, closely balancing the three infinitive clauses. "Not . . . nor . . . nor" (BDF §445.1; Robertson, 1179). The final phrase, Ἰουδαῖον ὁμολογεῖν εἶναι, essentially summarizes the rest of 6:6.

σαββατίζειν. Pres act inf σαββατίζω (substantival). The compound infinitival clause, οὔτε σαββατίζειν οὔτε πατρῴους ἑορτὰς διαφυλάττειν οὔτε ἁπλῶς Ἰουδαῖον ὁμολογεῖν εἶναι, functions as the subject of ἦν. From an Aramaic loanword (σάββατα), the verb also appears in the LXX Exod 16:30; Lev 23:32; 26:34, 35; 1 Esd 1:55; 2 Chr 36:21.

πατρῴους ἑορτὰς. Accusative direct object of διαφυλάττειν.

διαφυλάττειν. Pres act inf διαφυλάσσω (substantival). See comments on σαββατίζειν. On the meaning of the verb, see GE (517.1): "to obtain." On the Attic morphology, see 4:40 on ἧττον.

ἁπλῶς. Adverb of manner. See GELS (69): "in simple, not elaborate or devious manner."

Ἰουδαῖον. Predicate accusative of εἶναι. On the meaning of Ἰουδαῖος, see discussion in 1:1 on Τοῖς ἀδελφοῖς τοῖς . . . Ἰουδαίοις. Here, especially, it is clear that Ἰουδαῖος entails religious practice and/or commitment rather than purely ethnicity. Cf. 9:17, where Antiochus purportedly repents and pledges to "become a Jew" (Ἰουδαῖον ἔσεσθαι). Goldstein (276) suggests that "confessing to be Jewish" may allude to particular Jewish rituals, such as reciting the *Shema*, as acts of bearing witness (cf. Josephus, *Ant.* 4.212). In the biblical tradition, see also the book of Esther, where both Esther (2:10) and Mordecai (3:4) must decide whether to "reveal" (ὑποδείκνυμι) that they are Jews.

ὁμολογεῖν. Pres act inf ὁμολογέω (substantival). See comments on σαββατίζειν.

εἶναι. Pres act inf εἰμί (indirect discourse).

6:7 ἤγοντο δὲ μετὰ πικρᾶς ἀνάγκης εἰς τὴν κατὰ μῆνα τοῦ βασιλέως γενέθλιον ἡμέραν ἐπὶ σπλαγχνισμόν, γενομένης δὲ Διονυσίων ἑορτῆς ἠναγκάζοντο κισσοὺς ἔχοντες πομπεύειν τῷ Διονύσῳ.

ἤγοντο. Impf pass ind 3rd pl ἄγω. Although possibly middle, the context suggests passive: i.e., "they were brought" rather than "they brought."

δὲ. Development; see 1:10 on δέ.

μετὰ πικρᾶς ἀνάγκης. Manner.

εἰς τὴν ... γενέθλιον ἡμέραν. Temporal, specifying the time at which something takes place (cf. BDAG, 289.2.a.β). The collocation refers to a "birthday celebration" (BDAG, 192.2). VanderKam (1981, 67) notes that a monthly celebration of royal birthdays is well-attested from Ptolemaic Egypt, Pergamum, and Commagene.

κατὰ μῆνα. Temporal, marking a definite indication of time (BDAG, 512.B.2.a) or, better, distributive (BDAG, 512.B.2.c).

τοῦ βασιλέως. Objective genitive.

ἐπὶ σπλαγχνισμόν. Locative or, more likely, purpose: "for consumption of the entrails of sacrificial victim" (cf. GE, 1947). Nicklas (2011, 1392) suggests this refers to a pagan sacrificial altar ("pagane Opfermähler") (cf. Goldstein, 276; Doran 2012, 137). Thus, "[pagan] sacrifices."

γενομένης. Aor mid ptc gen fem sg γίνομαι (genitive absolute, temporal). γίνομαι is often used to describe festivals that "took place" (cf. BDAG, 197.4.a). On the genitive absolute, see 1:7 on βασιλεύοντος.

δὲ. Development; see 1:10 on δέ.

Διονυσίων. Subjective genitive. The plural "indicates that its referent has multiple components" (Muraoka §21k).

ἑορτῆς. Genitive subject of the participle γενομένης. The epitomizer's description of the festival of Dionysus probably indicates his diasporan context.

ἠναγκάζοντο. Impf pass ind 3rd pl ἀναγκάζω.

κισσοὺς. Accusative direct object of ἔχοντες. This refers to "ivy wreaths," which were commonly associated with Dionysus (OCD, 396).

ἔχοντες. Pres act ptc nom masc pl ἔχω. The participle could be either attributive (modifying the implicit subject of ἠναγκάζοντο) or, better, adverbial, describing the manner of the procession.

πομπεύειν. Pres act inf πομπεύω (complementary). The verb appears only here and in Wis 4:2 in the LXX.

τῷ Διονύσῳ. Dative of interest.

6:8 ψήφισμα δὲ ἐξέπεσεν εἰς τὰς ἀστυγείτονας Ἑλληνίδας πόλεις Πτολεμαίου ὑποθεμένου τὴν αὐτὴν ἀγωγὴν κατὰ τῶν Ιουδαίων ἄγειν καὶ σπλαγχνίζειν,

ψήφισμα. Nominative of ἐξέπεσεν. See *GE* (2403.A): "proposal that is approved *by the majority of votes, hence* decree, deliberation, decision." Cf. 10:28; 12:4; 15:36.

δὲ. Development; see 1:10 on δέ.

ἐξέπεσεν. Aor act ind 3rd sg ἐκπίπτω. As a metaphorical extension of ἐκπίπτω, here the word has the sense of "to be publicly announced" (*GELS*, 214). D. Schwartz (280) notes that ἐκπίπτω appears in connection with the result of a vote (cf. Xenophon, *Symp.* 5.10; Polybius, *Hist.* 30.32.10) and "refers both to the arrival at the decision and its publication."

εἰς τὰς ἀστυγείτονας Ἑλληνίδας πόλεις. Spatial. On ἀστυγείτων, see LEH (90): "neighboring."

Πτολεμαίου. Genitive subject of the participle ὑποθεμένου. While both R-H and the Göttingen edition read the singular Πτολεμαίου ("Ptolemy"), several MSS (*L*-542 62 *l* La^V Arm Lucif.) have the plural Πτολεμαιων ("[the city] of Ptolemais"), possibly indicating that the hostile people of Ptolemais took initiatives against Jews (cf. 13:25). The latter reading, although less plausible to be the early text, is probably the result of two factors: (1) the use of ψήφισμα in 6:8, which "usually refers to a decision [made] by a city" (D. Schwartz, 279), may have led some copyists to render the plural; (2) the reference to "neighboring Greek cities" (τὰς ἀστυγείτονας Ἑλληνίδας πόλεις) may have led copyists to understand Πτολεμαίου as a city reference as well, requiring the alteration to the plural. See especially D. Schwartz (279–80). Cf. the same Ptolemy in 4:45 and 8:8.

ὑποθεμένου. Aor mid ptc gen masc sg ὑποτίθημι (genitive absolute, causal). On the genitive absolute, see 1:7 on βασιλεύοντος.

τὴν αὐτὴν ἀγωγὴν. Accusative direct object of ἄγειν. αὐτός is intensive, modifying τὴν . . . ἀγωγήν and marking it as prominent in the discourse.

κατὰ τῶν Ιουδαίων. Opposition.

ἄγειν. Pres act inf ἄγω (indirect discourse).

σπλαγχνίζειν. Pres act inf σπλαγχνίζω (indirect discourse). *GE* (1947.1) suggests that here σπλαγχνίζω = σπλαγνεύω ("to eat the entrails of the victim, after sacrifice") (cf. Dorival, 291). Habicht (230) considers καὶ σπλαγχνίζειν to be incomprehensible ("unverständlich") in context, arguing that σπλαγχνίζειν describes actions of Jews, whereas ἄγειν and κατασφάζειν (6:9) describes actions of gentiles. Thus, despite the textual evidence, Habicht suggests that αὐτοὺς ἀναγκάσαι has fallen out. Cf. 6:7.

6:9 τοὺς δὲ μὴ προαιρουμένους μεταβαίνειν ἐπὶ τὰ Ἑλληνικὰ κατασφάζειν. παρῆν οὖν ὁρᾶν τὴν ἐνεστῶσαν ταλαιπωρίαν.

τοὺς . . . μὴ προαιρουμένους. Pres mid ptc acc masc pl προαιρέω (substantival). Object of κατασφάζειν. On the meaning of the verb, see *GELS* (584.2): "to select out of multiple alternatives as desirable, suited."

δὲ. Development; see 1:10 on δέ.

μεταβαίνειν. Pres act inf μεταβαίνω (complementary). Cf. 6:1.

ἐπὶ τὰ Ἑλληνικὰ. Locative.

κατασφάζειν. Pres act inf κατασφάζω (indirect discourse).

παρῆν. Impf act ind 3rd sg πάρειμι (impersonal). Used with the infinitive to convey "being possible, being permissible" (*GE*, 1576.C; cf. *GELS*, 533.3).

οὖν. Inferential. See 2:15 on οὖν.

ὁρᾶν. Pres act inf ὁράω (complementary).

τὴν ἐνεστῶσαν ταλαιπωρίαν. Accusative direct object of ὁρᾶν.

ἐνεστῶσαν. Aor act ptc acc fem sg ἐνίστημι (attributive).

6:10 δύο γὰρ γυναῖκες ἀνήχθησαν περιτετμηκυῖαι τὰ τέκνα· τούτων δὲ ἐκ τῶν μαστῶν κρεμάσαντες τὰ βρέφη καὶ δημοσίᾳ περιαγαγόντες αὐτὰς τὴν πόλιν κατὰ τοῦ τείχους ἐκρήμνισαν.

δύο . . . γυναῖκες. Nominative subject of ἀνήχθησαν.

γὰρ. Introduces an explanation-example that illustrates the "desperate situation" described in 6:9. See 1:12 on γάρ.

ἀνήχθησαν. Aor pass ind 3rd pl ἀνάγω. The sixth principal part of ἄγω is ἤχθην. Most MSS read ἀνήχθησαν, but a few MSS (V 55) read ἀνηνέχθησαν, but the meaning is very similar. Doran (2012, 143) suggests, but does not follow, an emendation to ἀπήχθησαν ("they were led away"). The connotation is that they were brought in to be punished.

περιτετμηκυῖαι. Prf act ptc nom fem pl περιτέμνω (causal). Note that the stative aspect refers to the women, not the children. Therefore, the text of 2 Maccabees suggests that the women themselves performed the circumcision.

τὰ τέκνα. Accusative direct object of περιτετμηκυῖαι. On the use of the Greek article like a pronoun, see 1:16 on τὰς κεφαλάς.

τούτων. Possessive genitive. The pronoun precedes the PP: "[from the breasts] *of them*" = "from their breasts."

δὲ. Development, marking a change of subject from the women (δύο . . . γυναῖκες) to those who threw them off the wall. See 1:10 on δέ.

ἐκ τῶν μαστῶν. Separation (cf. *GELS*, 201.1).

κρεμάσαντες. Aor act ptc nom masc pl κρεμάζω (temporal). This action of "hanging" (cf. *GE*, 1174.1.A) displays publicly the circumcised penis, thus displaying the reason for their execution (cf. D. Schwartz, 281). It is not clear how babies can be hung from breasts.

τὰ βρέφη. Accusative direct object of κρεμάσαντες. In keeping with Jewish law, boys were to be circumcised on the eighth day (Gen 17:12). Thus, it is not surprising that the epitomizer calls the children βρέφος, which denotes a "very small child, baby, infant" (BDAG, 184.2).

δημοσίᾳ. Feminine adjective used adverbially in an idiomatic expression: "in public view" (*GELS*, 147; cf. Muraoka §20f).

περιαγαγόντες. Aor act ptc nom masc pl περιάγω (temporal). On the meaning of the verb, see *GELS* (548.1): "to cause to move around, led by s[omebody] else . . . + acc[usative] loci." Cf. 4:38.

αὐτὰς. Accusative direct object of περιαγαγόντες.

τὴν πόλιν. Adverbial accusative, indicating extent of space (cf. Wallace, 201–2).

κατὰ τοῦ τείχους. Locative. See BDAG (511.A.2): "down upon, toward, against someone or someth[ing]."

ἐκρήμνισαν. Aor act ind 3rd pl κρημνίζω. The epitomizer contrasts κρεμάσαντες ("hanging") with ἐκρήμνισαν ("throwing").

6:11 ἕτεροι δὲ πλησίον συνδραμόντες εἰς τὰ σπήλαια λεληθότως ἄγειν τὴν ἑβδομάδα μηνυθέντες τῷ Φιλίππῳ συνεφλογίσθησαν διὰ τὸ εὐλαβῶς ἔχειν βοηθῆσαι ἑαυτοῖς κατὰ τὴν δόξαν τῆς σεμνοτάτης ἡμέρας.

ἕτεροι. Nominative subject of συνεφλογίσθησαν.

δὲ. Development, marking a change of subject from the women (δύο . . . γυναῖκες) in 6:10 to the "others" (ἕτεροι) in 6:11. See 1:10 on δέ.

πλησίον. Adverb of place.

συνδραμόντες. Aor act ptc nom masc pl συντρέχω (attributive, modifying ἕτεροι). On the meaning of the verb, see GE (2054.B): "to gather, assemble," with εἰς + accusative. Due to suppletion, the third principal part of (συν-) τρέχω is (συν-) ἔδραμον. The two συν- verbs in 6:11 emphasize the solidarity of the Jews (cf. D. Schwartz, 282).

εἰς τὰ σπήλαια. Spatial.

λεληθότως. Adverb of manner, formed from the perfect active participle of λανθάνω: "secretly." Cf. 8:1.

ἄγειν. Pres act inf ἄγω (purpose). The bare infinitive is typical after an intransitive verb of motion such as συντρέχω (cf. Wallace, 591). On the sense of "celebrate," see 1:9 on ἄγητε.

τὴν ἑβδομάδα. Accusative direct object of ἄγειν. Denotes "the seventh day of the week" = "Sabbath" (cf. GE, 578; GELS, 184.2). Cf. 12:38; 15:4 and many uses in Josephus (e.g., Ant. 8.234; 14.63).

μηνυθέντες. Aor pass ptc nom masc pl μηνύω (temporal or, perhaps, causal). See 3:7 on μηνυθέντων. Use of the passive voice allows the epitomizer to downplay that fellow Jews were likely involved in this betrayal.

τῷ Φιλίππῳ. Dative indirect object of μηνυθέντες.

συνεφλογίσθησαν. Aor pass ind 3rd pl συμφλογίζω. On the meaning of the verb, see GELS (649): "to burn together."

ἔχειν. Pres act inf ἔχω. Used with διὰ τό to denote cause. The neuter article τό indicates the case of ἔχειν (Burk, 27–46). The verb ἔχω is used with εὐλαβῶς with the sense "to be in some state or condition" (BDAG, 422.10). Thus, the collocation εὐλαβῶς ἔχειν is equivalent to εὐλαβέομαι ("to be concerned about a matter, *be concerned, be anxious*," BDAG, 407.2). See 1:24 on ἔχουσα for discussion of an idiom where ἔχω is followed by an adverb.

εὐλαβῶς. Adverb of manner.

βοηθῆσαι. Aor act inf βοηθέω (complementary). See CGCG (§51.8) on ἔχω + infinitive.

ἑαυτοῖς. Dative complement of βοηθῆσαι.

κατὰ τὴν δόξαν. Standard. The Göttingen edition lacks the article. Here δόξα means something like "status of honour and distinction" = "glory" (cf. GELS, 175.1).

τῆς σεμνοτάτης ἡμέρας. Objective genitive. The superlative form σεμνοτάτης comes from σεμνός ("a most sacred [day]," GELS 619.1).

2 Maccabees 6:12-17

[12]So then, I encourage those who happen to come across this book roll not to be discouraged because of the misfortunes, and to recognize that these punishments were not to destroy but to discipline our people. [13]For not to leave alone those acting wickedly for much time but to encounter punishments immediately is a sign of great kindness. [14]For just as concerning the other nations the Sovereign waits patiently until, after reaching the full measure of [their] sins, he punishes them; so he decided not to be against us [15]in order that, after our sins have reached their height, he might not take vengeance upon us later. [16]Therefore, he

never withdraws [his] mercy from us. Rather, even though disciplining [us] with calamity, he does not forsake his own people. ¹⁷In any case, let these things be said by us as a reminder. After a few words, it is necessary to go on to the narrative.

Here begins another digression (cf. 4:16-17; 5:17-20) that spans from 6:12-17 and is marked by a shift to the present tense (4 times). In the digression, the epitomizer explains that the calamities that befell the nation are not accidental but providential. These verses provide comfort after the troubling account in 6:1-11 and are preparatory for the extended description of the martyrdoms of Eleazar (6:18–31) and the seven brothers (7:1-42). Moreover, following from 5:17, where the epitomizer stated that "the Sovereign was angered briefly" and "there came about *neglect* concerning the place," there is a different emphasis here on God's disciplining *presence*. Cohesion is found in the digression through the repetition of key terms from 6:12 in 6:16 (e.g., συμφορά, παιδεία), as the epitomizer draws the digression to a close. For more on digressions, see the Introduction.

The epitomizer switches to the present tense throughout 6:12-17 because he is addressing the reader directly (παρακαλῶ), and making general statements that could be considered timeless (6:13, 14, 16) (cf. *CGCG* §33.14-16).

6:12 Παρακαλῶ οὖν τοὺς ἐντυγχάνοντας τῇδε τῇ βίβλῳ μὴ συστέλλεσθαι διὰ τὰς συμφοράς, λογίζεσθαι δὲ τὰς τιμωρίας μὴ πρὸς ὄλεθρον, ἀλλὰ πρὸς παιδείαν τοῦ γένους ἡμῶν εἶναι·

Παρακαλῶ. Pres act ind 1st sg παρακαλέω. The beginning of a new discourse-unit is marked by the present tense verb.

οὖν. Inferential, introducing commentary on the narrative from the epitomizer. Note also that Runge (43) comments that "[o]ne often finds οὖν at high-level boundaries in the discourse, where the next major topic is drawn from and builds upon what precedes." See 2:15 on οὖν.

τοὺς ἐντυγχάνοντας. Pres act ptc acc masc pl ἐντυγχάνω (substantival). Direct object of παρακαλῶ. On the meaning of the verb, see *GE* (706): "to meet (by accident), encounter." BDAG (341.2) notes that "the idea of 'coming across' or 'encountering' a book derives the sense *read*." Cf. 2:25; 15:39.

τῇδε τῇ βίβλῳ. Dative complement of ἐντυγχάνοντας (cf. BDAG, 341). The demonstrative pronoun refers to an object or entity that is in close proximity to the speaker/writer (cf. BDAG, 689.1; Doran 1981, 29). On the translation "book roll," see 2:13 on τὰ . . . βιβλία.

μὴ. See comment on the negation in 1:5.

συστέλλεσθαι. Pres pass inf συστέλλω (indirect discourse).

διὰ τὰς συμφοράς. Cause. Cf. 6:16.

λογίζεσθαι. Pres mid inf λογίζομαι (indirect discourse).

δὲ. Development, marking an addition of a new point in addition to (rather than a correction of) μὴ συστέλλεσθαι ("not to be discouraged"). Most commentators translate as "but" (cf. NETS). However, this obscures that the epitomizer is mounting an argument rather than correcting a previous statement. See 1:10 on δέ.

τὰς τιμωρίας. Accusative subject of an implied verb (εἶναι). Ellipsis of the verb is common in statements using ἀλλά (see BDF §479.1).

μὴ . . . ἀλλὰ. Point/counterpoint set. See 1:20 on μὴ . . . ἀλλά.

πρὸς ὄλεθρον. Purpose.

πρὸς παιδείαν. Purpose. On the theme of discipline as beneficial, see especially Deut 8:5 and Wis 3:5: "and having been *disciplined* [παιδευθέντες] a little, they will be greatly *benefited* [εὐεργετηθήσονται]" (NETS). Because παιδεία is often associated with training and education, this use is also ironic (Doran 2012, 164).

τοῦ γένους. Objective genitive.

ἡμῶν. Genitive of relationship. Here the epitomizer apparently self-identifies as a Jew: "*our* people." Cf. 14:34.

εἶναι. Pres act inf εἰμί (indirect discourse).

6:13 καὶ γὰρ τὸ μὴ πολὺν χρόνον ἐᾶσθαι τοὺς δυσσεβοῦντας, ἀλλ᾽ εὐθέως περιπίπτειν ἐπιτίμοις, μεγάλης εὐεργεσίας σημεῖόν ἐστιν.

καὶ γὰρ. Introduces an additional statement that "explains the preceding" (GELS, 125; cf. Denniston, 108; BDF §452.3; Mayser II 3.122–23). See 1:19 on καὶ γάρ.

τὸ . . . ἐᾶσθαι. Pres mid inf ἐάω (substantival). The infinitive clauses, τὸ μὴ πολὺν χρόνον ἐᾶσθαι τοὺς δυσσεβοῦντας, ἀλλ᾽ εὐθέως περιπίπτειν ἐπιτίμοις, function as the subject of ἐστιν. The article τό functions to mark the infinitive as the nominative subject (Burk, 54–58). On the meaning of the verb, see GELS (184.2): "to let alone in peace and undisturbed."

μὴ . . . ἀλλ᾽. Point/counterpoint set. See 1:20 on μὴ . . . ἀλλά.

πολὺν χρόνον. Adverbial accusative, indicating extent of time (cf. Wallace, 201–2). The use of εὐθέως in the contrasting expression below helps clarify the adverbial nature of πολὺν χρόνον.

τοὺς δυσσεβοῦντας. Pres act ptc acc masc pl δυσσεβέω (substantival). Direct object of ἐᾶσθαι.

εὐθέως. Adverb of manner (cf. BDF §102.2).

περιπίπτειν. Pres act inf περιπίπτω. The second element of the compound subject of ἐστιν. On the meaning of the verb, see *GELS* (551): "to encounter unintentionally: + dat[ive] (s[omething] undesirable, unpleasant)."

ἐπιτίμοις. Dative complement of περιπίπτειν.

μεγάλης εὐεργεσίας. Genitive of apposition. D. Schwartz (284): "[h]ere God is depicted as a benevolent Hellenistic king." Cf. 4:2.

σημεῖόν. Predicate nominative. σημεῖόν acquires its second accent from the enclitic ἐστιν. When following a word with a circumflex on the penult, the enclitic surrenders its accent, and it appears as an additional acute accent on the preceding word (Smyth §183.c).

ἐστιν. Pres act ind 3rd sg εἰμί.

6:14 οὐ γὰρ καθάπερ καὶ ἐπὶ τῶν ἄλλων ἐθνῶν ἀναμένει μακροθυμῶν ὁ δεσπότης μέχρι τοῦ καταντήσαντας αὐτοὺς πρὸς ἐκπλήρωσιν ἁμαρτιῶν κολάσαι, οὕτως καὶ ἐφ᾽ ἡμῶν ἔκρινεν εἶναι,

οὐ. As is common with comparative clauses, the negation appears outside of the principal sentence (cf. Robertson, 1159). Most commentators and translations take the negation with εἶναι: "he decided *not to be*" (cf. NETS).

γὰρ. Introduces an explanation of 6:13, showing how the Lord's patience with the Jews is not matched by patience toward the nations. See 1:12 on γάρ.

καθάπερ καὶ . . . οὕτως καὶ. Comparative. "Just as . . . so." This correlative construction compares the way that "the Sovereign" (ὁ δεσπότης) deals with the nations with the way the Lord will deal with Jews. Distinct from the construction καθάπερ . . . οὕτως (see 2:29), the dual uses of καί function to reinforce the comparison (cf. *GELS*, 354.2.d). Cf. 2:27, 29; 15:39.

ἐπὶ τῶν ἄλλων ἐθνῶν. Reference. BDAG (365.8) refers to this use of ἐπί as "a marker of perspective . . . *concerning, about*" (cf. *GELS*, 264.I.7). Here, again, the epitomizer apparently self-identifies as Jewish: "*our* people." Cf. 6:12; 14:34.

ἀναμένει. Pres act ind 3rd sg ἀναμένω.

μακροθυμῶν. Pres act ptc nom masc sg μακροθυμέω (manner). *GELS* (439.a) notes the collocation of ἀναμένω + μακροθυμέω means "bides the time patiently."

ὁ δεσπότης. Nominative subject of ἀναμένει. Cf. 5:17, 20.

κολάσαι. Aor act inf κολάζω. Used with μέχρι τοῦ to mark the "continuance in time up to a point" (BDAG, 644.2).

καταντήσαντας. Aor act ptc acc masc pl καταντάω (temporal). On the meaning of the verb, see *GELS* (378.1): "to arrive at . . . + πρός and acc[usative]." The participle is accusative because it agrees with αὐτούς. On circumstantial participles in oblique cases, see 3:27 on πεσόντα.

αὐτούς. Accusative direct object of κολάσαι.

πρὸς ἐκπλήρωσιν. Spatial (motion toward). See *GELS* (214): "act of reaching the full measure."

ἁμαρτιῶν. Objective genitive.

ἐφ᾽ ἡμῶν. Opposition.

ἔκρινεν. Aor act ind 3rd sg κρίνω. On the meaning of the verb, see *GELS* (413.6): "to decide: + inf[initive]."

εἶναι. Pres act inf εἰμί (indirect discourse). Negated by οὐ at the beginning of 6:14.

6:15 ἵνα μὴ πρὸς τέλος ἀφικομένων ἡμῶν τῶν ἁμαρτιῶν ὕστερον ἡμᾶς ἐκδικᾷ.

ἵνα μή. Introduces a negative purpose clause.

πρὸς τέλος. Goal. *GELS* (675.3) suggests the following definition of τέλος: "the close of a period or process," thus, "after our sins have reached *their height*."

ἀφικομένων. Aor mid ptc gen fem pl ἀφικνέομαι (genitive absolute, temporal). On the meaning of the verb, see *GELS* (107): "to reach." On the genitive absolute, see 1:7 on βασιλεύοντος.

ἡμῶν. Possessive (i.e., "the sins attributable *to us*") or, possibly, subjective genitive (i.e., "the sins *we* committed").

τῶν ἁμαρτιῶν. Genitive subject of the participle ἀφικομένων.

ὕστερον. The neuter adjective is used as an adverb: "afterward" (*GELS*, 707.II).

ἡμᾶς. Accusative direct object of ἐκδικᾷ.

ἐκδικᾷ. Aor act subj 3rd sg ἐκδικάζω. Subjunctive with ἵνα. The separation of ἵνα μή from ἐκδικᾷ is an example of hyperbaton.

6:16 διόπερ οὐδέποτε μὲν τὸν ἔλεον ἀφ᾽ ἡμῶν ἀφίστησιν, παιδεύων δὲ μετὰ συμφορᾶς οὐκ ἐγκαταλείπει τὸν ἑαυτοῦ λαόν.

διόπερ. Introduces a logical conclusion or inference following the digression (6:12-17): despite present circumstances God "never withdraws mercy from us." See 5:20 on διόπερ.

οὐδέποτε. Temporal adverb, denoting "an indefinite negated point of time" (LN 67.10).

μὲν . . . δέ. Point/counterpoint set. See 2:25 on μὲν . . . δέ.

τὸν ἔλεον. Accusative direct object of ἀφίστησιν.

ἀφ᾽ ἡμῶν. Separation.

ἀφίστησιν. Pres act ind 3rd sg ἀφίστημι.

παιδεύων. Pres act ptc nom masc sg παιδεύω (temporal or concessive).

μετὰ συμφορᾶς. Manner. Cf. 6:12.

οὐκ ἐγκαταλείπει τὸν ἑαυτοῦ λαόν. "He does not abandon his own people." Perhaps a loose quotation of LXX Ps 93:14, where God's inheritance is his people.

οὐκ. See 1:5 on the use of οὐ versus μή.

ἐγκαταλείπει. Pres act ind 3rd sg ἐγκαταλείπω.

τὸν . . . λαόν. Accusative direct object of ἐγκαταλείπει.

ἑαυτοῦ. Possessive genitive or genitive of relationship.

6:17 πλὴν ἕως ὑπομνήσεως ταῦθ᾽ ἡμῖν εἰρήσθω· δι᾽ ὀλίγων δ᾽ ἐλευστέον ἐπὶ τὴν διήγησιν.

πλὴν. The adverb is used as a conjunction. *GELS* (564.A.1) notes that πλήν can occur "[a]t the beginning of a clause, and interrupting a discourse and emphasizing what is important." The word helps signal a transition between the epitomizer's evaluation of events and the narrative of those events.

ἕως ὑπομνήσεως. Literally, "as far as reminding" = "as a reminder." Doran (2012, 150) notes that "[t]he use of ἕως here is unusual. Usually it has the sense of 'up to, as far as' with temporal or locative meaning. It can also be used to describe number or degree. . . . Here its use with a substantive denoting action reflects the same tendency as in Polybius for an abstract style."

ταῦθ᾽. Nominative subject of εἰρήσθω. The neuter plural subject is used commonly with a singular verb (cf. Smyth §958).

ἡμῖν. Dative of agency.

εἰρήσθω. Prf mid impv 3rd sg λέγω. Due to suppletion, the perfect principal part of λέγω is completed by εἴρηκα.

δι᾽ ὀλίγων. Means (cf. BDAG, 214.3.b): literally, "through a few [things]" = "through a few words." It is not clear whether this refers to what has already been said (6:12-17a) or what will be said (6:18–7:42). D. Schwartz (285) is probably right that "it seems that the author means to tell us that after he told us 'these things' (vv. 12-16) as a reminder, he will get back to his narrative, but only after giving us 'a few words'— which will turn out to be the two long martyrologies which take us to the end of Chapter 7." On the use of ὀλίγος in a PP, see BDAG (703.3). Cf. Josephus, *Ant.* 12.137 for a similar excursus.

δ'. Development; see 1:10 on δέ.

ἐλευστέον. The verbal adjective (cf. future of ἔρχομαι) is used as a predicate nominative after an implied copulative: "*to go on* [is necessary]" (see BDF §412.2). The copula is often omitted "in expressions of necessity, duty" (Smyth §944.b; cf. *CGCG* §26.13). See *GE* (660): "it is necessary to come, it is necessary to return."

ἐπὶ τὴν διήγησιν. Locative. Cf. the use of διήγησις in 2:32, where the epitomizer differentiated between the preface (2:19-32) and "the narrative."

2 Maccabees 6:18-23

[18]A certain Eleazar, one of the leading officials, a man already advanced in age and most honorable in the appearance of [his] countenance, was being compelled, when he opened his mouth, to eat pig flesh. [19]But he, welcoming death with honor rather than life with defilement, went up to the rack freely, [20]after spitting [it] out, as indeed it is necessary to approach [it] in the same manner as those who are determined to reject that which is not lawful to taste because of the intense desire to live. [21]Now those in charge of the unlawful entrail sacrifice, because of [their] knowledge of the man from times gone-by, after taking him aside, they were encouraging [him] privately to bring meat that was allowed for him to use, having been prepared by himself, and to pretend that he was eating the portions commanded by the king of the flesh from the sacrifice, [22]in order that by doing this, he might be delivered from death and, because of old friendships with them, he might obtain kindness. [23]But he made use of good reasoning—that is [reasoning that was] worthy of [his] age and of the dignity of old age and of his acquired and evident gray hair and of excellent behavior from childhood but still more, [worthy] of the holy and God ordained legislation—and he declared [it] quickly, saying to send [him] to Hades.

Following the digression (6:12-17), the story continues on without indicating a change of scene. The epitomizer tells a complex, but comprehensible, story of Eleazar's confrontation with the threats of Hellenization. Not only does Eleazar refuse to eat the flesh of pigs (6:18), he even refuses to give the impression that he has eaten it in order to preserve his life (6:21). The story of Eleazar's choice between life with defilement and death with honor parallels several stories in classical literature (e.g., Homer, *Il.* 9.410–916; Aeschylus, *Cho.* 349; Sophocles, *Aj.* 465). This should be understood as a further indication of the epitomizer's cultural milieu.

The narrative itself slows considerably here, probably because the epitomizer wants to focus on the martyrdom descriptions that follow and, thus, engage the reader in the emotion of the events. Additionally, the sufferings play a critical role in the narrative plotline: God's wrath will be turned to mercy and suffering/persecution will cease.

6:18 Ελεάζαρός τις τῶν πρωτευόντων γραμματέων, ἀνὴρ ἤδη προβεβηκὼς τὴν ἡλικίαν καὶ τὴν πρόσοψιν τοῦ προσώπου κάλλιστος, ἀναχανὼν ἠναγκάζετο φαγεῖν ὕειον κρέας.

Ελεάζαρός τις. Nominative subject of ἠναγκάζετο. The noun Ελεάζαρός appears with two accents because τις, an enclitic, loses its accent to the preceding word (Smyth §181–82). This "Eleazar" is otherwise unknown. On the function of the indefinite pronoun, see 3:4 on Σιμων . . . τις.

τῶν πρωτευόντων γραμματέων. Partitive genitive. Regarding the word γραμματεύς, Scham (34) notes the problem of "the creation of an artificial category of *Schriftgelehrte*/Torah scholars which was imposed on the ancient sources." γραμματεύς may denote a range of vocations and, unfortunately, the epitomizer does not describe the expertise from which Eleazar procured this title (cf. Schams, 123). It is possible that Eleazar was a "scribe" in the vein of "Near-Eastern-Jewish type of scribe sage which is described in Ben Sira" (Schams, 314), but without a description of his ability to write, it may be wiser to adopt the broader sense of "official." See especially Schams (312–21), who describes the range of uses of the term in the Hellenistic Period.

πρωτευόντων. Pres act ptc gen masc pl πρωτεύω (attributive). On the meaning of the verb, see *GELS* (604): "to hold the leading position." Cf. 13:15.

ἀνὴρ. Nominative in apposition to Ελεάζαρός.

ἤδη. Temporal adverb, modifying προβεβηκώς.

προβεβηκὼς. Prf act ptc nom masc sg προβαίνω (attributive).

τὴν ἡλικίαν καὶ τὴν πρόσοψιν. Accusatives of respect: "[advanced] *with respect to age* and [who was most honorable] *with respect to appearance*" = "[advanced] in age and [most honorable] in appearance." In 6:24 we learn that Eleazar was ninety.

τοῦ προσώπου. Subjective genitive, modifying πρόσοψιν.

κάλλιστος ἀναχανὼν ἠναγκάζετο. There is considerable discussion about the text critical issues (and implications) of these words. Doran (2012, 143) summarizes the issues well:

1. κάλλιστος ἀναχανὼν ἠναγκάζετο ("most honorable, opening his mouth he was being pressed") in La^LXVP Arm (cf. Hanhart; Abel; Goldstein, 286).
2. κάλλιστος ἠναγκάζετο ("most honorable, he was being pressed") in V La^BM Sy.
3. κάλλιστος τυγξάνων ἀναχανὼν ἠναγκάζετο ("most honorable, opening his mouth he was being pressed") in L 46-52 58 311.
4. κάλλιστος τυγξάνων ἠναγκάζετο ("most honorable, he was being pressed"), which is an emendation proposed by Katz (1960, 14) and followed by Habicht (231) and Doran (2012, 151).

Some scholars reject versions that include ἀναχανὼν (numbers 1 and 3) because of the violence implied in forcing Eleazar to open his mouth to eat pig flesh (cf. van Henten 1997, 96–97; Doran 2012, 151). They argue that the context, which portrays Eleazar's friends receiving accommodation to reason with Eleazar, suggests something less visceral and violent. Moreover, 4 Maccabees 5–7, which is an expanded retelling of this same narrative, does not include any use of force against Eleazar (cf. Habicht, 231).

κάλλιστος. Predicate adjective of an implied verb: "[being] most honorable" (cf. Doran 2012, 152). The description of his beautiful appearance functions to demonstrate his favor in God's sight (cf. Acts 6:15; Josephus, *Ant.* 2.224, 231–232).

ἀναχανὼν. Aor act ptc nom masc sg ἀναχάσκω (temporal). On the meaning of the verb, see LEH (46): "to open the mouth."

ἠναγκάζετο. Impf pass ind 3rd sg ἀναγκάζω.

φαγεῖν. Aor act inf ἐσθίω (complementary).

ὕειον κρέας. Accusative direct object of φαγεῖν. Rosenblum (40) notes that "[p]ork-related Jewish martyrdom at the hand of Antiochus appears in two texts (2 Macc 6:18–7:42 and 4 Macc 5–18)."

6:19 ὁ δὲ τὸν μετ᾽ εὐκλείας θάνατον μᾶλλον ἢ τὸν μετὰ μύσους βίον ἀναδεξάμενος, αὐθαιρέτως ἐπὶ τὸ τύμπανον προσῆγεν,

ὁ δὲ. The article functions as the nominative subject of προσῆγεν and refers to Eleazar. See 6:19 on ὁ δέ.

τὸν ... θάνατον. Accusative direct object of an implied ἀναδεξάμενος.

μετ᾽ εὐκλείας. Manner ("[to die] *with honor or fame*" = "[to die] *honorably*"). The meaning of εὔκλεια is "fame, glory, celebrity" (*GE*, 851). On the attributive position of the PP, see 1:1 on κατ᾽ Αἴγυπτον.

μᾶλλον ἢ. The comparative adverb + particle sets up a contrast between welcoming *death* and *life*. Cf. Tob 3:6 and Homer *Il.* 9.410-16, where the theme of death and glory is significant.

τὸν . . . βίον. Accusative direct object of ἀναδεξάμενος.

μετὰ μύσους. Manner. The meaning of μύσος is "filth, impurity, disgrace, contamination" (*GE*, 1373). Cf. 6:25. Although not the standard LXX term (i.e., ἀκάθαρτος) for ritual impurity, the context makes it clear that eating impure foods leads to a state of μύσος. μύσος appears only here and 6:25 and in Wis 12:6 in the LXX. On the attributive position of the PP, see 1:1 on κατ᾽ Αἴγυπτον.

ἀναδεξάμενος. Aor mid ptc nom masc sg ἀναδέχομαι (manner or, possibly, causal). Cf. 8:36. On the meaning of the verb, see BDAG (62.1): "to experience someth[ing] by being accepting, *accept, receive*."

αὐθαιρέτως. Adverb of manner.

ἐπὶ τὸ τύμπανον. Locative. Literally, τύμπανον refers to a "kettledrum, hand drum," but metaphorically it can denote "an instrument of torture" (*EDG*, 1518). The plural describes "instruments of punishment" (Doran 2012, 152). The article, apparently, refers to "a specific post of punishment" (Doran 2012, 152).

προσῆγεν. Impf act ind 3rd sg προσάγω.

6:20 προπτύσας δὲ καθ᾽ ὃν ἔδει τρόπον προσέρχεσθαι τοὺς ὑπομένοντας ἀμύνασθαι ὧν οὐ θέμις γεύσασθαι διὰ τὴν πρὸς τὸ ζῆν φιλοστοργίαν.

Many scholars note that the text of 6:20 is barely translatable ("kaum sinnvoll übersetzbar," Nicklas 2011, 1393; cf. Habicht, 231; Niese, 524), resulting in several conjectural proposals. For example, some emend προπτύσας to προτυπώσας (see below). Goldstein (286) provides a possible solution to the difficulties: "In Greek, 'He spat' is a participial phrase (προπτύσας δέ), which follows 'and of . . . to the whipping drum [= rack] [6:19]. The particle δέ probably indicates that προπτύσας is to be taken as parallel to the participial phrase at the beginning of vs. 19" (cf. Bartlett, 266). Goldstein's translation is reproduced here to illustrate the solution:

> [6:19a] He, however, preferred death with glory to life with defilement. [6:20] He spat, as one should when standing fast to resist the temptation to let love of life bring him to taste what religion forbids, [6:19b] and of his own free will he began to march to the whipping drum.

A helpful discussion of the problems of this verse also appear in D. Schwartz (287), under the entry "*to open his mouth*."

προπτύσας. Aor act ptc nom masc sg προπτύω (temporal). Katz (1961, 120), followed by Habicht (231) and Doran (2012, 143), proposes προτυπώσας ("modeling") because of the rarity of προπτύω. On the one hand, this solves the difficulty of Eleazar "spitting out" food after he has already gone up to the torture rack. Rather than "spitting out [the food]," Eleazar was "*modeling* how those should present themselves who stand firm to guard themselves from those things which it is not lawful to take" (Doran 2012, 143). This emended reading is also more desirable if 6:18 does not include ἀναχανών (MSS V La^BM Sy). See 6:18 on κάλλιστος ἀναχανὼν ἠναγκάζετο. On the other hand, rare terminology is not unusual for the epitomizer (cf. D. Schwartz, 288) and it is possible to understand προπτύσας parallel with ἀναδεξάμενος in 6:19 (see comments above).

δὲ. Development; see 1:10 on δέ.

καθ᾽ ὃν ... τρόπον. Standard. See *GELS* (688.2.b): "*just as, exactly as* emphasizing comparability and analogy."

ἔδει. Impf act ind 3rd sg δεῖ (impersonal). The imperfect is probably conative, denoting "what could, should or might have happened, but did not" (Muraoka §28c.vi; cf. BDAG, 214.2; *CGCG* §33.25).

προσέρχεσθαι. Pres mid inf προσέρχομαι. The infinitive is the subject of ἔδει.

τοὺς ὑπομένοντας. Pres act ptc acc masc pl ὑπομένω (substantival). Subject of the infinitive προσέρχεσθαι: "those waiting [to reject] to approach." On the meaning of the verb, see *GELS* (704.4): "*to submit* to a difficult or undesirable act: + inf[initive]."

ἀμύνασθαι. Aor mid inf ἀμύνομαι (complementary). Katz (1961, 118–24) suggests the reading μὴ μιαίνεσθαι, following the Syriac tradition. On the meaning of the verb, see *GELS* (33.2.b): "to reject s[omething] undesirable or unlawful."

ὧν. Genitive complement of γεύσασθαι. Although the likely antecedent is singular (ὕειον κρέας), the relative pronoun is plural because the construction "according to the sense" is used (cf. *CGCG* 50.8).

θέμις. Predicate adjective of an implied verb, negated by οὐ. θέμις is used as a synonym of the genuine adjective θέμιτος. Cf. 12:14.

γεύσασθαι. Aor mid inf γεύομαι. The infinitive clause, ὧν ... γεύσασθαι διὰ τὴν πρὸς τὸ ζῆν φιλοστοργίαν, is the subject of an implied verb (cf. Muraoka §94dba): "which [is not lawful] to taste because of the intense desire to live." Verbs of "tasting" often take the genitive case (cf. *CGCG* §30.21).

διὰ τὴν ... φιλοστοργίαν. Cause. See *GELS* (716): "intense desire." D. Schwartz (289) notes that "what is meant is that it is forbidden to taste such things *even* due to love of life."

ζῆν. Pres act inf ζάω (substantival). While πρὸς τό with the infinitive typically introduces a purpose or result clause (cf. Wallace, 611; BDF

§402.5), the position of the PP between the article (τήν) and the noun (φιλοστοργίαν) clarifies that πρός modifies φιλοστοργίαν.

6:21 οἱ δὲ πρὸς τῷ παρανόμῳ σπλαγχνισμῷ τεταγμένοι διὰ τὴν ἐκ τῶν παλαιῶν χρόνων πρὸς τὸν ἄνδρα γνῶσιν ἀπολαβόντες αὐτὸν κατ᾽ ἰδίαν παρεκάλουν ἐνέγκαντα κρέα, οἷς καθῆκον αὐτῷ χρᾶσθαι, δι᾽ αὐτοῦ παρασκευασθέντα, ὑποκριθῆναι δὲ ὡς ἐσθίοντα τὰ ὑπὸ τοῦ βασιλέως προστεταγμένα τῶν ἀπὸ τῆς θυσίας κρεῶν,

οἱ . . . τεταγμένοι. Prf pass ptc nom masc pl τάσσω (substantival). Subject of παρεκάλουν. On the meaning of the verb, see *GELS* (672.5): "to give charge (over)." On the morphology of the verb, see 5:3 on διατεταγμένας.

δὲ. Development; see 1:10 on δέ.

πρὸς τῷ παρανόμῳ σπλαγχνισμῷ. On the preposition, see *GELS* (590.II.4): "indicates engagement, involvement." Cf. 6:7.

διὰ τὴν . . . γνῶσιν. Cause.

ἐκ τῶν παλαιῶν χρόνων. Temporal. On παλαιός, see *GELS* (520): "[from] times (gone-by)."

πρὸς τὸν ἄνδρα. Reference (BDAG, 875.3.e).

ἀπολαβόντες. Aor act ptc nom masc pl ἀπολαμβάνω (temporal or, possibly, attendant circumstance). On the meaning of the verb, see BDAG (115.3): "to lead or take away from a particular point, *take away.*"

αὐτὸν. Accusative direct object of ἀπολαβόντες.

κατ᾽ ἰδίαν. The adverbial expression is an idiom: "by oneself, privately" (BDAG, 467.5).

παρεκάλουν. Impf act ind 3rd pl παρακαλέω.

ἐνέγκαντα. Aor act ptc acc masc sg φέρω (indirect discourse). Following a verb of communication (παρεκάλουν), the accusative participle functions as indirect discourse (Wallace, 645): "they were encouraging him privately *to bring.*" Alternatively, it is possible to understand the participle as circumstantial, expanding ὑποκριθῆναι and expressing means: "to pretend . . . *by bringing* meat that was allowed for him to eat" (cf. Muraoka §31dh).

κρέα. Accusative direct object of ἐνέγκαντα.

οἷς. Dative complement of χρᾶσθαι. The antecedent is κρέα.

καθῆκον. Pres act ind 3rd pl καθήκω (impersonal).

αὐτῷ. Dative of advantage.

χρᾶσθαι. Pres mid inf χράομαι. The infinitive clause, οἷς . . . χρᾶσθαι, functions as the subject of καθῆκον: literally, "which to use [is allowed for him]." On the meaning of the verb, see *GE* (2371): "to use" + dative. See 1:13 on χρησαμένων.

δι' αὐτοῦ. Agency.

παρασκευασθέντα. Aor pass ptc acc neut pl παρασκευάζω (causal). The adverbial participle modifies καθῆκον, but it is accusative because it agrees with κρέα. On the meaning of the verb, see BDAG (771): "to cause someth[ing] to be ready, *prepare*."

ὑποκριθῆναι. Aor pass inf ὑποκρίνομαι (indirect discourse). Eleazar's friends ask him "to pretend," cf. 5:25 where Apollonius "pretends" to be peaceful.

δὲ. Development, marking progress in the storyline: they asked Eleazar not only to bring kosher food but to eat it (thus, pretending to eat the non-kosher food). See 1:10 on δέ.

ὡς. Introduces a clausal complement (indirect discourse) of ὑποκριθῆναι.

ἐσθίοντα. Pres act ptc acc masc sg ἐσθίω (indirect discourse).

τὰ ... προστεταγμένα. Prf pass ptc acc neut pl προστάσσω (substantival). Direct object of ἐσθίοντα.

ὑπὸ τοῦ βασιλέως. Agency.

τῶν ... κρεῶν. Partitive genitive.

ἀπὸ τῆς θυσίας. Source.

6:22 ἵνα τοῦτο πράξας ἀπολυθῇ τοῦ θανάτου καὶ διὰ τὴν ἀρχαίαν πρὸς αὐτοὺς φιλίαν τύχῃ φιλανθρωπίας.

ἵνα. Introduces two purpose clauses (καί links both subjunctive verbs to ἵνα).

τοῦτο. Accusative direct object of πράξας. The neuter demonstrative pronoun has a clausal antecedent from 6:21 (cf. Wallace, 333). Thus, it is a "conceptual" antecedent and refers to pretending to eat pork.

πράξας. Aor act ptc nom masc sg πράσσω (means).

ἀπολυθῇ. Aor pass subj 3rd sg ἀπολύω. Subjunctive used with ἵνα.

τοῦ θανάτου. Genitive of separation.

διὰ τὴν ἀρχαίαν ... φιλίαν. Cause.

πρὸς αὐτοὺς. Association.

τύχῃ. Aor act subj 3rd sg τυγχάνω. Subjunctive used with ἵνα.

φιλανθρωπίας. Accusative direct object of τύχῃ. Cf. 14:9. *GE* (2274.A) suggests "cordiality, courtesy" or "concession, privilege." In context, those seeking to persuade Eleazar to pretend to eat pork want him to receive *kind* treatment rather than death.

6:23 ὁ δὲ λογισμὸν ἀστεῖον ἀναλαβὼν καὶ ἄξιον τῆς ἡλικίας καὶ τῆς τοῦ γήρως ὑπεροχῆς καὶ τῆς ἐπικτήτου καὶ ἐπιφανοῦς πολιᾶς καὶ τῆς ἐκ παιδὸς καλλίστης ἀναστροφῆς, μᾶλλον δὲ τῆς ἁγίας καὶ θεοκτίστου νομοθεσίας ἀκολούθως ἀπεφήνατο ταχέως λέγων προπέμπειν εἰς τὸν ᾅδην.

ὁ δὲ. The article functions as the nominative subject of ἀπεφήνατο and refers to Eleazar. See 6:19 on ὁ δέ.

λογισμὸν ἀστεῖον. Accusative direct object of ἀναλαβών. On the meaning of ἀστεῖος + λογισμός, see GELS (98.3): "showing signs of good upbringing and education."

ἀναλαβών. Aor act ptc nom masc sg ἀναλαμβάνω (attendant circumstance, modifying ἀπεφήνατο). On the meaning of the verb, see GELS (42.9): "to decide to make use of resources of. . . ."

καὶ. Epexegetical, explaining λογισμὸν ἀστεῖον or, less likely, ascensive. On the former sense, see GELS (354.13) and BDAG (493.1.c).

ἄξιον. Predicate adjective of an implied verb.

τῆς ἡλικίας καὶ τῆς . . . ὑπεροχῆς καὶ τῆς ἐπικτήτου καὶ ἐπιφανοῦς πολιᾶς καὶ τῆς . . . καλλίστης ἀναστροφῆς . . . τῆς ἁγίας καὶ θεοκτίστου νομοθεσίας. This string of genitives complements ἄξιον. As Goldstein (287) notes, it is possible to take many of these genitives complementing ἀκολούθως, but elsewhere ἀκολούθως takes the dative, not the genitive case (e.g., 1 Ezra 5:48; 7:6).

τοῦ γήρως. Genitive of apposition, qualifying τῆς . . . ὑπεροχῆς. Niese (524) and Habicht (232) prefer the reading γένους ("family"), arguing that in context γήρως is redundant. However, the use of synonymous expressions is not unusual for the epitomizer (cf. Goldstein, 287; Doran 2012, 144).

ἐκ παιδὸς. Temporal.

μᾶλλον δὲ. The combination "introduces an expr[ession] or thought that supplements and thereby corrects what has preceded" (BDAG, 614.3.d). After a long explanation of Eleazar's worthiness, the epitomizer introduces the most important qualification: Eleazar followed God's law. δέ, therefore, introduces a minor development in the argument and is (mildly) disjunctive when paired with μᾶλλον.

ἀκολούθως. Adverb, used with the genitive to denote "in conformity with" (GELS, 21). Doran (2012, 153) notes that this adverb is typically followed by the dative, not the genitive. So, it is best to take the adverb with ἀπεφήνατο.

ἀπεφήνατο. Aor mid ind 3rd sg ἀποφαίνω. On the meaning of the verb, see GELS (87.2): "to declare an opinion: + inf[initive]."

ταχέως. Temporal adverb.

λέγων. Pres act ptc nom masc sg λέγω (means). The adverbial participle introduces indirect discourse.

προπέμπειν. Pres act inf προπέμπω (indirect discourse). This verb, along with the following PP (εἰς τὸν ἅδην), is an idiom for killing. Concerning the verb, Doran (2012, 153) helpfully observes that "[t]he verb . . . is used to describe those who escort a corpse to the grave. . . . The author of 2 Maccabees thus has Eleazar ironically invite his persecutors to be his funeral escort."

εἰς τὸν ἅδην. Spatial. Here the Greek epitomizer uses this expression to refer to the underworld, despite the fact that the words are spoken by a Jewish character in the story (cf. Habicht, 232).

2 Maccabees 6:24-31

[24]"For to pretend is not worthy of our height [of age] in order that many of the young, supposing that Eleazar the ninety-year-old has turned to strange customs [25]and they, through my hypocrisy and for the sake of living a short and brief [moment longer], might be led astray because of me, and I might obtain defilement and a stain [on my] old age. [26]For even if in the present I will escape the punishment from humans, but neither living nor dying, will I escape the hands of the Almighty. [27]Therefore, courageously giving up [my] life now, I will be shown to be worthy of old age [28]and, for the youth, leaving behind a noble example of how to die willingly and nobly for the sake of the revered and holy laws." Having said that much, he went up on the torture rack immediately [29]as those leading him away changed good will toward him into bad will, because the aforementioned words, as they supposed, were madness. [30]Now, being about to die from the blows, he groaned and said, "It is clear to the Lord who has holy knowledge that, although I am able to be freed from death, I endure terrible sufferings in my body by being whipped; but in my soul, I suffer these things gladly because of fear of him." [31]And so this one died in this way, leaving—not only to the youth, but also to the great body of the nation—his own death as an example of nobility and a memorial of virtue.

The last section of 2 Maccabees 6 is comprised of Eleazar's final speech (6:24-28a; 30b) and a brief statement of his death (6:28b-30a, 31). Not only does Eleazar refuse to eat pork, he provides a rationale for his refusal, which gives the epitomizer an opportunity to address the key topics of suffering and punishment (Coetzer, 100). As noted previously, the present indicative is used with greater frequency (6:24, 30) because the section contains discourse.

6:24 Οὐ γὰρ τῆς ἡμετέρας ἡλικίας ἄξιόν ἐστιν ὑποκριθῆναι, ἵνα πολλοὶ τῶν νέων ὑπολαβόντες Ελεαζαρον τὸν ἐνενηκονταετῆ μεταβεβηκέναι εἰς ἀλλοφυλισμὸν,

Οὐ. See 1:5 on the use of οὐ versus μή.

γὰρ. The particle introduces direct discourse. The shift from narration to discourse is further attested by the first-person pronouns in 6:24-28.

τῆς ἡμετέρας ἡλικίας. Genitive complement of ἄξιόν. On the use of ἡλικία to denote "height of age," see the earlier uses in 4:40; 5:24; 6:18.

ἄξιόν. Stands in predicate position to the subject infinitive.

ἐστιν. Pres act ind 3rd sg εἰμί.

ὑποκριθῆναι. Aor pass inf ὑποκρίνομαι. The infinitive is the subject of ἐστιν. Doran (2012, 153) draws attention to the parallel with Apollonius in 5:25, who "*pretended* [ὑποκριθείς] to be peaceful."

ἵνα. Introduces a purpose clause.

πολλοὶ. Nominative subject of πλανηθῶσιν in 6:25. Part of a right-dislocation (Runge, 317–36), perhaps to shift attention away from the main figure Eleazar.

τῶν νέων. Partitive genitive.

ὑπολαβόντες. Aor act ptc nom masc pl ὑπολαμβάνω (attendant circumstance).

Ελεαζαρον. Accusative subject of the infinitive μεταβεβηκέναι.

τὸν ἐνενηκονταετῆ. Accusative in apposition to Ελεαζαρον. A combination of the numeral ἐνενήκοντα ("ninety") with the suffix -ετής ("year") = "ninety-year-old."

μεταβεβηκέναι. Prf act inf μεταβαίνω (indirect discourse). Cf. 6:1, 9.

εἰς ἀλλοφυλισμὸν. Direction. As in 4:13, here the sense is that of adopting non-Jewish customs. Thus, ἀλλοφυλισμός = Ἑλληνισμός. See 4:13 on ἀλλοφυλισμοῦ.

6:25 καὶ αὐτοὶ διὰ τὴν ἐμὴν ὑπόκρισιν καὶ διὰ τὸ μικρὸν καὶ ἀκαριαῖον ζῆν πλανηθῶσιν δι᾽ ἐμέ, καὶ μύσος καὶ κηλῖδα τοῦ γήρως κατακτήσωμαι.

αὐτοὶ. Nominative subject of πλανηθῶσιν.

διὰ τὴν ἐμὴν ὑπόκρισιν. Cause or, more likely, means. ὑπόκρισις has the negative connotation of "pretense, outward show" (BDAG, 1038).

μικρὸν καὶ ἀκαριαῖον. Accusative direct objects of ζῆν.

ζῆν. Pres act inf ζάω. Used with διὰ τό to denote cause.

πλανηθῶσιν. Aor pass subj 3rd pl πλανάω. Cf. 2:2 and 7:18.

δι᾽ ἐμέ. Cause.

μύσος καὶ κηλῖδα. Accusative direct objects of κατακτήσωμαι. κηλίς appears only here and in Wis 13:14 in the LXX.

τοῦ γήρως. Objective genitive, qualifying κηλῖδα.

κατακτήσωμαι. Aor mid subj 1st sg κατακτάομαι.

6:26 εἰ γὰρ καὶ ἐπὶ τοῦ παρόντος ἐξελοῦμαι τὴν ἐξ ἀνθρώπων τιμωρίαν, ἀλλὰ τὰς τοῦ παντοκράτορος χεῖρας οὔτε ζῶν οὔτε ἀποθανὼν ἐκφεύξομαι.

εἰ. Introduces a first-class conditional clause (Smyth §2298), using εἰ + present indicative in the protasis. This first-class conditional introduces a concessive clause where "[t]he realization of the action of the apodosis is presented as contrary to expectation given the realization of the action in the protasis, yet in the end not affected by that realization" (*CGCG* §49.19).

γὰρ. Introduces an explanation of 6:24-25, further explaining how escaping death by pretending will not ultimately work out for Eleazar. See 1:12 on γάρ.

καὶ. Ascensive. The use of καί in the construction εἰ + καί has the effect of putting emphasis on the action of the protasis (*CGCG* §49.19). On the many functions of καί in Greek literature, see Bonifazi, Drummen, and de Kreij (§93).

ἐπὶ τοῦ παρόντος. Temporal, expressing contemporaneous action with the main verb.

παρόντος. Pres act ptc gen neut sg πάρειμι (substantival).

ἐξελοῦμαι. Fut mid ind 1st sg ἐξαιρέω. The future is used because a prediction is made in the context of the conditional clause (cf. *CGCG* §33.43).

On the meaning of the verb, see BDAG (344.2): "to deliver someone from peril or confining circumstance, *set free, deliver, rescue.*"

τὴν . . . τιμωρίαν. Accusative direct object of ἐξελοῦμαι.

ἐξ ἀνθρώπων. Source or means.

ἀλλὰ. The contrastive conjunction introduces a concessive idea (cf. Grimm, 117; *GELS*, 26.3).

τὰς . . . χεῖρας. Accusative direct object of ἐκφεύξομαι.

τοῦ παντοκράτορος. Possessive genitive. Coetzer (100–101) notes that the use of παντοκράτωρ in the martyrdom narratives (e.g., 7:35, 38) sets up a theme that "the all-powerful God of the Jews will deal with individuals after their deaths in a manner that fits with their actions on earth."

οὔτε . . . οὔτε. Coordinating conjunctions, closely balancing the two participles: "Neither . . . nor."

ζῶν. Pres act ptc nom masc sg ζάω (means).

ἀποθανὼν. Aor act ptc nom masc sg ἀποθνῄσκω (means). The idea that sinners are punished in Hades is developed further in 12:43-45.

ἐκφεύξομαι. Fut mid ind 1st sg ἐκφεύγω.

6:27 διόπερ ἀνδρείως μὲν νῦν διαλλάξας τὸν βίον τοῦ μὲν γήρως ἄξιος φανήσομαι,

διόπερ. Inferential conjunction, introducing the conclusion of Eleazar's speech. See 5:20 on διόπερ.

ἀνδρείως. Adverb of manner, formed from the adjective ἀνδρεῖος (cf. "courageously," *GELS*, 49.3).

μὲν. Anticipatory. Although Doran (2012, 154) claims that μέν is "emphatic, stressing the courage of Eleazar," this is better explained as a normal prospective use of μέν (cf. Fresch 2017b, 277). See 4:11 on μέν.

νῦν. Temporal adverb. BDAG (681) notes two senses: (1) "temporal marker with focus on the moment as such"; or (2) "temporal marker with focus not so much on the present time as the situation pert[aining] at a given moment" (cf. *GELS*, 478.5). Although Eleazar's impending death in 6:31 may suggest the first meaning, it is the situation surrounding Eleazar's death that interests the epitomizer and not simply the timing of it. Thus, the second sense may be preferred here.

διαλλάξας. Aor act ptc nom masc sg διαλλάσσω (means). On the meaning of the verb, see *GELS* (153): "to give up in exchange: + acc[usative], τὸν βίον (in exchange for death)."

τὸν βίον. Accusative direct object of διαλλάξας.

τοῦ . . . γήρως. Genitive complement of ἄξιος.

μὲν . . . δὲ. Point/counterpoint set. The set, which is completed in 6:28, pairs Eleazar's "worth" (ἄξιος) with his "example" (ὑπόδειγμα). See 2:25 on μὲν . . . δέ.

ἄξιος. Predicate nominative of an implied verb. Muraoka (§69A.ac) notes that "the predicate nominal of an infinitive may remain in the nominative case when it is identical with that of the lead verb."

φανήσομαι. Fut pass ind 1st sg φαίνω. *GE* (225) notes that φαίνω sometimes occurs with the nominative and an implied infinitive, citing multiple examples from Homer:

Il. 9.94   οὗ καὶ πρόσθεν ἀρίστη φαίνετο βουλή

whose counsel even before seemed [to be] the best

Od. 6.137 ὅς τις φαίνηται ἄριστος

whoever seems [to be] best

6:28 τοῖς δὲ νέοις ὑπόδειγμα γενναῖον καταλελοιπὼς εἰς τὸ προθύμως καὶ γενναίως ὑπὲρ τῶν σεμνῶν καὶ ἁγίων νόμων ἀπευθανατίζειν. τοσαῦτα δὲ εἰπὼν ἐπὶ τὸ τύμπανον εὐθέως ἦλθεν.

τοῖς ... νέοις. Dative of advantage. The adjective is used as a substantive. Eleazar's example "for the youth" is immediately followed by the seven brothers in chapter 7. Cf. 15:17.

μὲν ... δὲ. See 6:27.

ὑπόδειγμα γενναῖον. Accusative direct object of καταλελοιπὼς. The word ὑπόδειγμα denotes "an example of behavior used for purposes of moral instruction, *example, model, pattern*" (BDAG, 1037.1).

καταλελοιπὼς. Prf act ptc nom masc sg καταλείπω. Some copyists added ἔσομαι (MSS *L′* 58 311 771), clarifying that καταλελοιπὼς should be understood as part of a future periphrastic construction indicating a future state arising from a prior action: "I will leave behind [a noble example]." Because the "future perfect act[ive] of most verbs is formed by combining the perfect active participle with ἔσομαι" (Smyth §600), sometimes εἰμί can be omitted in the construction. Understood in this way, the periphrastic construction takes the person, number, and mood from ἔσομαι; aspect, voice, and lexical form from καταλελοιπὼς. Thus, the synthetic form would be: καταλέλοιπα, prf act ind 1st sg. Given that ἔσομαι was added by some copyists (but does not belong to the early text), an alternative understanding would be to supply a form of φαίνομαι (cf. this verb in 6:27), which is sometimes used to form periphrastic constructions (cf. Smyth §1965). On motivations for periphrastic constructions, see comments in the Introduction.

προθύμως καὶ γενναίως. Adverbs of manner.

ὑπὲρ τῶν σεμνῶν καὶ ἁγίων νόμων. Advantage (lit. "[to die] for the sake of the revered and holy laws").

ἀπευθανατίζειν. Pres act inf ἀπευθανατίζω (epexegetical to ὑπόδειγμα). While εἰς τό with the infinitive is typically used to introduce a purpose or result clause, here it is better taken as introducing an epexegetical function (cf. Wallace, 611). On the meaning of the verb, see LEH (63): "to die well."

τοσαῦτα. Accusative direct object of εἰπών, emphasizing degree: "[having said] that much" (cf. *GELS*, 684.I.1; Muraoka §16a).

δὲ. Development; see 1:10 on δέ.

εἰπὼν. Aor act ptc nom masc sg εἶπον (temporal).

ἐπὶ τὸ τύμπανον. Locative. Cf. the same phrase in 6:19.

εὐθέως. Temporal adverb, demonstrating Eleazar's willingness to die.

ἦλθεν. Aor act ind 3rd sg ἔρχομαι. See 2:5 on ἐλθών.

6:29 τῶν δὲ ἀγόντων πρὸς αὐτὸν τὴν μικρῷ πρότερον εὐμένειαν εἰς
δυσμένειαν μεταβαλόντων διὰ τὸ τοὺς προειρημένους λόγους, ὡς
αὐτοὶ διελάμβανον, ἀπόνοιαν εἶναι,

According to Doran (2012, 144): "[t]he manuscripts here are quite
confused." Abel (368–69) suggests taking the participles in 6:29 with
εἶπεν in 6:30. However, another plausible (and preferable) way of understanding the grammar is to construe 6:29 with what precedes, taking
the genitive absolute construction as modifying the main verb in 6:28
(cf. Risberg, 19–22; Doran 2012, 144; Habicht, 232; Nicklas 2011, 1393).

τῶν . . . ἀγόντων. Pres act ptc gen masc pl ἄγω (substantival). Subject
of μεταβαλόντων. There is a text critical issue here: ἀγόντων (MS A) and
ἀπαγόντων (MS V). The latter implies "taking him away [to be executed]."
D. Schwartz (292–93) prefers ἀγόντων because "up until this point we
have not been told that Eleazar was to be executed." BDAG (16.2) refers to
this as a technical term "[o]f leading away to execution." Cf. 7:18.

δὲ. Development; see 1:10 on δέ.

πρὸς αὐτὸν. Spatial (direction toward).

τὴν . . . εὐμένειαν. Accusative direct object of μεταβαλόντων. In
context, it contrasts with δυσμένειαν as part of a wordplay (cf. 5:6).

μικρῷ πρότερον. Temporal adverbs.

εἰς δυσμένειαν. Goal (cf. BDAG, 290.4.b). On δυσ-compound words
in 2 Maccabees, see 2:24 on δυσχέρειαν.

μεταβαλόντων. Aor act ptc gen masc pl μεταβάλλω (genitive absolute, temporal). On the genitive absolute, see 1:7 on βασιλεύοντος.

τοὺς προειρημένους λόγους. Accusative subject of the infinitive
εἶναι.

προειρημένους. Prf pass ptc acc masc pl προεῖπον (attributive).

ὡς. Introduces a comparative clause ("*as* they supposed") or, less
likely, causal ("*because* they supposed").

αὐτοὶ. Nominative subject of διελάμβανον.

διελάμβανον. Impf act ind 3rd pl διαλαμβάνω. The Göttingen edition reads ὑπελάμβανον.

ἀπόνοιαν. Predicate accusative. See *GELS* (80): "madness." Unlike
a predicate accusative adjective, the predicate accusative (noun) need
only agree in case (cf. *CGCG* §26.8).

εἶναι. Pres act inf εἰμί. Used with διὰ τό to denote cause. The separation of διὰ τό from the infinitive is an example of hyperbaton.

6:30 μέλλων δὲ ταῖς πληγαῖς τελευτᾶν ἀναστενάξας εἶπεν Τῷ κυρίῳ τῷ τὴν ἁγίαν γνῶσιν ἔχοντι φανερόν ἐστιν ὅτι δυνάμενος ἀπολυθῆναι τοῦ θανάτου σκληρὰς ὑποφέρω κατὰ τὸ σῶμα ἀλγηδόνας μαστιγούμενος, κατὰ ψυχὴν δὲ ἡδέως διὰ τὸν αὐτοῦ φόβον ταῦτα πάσχω.

μέλλων. Pres act ptc nom masc sg μέλλω (temporal or, perhaps, causal). Here the verb + infinitive expresses an imminent event.

δὲ. Development, marking a change of subject from 6:29 back to Eleazar in 6:30. See 1:10 on δέ.

ταῖς πληγαῖς. Dative of means.

τελευτᾶν. Pres act inf τελευτάω (complementary). Death speeches were a common literary topos in antiquity (e.g., Homer, *Il.* 16.492–501; 16.844–854; 22.338–343).

ἀναστενάξας. Aor act ptc nom masc sg ἀναστενάζω (attendant circumstance). Other LXX uses of ἀναστενάζω (e.g., Lam 1:4; Sir 25:18; Sus 22 [Θ]) show that the term has negative connotations, thus "to groan" (*GELS*, 45) rather than just "sigh deeply" (BDAG, 72).

εἶπεν. Aor act ind 3rd sg εἶπον.

Τῷ κυρίῳ. Ethical dative (lit. "[it is clear] as far *the Lord* is concerned").

τῷ. . . . ἔχοντι. Pres act ptc dat masc sg ἔχω (attributive, modifying κυρίῳ).

τὴν ἁγίαν γνῶσιν. Accusative direct object of ἔχοντι. The choice of γνῶσις parallels 6:21, where the "knowledge" of the oppressors leads them to urge Eleazar to betray his convictions. Here, in 6:30, the expression of God's "knowledge" functions much like the expression "God is witness" (cf. Lucian, *Phal.* 1.1; Wis 1:6; Philo, *Ebr.* 139; Josephus, *Ant.* 5.113; etc.), which was a common type of expression for evoking divine testimonies (Novenson 2010, 373–74; cf. D. Schwartz, 293).

φανερόν. Predicate adjective, agreeing with the implied subject of ἐστιν.

ἐστιν. Pres act ind 3rd sg εἰμί.

ὅτι. Introduces a clausal complement (indirect discourse) of ἐστιν.

δυνάμενος. Pres mid ptc nom masc sg δύναμαι (concessive).

ἀπολυθῆναι. Aor pass inf ἀπολύω (complementary). Cf. 6:22 for the collocation of ἀπολύω and τοῦ θανάτου.

τοῦ θανάτου. Genitive of separation.

σκληρὰς . . . ἀλγηδόνας. Accusative direct object of ὑποφέρω. The separation of the modifier from the head is an example of hyperbaton where the modifier (σκληράς) is emphasized.

ὑποφέρω. Pres act ind 1st sg ὑποφέρω.

κατὰ τὸ σῶμα. Reference. The body-soul distinction introduced in 6:30 is preparatory for the theme of life after death (cf. Wis 3:1-4). See further 14:38 on the distinction between body and soul.

μαστιγούμενος. Pres pass ptc nom masc sg μαστιγόω (manner).

κατὰ ψυχὴν. Reference.

δὲ. Development, setting up a contrast between "body" and "soul." See 1:10 on δέ.

ἡδέως. Adverb of manner.

διὰ τὸν . . . φόβον. Cause. D. Schwartz (293) suggests that the use of φόβος rather than something from the σεβ-root (cf. εὐσέβεια, δυσσεβή, ἀσεβής) is a Hebraism. This does not suggest anything about the source language of 2 Maccabees (*pace* Habicht). Rather, it likely represents the epitomizer's choice to mirror biblical diction. Cf. Prov 1:7 on the theme of fearing God.

αὐτοῦ. Objective genitive.

ταῦτα. Accusative direct object of πάσχω.

πάσχω. Pres act ind 1st sg πάσχω.

6:31 καὶ οὗτος οὖν τοῦτον τὸν τρόπον μετήλλαξεν οὐ μόνον τοῖς νέοις, ἀλλὰ καὶ τοῖς πλείστοις τοῦ ἔθνους τὸν ἑαυτοῦ θάνατον ὑπόδειγμα γενναιότητος καὶ μνημόσυνον ἀρετῆς καταλιπών.

Much of the Latin tradition of 2 Maccabees (LA^LXBM) concludes Eleazar's martyrdom story after the opening summary: "and so this one died in this way."

οὗτος. Nominative subject of μετήλλαξεν.

οὖν. Inferential, introducing commentary on the narrative about Eleazar's death in 6:18-30. Note also that Runge (43) comments that "[o]ne often finds οὖν at high-level boundaries in the discourse, where the next major topic is drawn from and builds upon what precedes." See also 2:15 on οὖν.

τοῦτον τὸν τρόπον. Τρόπον is used in various adverbial expressions: "in this manner" (cf. Muraoka §22xg).

μετήλλαξεν. Aor act ind 3rd sg μεταλλάσσω. On the meaning of μεταλλάσσω, see 4:7 on Μεταλλάξαντος.

οὐ μόνον . . . ἀλλὰ καί. This construction is used to contrast and expand upon a preceding idea (cf. Ehorn and Lee, 12). Ellipsis of the verb is common in this construction (cf. BDF §479.1).

τοῖς νέοις. Dative of advantage.

τοῖς πλείστοις. Dative of advantage. Superlative of πολύς.

τοῦ ἔθνους. Genitive of apposition.

τὸν ... θάνατον. Accusative direct object of καταλιπών in an object-complement double accusative construction.

ἑαυτοῦ. Subjective genitive.

ὑπόδειγμα ... καὶ μνημόσυνον. Complements in an object-complement double accusative construction.

γενναιότητος. Genitive of apposition (i.e., "an example of nobility") or, perhaps, attributive genitive (i.e., "a noble example"). See BDAG (193): "the quality associated with one who is γενναῖος, *nobility, bravery*."

ἀρετῆς. Genitive of apposition or, perhaps, attributive genitive.

καταλιπών. Aor act ptc nom masc sg καταλείπω (purpose). Given that Eleazar aimed to provide a "noble example" (ὑπόδειγμα γενναῖον, 6:28), it is best to understand the participle as denoting purpose in this context. On the meaning of the verb, see BDAG (520.5): "to leave someth[ing] with design before departing, *leave behind* of an inheritance." D. Schwartz (294): "[i]n Greek this is the last word of the chapter, ending it, and Eleazar's martyrdom, with finality."

2 Maccabees 7:1-6

[1]Now it also came about [that] seven brothers with their mother were arrested and forced by the king to touch the unlawful pig flesh, being tortured by whips and cords. [2]One of them, becoming a spokesman, said as follows, "What are you going to ask and to learn from us? For we are ready to die rather than transgress the ancestral laws." [3]Then, becoming incensed, the king ordered [some] to heat pans and cauldrons. [4]When they were instantly heated, he ordered [some] to cut off the tongue of the one who had become their spokesman and, after scalping [him], to cut off his extremities, while the rest of the brothers and [their] mother were looking on. [5]Then, after he was useless in every way, he ordered [some] to bring [him] to the fire, breathing and alive, and to fry [him]. And as the smoke spread about from the pan for a long time, they were exhorting one another with [their] mother to die nobly, saying as follows, [6]"The Lord God is watching and in truth is becoming compassionate toward us, just as through the song of witness against the face [of the people], Moses declared, saying, 'And to his slaves he will be compassionate.'"

The account of the martyrdom of the seven brothers (7:1-42) is one of the most well-known stories of 2 Maccabees and is retold in later Jewish works (e.g., 4 Macc 8:1-17:6; *b. Giṭ.* 57b). Despite its popularity, the originality of the story is sometimes questioned. Many scholars (e.g., Habicht, 176–77) believe that the text was added by a later redactor/editor of the text and that the summary in 7:42 belongs directly after 6:31. Alternatively, D. Schwartz (19) argues that chapter 7 along with 6:18-42 reflect the use of a different source than the rest of the book. However, Domazakis (341–49) plausibly argues that "[o]ne and the same person penned chapter 7 and the rest of the epitome." This judgment is based on linguistic connections with the rest of 2 Maccabees. For example, Domazakis (398–400) lists thirty-three "non-trivial word combinations" found in chapter 7 and elsewhere in 2 Maccabees. Moreover, many rare individual words in chapter 7 are employed elsewhere in the epitome, suggesting that whoever wrote chapter 7 was intimately familiar with the language of the rest of the book. One plausible (and in my view the most plausible) explanation for these shared linguistic connections is that the martyrdom narratives were written by the same author.

The martyrdom account is linked to the preceding story because Eleazar wanted to "leave *to the young* [τοῖς νέοις] a noble example of how to die a good death" (6:28, NETS; cf. 6:31). While the connection to the brothers in the immediately following narrative may be obvious, the epitomizer makes the connection more explicit by referring to "*the youngest* [τοῦ νεωτέρου] brother" (7:24, NETS) in the digression that comprises 7:20-29. The rest of the martyrdom account includes speeches that not only give voice to the characters, but also allow the epitomizer to communicate his own agenda. In particular, the epitomizer explains why tragedy strikes the brothers and also what obedience to ancestral tradition will attain (cf. Coetzer, 109–10). The result of obedience is twofold. First, God is reconciled to the nation (e.g., 7:6, 16, 33, 37-38) in accordance with the Deuteronomistic notion of sin, punishment, suffering, and reconciliation (cf. D. Schwartz, 299). Second, the brothers also hold out hope that God will raise them to new life after they die (7:9, 11, 14, 23, 29, 36).

Throughout chapter 7 most of the plotline of the narrative is conveyed using the aorist indicative (e.g., 7:1, 2, 3, 4, 5, 6). Whenever discourse is introduced into the narrative, the tense switches to the present (e.g., 7:2, 6).

7:1 Συνέβη δὲ καὶ ἑπτὰ ἀδελφοὺς μετὰ τῆς μητρὸς συλλημφθέντας ἀναγκάζεσθαι ὑπὸ τοῦ βασιλέως ἀπὸ τῶν ἀθεμίτων ὑείων κρεῶν ἐφάπτεσθαι μάστιξιν καὶ νευραῖς αἰκιζομένους.

Συνέβη. Aor act ind 3rd sg συμβαίνω. See 3:2 on συνέβαινεν.

δέ. Development; see 1:10 on δέ. Unlike chapters 5, 6, 9, 11, 13, and 14, the fact that the narrative simply continues on without mentioning any passage of time indicates that the present story is still part of the "few words" (6:17) that the epitomizer wanted to communicate before returning to the main storyline (cf. D. Schwartz, 300).

καί. Adverbial.

ἑπτὰ ἀδελφοὺς. Accusative subject of the infinitive ἀναγκάζεσθαι. The historicity of the story is not of concern here. However, Doran (2012, 155) suggests that "[t]he number seven is a round number for completion." It is also possible that the number seven was selected based on Jer 15:9, which refers to a mother who dies in the same way that her seven children did.

μετὰ τῆς μητρὸς. Accompaniment. On the use of the Greek article like a pronoun, see 1:16 on τὰς κεφαλάς.

συλλημφθέντας. Aor pass ptc acc masc pl συλλαμβάνω (attendant circumstance). The participle is accusative because it agrees with the ἑπτὰ ἀδελφούς, the accusative subject of the infinitive. On circumstantial participles in oblique cases, see 3:27 on πεσόντα.

ἀναγκάζεσθαι. Pres pass inf ἀναγκάζω (indirect discourse).

ὑπὸ τοῦ βασιλέως. Agency. See D. Schwartz (300) on the problem that the king, Antiochus, is apparently in Jerusalem when earlier we were told that he returned to Antioch (cf. 5:21).

ἀπὸ τῶν ἀθεμίτων. Source or, more likely, partitive ("[part of] the unlawful").

ὑείων κρεῶν. Genitive in apposition to τῶν ἀθεμίτων.

ἐφάπτεσθαι. Pres mid inf ἐφάπτω (complementary). Muraoka (§22p): here "ἀπό combined with ἐφάπτομαι, which is semantically and derivationally affiliated with ἅπτομαι, shows the ablative nature of the genitive rection of the latter." While Habicht (233) considers the collocation of ἐφάπτω + ἀπό to be poor Greek (cf. Nicklas 2011, 1394), Coetzer (102) is correct that "the author of 2 Maccabees represented himself as a proper Hellenistic writer and thus one who is aware of the finer details of the language and its progression."

Although many translate the verb ἐφάπτω here as "to taste" or "to partake" (cf. NETS, Zeitlin and Tedesche, 159; Goldstein, 289; Bartlett, 270; Grimm, 118), the sense of "touch" is a better translation (cf. *GE*, 876.2) and is reflected in the Latin versions of 2 Maccabees (i.e., *contingere*). D. Schwartz (300) helpfully points out that this is an example of rhetorical intensification: "the king wanted to force them (as Eleazar) to eat the forbidden meat, but they refused even to touch it."

μάστιξιν καὶ νευραῖς. Datives of instrument.

αἰκιζομένους. Pres pass ptc acc masc pl αἰκίζω (manner). The switch to imperfective verbal aspect helps indicate an ongoing or repeated action: "*being tortured* by whips and cords." On the accusative case of the participle, see comments above on συλλημφθέντας.

7:2 εἷς δὲ αὐτῶν γενόμενος προήγορος οὕτως ἔφη Τί μέλλεις ἐρωτᾶν καὶ μανθάνειν ἡμῶν; ἕτοιμοι γὰρ ἀποθνήσκειν ἐσμὲν ἢ παραβαίνειν τοὺς πατρίους νόμους.

εἷς. Nominative subject of ἔφη.

αὐτῶν. Partitive genitive.

γενόμενος. Aor mid ptc masc nom masc sg γίνομαι (manner).

προήγορος. Predicate nominative. See *GE* (1763): "spokesman."

οὕτως. The adverb is cataphoric, pointing forward to the discourse that follows (cf. BDAG, 742.2).

ἔφη. Aor act ind 3rd sg φημί.

Τί. Accusative direct object of ἐρωτᾶν. Introduces an indirect question.

μέλλεις. Pres act ind 2nd sg μέλλω. The collocation of τί + μέλλεις can also mean "why are you delaying?" (BDAG, 628.4). After direct discourse has been introduced (ἔφη), a switch to the present tense is expected in narrative (cf. Campbell, 76).

ἐρωτᾶν. Pres act inf ἐρωτάω (complementary).

μανθάνειν. Pres act inf μανθάνω (complementary).

ἡμῶν. Genitive of source.

ἕτοιμοι γὰρ ἀποθνήσκειν ἐσμὲν. Cf. 8:21, where a similar phrase describes Judas Maccabeus' men.

ἕτοιμοι. Predicate adjective.

γὰρ. Introduces an explanation of the question: Τί μέλλεις ἐρωτᾶν καὶ μανθάνειν ἡμῶν ("What are you going to ask and to learn from us?"). See 1:12 on γάρ.

ἀποθνήσκειν. Pres act inf ἀποθνῄσκω (epexegetical to ἕτοιμοι).

ἐσμὲν. Pres act ind 1st pl εἰμί.

ἢ. The conjunction marks a preference: "[this] *rather than* [that]" (cf. Muraoka §23bdb).

παραβαίνειν. Pres act inf παραβαίνω (epexegetical to ἕτοιμοι).

τοὺς πατρίους νόμους. Accusative direct object of παραβαίνειν. The epitomizer uses the adjective πάτριος six times in chapter 7 to describe "ancestral laws" (7:2, 24, 37) or "ancestral language" (7:8, 21, 27).

7:3 ἔκθυμος δὲ γενόμενος ὁ βασιλεὺς προσέταξεν τήγανα καὶ λέβητας ἐκπυροῦν.

ἔκθυμος. Predicate adjective of γενόμενος. D. Schwartz (301) notes that although the term is typically positive in other Greek contexts (cf. *GE*, 630), the epitomizer uses it with a negative sense: "incensed" (*GELS*, 208). The word appears with a similar meaning in Esth 7:9 (AT). Cf. 7:39, where the king becomes angry again.

δὲ. Development; see 1:10 on δέ.

γενόμενος. Aor mid ptc nom masc sg γίνομαι (temporal or, perhaps, causal).

ὁ βασιλεὺς. Nominative subject of προσέταξεν.

προσέταξεν. Aor act ind 3rd sg προστάσσω. BDAG (885) notes that προστάσσω is sometimes followed by the accusative and infinitive. Here, although no accusative subject of the infinitive is stated, logically the clause requires it: "he ordered [*some*] to heat pans and cauldrons."

τήγανα καὶ λέβητας. Accusative direct objects of ἐκπυροῦν. τήγανον refers to "a cooking instrument which would be heated by cauldrons underneath it in which a fire would be started" (Coetzer, 102; cf. Doran 2012, 156).

ἐκπυροῦν. Pres act inf ἐκπυρόω (indirect discourse). This rare verb occurs only in 7:3 and 7:4 in the Greek of the LXX. Cf. Polybius (*Hist.* 12.25.2), where the same verb is used of a torture instrument.

7:4 τῶν δὲ παραχρῆμα ἐκπυρωθέντων τὸν γενόμενον αὐτῶν προήγορον προσέταξεν γλωσσοτομεῖν καὶ περισκυθίσαντας ἀκρωτηριάζειν τῶν λοιπῶν ἀδελφῶν καὶ τῆς μητρὸς συνορώντων.

τῶν δὲ. The article functions as the genitive subject of the participle ἐκπυρωθέντων and functions like an anaphoric third person pronoun, agreeing with the neuter antecedents τήγανα καὶ λέβητας in 7:3. See 6:19 on ὁ δέ.

ἐκπυρωθέντων. Aor pass ptc gen masc pl ἐκπυρόω (genitive absolute, temporal). On the genitive absolute, see 1:7 on βασιλεύοντος.

παραχρῆμα. Temporal adverb.

τὸν γενόμενον. Aor mid ptc acc masc sg γίνομαι (substantival). Direct object of γλωσσοτομεῖν.

αὐτῶν. Objective genitive.

προήγορον. Predicate accusative of γενόμενον. Cf. 7:2 on προήγορος.

προσέταξεν. Aor act ind 3rd sg προστάσσω. See comments in 7:3 on προσέταξεν.

γλωσσοτομεῖν. Pres act inf γλωσσοτομέω (indirect discourse). The word is built from γλῶσσα + τομή (i.e., "cutting"). On the meaning of the verb, see *GE* (435): "to cut out the tongue."

περισκυθίσαντας. Aor act ptc acc masc pl περισκυθίζω (temporal). The circumstantial participle expands upon the infinitive (cf. Muraoka §31dh). As with most -ιζω verbs, περισκυθίζω is built on a noun stem of a region or an ethnos (i.e., Σκυθία, "Scythia") and may have three basic meanings: (1) to lend support (politically); (2) to adopt customs; or (3) to speak a language (Cohen 1999, 175–78). Here, the cultural sense is most appropriate: "[to adopt the Scythian custom of] scalping." In particular, περισκυθίζω refers to "cutting all the way around at the level of the ears and removing the scalp by pulling and shaking" (Goldstein, 304). This method of scalping was regularly associated with Scythians in both literary (cf. Herodotus, *Hist.* 4.64; Pliny, *Hist. Nat.* 6.53; 7.9–11) and archeological sources (Rolle, 82–85; cf. D. Schwartz, 302).

Domazakis (145–54, esp. 150), who discusses the term at length, rightly notes that περισκυθίζω refers to "a method of torture instigated by the Seleucid Greek king Antiochus IV, whom the author of the book, in his effort to invert the established stereotypes about Greek and barbarians, portrays as a sadistic ogre, who out-savages the savages." See also the circumlocution for scalping in 7:7: τὸ τῆς κεφαλῆς δέρμα σὺν ταῖς θριξὶν περισύραντες ("tearing off the skin of his head with his hair").

ἀκρωτηριάζειν. Pres act inf ἀκρωτηριάζω (indirect discourse). On the meaning of the verb, see *GE* (79.1): "to cut off the extremities" (i.e., the hands and feet).

τῶν λοιπῶν ἀδελφῶν καὶ τῆς μητρὸς. Genitive subjects of the participle συνορώντων. If λοιπῶν is taken as a substantive, then ἀδελφῶν would be a partitive genitive ("the rest of the brothers"). Alternatively, λοιπῶν may be taken as an attributive adjective ("the remaining brothers").

συνορώντων. Pres act ptc gen masc pl συνοράω (genitive absolute, temporal). Less commonly, the genitive absolute follows the main verb (cf. Muraoka §31h), but this may be because two genitive participles (see earlier ἐκπυρωθέντων) depend upon προσέταξεν. The mother's "looking" is mentioned here at the beginning of the ordeal as well as at 7:20, before the seventh son dies. On the genitive absolute, see 1:7 on βασιλεύοντος.

7:5 ἄχρηστον δὲ αὐτὸν τοῖς ὅλοις γενόμενον ἐκέλευσεν τῇ πυρᾷ προσάγειν ἔμπνουν καὶ τηγανίζειν. τῆς δὲ ἀτμίδος ἐφ᾽ ἱκανὸν διαδιδούσης τοῦ τηγάνου ἀλλήλους παρεκάλουν σὺν τῇ μητρὶ γενναίως τελευτᾶν λέγοντες οὕτως.

ἄχρηστον. Predicate accusative of γενόμενον. After cutting off his extremities (7:4), the first brother was "useless" (*GELS*, 110).

δὲ. Development; see 1:10 on δέ.

αὐτὸν. Accusative subject of the infinitive γενόμενον.

τοῖς ὅλοις. Dative of manner. This could be masculine (e.g., "in all [his members]") or, more likely, neuter and thus adverbial (i.e., "in every way"). Cf. 6:3.

γενόμενον. Aor mid ptc acc masc sg γίνομαι (temporal). The participle is accusative because it agrees with the implied accusative subject of the infinitive προσάγειν. On circumstantial participles in oblique cases, see 3:27 on πεσόντα.

ἐκέλευσεν. Aor act ind 3rd sg κελεύω.

τῇ πυρᾷ. Dative indirect object of προσάγειν.

προσάγειν. Pres act inf προσάγω (indirect discourse). Often the accusative direct object needs to be supplied from context (BDAG, 875.1.a).

ἔμπνουν. Adverbial accusative of manner. See *GELS* (229): "breathing and alive."

τηγανίζειν. Pres act inf τηγανίζω (indirect discourse).

τῆς ... ἀτμίδος. Genitive subject of the participle διαδιδούσης. Nicklas (2011, 1394) notes that ἀτμίς designates not only "smoke," but also the smell of burning.

δὲ. Development, indicating a change of grammatical subject. See 1:10 on δέ.

ἐφ᾽ ἱκανὸν. Temporal, denoting "for a long time" (BDAG, 472.3). Cf. 8:25.

διαδιδούσης. Pres act ptc gen fem sg διαδίδωμι (genitive absolute, temporal). On the meaning of the verb, see *GELS* (150.3): "to spread about." On the genitive absolute, see 1:7 on βασιλεύοντος.

τοῦ τηγάνου. Genitive of separation.

ἀλλήλους. Accusative subject of the infinitive τελευτᾶν.

παρεκάλουν. Impf act ind 3rd pl παρακαλέω. The exhortation (παρακαλέω) "to die nobly" here contrasts starkly with the exhortation (παρακαλέω) "to bring meat that was allowed for him to use" (6:21).

σὺν τῇ μητρὶ. Association. On the use of the Greek article like a pronoun, see 1:16 on τὰς κεφαλάς.

γενναίως. Adverb of manner. Cf. 7:11.

τελευτᾶν. Pres act inf τελευτάω (indirect discourse).

λέγοντες. Pres act ptc nom masc pl λέγω (attendant circumstance or, more likely, means). Although λέγοντες often signals direct speech when it follows the main verb, in this context it probably denotes the means by which the brothers exhorted one another.

οὕτως. The adverb is cataphoric, pointing forward to the discourse in 7:6 (cf. BDAG, 742.2).

7:6 Ὁ κύριος ὁ θεὸς ἐφορᾷ καὶ ταῖς ἀληθείαις ἐφ᾽ ἡμῖν παρακαλεῖται, καθάπερ διὰ τῆς κατὰ πρόσωπον ἀντιμαρτυρούσης ᾠδῆς διεσάφησεν Μωυσῆς λέγων Καὶ ἐπὶ τοῖς δούλοις αὐτοῦ παρακληθήσεται.

ὁ κύριος ὁ θεός. Nominative subject of ἐφορᾷ.

ἐφορᾷ. Pres act ind 3rd sg ἐφοράω. On the theme of God watching over his people while they suffer, see 3:39; 12:22; 15:2; Gen 16:13; Exod 2:25; Ps 30:7; etc. After direct discourse has been introduced (cf. λέγοντες in 7:5), a switch to the present tense is expected in narrative (cf. Campbell, 76).

ταῖς ἀληθείαις. Dative of manner.

ἐφ᾽ ἡμῖν. Locative.

παρακαλεῖται. Pres pass ind 3rd sg παρακαλέω. Goldstein (304) notes that the use of the present tense is striking because the brothers believe that Deut 32:6 is being fulfilled. As noted just above, the present tense is not unusual at all. However, the application of Deuteronomy 32 to the present situation is certainly noteworthy.

καθάπερ. The conjunction introduces a comparative clause. See 2:27 on καθάπερ.

διὰ τῆς κατὰ πρόσωπον ἀντιμαρτυρούσης ᾠδῆς. The "song of witness against the face [of the people]" is taken from LXX Deut 31:21: καὶ ἀντικαταστήσεται ἡ ᾠδὴ αὕτη κατὰ πρόσωπον μαρτυροῦσα.

διὰ τῆς . . . ἀντιμαρτυρούσης ᾠδῆς. Means.

ἀντιμαρτυρούσης. Pres act ptc fem sg gen ἀντιμαρτυρέω (attributive). On the meaning of the verb, see *GELS* (59): "to make a case in front of a hostile audience."

κατὰ πρόσωπον. Locative. This is an idiom meaning "a position in front of an object, with the implication of direct sight" (LN 83.34; cf. BDAG, 888.1.b.β.7).

διεσάφησεν. Aor act ind 3rd sg διασαφέω.

Μωυσῆς. Nominative subject of διεσάφησεν.

λέγων. Pres act part masc sg nom λέγω (attendant circumstance or, perhaps, manner). The adverbial participle that relates to διεσάφησεν.

Καὶ ἐπὶ τοῖς δούλοις αὐτοῦ παρακληθήσεται. A quotation from LXX Deut 32:36 (cf. Ps 135:14). By using this quotation, the martyrs identify themselves with "the slaves" in the text and, thus, there is a hint of future hope. Cf. 7:33 and 8:29 for additional allusions to Deut 32:36.

ἐπὶ τοῖς δούλοις. Locative. Although translated here as "slaves," the source text of the quotation, where δοῦλος and λαός are parallel, may suggest the softer "servants" (e.g., NRSV).

αὐτοῦ. Possessive genitive.

παρακληθήσεται. Fut pass ind 3rd sg παρακαλέω.

2 Maccabees 7:7-19

[7]Now after the first [brother] died in this manner, they were bringing the second for torture and, tearing off the skin of his head with his hair, they were asking [him], "Will you eat rather than have your body punished limb by limb." [8]But he, answering in his ancestral language, said, "No!" Therefore, even this one received the next torture as the first. [9]But, when he came to [his] last breath, he said, "You wretch! From our present life you release us, but the king of the world, because we die for his laws, will raise us up to an everlasting renewal of life." [10]Then, after this one, the third [brother] was tortured and, when it was demanded, he immediately stuck out his tongue and courageously stretched out his hands. [11]And nobly he said, "From heaven I obtained these, and because of his laws, I disregard these, and from him I hope to receive back these again." [12]As a result, the king himself and those with him were amazed at the spirit of the young man; he was regarding the sufferings as nothing. [13]And, after this one died also, they were torturing the fourth [brother] similarly, maltreating [him]. [14]And when he came near to death, he spoke thusly, "It is better, even though being put to death by men, to look for the hopes [given] by God to be raised up again by him. Indeed, for you there will be no resurrection unto life." [15]Next, they were bringing forward the fifth [brother] and mistreating [him]. [16]But he, looking toward him, said, "Because you have authority among men, even though you are mortal, you do what you please. But do not think that our people have been forsaken by God. [17]You wait and see his magnificent strength, which will torture you and your seed." [18]Then after this one, they were bringing the sixth [brother], and when he was about to die, he said, "Do not deceive yourselves vainly; for we are suffering these things because of our own [sins], having sinned against our own God. Amazing things have happened. [19]But you should not suppose [that] you are innocent because you tried to fight against God."

Although the first brother dies with his tongue cut out (7:4) and, thus, is unable to give a final speech, the remaining brothers are afforded the opportunity to speak; this heightens the emotion of the narrative (cf. Doran 2012, 156). The narrative coheres through the use of similar terminology in multiple deaths: μεταλλάσσω (7:7, 13-14); βάσανος and βασανίζω (7:8, 13); ἀνίστημι and ἀνάστασις (7:9, 14). Moreover, the martyrdom account has connections with other parts of 2 Maccabees. For instance, the sixth son's speech reiterates the theme of the digression in 5:17-20 by stating clearly that Antiochus' success against the Jews is only because he is an instrument of God's punishment. The theme of "ancestry" (πάτριος) also plays a significant role here and elsewhere (7:2, 8, 21, 27, 24, 37). On the use of the present tense in the narrative, see comments following the translation of 7:1-6.

7:7 Μεταλλάξαντος δὲ τοῦ πρώτου τὸν τρόπον τοῦτον τὸν δεύτερον ἦγον ἐπὶ τὸν ἐμπαιγμὸν καὶ τὸ τῆς κεφαλῆς δέρμα σὺν ταῖς θριξὶν περισύραντες ἐπηρώτων Εἰ φάγεσαι πρὸ τοῦ τιμωρηθῆναι τὸ σῶμα κατὰ μέλος;

Μεταλλάξαντος. Aor act ptc gen masc sg μεταλλάσσω (genitive absolute, temporal). On the genitive absolute, see 1:7 on βασιλεύοντος.

δὲ. Development; see 1:10 on δέ.

τοῦ πρώτου. Genitive subject of the participle μεταλλάξαντος.

τὸν τρόπον τοῦτον. Τρόπον is used in various adverbial expressions: "in this manner" (cf. Muraoka §22xg).

τὸν δεύτερον. Accusative direct object of ἦγον.

ἦγον. Impf act ind 3rd pl ἄγω.

ἐπὶ τὸν ἐμπαιγμὸν. Purpose. While "mocking" is a common translation of ἐμπαιγμός (cf. GE, 671; BDAG, 323; GELS, 226; NETS; Habicht, 234; D. Schwartz, 296; Doran 2012, 145–46), this is not really warranted by the context, where it is the martyrs who mock Antiochus rather than the other way around (cf. Domazakis, 283). The alternative sense of "torturing" (cf. Abel, 373; Goldstein, 289) makes better sense in a context where the oppressors scalp the second brother and threaten to have his "body punished limb by limb" (πρὸ τοῦ τιμωρηθῆναι τὸ σῶμα κατὰ μέλος, 7:7). Moreover, comparison with 6:7 is instructive:

6:7 ἤγοντο . . . ἐπὶ σπλαγχνισμόν

they were brought for the [consumption of] sacrifices

7:7 ἦγον ἐπὶ τὸν ἐμπαιγμόν

they were bringing [the second] for torture

Based on the linguistic parallels, Domazakis (285) notes that ἐμπαιγμός "refers to the entire degrading session of σπλαγχνισμός, which included the participation in a pagan sacrifice, the trial-like questioning . . . , the forced eating of pork meat . . . , and not solely to its conclusion, the infliction of physical violence, culminating in the execution of the recalcitrant." Cf. ἐμπαίζω in 7:10.

τὸ . . . δέρμα. Accusative direct object of περισύραντες.

τῆς κεφαλῆς. Partitive genitive.

σὺν ταῖς θριξὶν. Association or means (i.e., "by involving and making use of"; GELS, 650.3). The sense is either that his scalp was torn off *along with* his hair or, better, that his scalp was torn off by pulling his hair.

περισύραντες. Aor act ptc nom masc pl περισύρω (temporal). Cf. the scalping in 7:4. See also Herodotus (*Hist.* 7.26) for more on this form of torture.

ἐπηρώτων. Impf act ind 3rd pl ἐπερωτάω.

Εἰ. Conditional conjunction, introducing an indirect question (cf. Grimm, 121; CGCG §42.3). The rarity of εἰ introducing a question in classical Greek led Muraoka (§88) to suggest that "the particle in [2 Maccabees] introducing a direct question is most likely an influence of Septuagint books introduced earlier." But, as both Muraoka (§88) and Doran (2012, 156) note, it is very unlikely that this use of εἰ is simply a semiticism because the particle εἰ appears in multiple instances where no corresponding Hebrew particle (e.g., אִם) is found (e.g., Jonah 3:9). See 15:3 for a similar construction.

φάγεσαι. Fut mid ind 2nd sg ἐσθίω. Deliberative.

τιμωρηθῆναι. Aor pass inf τιμωρέω. Although πρὸ τοῦ is often used to denote subsequent time (Wallace, 596), there are examples in classical literature where it means "rather than" (e.g., Herodotus, *Hist.* 7.152.3; Thucydides, *Hist.* 5.36.1). Accordingly, here NETS translates "rather than have your body punished," which is supported by GE (1741.II.D): "with idea of preference . . . rather than."

τὸ σῶμα. Accusative direct object of τιμωρηθῆναι. Cf. the description of Antiochus in 9:7.

κατὰ μέλος. Distributive, "indicating repetition of same process with multiple entities" (*GELS*, 367.II.8).

7:8 ὁ δὲ ἀποκριθεὶς τῇ πατρίῳ φωνῇ προσεῖπεν Οὐχί. διόπερ καὶ οὗτος τὴν ἑξῆς ἔλαβεν βάσανον ὡς ὁ πρῶτος.

ὁ δὲ. The article functions as the nominative subject of προσεῖπεν and refers to the second brother. See 6:19 on ὁ δέ.

ἀποκριθεὶς. Aor pass ptc nom masc sg ἀποκρίνομαι (attendant circumstance).

τῇ πατρίῳ φωνῇ. Dative of manner. See BDAG (1072.3) on φωνή: "a verbal code shared by a community to express ideas and feelings, *language.*" Here, the language is most assuredly Hebrew rather than Aramaic (cf. 15:36). Himmelfarb (37) notes that the reference to ancestral language is a further act of defiance because even a diaspora Jew could say, "no!" in Greek. Cf. 7:21 and 7:27.

προσεῖπεν. Aor act ind 3rd sg προσεῖπον.

Οὐχί. When used in a negative reply, οὐχί is the standard form of the negation (cf. BDAG, 742.2).

διόπερ. Inferential conjunction, introducing a logical conclusion (cf. *GELS*, 171). See 5:20 on διόπερ.

καὶ. Ascensive.

οὗτος. The anaphoric demonstrative pronoun is the nominative subject of ἔλαβεν.

τὴν ἑξῆς . . . βάσανον. Accusative direct object of ἔλαβεν. The adverb ἑξῆς modifies the noun. Muraoka (§24b) notes that "the adverb cannot mean 'one after another,' modifying ἔλαβεν, for that would make the article, τήν, stand alone, separated from βάσανον, a highly unlikely hyperbaton."

ἔλαβεν. Aor act ind 3rd sg λαμβάνω.

ὡς. Introduces a comparative clause, involving ellipsis: "this one received the next torture *as* the first [received torture]." While Abel (373; cf. Goldstein, 305) argues that ὡς ὁ πρῶτος must be a gloss because the second brother could not have died "as the first [died]," it is likely that the epitomizer is only making a general comparison between the deaths of the two brothers (cf. Doran 2012, 156).

ὁ πρῶτος. Nominative subject of an implied form of λαμβάνω. The ordinal number is substantivized.

7:9 ἐν ἐσχάτῃ δὲ πνοῇ γενόμενος εἶπεν Σὺ μέν, ἀλάστωρ, ἐκ τοῦ παρόντος ἡμᾶς ζῆν ἀπολύεις, ὁ δὲ τοῦ κόσμου βασιλεὺς ἀποθανόντας ἡμᾶς ὑπὲρ τῶν αὐτοῦ νόμων εἰς αἰώνιον ἀναβίωσιν ζωῆς ἡμᾶς ἀναστήσει.

ἐν ἐσχάτῃ . . . πνοῇ. Locative.

δὲ. Development; see 1:10 on δέ.

γενόμενος. Aor mid ptc nom masc sg γίνομαι (temporal).

εἶπεν. Aor act ind 3rd sg εἶπον.

Σὺ. Nominative subject of ἀπολύεις.

μέν . . . δὲ. Point/counterpoint set, contrasting the earthly king, Antiochus, with the God who is king of the world. See 2:25 on μὲν . . . δέ.

ἀλάστωρ. Vocative. Taken actively, this may denote an "avenger" (GE, 82.B); passively, "a person whose evil deeds merit vengeance" (LSJ, 61.II). As Doran (2012, 156) notes, ἀλάστωρ may refer to the one who suffers vengeance from an avenging deity (cf. Aeschylus, Eum. 236; Sophocles, Aj. 374). Goldstein (305) observes that the brother "pointedly refrains from addressing Antiochus as 'King.'"

ἐκ τοῦ παρόντος . . . ζῆν. Separation.

παρόντος. Pres act ptc gen masc sg πάρειμι (attributive).

ζῆν. Pres act inf ζάω (substantival).

ἡμᾶς. Accusative direct object of ἀπολύεις.

ἀπολύεις. Pres act ind 2nd sg ἀπολύω. Cf. the uses of ἀπολύω in 6:22 and 6:30. After direct discourse has been introduced (cf. εἶπεν), a switch to the present tense is expected in narrative (cf. Campbell, 76).

ὁ . . . βασιλεὺς. Nominative subject of ἀναστήσει.

τοῦ κόσμου. Genitive of subordination ("[king] over the world").

ἀποθανόντας. Aor act ptc acc masc pl ἀποθνήσκω (causal). The participle is accusative because it agrees with ἡμᾶς. On circumstantial participles in oblique cases, see 3:27 on πεσόντα.

ἡμᾶς. Accusative direct object of ἀναστήσει.

ὑπὲρ τῶν . . . νόμων. Advantage (i.e., "on behalf of his laws").

αὐτοῦ. Genitive of source, qualifying τῶν . . . νόμων.

εἰς αἰώνιον ἀναβίωσιν. Goal (cf. BDAG, 290.4.a). It is unusual that αἰώνιον agrees with ἀναβίωσιν rather than ζωῆς. Some conjecture that αἰώνιον should be αἰωνιου (cf. Habicht, 234), but this is unnecessary (Nicklas 2011, 1394). This is likely a case of the rhetorical figure of hypallage, which is when "a word, instead of agreeing with the case it logically qualifies, is made to agree with another case" (Smyth §3027; cf. Doran 2012, 157). Goldstein notes that the Greek is redundant because the epitomizer wanted to mimic the language of LXX Dan 12:2: οἱ μὲν εἰς ζωὴν αἰώνιον, οἱ δὲ εἰς ὀνειδισμόν, οἱ δὲ εἰς διασπορὰν καὶ αἰσχύνην αἰώνιον ("some to everlasting life but others to shame and others to dispersion [and contempt] everlasting").

ἀναβίωσις, which is a neologism, means "return to life, resurrection" (LEH, 35) or "revival, resurrection" (GE, 128). The translation in NETS is adopted here: "to an everlasting renewal [of life]."

ζωῆς. Objective genitive.

ἡμᾶς. Accusative direct object of ἀναστήσει.

ἀναστήσει. Fut act ind 3rd pl ἀνίστημι. On resurrection belief in this period, see Dan 12:2 and 1 En. 91:10.

7:10 Μετὰ δὲ τοῦτον ὁ τρίτος ἐνεπαίζετο καὶ τὴν γλῶσσαν αἰτηθεὶς ταχέως προέβαλεν καὶ τὰς χεῖρας εὐθαρσῶς προέτεινεν,

Μετὰ ... τοῦτον. Temporal. Cf. 7:18.

δὲ. Development; see 1:10 on δέ.

ὁ τρίτος. Nominative subject of ἐνεπαίζετο.

ἐνεπαίζετο. Impf pass ind 3rd sg ἐμπαίζω. Cf. 7:7 on ἐπὶ τὸν ἐμπαιγμόν.

τὴν γλῶσσαν. Accusative direct object of αἰτηθεὶς ("demanding *his tongue*") or, perhaps, προέβαλεν ("he put out *his tongue*"). D. Schwartz (305) notes that sticking out the tongue later becomes a martyrological *topos* (e.g., Eusebius, *Mart. Pal.* 2.3). On the use of the article like a pronoun, see 1:16 on τὰς κεφαλάς.

αἰτηθεὶς. Aor pass ptc nom masc sg αἰτέω (temporal or, perhaps, causal).

ταχέως. Adverb of manner.

προέβαλεν. Aor act ind 3rd sg προβάλλω.

τὰς χεῖρας. Accusative direct object of προέτεινεν. On the use of the Greek article like a pronoun, see 1:16 on τὰς κεφαλάς.

εὐθαρσῶς. Adverb of manner.

προέτεινεν. Aor act ind 3rd sg προτείνω.

7:11 καὶ γενναίως εἶπεν Ἐξ οὐρανοῦ ταῦτα κέκτημαι καὶ διὰ τοὺς αὐτοῦ νόμους ὑπερορῶ ταῦτα καὶ παρ᾽ αὐτοῦ ταῦτα πάλιν ἐλπίζω κομίσασθαι·

Some later copyists of the Latin tradition and some scholars (e.g., Katz 1960, 19–20) omit 7:11, probably because it is impossible to give a final speech with one's tongue cut out (cf. 7:10). Additionally, if 7:11 were omitted, the result clause that begins in 7:12 would relate to the third brother's actions of sticking out his tongue and stretching out his hands (7:10). As D. Schwartz (305) plausibly suggests, it is possible that this speech was given prior to the violent act or that such critical questions are not relevant to the writer's purpose (cf. Habicht, 235; Doran 2012, 157).

γενναίως. Adverb of manner. Cf. 7:5.

εἶπεν. Aor act ind 3rd sg εἶπον.

Ἐξ οὐρανοῦ. Source. "Heaven" is used as a circumlocution for "God" rather than a simple reference to God's dwelling place (Doran 2012, 157; cf. Marcus, 96–97; D. Schwartz, 305).

ταῦτα. Accusative direct object of κέκτημαι. The neuter demonstrative pronoun refers back to τὴν γλῶσσαν and τὰς χεῖρας from 7:10 (cf. BDF §131). The three-fold repetition of ταῦτα "underscores that the brother hopes to regain the same limbs" (Doran 2012, 157).

κέκτημαι. Prf mid ind 1st sg κτάομαι. This middle verb conveys the self-interest of the subject.

διὰ τοὺς . . . νόμους. Cause.

αὐτοῦ. Genitive of source, qualifying τοὺς . . . νόμους.

ὑπερορῶ. Pres act ind 1st sg ὑπεροράω. GELS (699.c) suggests the following meaning: "to be willing to part with" = "to disregard." The earlier reference to "heaven" may imply that the third brother is looking upward and, thus, the compound verb beginning with ὑπέρ should be understood as looking *above* or *upward* toward the heavens (cf. D. Schwartz, 305). After direct discourse has been introduced (cf. εἶπεν), a switch to the present tense is expected in narrative (cf. Campbell, 76).

ταῦτα. Accusative direct object of ὑπερορῶ.

παρ᾽ αὐτοῦ. Source.

ταῦτα. Accusative direct object of κομίσασθαι.

πάλιν. Adverbial, functioning as a "marker of a discourse or narrative item added to items of a related nature" (BDAG, 753.3).

ἐλπίζω. Pres act ind 1st sg ἐλπίζω.

κομίσασθαι. Aor mid inf κομίζω (complementary).

7:12 ὥστε αὐτὸν τὸν βασιλέα καὶ τοὺς σὺν αὐτῷ ἐκπλήσσεσθαι τὴν τοῦ νεανίσκου ψυχήν, ὡς ἐν οὐδενὶ τὰς ἀλγηδόνας ἐτίθετο.

ὥστε. Introduces a result clause.

αὐτὸν τὸν βασιλέα καὶ τοὺς σὺν αὐτῷ. Compound accusative subjects of the infinitive ἐκπλήσσεσθαι.

αὐτόν. Intensive adjective ("the king *himself*").

τούς. The article functions as a nominalizer, changing the PP (σὺν αὐτῷ) into the second element of the compound accusative subject of the infinitive ἐκπλήσσεσθαι.

σὺν αὐτῷ. Association.

ἐκπλήσσεσθαι. Pres pass inf ἐκπλήσσω (result). Used with ὥστε to indicate a result. Astonishment or amazement is an ancient literary *topos* (e.g., Josephus, *Ag. Ap.* 1.190-93; Arrian, *Anab.* 7.3.5) and Coetzer (104) notes that the presence of the *topos* here serves to invite a similar reaction from readers of 2 Maccabees.

τὴν ... ψυχήν. Accusative direct object of ἐκπλήσσεσθαι.

τοῦ νεανίσκου. Possessive genitive or genitive of apposition.

ὡς. Used with a verb of perception, ὡς refers to "perceiving an object in a certain state" (*GELS*, 748.7.c). Ultimately, the meaning is similar to the double-accusative construction in 5:21 using τίθημι:

τὴν μὲν γῆν πλωτὴν καὶ τὸ πέλαγος πορευτὸν θέσθαι

to make the land navigable and the sea passable

See also LXX Hos 9:10; Ps 20:10.

ἐν οὐδενὶ. Manner. Cf. 4:15.

τὰς ἀλγηδόνας. Accusative direct object of ἐτίθετο.

ἐτίθετο. Impf mid ind 3rd sg τίθημι.

7:13 Καὶ τούτου δὲ μεταλλάξαντος τὸν τέταρτον ὡσαύτως ἐβασάνιζον αἰκιζόμενοι.

Καὶ. Adverbial.

τούτου. Genitive subject of the participle μεταλλάξαντος.

δὲ. Development, marking a change of grammatical subject in 7:13. See 1:10 on δέ.

μεταλλάξαντος. Aor act ptc gen masc sg μεταλλάσσω (genitive absolute, temporal). See 4:7 on Μεταλλάξαντος. On the genitive absolute, see 1:7 on βασιλεύοντος.

τὸν τέταρτον. Accusative direct object of ἐβασάνιζον.

ὡσαύτως. Adverb of manner.

ἐβασάνιζον. Impf act ind 3rd pl βασανίζω. See 1:28 on βασάνισον. Cf. 7:17; 9:6.

αἰκιζόμενοι. Pres mid ptc nom masc pl αἰκίζω (manner). A synonym of βασανίζω, with the sense of "to maltreat, outrage, torture, mutilate" (*GE*, 50.2). The verb is middle because the action implies negative interaction between the oppressors and the fourth brother (cf. N. Miller, 427).

7:14 καὶ γενόμενος πρὸς τὸ τελευτᾶν οὕτως ἔφη Αἱρετὸν μεταλλάσσοντας ὑπ' ἀνθρώπων τὰς ὑπὸ τοῦ θεοῦ προσδοκᾶν ἐλπίδας πάλιν ἀναστήσεσθαι ὑπ' αὐτοῦ· σοὶ μὲν γὰρ ἀνάστασις εἰς ζωὴν οὐκ ἔσται.

γενόμενος. Aor mid ptc nom masc sg γίνομαι (temporal). When used with an adverbial predicate, "to make a change of location in space" (BDAG, 198.6.e; cf. *GE*, 429).

πρὸς τὸ τελευτᾶν. Although the construction πρὸς τό + infinitive often indicates purpose, the PP phrase here indicates goal or direction. See *GELS* (589.III.a): "in the direction of, towards: with verbs of physical movement."

τελευτᾶν. Pres act inf τελευτάω (substantival).

οὕτως. The adverb is cataphoric, pointing forward to the discourse that follows (cf. BDAG, 742.2).

ἔφη. Aor act ind 3rd sg φημί.

Αἱρετὸν. Predicate adjective of an implied verb.

μεταλλάσσοντας. Pres act ptc acc masc pl μεταλλάσσω (temporal or, perhaps, concessive). The circumstantial participle expands the infinitive προσδοκᾶν (cf. Muraoka §31dh): "[to look for the hopes] even though being put to death." See 4:7 on Μεταλλάξαντος.

ὑπ᾽ ἀνθρώπων. Intermediate agency. The Göttingen edition, following MS A, reads ἀπ᾽ rather than ὑπ᾽, which alters the sense to "[to die] among men." Neither preposition is particularly well-attested in collocation with μεταλλάσσω. The orthographic similarity makes either preposition possible.

τὰς . . . ἐλπίδας. Accusative direct object of προσδοκᾶν. The use of the plural "hopes" is a normal use of the Greek plural (MHT 3:25–28).

ὑπὸ τοῦ θεοῦ. Intermediate agency, paralleling the earlier PP. *GELS* (701.I.2.d) suggests that in 7:14 "a passive verb [should be] understood."

προσδοκᾶν. Pres act inf προσδοκάω. The infinitive clause, τὰς ὑπὸ τοῦ θεοῦ προσδοκᾶν ἐλπίδας, functions as the subject on an implied verb (cf. BDF §393.2). BDAG (877) suggests the sense of "wait for" or "look for" and further states that "the context indicates whether one does this in longing, in fear, or in a neutral state of mind." Here, with the explicit mention of hope, the sense of longing is clear.

πάλιν. Adverbial, functioning as a "marker of a discourse or narrative item added to items of a related nature" (BDAG, 753.3).

ἀναστήσεσθαι. Fut mid inf ἀνίστημι (epexegetical to ἐλπίδας).

ὑπ᾽ αὐτοῦ. Intermediate agency.

σοί. Dative of advantage.

μὲν γὰρ. "Indeed" (*GE*, 1311.3.B). See 6:4 on μὲν γάρ.

ἀνάστασις. Nominative subject of ἔσται.

εἰς ζωὴν. Goal/direction.

οὐκ. See comment on the negation in 1:5.

ἔσται. Fut mid ind 3rd sg εἰμί.

7:15 Ἐχομένως δὲ τὸν πέμπτον προσάγοντες ᾐκίζοντο.

Ἐχομένως. Temporal adverb, formed from the present middle participle of ἔχω: "immediately thereafter" = "next" (cf. *GELS*, 310). Cf. 8:1.

δὲ. Development; see 1:10 on δέ.

τὸν πέμπτον. Accusative direct object of προσάγοντες.

προσάγοντες. Pres act ptc nom masc pl προσάγω (attendant circumstance).

ᾐκίζοντο. Impf act ind 3rd pl αἰκίζω.

7:16 ὁ δὲ πρὸς αὐτὸν ἰδὼν εἶπεν Ἐξουσίαν ἐν ἀνθρώποις ἔχων φθαρτὸς ὢν ὃ θέλεις ποιεῖς· μὴ δόκει δὲ τὸ γένος ἡμῶν ὑπὸ τοῦ θεοῦ καταλελεῖφθαι·

ὁ δὲ. The article functions as the nominative subject of εἶπεν and refers to the fifth brother. See 6:19 on ὁ δέ.

πρὸς αὐτὸν. Goal or direction. See *GELS* (589.III.a): "in the direction of, towards: with verbs of physical movement."

ἰδὼν. Aor act ptc nom masc sg ὁράω (temporal).

εἶπεν. Aor act ind 3rd sg εἶπον.

Ἐξουσίαν. Accusative direct object of ἔχων.

ἐν ἀνθρώποις. Sphere. The sense is not simply that Antiochus has authority in the sphere of humankind, but *over* them (cf. Abel, 375; D. Schwartz, 306). Nevertheless, the point of the text seems to be that while Antiochus has authority over humans, God has authority over Antiochus.

ἔχων. Pres act ptc nom masc sg ἔχω (causal).

φθαρτὸς. Predicate nominative before ὤν. As a substantive, the adjective refers to that which is "perishable" or "mortal" (cf. BDAG, 1053).

ὤν. Pres act ptc nom masc sg εἰμί (concessive). The circumstantial participle expands upon another participle (cf. Muraoka §31di).

ὃ. Accusative direct object of θέλεις. The relative clause lacks an antecedent.

θέλεις. Pres act ind 2nd sg θέλω. After direct discourse has been introduced (cf. εἶπεν), a switch to the present tense is expected in narrative (cf. Campbell, 76).

ποιεῖς. Pres act ind 2nd sg ποιέω. Serves as a clausal complement of θέλεις.

μὴ. See 1:5 on μή for further comments on the negation.

δόκει. Pres act impv 2nd sg δοκέω.

δὲ. Development; see 1:10 on δέ.

τὸ γένος. Accusative subject of the infinitive καταλελεῖφθαι.

ἡμῶν. Genitive of relationship.

ὑπὸ τοῦ θεοῦ. Agency.

καταλελεῖφθαι. Prf pass inf καταλείπω (indirect discourse with a verb of cognition). On the theme of God not forsaking his people, see esp. 6:16; Isa 54:7-8.

7:17 σὺ δὲ καρτέρει καὶ θεώρει τὸ μεγαλεῖον αὐτοῦ κράτος, ὡς σὲ καὶ τὸ σπέρμα σου βασανιεῖ.

σὺ. Nominative subject of καρτέρει.

δὲ. Development; see 1:10 on δέ.

καρτέρει. Pres act impv 2nd sg καρτερέω. The more passive translation "be patient" (cf. Bartlett, 271) does not capture fully the irony of this request. D. Schwartz (306) plausibly suggests the translation "you just wait," which conveys the idea of a threat.

θεώρει. Pres act impv 2nd sg θεωρέω.

τὸ μεγαλεῖον ... κράτος. Accusative direct object of θεώρει.

αὐτοῦ. Subjective genitive. Cf. 15:5.

ὡς. Introduces a clausal complement (object clause) of θεώρει.

σὲ καὶ τὸ σπέρμα. Accusative direct objects of βασανιεῖ. On the theme of children bearing the iniquities of their parents, see Deut 28:4, 18; Jer 31:29; Ezek 18:2.

σου. Genitive of relationship.

βασανιεῖ. Fut act ind 3rd sg βασανίζω. See 1:28 on βασάνισον. Cf. 7:13; 9:6.

7:18 Μετὰ δὲ τοῦτον ἦγον τὸν ἕκτον, καὶ μέλλων ἀποθνήσκειν ἔφη Μὴ πλανῶ μάτην, ἡμεῖς γὰρ δι᾽ ἑαυτοὺς ταῦτα πάσχομεν ἁμαρτόντες εἰς τὸν ἑαυτῶν θεόν, ἄξια θαυμασμοῦ γέγονεν·

Μετὰ ... τοῦτον. Temporal. Cf. 7:10.

δὲ. Development; see 1:10 on δέ.

ἦγον. Impf act ind 3rd pl ἄγω. BDAG (16.2) notes that ἄγω is used "[o]f leading away to execution."

τὸν ἕκτον. Accusative direct object of ἦγον.

μέλλων. Pres act ptc nom masc sg μέλλω (temporal).

ἀποθνήσκειν. Pres act inf ἀποθνήσκω (complementary).

ἔφη. Aor act ind 3rd pl φημί.

Μὴ. See comment on the negation in 1:5.

πλανῶ. Pres mid impv 2nd pl πλανάω. The middle voice is used because the sense is reflexive: "do not deceive *yourselves*."

μάτην. Adverbial accusative of μάτη (Cf. BDAG, 621). Cf. 7:34.

ἡμεῖς. Nominative subject of πάσχομεν.

γὰρ. Introduces the reason why the king should not be self-deceived; namely, the current affliction is ultimately from God. See 1:12 on γάρ.

δι᾽ ἑαυτοὺς. Cause. The twofold use of ἑαυτός "stresses the communal sense of sinning as the people stand in covenant relationship with God" (Doran 2012, 158).

ταῦτα. Accusative direct object of πάσχομεν.

πάσχομεν. Pres act ind 1st pl πάσχω. Although in Hellenistic Greek the idea of suffering is the common sense of the term, there is some evidence that πάσχω served as a euphemism to further denote *death* (e.g., Josephus, *Ant.* 15.65; Xenophon, *Cyr.* 2.1.8; Euripides, *Phoen.* 244; cf. *GE*, 1594.B). After direct discourse has been introduced (cf. ἔφη), a switch to the present tense is expected in narrative (cf. Campbell, 76).

ἁμαρτόντες. Aor act ptc nom masc pl ἁμαρτάνω (causal).

εἰς τὸν . . . θεόν. Disadvantage.

ἑαυτῶν. Genitive of subordination.

ἄξια θαυμασμοῦ γέγονεν. Because these words are lacking in a few MSS (58 Laˣ), commentators are divided over whether this sentence is original (Abel, 375; Goldstein, 306–7) or a marginal gloss (Katz 1960, 19–20; Nicklas 2011, 1395; Doran 2012, 146). Habicht (235) even suggests that the marginal note was meant to refer to 7:20, where the mother was described as "exceedingly marvelous and worthy of noble memory" (θαυμαστὴ καὶ μνήμης ἀγαθῆς ἀξία). Some MSS also have δίο (*L* 311 Sy) or γάρ (*q* 46-52) preceding ἄξια θαυμασμοῦ γέγονεν, which helps connect the sentence to the rest of 7:18. If original, the "amazing things" that have happened to the Jews should likely be set in contrast with 7:19, where the king is still responsible for fighting against God despite the "amazing things" that came about (cf. D. Schwartz, 307). That is, being an instrument of God's discipline does not relieve Antiochus of any responsibility for his actions.

ἄξια. Nominative subject of γέγονεν.

θαυμασμοῦ. Genitive complement of ἄξια. See *GELS* (325): "act of being astonished."

γέγονεν. Prf act ind 3rd sg γίνομαι.

7:19 σὺ δὲ μὴ νομίσῃς ἀθῷος ἔσεσθαι θεομαχεῖν ἐπιχειρήσας.

σὺ. Nominative subject of νομίσῃς.

δὲ. Development, marking a change of subject from 7:18 to address the king in 7:19. As noted in 7:18 under ἄξια θαυμασμοῦ γέγονεν, there is probably a slight contrast implied: "amazing things have happened [to us] . . . *But* you . . . ." See 1:10 on δέ.

μὴ. See comment on the negation in 1:5.

νομίσῃς. Aor act subj 2nd sg νομίζω (prohibitive subjunctive).

ἀθῷος. Predicate adjective.

ἔσεσθαι. Fut mid inf εἰμί (indirect discourse).

θεομαχεῖν. Pres act inf θεομαχέω (complementary). Built from θεός + μάχομαι ("to fight against divinity, *or* the god *or* god," *GE*, 932). On the literary *topos* of fighting god(s), see Josephus, *J. W.* 5.378. Cf. 7:34, where Antiochus lifts his hands "against the heavenly children."

ἐπιχειρήσας. Aor act ptc nom masc sg ἐπιχειρέω (causal). On the meaning of the verb, see BDAG (386): "set one's hand to, *endeavor, try* w[ith] inf[initive]."

2 Maccabees 7:20-29

20The mother was exceedingly marvelous and worthy of good memory, who, after witnessing the seven sons who perished in the course of a single day, was enduring courageously because of her hope in the Lord. 21Now, she was encouraging each of them in their ancestral language; filled with noble purpose and awakening her womanly reasoning with manly fervor, she said to them, 22"I do not know how you appeared in my womb, nor did I give breath and life to you. And the elements of each [of you] I did not arrange. 23Therefore, the creator of the world, the one who formed the genesis of humanity and who invented the genesis of all things, will return both breath and life to you again with mercy just as you are now disregarding yourselves because of his laws." 24But Antiochus—thinking [that] he was being despised and suspecting the reproachful voice—because the youngest [brother] still remained, not only was exhorting with words but also promising with oaths both to make rich and to make most blessed if he would change from the ancestral [ways] and to have a friend and to entrust [him] with an office. 25But because the young man paid no attention at all, the king, after summoning [her], was exhorting the mother to be an advisor of the boy for [his] safety. 26And because he exhorted [her] intensely, she agreed to persuade her son. 27But, leaning toward him, scoffing at the cruel tyrant, she spoke as follows in their ancestral language, "Son, take pity on me, the one who carried you in the womb nine months and the one who nursed you three years and the one who reared you and the one who brought [you] to this age and the one who sustained [you]. 28I ask you, child, to look up at heaven and earth and, seeing everything in them, to know that God did not make them out of existing things; and in the same manner the human race came into being. ²⁹Do not fear this executioner, but, being worthy of your brothers, accept death, so that by mercy I might receive you back with your brothers."

Second Maccabees 7:20-29 is a digression from the main narrative (cf. 4:16-17; 5:17-20; 6:12-17). This is signaled in several ways. First, the sequence of a son's speech followed by death (e.g., 7:2-7a; 7:7b-9; 7:10-12; 7:13-14; 7:15-17; 7:18-19) is interrupted by a story about their mother (7:20-29). Second, the digression steps outside of the temporal sequence established in 7:2-19. The mother's story is not situated between the martyrdom of the sixth and seventh son. Rather, the story is retrospective and looks back at what happened μιᾶς ὑπὸ καιρὸν ἡμέρας ("in the course of a single day," 7:20). This is further signaled by the fact that the mother is said to encourage *each of her sons* to be faithful in the face of death (7:21).

Regarding the placement of this digression, ancient authors such as Hermagoras (*Prol. Herm.* 4.12), Quintilian (*Inst.* 4.3.4), and Cicero (*Inv.* 1.51.91) discussed the location of a digression within a composition. The purpose of the digression in 7:20-29 seems to be to sustain the emotion evoked by the mother's six sons dying before moving to narrate the death of the seventh son (cf. Perry, 170–72). In her speech, the mother emphasizes God as one who creates. While it is debated whether or not the text refers to creation out of nothing (7:28), the point of the analogy is that Israel's God can reconstitute human bodies that suffer martyrdom (cf. Doran 2012, 161). See the Introduction for additional comments on digressions in 2 Maccabees.

7:20 Ὑπεραγόντως δὲ ἡ μήτηρ θαυμαστὴ καὶ μνήμης ἀγαθῆς ἀξία, ἥτις ἀπολλυμένους υἱοὺς ἑπτὰ συνορῶσα μιᾶς ὑπὸ καιρὸν ἡμέρας εὐψύχως ἔφερεν διὰ τὰς ἐπὶ κύριον ἐλπίδας.

Ὑπεραγόντως. The adverb is built from a participial form of the verb ὑπεράγω: "to the highest degree, exceedingly" (*GE*, 2194).

δὲ. Development, marking a shift of grammatical subject from the sons in 7:7-19 to the mother in 7:20. See 1:10 on δέ.

ἡ μήτηρ. Nominative subject of an implied verb. Although the mother is mentioned earlier in 7:1 (μετὰ τῆς μητρὸς), 7:4 (καὶ τῆς μητρὸς), and 7:5 (σὺν τῇ μητρὶ), she is generally de-emphasized as the main subject of the narrative until here in 7:20, when the story focuses on her.

θαυμαστὴ καὶ ... ἀξία. Predicate adjectives of an implied verb.

μνήμης ἀγαθῆς. Genitive complement of ἀξία.

ἥτις. Nominative subject of ἔφερεν. The relative pronoun stands in for the antecedent ἡ μήτηρ.

ἀπολλυμένους υἱοὺς ἑπτά. Accusative direct object of συνορῶσα. Although only six sons have died in the narrative thus far, the reference to *seven* sons anticipates the final martyrdom (cf. D. Schwartz, 308).

ἀπολλυμένους. Pres mid ptc acc masc pl ἀπόλλυμι (attributive).

συνορῶσα. Pres act ptc nom fem sg συνοράω (temporal).

μιᾶς ὑπὸ καιρὸν ἡμέρας. An idiom, meaning "in the course of a single day" (*GELS*, 701.II.3). Cf. 3 Macc 4:14; Esth 3:13.

μιᾶς ... ἡμέρας. Genitive of time. Signals the time within which something takes place (cf. Smyth §1325).

ὑπὸ καιρὸν. Temporal. See *GE* (221.II.C.E): "of time or duration."

εὐψύχως. Adverb of manner.

ἔφερεν. Impf act ind 3rd sg φέρω. Due to the unfortunate circumstances in context, the verb means "to endure, tolerate, bear" (*GE*, 2263.1.B).

διὰ τὰς ... ἐλπίδας. Cause.

ἐπὶ κύριον. Basis. The preposition is used to introduce the object of the verbal idea implicit in τὰς ... ἐλπίδας (cf. 2:18: ἐλπίζομεν ... ἐπὶ τῷ θεῷ).

7:21 ἕκαστον δὲ αὐτῶν παρεκάλει τῇ πατρίῳ φωνῇ γενναίῳ πεπληρωμένη φρονήματι καὶ τὸν θῆλυν λογισμὸν ἄρσενι θυμῷ διεγείρασα λέγουσα πρὸς αὐτούς,

ἕκαστον. Accusative direct object of παρεκάλει.

δὲ. Development; see 1:10 on δέ.

αὐτῶν. Partitive genitive.

παρεκάλει. Impf act ind 3rd sg παρακαλέω.

τῇ πατρίῳ φωνῇ. Dative of manner. Cf. 7:8. On the use of the article like a pronoun, see 1:16 on τὰς κεφαλάς.

γενναίῳ ... φρονήματι. Dative of content (Wallace 170–71), used with πληρόω (lit. "filled *with a noble spirit*"). However, Muraoka (§58aa) refers to this as an instrumental dative. The description of the mother as "noble" links her with Eleazar (6:28), her sons (7:5, 11), and later with Judas Maccabeus (12:42). The separation of the modifier from the head is an example of hyperbaton where the modifier (γενναίῳ) is emphasized.

πεπληρωμένη. Prf pass ptc nom fem sg πληρόω (temporal).

τὸν θῆλυν λογισμὸν. Accusative direct object of διεγείρασα. The mention of "reasoning" links the mother with Eleazar (6:23) and Judas Maccabeus (15:10).

ἄρσενι θυμῷ. Dative of manner. This unusual expression betrays the epitomizer's (and most ancient people's) way of thinking about women as weaker or lesser than men. Thus, in order to accomplish her task, she must act "with manly fervor" (cf. *GELS*, 334.2) and thus align herself more with Eleazar (6:31) and her sons. Doran (2012, 159) rightly notes that the fact that a king is bested by a woman "is even stronger evidence of the rightness of the Jewish cause." See also D. Schwartz (308–9) on ancient attitudes toward women.

διεγείρασα. Aor act ptc nom fem sg διεγείρω (temporal).

λέγουσα. Pres act ptc nom fem sg λέγω (attendant circumstance or, more likely, means). Although λέγοντες often signals direct speech when it follows the main verb, in this context it probably denotes the means by which the mother encouraged her sons.

πρὸς αὐτούς. The PP takes the place of the dative (αὐτῷ) and functions as the indirect object of λέγουσα.

7:22 Οὐκ οἶδ᾽ ὅπως εἰς τὴν ἐμὴν ἐφάνητε κοιλίαν, οὐδὲ ἐγὼ τὸ πνεῦμα καὶ τὴν ζωὴν ὑμῖν ἐχαρισάμην, καὶ τὴν ἑκάστου στοιχείωσιν οὐκ ἐγὼ διερρύθμισα·

Οὐκ. See 1:5 on the use of οὐ versus μή.

οἶδ᾽. Prf act ind 1st sg οἶδα. In the perfect οἶδα marks the "enduring result rather than the completed act" and is best translated as if present (Smyth §1946). Thus, Porter (1999, 40) is correct that the perfect of οἶδα means "I know" or "I am in a knowledgeable state."

ὅπως. Introduces an indirect question after a verb of cognition (cf. *GELS*, 502.5).

εἰς τὴν ἐμὴν . . . κοιλίαν. Locative.

ἐφάνητε. Aor pass ind 2nd pl φαίνω. Following οἶδα the indicative mood is normal in indirect questions (just as in clauses in indirect discourse) (cf. Smyth §2677). The fact that the mother does "not know how you appeared in my womb" does not indicate her ignorance about the facts of procreation, but rather indicates that God (and no named father) is the true father of her children (cf. Doran 2012, 166). Katz (1960, 14) and Habicht (236) conjecture ὑφάνθητε ("was formed") rather than ἐφάνητε, but this is unnecessary to make sense of the meaning.

οὐδὲ. The combination of the negative particle οὐ and the postpositive δέ signals negation + development (cf. Olmstead, 123).

ἐγώ. Nominative subject of ἐχαρισάμην.

τὸ πνεῦμα καὶ τὴν ζωὴν. Accusative direct objects of ἐχαρισάμην. Either "spirit and life" (cf. D. Schwartz, 310) or "breath and life" (cf. NETS; Zeitlin and Tedesche, 165; Doran 2012, 147; Habicht, 236). If the latter, as is likely, then perhaps an example of hendiadys: "the breath of life." Cf. 7:23; 14:46. Doran (2012, 159) argues that "breath and life" is an allusion to Genesis, which makes sense in the literary context that describes God as "creator of the world" (7:23).

ὑμῖν. Dative indirect object of ἐχαρισάμην.

ἐχαρισάμην. Aor mid ind 1st sg χαρίζομαι.

τὴν ... στοιχείωσιν. Accusative direct object of διερρύθμισα. The gloss in GELS (637) is "teaching of fundamentals," which does not fit the context well. Rather, one common sense found in classical literature is illuminating: "how is generation possible for flesh and bone or any other continuous body? *They cannot be composed of the elements themselves* [οὔτε γὰρ ἐξ αὐτῶν τῶν στοιχείων ἐγχωρεῖ] since nothing continuous can result from their collocation, nor of a collocation of the surfaces, since that generates *the elements* [τὰ ... στοιχεῖα], not their compounds" (Aristotle, *Cael.* 3.8 306b22-29). Cf. GELS (637) on στοιχεῖον: "*basic component* . . . of hum[an] body" (cf. 4 Macc 12:13).

ἑκάστου. Possessive genitive.

οὐκ. See above.

ἐγώ. Nominative subject of διερρύθμισα.

διερρύθμισα. Aor act ind 1st sg διαρρυθμίζω. On the meaning of the verb, see GE (506): "to set in order."

7:23 τοιγαροῦν ὁ τοῦ κόσμου κτίστης ὁ πλάσας ἀνθρώπου γένεσιν καὶ πάντων ἐξευρὼν γένεσιν καὶ τὸ πνεῦμα καὶ τὴν ζωὴν ὑμῖν πάλιν ἀποδίδωσιν μετ᾽ ἐλέους, ὡς νῦν ὑπερορᾶτε ἑαυτοὺς διὰ τοὺς αὐτοῦ νόμους.

Although the Greek ὁ πλάσας ἀνθρώπου γένεσιν καὶ πάντων ἐξευρὼν γένεσιν is awkward, it is comprised of allusions to Genesis. Specifically, in LXX Gen 2:7 the text states that "God formed man" (ἔπλασεν ὁ θεὸς τὸν ἄνθρωπον, cf. 2:8, 15) and LXX Gen 5:1 states that "this is the book of the genesis of mankind" (Αὕτη ἡ βίβλος γενέσεως ἀνθρώπων) (cf. Goldstein, 313). Once these allusions are recognized, the various emendations (see below) to the text proposed by scholars are no longer necessary.

τοιγαροῦν. The compound particle (τοί + γάρ + οὖν) introduces an inference: "for that very reason, then, therefore" (cf. BDAG, 1009). Denniston (566) notes it is "strongly emphatic, and sometimes even convey[s] the effect that the logical connexion is regarded as more important than the ideas connected."

ὁ . . . κτίστης. Nominative subject of ἀποδίδωσιν.

τοῦ κόσμου. Objective genitive.

ὁ πλάσας. Aor act ptc nom masc sg πλάσσω (attributive).

ἀνθρώπου. Genitive of relationship. Katz (1960, 14) conjectures ἄνθρωπον or ἀνθρώπους (i.e., "[the one who forms] the man"), but this is unnecessary.

γένεσιν. Accusative direct object of πλάσας. Katz (1960, 14) and Habicht (236) argue that the repetition of γένεσιν is unacceptable and some of the MS tradition (*L* 534*) reads "family" (γένος or γένους). Doran (2012, 147) is probably correct that the repetition underscores a connection with the text of Genesis.

πάντων. Objective genitive.

ἐξευρὼν. Aor act ptc nom masc sg ἐξευρίσκω (attributive). Linked by καί to the article ὁ. Doran (2012, 160) notes that "invented" is more appropriate than "discovered" in a context that describes God's knowledge (cf. Bar 3:35-36).

γένεσιν. Accusative direct object of ἐξευρών. See above.

καὶ . . . καί. Correlative construction: "both . . . and" (BDF §444.3; BDAG, 495.1.f).

τὸ πνεῦμα καὶ τὴν ζωήν. Accusative direct objects of ἀποδίδωσιν. Cf. 7:22 on the meaning of this expression.

ὑμῖν. Dative indirect object of ἀποδίδωσιν.

πάλιν. Adverbial, functioning as a "marker of a discourse or narrative item added to items of a related nature" (BDAG, 753.3).

ἀποδίδωσιν. Pres act ind 3rd sg ἀποδίδωμι. Goldstein (314) calls this the "oracular present, to be translated as future." Abel (377) and Habicht (236) prefer ἀποδώσει, which is supported by some MSS (e.g., *L*⁻⁵⁴²) and would still express a general truth (i.e., gnomic future).

μετ᾽ ἐλέους. Manner.

ὡς. Introduces a clause of comparison.

νῦν. Temporal adverb. See esp. 6:27 on νῦν.

ὑπερορᾶτε. Pres act ind 2nd pl ὑπεροράω.

ἑαυτοὺς. Accusative direct object of ὑπερορᾶτε.

διὰ τοὺς . . . νόμους. Cause. On the theme of dying for God's laws, see 7:2, 9.

αὐτοῦ. Genitive of source, qualifying τοὺς . . . νόμους.

7:24 Ὁ δὲ Ἀντίοχος οἰόμενος καταφρονεῖσθαι καὶ τὴν ὀνειδίζουσαν ὑφορώμενος φωνὴν ἔτι τοῦ νεωτέρου περιόντος οὐ μόνον διὰ λόγων ἐποιεῖτο τὴν παράκλησιν, ἀλλὰ καὶ δι᾽ ὅρκων ἐπίστου ἅμα πλουτιεῖν καὶ μακαριστὸν ποιήσειν μεταθέμενον ἀπὸ τῶν πατρίων καὶ φίλον ἕξειν καὶ χρείας ἐμπιστεύσειν.

Because the conditional sense of the circumstantial participle (μετα-θέμενον) in context may be difficult to follow in the Greek text, it is presented here in English to clarify its logic:

> if he would change from the ancestral ways,
> then he would make him rich
> and make him blessed
> and consider him a friend
> and entrust him with an office.

Ὁ ... Ἀντίοχος. Nominative subject of ἐποιεῖτο.

δὲ. Development; see 1:10 on δέ.

οἰόμενος. Pres mid ptc nom masc sg οἴομαι (causal or, less likely, concessive). On the meaning of the verb, see *GELS* (490): "to assume as probable though not absolutely certain" + infinitive. Cf. 5:21. Verbs of self-involvement are typically middle (N. Miller, 428).

καταφρονεῖσθαι. Pres pass inf καταφρονέω (indirect discourse).

τὴν ὀνειδίζουσαν ... φωνὴν. Accusative direct object of ὑφορώμενος. Because the mother speaks in her "ancestral language" (τῇ πατρίῳ φωνῇ, 7:21), it is unlikely that Antiochus understands her language as a rebuke (*pace* Abel, 377). Nevertheless, the "reproachful voice" of the mother leads Antiochus to suspect her tone (cf. Habicht, 236; D. Schwartz, 310). The separation of the modifier (ὀνειδίζουσαν) from the head (φωνήν) is an example of hyperbaton where the modifier is emphasized.

ὀνειδίζουσαν. Pres act ptc acc fem sg ὀνειδίζω (attributive). Following from the speech in 7:20-23, it is not entirely clear if "the reproachful voice" is directed toward Antiochus or her sons (cf. Doran 2012, 160).

ὑφορώμενος. Pres act ptc nom masc sg ὑφοράω (causal or, less likely, concessive).

ἔτι. Temporal adverb.

τοῦ νεωτέρου. Genitive subject of the participle περιόντος. The comparative form is superlative in meaning.

περιόντος. Pres act ptc gen masc sg περίειμι (genitive absolute, causal). On the genitive absolute, see 1:7 on βασιλεύοντος.

οὐ μόνον ... ἀλλὰ καί. This construction is used to contrast and expand upon a preceding idea (cf. Ehorn and Lee, 12).

διὰ λόγων. Means.

ἐποιεῖτο. Impf mid ind 3rd sg ποιέω. When the middle of ποιέω is used with a verbal noun (παράκλησιν), this can be a periphrasis for the verb itself: παρακαλέω (*GELS*, 570.II; BDF §310.1; BDAG, 839.2.d). See 1:23 on ἐποιήσαντο.

τὴν παράκλησιν. Accusative direct object of ἐποιεῖτο. The epitomizer is cleverly exploiting the semantic possibilities of the term παράκλησις and its cognate παρακαλέω. Whereas the brothers and their mother "exhorted/encouraged" (7:5, 21) one another to "resist the king," here the king "encourages" the seventh son to switch sides (D. Schwartz, 311).

δι᾽ ὅρκων. Means. As seen already in the narrative, "oaths" are not necessarily reliable (4:34; cf. 15:10).

ἐπίστου. Impf act ind 3rd sg πιστόω.

ἅμα . . . καὶ. Correlative. The adverb is part of a formula: ἅμα A καὶ B ("both . . . and") (cf. *GELS*, 30.I.c; *GE*, 100.A).

πλουτιεῖν. Pres act inf πλουτίζω (indirect discourse or complementary).

μακαριστὸν. Accusative direct object of ποιήσειν.

ποιήσειν. Fut act inf ποιέω (indirect discourse or complementary). On the future infinitive, see 2:23 on ἐπιτεμεῖν.

μεταθέμενον. Aor mid ptc acc masc sg μετατίθημι (conditional, modifying ποιήσειν). The participle is accusative because it agrees with the implied object pronouns of the two infinitives (πλουτιεῖν and ποιήσειν) (cf. Muraoka §69A.ag). Cf. 4:46. On circumstantial participles in oblique cases, see 3:27 on πεσόντα.

ἀπὸ τῶν πατρίων. Separation.

φίλον. Accusative direct object of ἕξειν. On the meaning of φίλος, see 1:14 on φίλοι.

ἕξειν. Fut act inf ἔχω (indirect discourse or complementary).

χρείας. Accusative direct object of ἐμπιστεύσειν. Here the noun refers to "an activity that is needed, *office, duty, service*" (BDAG, 1088.4).

ἐμπιστεύσειν. Fut act inf ἐμπιστεύω (indirect discourse or complementary).

7:25 τοῦ δὲ νεανίου μηδαμῶς προσέχοντος προσκαλεσάμενος ὁ βασιλεὺς τὴν μητέρα παρῄνει γενέσθαι τοῦ μειρακίου σύμβουλον ἐπὶ σωτηρίᾳ.

τοῦ . . . νεανίου. Genitive subject of the participle προσέχοντος.

δὲ. Development; see 1:10 on δέ.

μηδαμῶς. Adverb, negating the verb. See *GELS* (459): "*certainly no, oh no*, expressing strong negative reaction and protest."

προσέχοντος. Pres act ptc gen masc sg προσέχω (genitive absolute, causal). On the genitive absolute, see 1:7 on βασιλεύοντος.

προσκαλεσάμενος. Aor mid ptc nom masc sg προσκαλέομαι (temporal). The repetition of the prefix πρός (i.e., προσέχοντος προσκαλεσάμενος) is an example of paronomasia.

ὁ βασιλεύς. Nominative subject of παρήνει.

τὴν μητέρα. Accusative direct object of παρήνει.

παρήνει. Impf act ind 3rd sg παραινέω.

γενέσθαι. Aor mid inf γίνομαι (indirect discourse).

τοῦ μειρακίου. Objective genitive. The switch from discussing the "young man" (νεανίας) to the "boy" (μειράκιον) may be for stylistic variation or rhetorical purposes.

σύμβουλον. Predicate accusative. This term contrasts with ἐπίβουλος ("plotter") in 3:38; 4:2, 50; 14:26.

ἐπὶ σωτηρίᾳ. Purpose (cf. BDAG, 366.16; LN §89.60). While the noun σωτηρία is commonly used to denote the physical safety or well-being of someone (cf. Doran 2012, 160; GELS 668.2), it is ambiguous in this context where Antiochus speaks of σωτηρία from torture and death and immediately following the mother speaks of eternal salvation (cf. Nicklas 2011, 1395). Cf. 3:29, 32; 12:25.

7:26 πολλὰ δὲ αὐτοῦ παραινέσαντος ἐπεδέξατο πείσειν τὸν υἱόν·

πολλά. Either the accusative direct object of παραινέσαντος ("[exhorting] many things") or, better, a substantive used as an adverbial accusative ("[exhorting] intensely") (cf. BDAG, 849.3.a.β).

δέ. Development, marking a change of subject from 7:25. See 1:10 on δέ.

αὐτοῦ. Genitive subject of the participle παραινέσαντος.

παραινέσαντος. Aor act ptc gen masc sg παραινέω (genitive absolute, temporal, or causal).

ἐπεδέξατο. Aor mid ind 3rd sg ἐπιδέχομαι. On the meaning of the verb, see GELS (271): "to accept willingly and approvingly." However, in the following context it becomes clear that the mother's willingness to persuade her son is shown to be a ruse. D. Schwartz (311) notes the irony: "at v. 24 the king thought he was being mocked, which was not really the case . . . and now, when he thought the mother was doing his bidding, she was in fact mocking him. This king is always wrong!" Cf. 7:29. On the genitive absolute, see 1:7 on βασιλεύοντος.

πείσειν. Fut act inf πείθω (indirect discourse or complementary). Although Antiochus convinces the mother "to persuade" (πείσειν) her

son, he nevertheless dies "having confidence" (πεποιθώς) in the Lord
(7:40). On the future infinitive, see 2:23 on ἐπιτεμεῖν.

τὸν υἱόν. Accusative direct object of πείσειν. On the use of the article
like a pronoun, see 1:16 on τὰς κεφαλάς.

7:27 προσκύψασα δὲ αὐτῷ χλευάσασα τὸν ὠμὸν τύραννον οὕτως
ἔφησεν τῇ πατρίῳ φωνῇ Υἱέ, ἐλέησόν με τὴν ἐν γαστρὶ περιενέγκασάν
σε μῆνας ἐννέα καὶ θηλάσασάν σε ἔτη τρία καὶ ἐκθρέψασάν σε καὶ
ἀγαγοῦσαν εἰς τὴν ἡλικίαν ταύτην καὶ τροφοφορήσασαν.

προσκύψασα. Aor act ptc nom fem sg προσκύπτω (attendant
circumstance).

δὲ. Development; see 1:10 on δέ.

αὐτῷ. Dative complement of προσκύψασα (cf. LEH, 526).

χλευάσασα. Aor act ptc nom fem sg χλευάζω (manner). On the
meaning of the verb, see *GELS* (733): "to scoff at."

τὸν ὠμὸν τύραννον. Accusative direct object of χλευάσασα. See 4:25
on ὠμοῦ τυράννου.

οὕτως. The adverb is cataphoric, pointing forward to the discourse
that follows (cf. BDAG, 742.2).

ἔφησεν. Aor act ind 3rd sg φημί.

τῇ πατρίῳ φωνῇ. Dative of manner. Cf. 7:8, 21.

Υἱέ. Vocative.

ἐλέησόν. Aor act impv 2nd sg ἐλεέω. The verb has two acute accents
because it is followed by an enclitic (με). When following a word with an
acute accent on the antepenult, the enclitic surrenders its accent and it
appears as an additional acute accent on the preceding word (Smyth §183.c).

με. Accusative direct object of ἐλέησόν.

τὴν . . . περιενέγκασάν. Aor act ptc acc fem sg περιφέρω (substantival). Accusative in apposition to με (cf. Muraoka §31bb). On the two
accents, see just above.

ἐν γαστρὶ. Locative.

σε. Accusative direct object of τὴν . . . περιενέγκασάν.

μῆνας ἐννέα. Adverbial accusative, indicating extent of time (cf.
Wallace, 201–2).

θηλάσασάν. Aor act ptc acc fem sg θηλάζω (substantival). Accusative
in apposition to με. On the two accents, see just above. On the meaning
of the verb, see *GELS* (329): "*to give milk to*, 'suckle.'"

σε. Accusative direct object of θηλάσασάν.

ἔτη τρία. Adverbial accusative, indicating extent of time (cf. Wallace,
201–2).

ἐκθρέψασάν. Aor act ptc acc fem sg ἐκτρέφω (substantival). Accusative in apposition to με. On the two accents, see just above. On the meaning of the verb, see *GELS* (218): "to rear, nurture."

σε. Accusative direct object of ἐκθρέψασάν.

ἀγαγοῦσαν. Aor act ptc acc fem sg ἄγω (substantival). Accusative in apposition to με.

εἰς τὴν ἡλικίαν ταύτην. Locative. See 4:40 on τὴν ἡλικίαν.

τροφοφορήσασαν. Aor act ptc acc fem sg τροφοφορέω (substantival). Accusative in apposition to με. On the meaning of the verb, see *GELS* (688): "to sustain by providing food." Following ἐκθρέψασαν, the participle τροφοφορήσασαν may be pleonastic. Alternatively, the word may have originally been a marginal gloss (e.g., Abel, 378; Katz 1960, 19; Habicht, 236; Goldstein, 315), which finds some support from the MS tradition that omits the verb (71-107 347 La⁻ᵖ). However, Doran (2012, 147) argues that τροφοφορήσασαν sums up the previous actions.

7:28 ἀξιῶ σε, τέκνον, ἀναβλέψαντα εἰς τὸν οὐρανὸν καὶ τὴν γῆν καὶ τὰ ἐν αὐτοῖς πάντα ἰδόντα γνῶναι ὅτι οὐκ ἐξ ὄντων ἐποίησεν αὐτὰ ὁ θεός, καὶ τὸ τῶν ἀνθρώπων γένος οὕτω γίνεται.

See Goldstein (307) for further analysis of the creation language in this verse.

ἀξιῶ. Pres act ind 1st sg ἀξιόω. After discourse is introduced (cf. ἔφησεν in 7:27), the present tense is used.

σε. Accusative direct object of ἀξιῶ.

τέκνον. Vocative. Reference to the son as τέκνον indicates nothing about his age (cf. D. Schwartz, 312). This is a common way for a parent to refer to a child, regardless of their age.

ἀναβλέψαντα. Aor act ptc acc masc sg ἀναβλέπω (indirect discourse). After a verb of communication, the accusative participle indicates indirect discourse (cf. Wallace, 645).

εἰς τὸν οὐρανὸν καὶ τὴν γῆν. Spatial (toward).

τὰ . . . πάντα. Accusative direct object of ἰδόντα.

ἐν αὐτοῖς. Locative.

ἰδόντα. Aor act ptc acc masc sg ὁράω (temporal).

γνῶναι. Aor act inf γινώσκω (indirect discourse).

ὅτι. Introduces the clausal complement (indirect discourse with a verb of cognition) of γνῶναι.

οὐκ. See 1:5 on the use of οὐ versus μή. Rather than the text of R-H, οὐκ . . . ἐποίησεν ("[God] did not make"), some of the MS tradition (e.g., L 55 311) has a different word order, which slightly alters the sense: ἐξ οὐκ ὄντων ("from things that do not exist").

ἐξ ὄντων. Source. Beginning with Origen (*Princ.* 2.1.5), a long interpretive tradition posits that a doctrine of creation *ex nihilo* is found in this text. But D. Schwartz (312–13) correctly notes that "[t]he point of the analogy is that just as God's power is demonstrated by the creation of a fetus with no participation by the fetus itself, so too is it demonstrated by the world which too did not participate in its own creation; such demonstrations of God's power are meant to arouse in the believer's mind the conviction that God will be able to reward him for his devotion." On the question of creation *ex nihilo*, see Copan (75–93) and Goldstein (310).

ὄντων. Pres act ptc gen neut pl εἰμί (substantival).

ἐποίησεν. Aor act ind 3rd sg ποιέω.

αὐτά. Accusative direct object of ἐποίησεν. Agrees with τὰ . . . πάντα.

ὁ θεός. Nominative subject of ἐποίησεν.

τὸ . . . γένος. Nominative subject of γίνεται.

τῶν ἀνθρώπων. Genitive of apposition.

οὕτω. The adverb is anaphoric, clarifying that the human race came into being "in the same manner" that heaven and earth came into being.

γίνεται. Pres mid ind 3rd sg γίνομαι.

7:29 μὴ φοβηθῇς τὸν δήμιον τοῦτον, ἀλλὰ τῶν ἀδελφῶν ἄξιος γενόμενος ἐπίδεξαι τὸν θάνατον, ἵνα ἐν τῷ ἐλέει σὺν τοῖς ἀδελφοῖς σου κομίσωμαί σε.

μὴ . . . ἀλλά. Point/counterpoint set. See 1:20 on μὴ . . . ἀλλά.

φοβηθῇς. Aor pass subj 2nd sg φοβέω (hortatory).

τὸν δήμιον τοῦτον. Accusative direct object of φοβηθῇς. Goldstein (315) points out the irony that δήμιος, which refers to a public slave "owned by the state [who] carried out executions," is used by the mother to refer to Antiochus. Cf. 5:8 where Jason is called δήμιος.

τῶν ἀδελφῶν. Genitive complement of ἄξιος. On the use of the article like a pronoun, see 1:16 on τὰς κεφαλάς.

ἄξιος. Predicate adjective.

γενόμενος. Aor mid ptc nom masc sg γίνομαι (manner).

ἐπίδεξαι. Aor mid impv 2nd sg ἐπιδέχομαι. Cf. 7:26.

τὸν θάνατον. Accusative direct object of ἐπίδεξαι.

ἵνα. Introduces a purpose clause.

ἐν τῷ ἐλέει. Cause. The article is anaphoric, referring to the "mercy" (μετ᾽ ἐλέους) mentioned in 7:23. However, D. Schwartz (313) notes that "[w]hat seems to be meant is the *time* of mercy, namely, the one promised at Isaiah 54:7."

σὺν τοῖς ἀδελφοῖς. Association.

σου. Genitive of relationship.

κομίσωμαί. Aor mid subj 1st sg κομίζω. Subjunctive used with ἵνα. On the two accents, see comments in 7:27. This verb implies not only that the brothers will be resurrected, but also that the mother will too (cf. D. Schwartz, 313).

σε. Accusative direct object of κομίσωμαί.

2 Maccabees 7:30-42

[30]Now, when this one was stopped [speaking], the young man said, "What are you waiting for? I will not obey the command of the king, but I obey the command of the law that was given to our fathers by Moses. [31]But you, having become an instigator of all kinds of evil against the Hebrews, will certainly not escape the hands of God. [32]For we are suffering because of our own sins. [33]And if, for the sake of reproof and discipline, our living Lord has become angry briefly, he will be reconciled again to his slaves. [34]But you, O impious and most impure of all men, do not be elated in vain and puffed up by uncertain hopes, lifting up hands against the heavenly children. [35]For you have not yet escaped the judgment of the Almighty, all-seeing God. [36]For indeed, our brothers, now having endured brief suffering for everlasting life, have fallen under the covenant of God; but you will receive just punishment by the judgment of God for your arrogance. [37]But I, just as my brothers, give up both body and soul for the sake of the ancestral laws, calling upon God quickly to be merciful to our nation; and you with torments and plagues to acknowledge that he alone is God [38]and [that] with me and my brothers, the wrath of the Almighty that has justly come upon our whole nation shall be ended." [39]Now, becoming angry, the king dealt with this one more severely than the others, being embittered because of the scorn. [40]And so this one died in purity, having complete confidence in the Lord. [41]And after [her] sons, the mother died.

[42]Therefore, let this be enough said about the eating of pagan sacrifices and the tortures that exceed all bounds.

As noted earlier, the martyrdom story is integrated into the narrative through the use of shared terminology, especially with the epitomizer's reflections found in the digressions: παιδεία (6:12; 7:33), βραξέως ἀ(ἐ) πώργισται (5:17; 7:33), μετεωρίζω (5:17; 7:34), ὀργή–ἔλεος (5:20; 6:16; 7:37-38; 8:5) (Doran 2012, 165). This section of the narrative ends with a vivid portrayal of Antiochus and the seventh son, using a number of similarly-ending adverbs (-ως): Antiochus "dealt with this one *more severely* [χειρίστως]" and was "*embittered* [πικρῶς]." In contrast, the son "died *in purity* [καθαρῶς]" and had "*complete* [παντελῶς] confidence in the Lord" (cf. Coetzer, 109). On the use of the present tense in the narrative to introduce discourse, see comments following the translation of 7:1-6.

7:30 Ἔτι δὲ ταύτης καταληγούσης ὁ νεανίας εἶπεν Τίνα μένετε; οὐχ ὑπακούω τοῦ προστάγματος τοῦ βασιλέως, τοῦ δὲ προστάγματος ἀκούω τοῦ νόμου τοῦ δοθέντος τοῖς πατράσιν ἡμῶν διὰ Μωυσέως.

Ἔτι. Temporal adverb. Kappler (64), followed by Doran (2012, 147), D. Schwartz (313), and Habicht (237) argue(s) that the text should read ἄρτι δὲ ταύτης καταληγούσης, as in 9:5. But, in agreement with Goldstein (315), changing ἔτι to ἄρτι is not necessary because ἔτι can be plausibly rendered with καταληγούσης. Cf. Katz (1960, 14).

δέ. Development, marking a change of grammatical subject. See 1:10 on δέ. The digression ends and it would be typical for a line of argument or narrative to resume using οὖν. See Runge (54).

ταύτης. Genitive subject of the participle καταληγούσης. The demonstrative pronoun is anaphoric, pointing back to the mother who was the main focus in 7:20-29.

καταληγούσης. Pres act ptc gen fem sg καταλήγω (genitive absolute, temporal). NETS translates "while she was still speaking," following several manuscripts that read καταλεγουσης (MSS *L* 46ᶜ -52ᶜ 311 La). On the meaning of the verb, see *GELS* (376): "*to leave off* speaking." On the genitive absolute, see 1:7 on βασιλεύοντος.

ὁ νεανίας. Nominative subject of εἶπεν.

εἶπεν. Aor act ind 3rd sg εἶπον.

Τίνα. Accusative direct object of μένετε.

μένετε. Pres act ind 2nd pl μένω. On the meaning of the verb, see BDAG (631.3): "wait for, await." The plural presumably refers to the executioners. After discourse has been introduced (cf. εἶπεν), the epitomizer switches to the present tense.

οὐχ. See 1:5 on μή for further comments on the negation.

ὑπακούω. Pres act ind 1st sg ὑπακούω.

τοῦ προστάγματος. Genitive complement of ὑπακούω. The epitomizer employs both the genitive case (cf. 7:30) and the accusative case (cf. 11:24; 14:15) as the object of (ὑπο-) ἀκούω.

τοῦ βασιλέως. Subjective genitive.

τοῦ . . . προστάγματος. Genitive complement of ἀκούω. See above.

δέ. Development; see 1:10 on δέ.

ἀκούω. Pres act ind 1st sg ἀκούω.

τοῦ νόμου. Subjective genitive, qualifying τοῦ προστάγματος.

τοῦ δοθέντος. Aor pass ptc gen masc sg δίδωμι (attributive).

τοῖς πατράσιν. Dative indirect object of δοθέντος.

ἡμῶν. Genitive of relationship.

διὰ Μωυσέως. Means. Because names definitionally refer to unique entities, the use (or lack) of the article is not always predicable (cf. *CGCG* §28.8). However, Muraoka (§5cab) notes that "[a]ttached to a preposition it is always anarthrous."

7:31 σὺ δὲ πάσης κακίας εὑρετὴς γενόμενος εἰς τοὺς Εβραίους οὐ μὴ διαφύγῃς τὰς χεῖρας τοῦ θεοῦ.

σὺ. Nominative subject of διαφύγῃς.

δὲ. Development, marking shift of grammatical subject to the Antiochus (σύ). See 1:10 on δέ.

πάσης κακίας εὑρετὴς. Cf. the description of Menelaus in 4:47; 13:4.

πάσης κακίας. Objective genitive. The meaning of κακία is probably generic, summarizing the "all kinds of evil" that Antiochus committed against the Jews in the preceding context.

εὑρετὴς. Predicate nominative. See *GELS* (304): "one who has designed and brought about [something]" = "instigator." In LXX Prov 16:20, εὑρετὴς ἀγαθῶν ("discoverer of good things," NETS) describes someone who is capable in business.

γενόμενος. Aor mid ptc nom masc sg γίνομαι (temporal or causal).

εἰς τοὺς Εβραίους. Disadvantage. Normally the word γένος (e.g., 6:12) or λαός (e.g., 6:16) is used to refer to "the people." The reference to "Hebrews" may be conditioned by the recent mention of Moses in 7:30 (cf. Exod 1:15, 16, 19; etc.). Cf. 11:13 and 15:37.

διαφύγῃς. Aor act subj 2nd sg διαφεύγω. Subjunctive used with οὐ μή to express emphatic negation. Cf. 6:26 on ἐκφεύγω + χείρ.

τὰς χεῖρας. Accusative direct object of διαφύγῃς.

τοῦ θεοῦ. Possessive genitive.

7:32 ἡμεῖς γὰρ διὰ τὰς ἑαυτῶν ἁμαρτίας πάσχομεν.

ἡμεῖς. Nominative subject of πάσχομεν.

γὰρ. Causal, explaining the reason why Antiochus will be judged by God: the Jews are suffering for their own sins and Antiochus will suffer for his, too. See 1:12 on γάρ.

διὰ τὰς ... ἁμαρτίας. Cause.

ἑαυτῶν. Subjective genitive (i.e., "the sins we committed") or, less likely, possessive (i.e., "the sins attributable to us")

πάσχομεν. Pres act ind 1st pl πάσχω.

7:33 εἰ δὲ χάριν ἐπιπλήξεως καὶ παιδείας ὁ ζῶν κύριος ἡμῶν βραχέως ἐπώργισται, καὶ πάλιν καταλλαγήσεται τοῖς ἑαυτοῦ δούλοις.

This verse repeats the main idea of the digression in 5:17-20.

εἰ. Introduces a first-class conditional clause (Smyth §2298), using εἰ + perfect indicative in the protasis. The first-class conditional introduces a neutral condition where the writer or speaker "gives no indication of the likelihood of the realization of the action in the protasis" (*CGCG* §49.4). Thus, the reality of the protasis is assumed for the sake of argument.

δὲ. Development; see 1:10 on δέ.

χάριν ἐπιπλήξεως καὶ παιδείας. Goal, indicating that the Lord's anger is to bring about reproof and discipline. The noun ἐπίπληξις appears only here in the LXX, but in near context with παιδεία, it likely refers to "the act of rebuking" (*GELS*, 278). See also 6:12 on πρὸς παιδείαν.

ὁ ζῶν κύριος. Nominative subject of ἐπώργισται. Cf. 15:4.

ζῶν. Pres act ptc nom masc sg ζάω (attributive).

ἡμῶν. Genitive of subordination.

βραχέως. Temporal adverb.

ἐπώργισται. Prf mid ind 3rd sg ἐποργίζομαι. While in 5:17 the epitomizer used the similar verb ἀποργίζομαι, here the similar verb (prefixed with ἐπί) "may be intended to show that divine wrath falls directly *upon* the Jews and that Yahweh assumes for Himself the role of punisher" (Domazakis, 291; cf. D. Schwartz, 68).

καὶ. Adverbial.

πάλιν. Adverb modifying καταλλαγήσεται.

καταλλαγήσεται. Fut mid ind 3rd sg καταλλάσσω. On the meaning of this verb, see 1:5 on καταλλαγείη.

τοῖς . . . δούλοις. Dative of association. On καταλλάσσω with the dative, see 1:5 on ὑμῖν.

ἑαυτοῦ. Possessive genitive.

7:34 σὺ δέ, ὦ ἀνόσιε καὶ πάντων ἀνθρώπων μιαρώτατε, μὴ μάτην μετεωρίζου φρυαττόμενος ἀδήλοις ἐλπίσιν ἐπὶ τοὺς οὐρανίους παῖδας ἐπαιρόμενος χεῖρα·

σὺ. Nominative subject of μετεωρίζου.

δέ. Development, marking shift of grammatical subject to the Antiochus (σύ). See 1:10 on δέ.

ὦ. Interjection: "O. . . ." (BDAG, 1101.1). Nordgren (16–23) describes three categories of Greek interjections: (1) *expressive*, indicating the speaker's mental state, action, or attitude, or a reaction to some event in the discourse; (2) *conative*, indicating the speaker's desire or will (rather than the mental state); and (3) *phatic*, expressing the speaker's mental state toward the discourse itself without making reference to any addressee. Here the interjection expresses vexation or, perhaps, disdain (cf. Muraoka §22yc). Prefixed to the vocative, ὦ is "a mark of high register" (Muraoka §22yc).

ἀνόσιε καὶ . . . μιαρώτατε. Vocatives. Negated with ἀ(ν) (cf. Smyth §885.1), the word ὅσιος ("devout," "pious," etc.) refers to someone who is "opposed to piety" (*GELS*, 56). In the LXX, the word is used to describe wicked enemies of the Jews (e.g., 8:32; 3 Macc 2:2; 5:8; 4 Macc 12:11) and people whom God hates due to detestable practices such as child sacrifice and cannibalism (Wis 12:4-5). In Ezek 22:9 it refers to Israelites who sin against God in detestable ways. Doran (2012, 162) notes the parallel with Sophocles (*Oed. tyr.*, 353), where Teiresias accuses Oedipus as an "unholy polluter" (ἀνοσίῳ μιάστορι).

On the meaning of the superlative adjective μιαρώτατε, see 4:19 on Ἰάσων ὁ μιαρός.

πάντων ἀνθρώπων. Partitive genitive. Because μιαρώτατε is the superlative adjective, the genitives are partitive ("most impure *of all mortals*") rather than comparative ("more impure *than all mortals*").

μὴ. See 1:5 on μή for further comments on the negation.

μάτην. Adverbial accusative of μάτη (Cf. BDAG, 621). Cf. 7:18.

μετεωρίζου. Pres mid impv 2nd sg μετεωρίζομαι. On the meaning of the verb, see 5:17 on ἐμετεωρίζετο.

φρυαττόμενος. Pres mid ptc nom masc sg φρυάσσω (means). The participle elaborates the meaning of μετεωρίζου, clarifying that "[you should not] be puffed up." Morphologically, Smyth (§515) notes that sometimes presents ending in -σσω are formed from stems that end in τ (e.g., φρυάττω) (cf. *MBG* §26.4).

ἀδήλοις ἐλπίσιν. Dative of means or, perhaps, cause.

ἐπὶ τοὺς οὐρανίους παῖδας. Opposition. Although "heavenly children" can refer to angels (e.g., 1QS 4.22; 11.8), this is better taken as a description of the Jews as "heavenly children" (cf. Jub. 1:25; 3 Macc 6:28; Wis 2:13; 12:6) and may connect to the larger theme of God as the heavenly victor. See Doran (2012, 162) and D. Schwartz (315–16) for extended discussion.

ἐπαιρόμενος. Pres mid ptc nom masc sg ἐπαίρω (attendant circumstance or, better, result). The close relationship between Antiochus' vain hopes and his attacks against God's children may suggest that ἐπαιρόμενος is coordinate with the main verb (i.e., attendant circumstance). However, it is probably better to understand ἐπαιρόμενος as denoting a result: i.e., Antiochus' elation resulted in him lifting his hands against God's children. Lifting up one's hands can be a sign of rebellion (e.g., 2 Kgdms 18:28; 20:21; Ps 73:3).

χεῖρα. Accusative direct object of ἐπαιρόμενος.

7:35 οὔπω γὰρ τὴν τοῦ παντοκράτορος ἐπόπτου θεοῦ κρίσιν ἐκπέφευγας.

οὔπω. Temporal adverb.

γὰρ. Causal, giving the reason why Antiochus should avoid elation and conceit (cf. 7:34). See 1:12 on γάρ.

τὴν . . . κρίσιν. Accusative direct object of ἐκπέφευγας.

τοῦ παντοκράτορος ἐπόπτου θεοῦ. Subjective genitive. ἐπόπτης refers to "one who sees or attends to, with implication of careful scrutiny" (BDAG, 387.1) and was "widely used in pagan Greek as an epithet for a god" (Goldstein, 316): i.e., "the all-seeing God." See 1:25 on δίκαιος καὶ παντοκράτωρ καὶ αἰώνιος.

ἐκπέφευγας. Prf act ind 2nd sg ἐκφεύγω.

7:36 οἱ μὲν γὰρ νῦν ἡμέτεροι ἀδελφοὶ βραχὺν ὑπενέγκαντες πόνον ἀενάου ζωῆς ὑπὸ διαθήκην θεοῦ πεπτώκασιν· σὺ δὲ τῇ τοῦ θεοῦ κρίσει δίκαια τὰ πρόστιμα τῆς ὑπερηφανίας ἀποίσῃ.

The final clause of 7:36 is syntactically ambiguous ("uneindeutig," Nicklas 2011, 1395).

οἱ . . . ἡμέτεροι ἀδελφοί. Nominative subject of πεπτώκασιν.

μὲν γὰρ . . . δέ. Point/counterpoint. See 2:25 on μὲν . . . δέ. Used with γάρ (which introduces an explanation), the construction means: "for indeed . . . but" (BDAG, 629.1.a.α; GELS, 125; cf. Denniston, 108; BDF §452.3; Mayser II 3:122–23). Cf. 6:4.

νῦν. Temporal adverb used with the aorist to convey a contrast with the past (cf. BDAG, 681.1.a.α.‫ב‬). The temporal adverb οὔπω ("not yet") in 7:35 helped signal the impending judgment of God. Here the temporal adverb νῦν ("now") helps signal the status of the seven brothers.

βραχὺν . . . πόνον. Accusative direct object of ὑπενέγκαντες. The "brief suffering" in view is the torture associated with martyrdom. The separation of the modifier from the head is an example of hyperbaton where the modifier (βραχύν) is emphasized.

ὑπενέγκαντες. Aor act ptc nom masc pl ὑποφέρω (temporal).

ἀενάου ζωῆς. It is possible to take ἀενάου ζωῆς either with πόνον ("brief suffering for everlasting life," cf. Doran 2012, 148) or as a second genitive (with θεοῦ) modifying διαθήκην ("[God's] covenant of eternal life"; cf. D. Schwartz, 298). The former reading would be classified as a genitive of value (cf. Doran 2012, 163; Goldstein, 317), signifying that "once the brothers paid the price for eternal life, a covenant-keeping God must bestow it upon them" (D. Schwartz, 317). The latter reading would be classified as a genitive of apposition (cf. D. Schwartz, 316–17), where "eternal life" (ἀενάου ζωῆς) clarifies the more ambiguous term διαθήκην. Because of the syntactical ambiguity, it is difficult to decide. However, due to concerns of word order, it is perhaps best to take ἀενάου ζωῆς with πόνον (cf. Habicht, 237; Nicklas 2011, 1395).

ὑπὸ διαθήκην. Subordination. While a locative sense for ὑπό might be expected, an earlier occurrence of πίπτω + ὑπό helps clarify the meaning here: ὑπὸ τὴν τοῦ βασιλέως ἐξουσίαν πεσεῖν ταῦτα ("these things fell under the authority of the king," 3:6). D. Schwartz (317) translates διαθήκην as "covenant," but helpfully notes that the idea of "testament" helps develop the image that God "bequeathed eternal life to the martyrs."

θεοῦ. Possessive genitive.

πεπτώκασιν. Prf act ind 3rd pl πίπτω. A popular conjecture is to read πεπώκασιν (i.e., "[the brothers] have drunk [of eternal life]") rather than πεπτώκασιν (cf. Bartlett, 276). While it is true that πίνω can take the genitive case (e.g., Num 20:19; Isa 55:1), the separation of the verb and its complement by a PP (ὑπὸ διαθήκην θεοῦ) probably cautions against making this conjectural emendation (cf. Doran 2012, 148). Goldstein (316) humorously comments that "[t]he scribes may have known their Greek better than the translators, since the Greek manuscripts have no variants affecting the points of difficulty."

Πίπτω should be understood as "to fall defeated" (*GELS*, 558.2), which is the clear meaning of the word in 12:34 and 12:40. The perfect "has the sense that the brothers have already begun to enjoy eternal life, which seems contrary to the future hope expressed in 7:11, 14, and 23" (Doran 2012, 148).

σὺ. Nominative subject of ἀποίσῃ.

τῇ ... κρίσει. Dative of manner. Cf. 7:35.

τοῦ θεοῦ. Subjective genitive.

δίκαια τὰ πρόστιμα. Accusative direct object of ἀποίσῃ.

τῆς ὑπερηφανίας. Objective genitive, qualifying δίκαια τὰ πρόστιμα. For the combination of "arrogance" (ὑπερηφανία) and "judgment" (κρίσις) elsewhere in 2 Maccabees, see 5:21; 9:4, 7-8, 11.

ἀποίσῃ. Fut mid ind 2nd sg ἀποφέρω.

7:37 ἐγὼ δέ, καθάπερ οἱ ἀδελφοί, καὶ σῶμα καὶ ψυχὴν προδίδωμι περὶ τῶν πατρίων νόμων ἐπικαλούμενος τὸν θεὸν ἵλεως ταχὺ τῷ ἔθνει γενέσθαι καὶ σὲ μετὰ ἐτασμῶν καὶ μαστίγων ἐξομολογήσασθαι διότι μόνος αὐτὸς θεός ἐστιν,

ἐγὼ. Nominative subject of προδίδωμι. Fronted for emphasis.

δέ. Development, marking a change of grammatical subject from the king in 7:36 to the seventh son in 7:37. See 1:10 on δέ.

καθάπερ. The conjunction introduces a comparative clause. On the function, see 2:27 on καθάπερ.

οἱ ἀδελφοί. Nominative subject of an implied form of προδίδωμι in an elliptical phrase with καθάπερ: "But I, just as [my] brothers [give up], give up. . . ." On the use of the article like a pronoun, see 1:16 on τὰς κεφαλάς.

καὶ . . . καὶ. Correlative construction: "both . . . and" (BDF §444.3; BDAG, 495.1.f).

σῶμα καὶ ψυχὴν. Accusative direct objects of προδίδωμι.

προδίδωμι. Pres act ind 1st sg προδίδωμι.

περὶ τῶν πατρίων νόμων. Advantage/representation. The epitomizer uses the adjective πάτριος six times in chapter 7 to describe "ancestral laws" (7:2, 24, 37) or "ancestral language" (7:8, 21, 27).

ἐπικαλούμενος. Pres mid ptc nom masc sg ἐπικαλέω (purpose). Following the present controlling verb (προδίδωμι), here the present participle indicates purpose: "I give up both body and soul [for the purpose of] calling upon God to be merciful." On the use of the middle voice to invoke a deity in prayer, see 3:15 on ἐπεκαλοῦντο.

τὸν θεὸν. Accusative subject of the infinitive γενέσθαι.

ἵλεως. Predicate of γενέσθαι. The Göttingen edition reads ἵλεων (accusative), which improves the text to agree with τὸν θεὸν. Cf. 2:22 on ἵλεω.

ταχὺ. Temporal adverb.

τῷ ἔθνει. Dative of advantage (cf. BDAG, 199.7).

γενέσθαι. Aor mid inf γίνομαι (indirect discourse).

σὲ. Accusative subject of the infinitive ἐξομολογήσασθαι.

μετὰ ἐτασμῶν καὶ μαστίγων. Manner.

ἐξομολογήσασθαι. Aor mid inf ἐξομολογέω (indirect discourse).

διότι. Marker of discourse content (BDAG, 251.4; Muraoka §79a).

μόνος αὐτὸς. Nominative subject of ἐστιν.

θεός. Predicate nominative.

ἐστιν. Pres act ind 3rd sg εἰμί.

7:38 ἐν ἐμοὶ δὲ καὶ τοῖς ἀδελφοῖς μου στῆσαι τὴν τοῦ παντοκράτορος ὀργὴν τὴν ἐπὶ τὸ σύμπαν ἡμῶν γένος δικαίως ἐπηγμένην.

ἐν ἐμοὶ . . . καὶ τοῖς ἀδελφοῖς. Cause or, less likely, instrumental.

δὲ. Development; see 1:10 on δέ.

μου. Genitive of relationship.

στῆσαι. Aor act inf ἵστημι (indirect discourse, modifying ἐπικαλούμενος from 7:37).

τὴν . . . ὀργὴν. Accusative subject of the infinitive στῆσαι.

τοῦ παντοκράτορος. Genitive of source (indicating a judgment) or, perhaps, subjective genitive (indicating an action). See 5:20 on τοῦ παντοκράτορος.

τὴν . . . ἐπηγμένην. Prf pass ptc acc fem sg ἐπάγω (attributive, modifying τὴν . . . ὀργήν).

ἐπὶ τὸ σύμπαν . . . γένος. Locative.

ἡμῶν. Genitive of relationship. On its position, see Muraoka (§41ab).

δικαίως. δικαίως is an adverbial adjunct.

7:39 Ἔκθυμος δὲ γενόμενος ὁ βασιλεὺς τούτῳ παρὰ τοὺς ἄλλους χειρίστως ἀπήντησεν πικρῶς φέρων ἐπὶ τῷ μυκτηρισμῷ.

Ἔκθυμος. Predicate adjective of γενόμενος. Cf. 7:3 on ἔκθυμος.

δὲ. Development, marking a shift of grammatical subject to the king in 7:39. See 1:10 on δέ.

γενόμενος. Aor mid ptc nom masc sg γίνομαι (attendant circumstance).

ὁ βασιλεὺς. Nominative subject of ἀπήντησεν.

τούτῳ. Dative complement of ἀπήντησεν.

παρὰ τοὺς ἄλλους. Comparison.

χειρίστως. Adverb of manner.

ἀπήντησεν. Aor act ind 3rd sg ἀπαντάω. On the meaning of the verb, see LEH (60): "to deal with [τινι]."

πικρῶς. The adverb is used substantively and functions as the object of φέρων (cf. Muraoka §24). Cf. the adjective πικρός in 6:7; 9:5.

φέρων. Pres act ptc nom masc sg φέρω (manner). On the meaning of the verb, see BDAG (1051.1.b.α): "[to] carry a burden." The collocation of φέρω + an adverb is common for the epitomizer: βαρέως (11:1; 14:27), συωφόρως (14:28).

ἐπὶ τῷ μυκτηρισμῷ. Cause.

7:40 καὶ οὗτος οὖν καθαρὸς μετήλλαξεν παντελῶς ἐπὶ τῷ κυρίῳ πεποιθώς.

οὗτος. Nominative subject of μετήλλαξεν.

οὖν. Inferential, transitioning to the final death scene of the martyr-dom account. See 2:15 and 2:16 on οὖν.

καθαρὸς. The Göttingen edition reads καθαρῶς rather καθαρός (MSS V 236-93). On such spelling variations, see Caragounis (538–46). If καθαρῶς is taken as the early text, then it modifies μετήλλαξεν: "this one died *in purity*." The description of the youngest son as "undefiled" contrasts with the regular description of polluted people (4:13, 19; 5:16; 7:34; 9:13; 14:13) and objects (6:2; 8:2; 10:5) in 2 Maccabees.

μετήλλαξεν. Aor act ind 3rd sg μεταλλάσσω. See 4:7 on μεταλλάξαντος.

παντελῶς. Adverb.

ἐπὶ τῷ κυρίῳ. Locative. The collocation of πείθω + dative (person or thing) denotes what someone depends on or trusts in (BDAG, 792.2.a): "confidence *directed toward* the Lord" = "confidence in the Lord." See 4:34 on ἐπὶ δόλῳ.

πεποιθώς. Prf pass ptc nom masc sg πείθω (manner).

7:41 Ἐσχάτη δὲ τῶν υἱῶν ἡ μήτηρ ἐτελεύτησεν.

Ἐσχάτη. Temporal. The noun ἔσχατος is used as a preposition with the genitive (cf. *GELS*, 294.1.e). Muraoka (§26f) further notes that there is "a contamination of a predicative, adverbial use of ἐσχάτη and a pseudo-preposition ἐσχάτον formally adjusted to ἡ μήτηρ." Cf. Deut 31:27, 29; Prov 29:21.

δὲ. Development, marking a shift of grammatical subject from the seventh son (lit. οὗτος καθαρός) in 7:40 to μήτηρ in 7:41.

τῶν υἱῶν. Either the genitive object of ἔσχατος (i.e., "after the sons") or a genitive modifying ἡ μήτηρ denoting relationship (i.e., "the mother of the sons"). On the use of the article like a pronoun, see 1:16 on τὰς κεφαλάς.

ἡ μήτηρ. Nominative subject of ἐτελεύτησεν.

ἐτελεύτησεν. Aor act ind 3rd sg τελευτάω. Although D. Schwartz (318) suggests that the lack of description of the mother's death here contrasts with the epitomizer's interest in presenting more vivid descriptions of women who suffer (e.g., 3:19; 6:10), the fact that the mother's death is stated but not described keeps the narrative focus on the seven sons.

7:42 Τὰ μὲν οὖν περὶ τοὺς σπλαγχνισμοὺς καὶ τὰς ὑπερβαλλούσας αἰκίας ἐπὶ τοσοῦτον δεδηλώσθω.

Τὰ. The neuter article functions as a nominalizer, changing the PP (περὶ τοὺς σπλαγχνισμούς) into the accusative direct object of δεδηλώσθω.

μὲν . . . δὲ. Transitional. The sequence is completed in 8:1. See 3:40 on μὲν . . . δέ as well as comments in the Introduction on the transitional use of μέν/δέ.

οὖν. Inferential. See 2:15 on οὖν.

περὶ τοὺς σπλαγχνισμοὺς. Reference. Cf. 6:7-8, 21.

τὰς ὑπερβαλλούσας αἰκίας. Accusative direct object of δεδηλώσθω.

ὑπερβαλλούσας. Pres act ptc acc fem pl ὑπερβάλλω (attributive).

ἐπὶ τοσοῦτον. Direction. See 4:3 on ἐπὶ τοσοῦτον.

δεδηλώσθω. Prf pass impv 3rd sg δηλόω. Muraoka (§28hca) notes the perfect imperative "is rare and used with a sense of urgency and insistence." See 2:23 on δεδηλωμένα.

GLOSSARY

Adjectivizer—An article used to change a nonadjective into an adjectival modifier.

Anacoluthon—A grammatical interruption or lack of implied sequence within a sentence.

Anaphoric—Referring back to a preceding word or groups of words. Thus, pronouns are anaphoric references to participants that have already been introduced into the discourse.

Anarthrous—Lacking an article.

Antecedent—An element that is referred to by another expression that follows it. Thus, the antecedent of a relative pronoun is that element in the preceding context with reference to which the relative clause provides additional information.

Apodosis—The second part ("then" clause) in a conditional construction.

Arthrous/articular—Including an article.

Ascensive—Being intensive or expressing a final addition or point of focus. In Greek, this term is most often used in relation to conjunctions, especially καί. In such instances, the conjunction is typically translated "even."

Aspect—The writer's/speaker's viewpoint of an action, event, or state. Specifically, how the writer or speaker presents the action unfolding in time.

Asyndeton—The omission of conjunctions between clauses, often resulting in a hurried rhythm or vehement effect.

Attendant Circumstance—A verbal participle expressing an action or circumstance that prepares for or accompanies the action of the main verb. Although the participle is semantically dependant on the main verb, it is often translated as a finite

281

verb conjoined to the main verb by *and*. Structural clues
include the following: tense of both the participle and main
verb is aorist, mood of main verb is imperative or indicative,
participle precedes the main verb in word order and time,
typically found in narrative and infrequently elsewhere.

Background—Information that is off the event line, or storyline—that
is, those events or materials that do not move the narrative
forward. Instead, background information comments on,
amplifies, or otherwise supports the narration.

Brachylogy—Condensed, abbreviated writing or speech, usually
involving the omission of an element of language that must
be supplied into the context to fully complete the meaning.

Cataphoric—Referring forward to a following word or group of
words.

Clausal complement—A direct object expressed in the form of
a clause rather than a noun phrase. For example, ὅτι is
often used to introduce complement clauses after verbs of
speech.

Clitic—A word that is written as a separate word in the syntax but that
is pronounced and accented as if it were part of another word.
There are two types. Enclitics shift their accents to the preceding
word; proclitics shift their accents to the following word.

Cognition—A verb that refers to some sort of mental process.

Collocation—The conventional association of two or more words so as
to produce a particular nuance.

Complement—In addition to its use in the phrase "clausal
complement," this term is also used in two additional ways. It
may refer to (1) a constituent, other than an accusative direct
object, that is required to complete a verb phrase. Verbs that
include a propositional prefix often take a complement whose
case is determined by the prefix. For example, verbs with the
prefix συν- characteristically take a dative complement; or
(2) the second element in a double accusative construction,
which completes the verbal idea.

Construction ad sensum—Literally "construction according to sense."
A construction that follows the sense of the expression rather
than strict grammatical rules, as when a plural verb is used
with a collective singular subject.

Copula/copular clause—A linking verb that joins a subject and
predicate into an equative or copular clause.

Crasis—The merging of two words through the use of contraction.

Development—The use of δέ does not mark either semantic continuity or discontinuity (since either can be present) but instead signals a new development in the narrative or argument.

Direct discourse—A direct object clause often introduced by ὅτι that records direct speech.

Double accusative construction—Constructions in which a verb takes two accusatives. There are two types. In a double accusative of person and thing, the verb is often thought to have two accusative direct objects, a thing and a person. But many of these constructions are better understood as instances of the cross-linguistic phenomenon of advancement. In a double accusative of object-complement construction a verb will have an object and the complement of that object in the accusative case, the latter predicating something about the former.

Digression—Refers to a temporary departure from the topic of a speech or writing or, in the case of narrative, a departure from the narrative proper. Digressions are sometimes used as intentional rhetorical devices, permitting the writer/speaker to inject personal opinions and/or evoke emotional responses from readers/listeners.

Elative—An adjectival form denoting intensity or superiority.

Ellipsis—The omission of an element of language that technically renders the sentence ungrammatical but that is usually understood in context.

Enclitic—A clitic is a word that is written as a separate word in the syntax but that is pronounced and accented as if it were part of another word. Enclitics donate their accent to the preceding word.

Epexegetical—In reference to an infinitive, refers to its function in clarifying, explaining, or qualifying. Regarding a clause beginning with the conjunction ἵνα or ὅτι, refers to a clause that completes the idea of a noun, verb, or adjective. Epexegetical genitives specify a particular example of the category introduced in the head noun.

Equative verb/clause—An equative verb joins a subject and predicate to form an equative clause.

Epitome—A shortened version of the work of one author.

First-class conditional—Used to introduce neutral conditions where the realization of the action in the protasis is assumed for the sake of argument.

Foreground—Information that is on the event line, or storyline—that is, those events that move the narrative forward.

Genitive absolute—A participial construction consisting of a genitive substantive and anarthrous genitive participle, typically at the beginning of a sentence, and (usually) grammatically independent of the main clause verb. It can express any adverbial idea attested for participles but is most often temporal.

Gloss—A brief explanation or short definition of a word that may not reflect the wider range of meaning of the word.

Hapax legomenon—A word that occurs only one time in the designated corpus (e.g., LXX) or, in the case of *absolute hapax legomenon*, occurs only once in a language as a whole.

Haplography—The accidental omission of text.

Homoiarchton—In textual criticism, an unintentional error of eyesight committed when copying a text, due to words or lines that begin similarly.

Homoiteleuton—Used in rhetoric to refer to the use of similar sound endings to words, phrases, or sentences.

Hendiadys—Two words joined by καί and used to express a single idea.

Hyperbaton—Refers to the "separation of two or more syntactically closely connected words or groups of words, for signaling or reinforcing the end of syntactical and semantic units in the Greek (and, by analogy, Latin) literary sentence" (Markovic, 127).

Hypotaxis—The subordinate relationship of clauses, indicated by conjuctions or other grammatical relationships (e.g., genitive absolute construction).

Imperfective (verbal aspect)—A semantic value, associated with verbs in the present and imperfect tenses, with which the writer/speaker means to portray the action as a process or as continuous. See also *perfective* (*verbal aspect*) and *stative* (*verbal aspect*).

Indirect discourse—Reported speech or thought.

Intermediate agent—The agent (introduced with διά + the agent in the genitive case) is not the ultimate cause of the action; the action took place *through* him/her/it.

Intransitive—A type of verb that does not require a direct object. Some verbs may function either transitively or intransitively depending on the statement in which they are used.

Left-dislocation—An information-structuring device that introduces "the next primary topic of the discourse" (Runge, 289) by placing it at the beginning of the sentence and then picking it up with a resumptive pronoun in the actual sentence.

Litotes—A figure of speech in which a statement is made by negating the opposite idea. For example, οὐκ ὀλίγους τῶν πολεμίων τροπούμενος (2 Macc 8:6) translates as "putting to flight *not a few* of the enemies" = "putting to flight *many* enemies."

Neologism—A word not attested prior to the work (e.g., 2 Maccabees) in question. This definition includes (a) words that the epitomizer coins himself and (b) words that may have existed but are not attested prior to 2 Maccabees in extant Greek literary, epigraphical, or papyrological texts. See especially Domazakis (95–96).

Nominalizer—An article that is used to change a word, phrase, or clause into a substantive. Most commonly, nominalizers are used to make an adjective or participle subsantival.

Parachesis—Refers to the repetition of the same sound in multiple words, especially in close context.

Parataxis—The linking of clauses or phrases together without utilizing conjunctions that mark subordinate relationships.

Parenthesis—Describes a distinct thought not completely unrelated to the ideas in the discourse but somewhat disruptive.

Paronomasia—Refers to the repetition of the same word root in order to make a connection or word-play.

Perfective (verbal aspect)—A semantic value associated with verbs in the aorist tense with which the writer/speaker means to portray the action in summary or as a complete whole, without reference to any process that might be involved. See also *imperfective (verbal aspect)* and *stative (verbal aspect)*.

Periphrasis—An indirect way of saying something. For example, ποιέω + abstract noun (e.g., λιτανείαν) when the verb alone (e.g., λιτανεύω) would have sufficed.

Periphrastic construction—An anarthrous participle used with a verb of being to constitute a finite verbal idea, yielding a roundabout way of saying something that could have been expressed with a single verb.

Point/counterpoint set—A construction typically involving a negated statement (with οὐ or μή) followed by a corresponding phrase or clause initiated by ἀλλά. Such sets are one particular type of correlative emphasis.

Predicate nominative/accusative/adjective—An anarthrous noun or adjective sharing the same case as the subject and connected to the subject with an equative verb (expressed or implied).

Prolepsis—The use of a descriptive word or phrase in anticipation of its becoming applicable.

Prominence—The "semantic and grammatical elements of discourse that serve to set aside certain subjects, ideas or motifs of the author as more or less semantically or pragmatically significant than others" (Reed, 75–76).

Protasis—The first part ("if" clause) in a conditional construction.

Right-dislocation—A device that refers to a participant in the midst of a clause using a pronoun or generic NP and then adding more information about the same participant at the end of the clause. This serves the purpose of highlighting particular thematic information that the writer wants the reader to consider at that particular point in the discourse.

Second-class conditional—Used to introduce counterfactual conditions where the realization of the action in the protasis is impossible or no longer possible.

Semitism—The influence of a Semitic language (Hebrew or Aramaic) on a Greek writer. This phenomenon sometimes produces a form of expression that is atypical of a native Greek speaker.

Solecism—A violation of standard grammatical usage.

Stative (verbal aspect)—A semantic value associated with verbs in the perfect and pluperfect tenses with which the writer/speaker means to portray the action as a state or condition, without reference to any process or expenditure of energy. See also *perfective (verbal aspect)* and *imperfective (verbal aspect)*.

Storyline (discourse structure)—Information that moves the narrative forward. In the narrative genre, this is most commonly expressed with aorist tense forms.

Third-class conditional— Used to introduce prospective conditions, where the fulfillment of the condition is likely.

Ultimate agent—The person ultimately responsible for the action without necessarily being directly involved. The agent may be introduced in the gentivie case with ὑπο, ἀπό, or παρά.

Vorlage—A prototype or source document behind a manuscript copy or recension; or an underlying tradition.

WORKS CITED

Abel, Félix-Marie. *Les livres des Maccabées*. Études Bibliques. Paris: Gabalda, 1949.

Aejmelaeus, Anneli. *Parataxis in the Septuagint*. Annales Academiae Scientiarum Fennicae, 31. Helsinki: Suomalainen Tiedeakatemia, 1982.

Aitken, J. K. *No Stone Unturned: Greek Inscriptions and Septuagint Vocabulary*. Corpus Scriptorum Historiae Byzantinae, 5. Winona Lake, Ind.: Eisenbrauns, 2014.

Aubrey, Rachel. "Motivated Categories, Middle Voice, and Passive Morphology." Pages 563–625 in *The Greek Verb Revisited: A Fresh Approach for Biblical Exegesis*. Edited by Steven E. Runge and Christopher J. Fresch. Bellingham, Wash.: Lexham Press, 2016.

Bar-Kochva, Bezalel. *Judas Maccabaeus: The Jewish Struggle against the Seleucids*. Cambridge: Cambridge University Press, 1989.

Barclay, John M. G. *Jews in the Mediterranean Diaspora: From Alexander to Trajan (323 BCE – 11 CE)*. Berkeley: University of California Press, 1996.

Bartlett, John R. *The First and Second Book of the Maccabees*. The Cambridge Bible Commentary. Cambridge: Cambridge University Press, 1973.

Bauer, Walter, Frederick W. Danker, William F. Arndt, and F. Wilbur Gingrich. *Greek-English Lexicon of the New Testament and Other Early Christian Literature*. 3rd ed. Chicago: University of Chicago Press, 2000.

Baugh, S. M. "Hyperbaton and Greek Literary Style in Hebrews." *Novum Testamentum* 59, no. 2 (2017): 194–213.

Beckwith, I. T. "The Articular Infinitive with εἰς." *Journal of Biblical Literature* 15, no. 1 (1896): 155–67.

Beekes, Robert, and Lucien Van Beek. *Etymological Dictionary of Greek*. Leiden: Brill, 2009.

Bentein, Klaas. *Verbal Periphrasis in Ancient Greek: Have- and Be- Constructions*. Oxford: Oxford University Press, 2016.

Bergren, Theodore A. "Nehemiah in 2 Maccabees 1:10–2:18." *Journal for the Study of Judaism* 28, no. 3 (1997): 249–70.

Bickermann, E. "Ein jüdischer Festbrief vom Jahre 124 v. Chr. (II *Macc.* 1, 1-9)." *Zeitschrift für die neutestamentliche Wissenschaft und die Kunde der älteren Kirche* 32 (1933): 233–54.

———. *Studies in Jewish and Christian History*, vol. 1: *A New Edition in English including The God of the Maccabees*. AJEC, 68/1. Edited by Amram Tropper. Leiden: Brill, 2007.

Black, Stephanie L. *Sentence Conjunctions in the Gospel of Matthew: καί, δέ, τότε, γάρ, οὖν, and Asyndeton in Narrative Discourse*. Journal for the Study of the New Testament Supplement Series, 216. London: Sheffield Academic Press, 2002.

Bolyki, János. "'As Soon as the Signal Was Given' (2 Macc 4:14): Gymnasia in the Service of Hellenism." Pages 131–39 in *The Books of the Maccabees: History, Theology, Ideology: Papers of the Second International Conference on the Deuterocanonical Books, Pápa, Hungary, 9–11 June 2005*. Edited by Géza G. Xeravits and József Zsengellér. Journal for the Study of Judaism Supplement Series, 118. Leiden: Brill, 2007.

Bonifazi, A., A. Drummen, and M. de Kreij. "Particles in Ancient Greek Discourse: Five Volumes Exploring Particle Use across Genres," §93. Hellenic Studies, 74. Center for Hellenic Studies, Harvard University: http://chs.harvard.edu/CHS/article/display/6391.

Boyd-Taylor, Cameron. *Reading between the Lines: The Interlinear Paradigm for Septuagint Studies*. Leuven: Peeters, 2011.

Brock, Roger W. "Authorial Voice and Narrative Management in Herodotus." Pages 3–16 in *Herodotus and His World: Essays from a Conference in Memory of George Forrest*. Edited by P. Derow and R. Parker. Oxford: Oxford University Press, 2003.

Brookins, Timothy A., and Bruce W. Longenecker. *1 Corinthians 1–9: A Handbook on the Greek Text*. Baylor Handbook on the Greek New Testament. Waco, Tex.: Baylor University Press, 2016.

Broshi, M. "La population de l'ancienne Jérusalem." *Revue biblique* 82 (1975): 5–14.

De Bruyne, D., with B. Sodar. *Les anciennes traductions latines des Machabées*. Anecdota Maredsolana, 4. Maredsous: Abbaye de Maredsous, 1932.

Bugh, Glenn R. "Hellenistic Military Developments." Pages 265–94 in *The Cambridge Companion to the Hellenistic World*. Edited by Glenn R. Bugh. Cambridge: Cambridge University Press, 2006.

Burk, Denny. *Articular Infinitive in the Greek of the New Testament: On the Benefit of Grammatical Precision*. New Testament Monographs, 14. Sheffield: Sheffield Phoenix Press, 2006.

Cadoux, C. J. "The Imperatival Use of ἵνα in the New Testament." *Journal of Theological Studies* 42, nos. 167–68 (1941): 165–73.

Calder, W. M., and J. M. R. Cormack, eds. *Monumenta Asiae Minoris Antiqua*, vol. 8, *Monuments from Lycaonia, the Pisido-Phrygian Borderland, Aphrodisias*. Publications of the American Society for Archaeological Research in Asia Minor 8. Manchester: University Press, 1962.

Campbell, Constantine R. *Verbal Aspect, the Indicative Mood, and Narrative: Soundings in the Greek of the New Testament*. Studies in Biblical Greek, 13. New York: Lang, 2007.

Caragounis, Chrys C. *The Development of Greek and the New Testament: Morphology, Syntax, Phonology, and Textual Transmission*. Wissenschaftliche Untersuchungen zum Neuen Testament, 1/167. Tübingen: Mohr Siebeck, 2004.

Clines, David J. A. *The Dictionary of Classical Hebrew*. 8 vols. Sheffield: Sheffield Academic Press, 1993–2011.

Coetzer, Eugene. "A Rhetorical Analysis of 2 Maccabees." PhD diss., North-West University, 2014.

Cohen, Shaye J. D. *The Beginnings of Jewishness: Boundaries, Varieties, Uncertainties*. Berkeley: University of California Press, 1999.

———. "Respect for Judaism by Gentiles According to Josephus." *Harvard Theological Review* 80 (1987): 412–15.

Conybeare, F. C., and St. George Stock. *Grammar of the Septuagint: With Selected Readings, Vocabularies, and Updated Indexes*. Boston: Ginn, 1905. Repr. Peabody, Mass.: Hendrickson, 1995.

Copan, Paul. "Is *Creatio ex Nihilo* a Post-Biblical Invention? An Examination of Gerhard May's Proposal." *Trinity Journal* n.s. 17 (1996): 75–93.

Coulton, J. J. *Ancient Greek Architects at Work: Problems of Structure and Design*. New York: Cornell University Press, 1982.

Culy, Martin M. "The Clue Is in the Case: Distinguishing Adjectival and Adverbial Participles." *Perspectives in Religious Studies* 30 (2003): 441–53.

Denniston, J. D. *The Greek Particles*. 2nd ed. Revised by K. J. Dover. Indianapolis: Hackett, 1950.

Dexinger, Ferdinand. "Der Ursprung der Samaritaner im Spiegel der frühen Quellen." Pages 67–140 in *Die Samaritaner*. Edited by Ferdinand Dexinger and Reinhard Pummer. Darmstadt: Wissenschaftliche Buchgesellschaft, 1992.

Dhont, Marieke. *Style and Context of Old Greek Job.* Journal for the Study of Judaism Supplement Series, 183. Leiden: Brill, 2018.

Doering, Lutz. *Ancient Jewish Letters and the Beginnings of Christian Epistolography.* Wissenschaftliche Untersuchungen zum Neuen Testament, 1/298. Tübingen: Mohr Siebeck, 2012.

Domazakis, Nikolaos. *The Neologisms in 2 Maccabees.* Studia Graeca et Latina Lundensia, 23. Sweden: Lund University. 2018.

Dommershausen, Werner. *1 und 2 Makkabäer.* Die Neue Echter Bibel, 12. Wërzburg: Echter-Verlag, 1985.

Doran, Robert. *2 Maccabees: A Critical Commentary.* Minneapolis: Fortress, 2012.

———. *Temple Propaganda: The Purpose and Character of 2 Maccabees.* Catholic Biblical Quarterly Monograph Series, 12. Washington, D.C.: Catholic Biblical Association of America, 1981.

Dorival, Gilles. "La Lexicographie de la Septante entre Sem et Japhet." Pages 227–41 in *Biblical Lexicology: Hebrew and Greek: Semantics–Exegesis–Translation.* Edited by Eberhard Bons, Jan Joosten, and Regine Hunziker-Rodewald. Beihefte zur Zeitschrift für die alttestamentliche Wissenschaft, 443. Berlin: de Gruyter, 2015.

Ehorn, Seth M., and Mark Lee. "The Syntactical Function of ἀλλὰ καί in Phil. 2.4." *Journal of Greco-Roman Christianity and Judaism* 12 (2016): 9–16.

Ellis, Nicholas J. "Aspect Prominence, Morpho-Syntax, and a Cognitive-Linguistic Framework for the Greek Verb." Pages 122–60 in *The Greek Verb Revisited: A Fresh Approach for Biblical Exegesis.* Edited by Steven E. Runge and Christopher J. Fresch. Bellingham, Wash.: Lexham Press, 2016.

van Emde Boas, Evert, Albert Rijksbaron, Luuk Huitink, and Mathieu de Bakker. *The Cambridge Grammar of Classical Greek.* Cambridge: Cambridge University Press, 2019.

Engel, Georg. *De antiquorum epicorum didacticorum historicorum prooemiis.* PhD diss., Marburg, 1910.

Evans, Craig A. *Ancient Texts for New Testament Studies: A Guide to the Background Literature.* Peabody, Mass.: Hendrickson, 2005.

Fanning, Buist M. *Verbal Aspect in New Testament Greek.* Oxford Theological Monographs. Oxford: Oxford University Press, 1990.

Flusser, David. *Judaism and the Origins of Christianity.* Jerusalem: Magnes, 1988.

Fredriksen, Paula. "Arms and The Man: A Response to Dale Martin's 'Jesus in Jerusalem: Armed and Not Dangerous.'" *Journal for the Study of the New Testament* 37, no. 3 (2015): 312–25.

Fresch, Christopher J. "Discourse Markers in the Septuagint and Early Koine Greek with Special Reference to the Twelve." *Tyndale Bulletin* 68, no. 2 (2017a): 313–16.

———. "Is There an Emphatic μέν? A Consideration of the Particle's Development and Its Function in Koine." *New Testament Studies* 63 (2017b): 261–78.

Fuller, Lois K. "The 'Genitive Absolute' in New Testament/Hellenistic Greek: A Proposal for Clearer Understanding." *Journal of Greco-Roman Christianity and Judaism* 3 (2006): 142–67.

Gignac, Francis T. *A Grammar of the Greek Papyri of the Roman and Byzantine Periods*. 2 vols. Rome: Istituto editoriale cisalpino-La goliardica, 1976, 1981.

Goldstein, Jonathan A. *II Maccabees: A New Translation with Introduction and Commentary*. Anchor Bible, 41A. Garden City, N.Y.: Doubleday, 1983.

Grimm, Carl Ludwig. *Das zweite, dritte und vierte Buch der Maccabäer*. Kurzgefasstes Exegetisches Handbuch zu den Apokryphen, 4. Leipzig: Hirzel, 1857.

Habicht, Christian. *2 Makkabäerbuch*. Jüdische Schriften aus hellenistisch-römischer Zeit, 1/3. Gütersloh: Mohn, 1976.

Hamilton, Neill Q. "Temple Cleansing and Temple Bank." *Journal of Biblical Literature* 83, no. 4 (1964): 365–72.

Hanhart, Robert, ed. *Maccabaeorum liber II*. Copiis usus quas reliquit Werner Kappler. Septuaginta: Vetus Testamentum Graecum, vol. IX/2. Vierte Auflage. Göttingen: Vandenhoeck & Ruprecht, 2017.

———. *Zum Text des 2. und 3. Makkabäerbuches. Probleme der Überlieferung, der Auslegung und der Ausgabe*. Nachrichten der Akademie der Wissenschaften in Göttingen, I. Philosophisch-historische Klasse. Nr. 13. Göttingen: Vandenhoeck & Ruprecht, 1961.

Hansen, Mogens Herman. "City-Ethnics as Evidence for *Polis* Identity." Pages 169–96 in *More Studies in the Ancient Greek Polis*. Historia Einzelschriften, 108. Edited by Mogens Herman Hansen and Kurt Raaflaub. Stuttgart: Franz Steiner, 1996.

Hatch, Edwin, and Henry A. Redpath. *A Concordance to the Septuagint and Other Greek Versions of the Old Testament*. 2nd ed. Grand Rapids: Baker, 2005.

Hayes, Christine E. *Gentile Impurities and Jewish Identities*. Oxford: Oxford University Press, 2002.

Heckert, Jacob K. *Discourse Function of Conjoiners in the Pastoral Epistles*. Dallas: SIL International, 1996.

Hengel, Martin. *Judaism and Hellenism: Studies in their Encounter in Palestine during the Early Hellenistic Period.* London: SCM Press, 1974.

van Henten, Jan Willem. *The Maccabean Martyrs as Saviours of the Jewish People: A Study of 2 & 4 Maccabees.* Journal for the Study of Judaism Supplement Series, 57. Leiden: Brill, 1997.

———. "ΠΑΝΤΟΚΡΑΤΩΡ ΘΕΟΣ in 2 Maccabees." Pages 117–26 in *YHWH-Kyrios: Antitheism or the Power of the Word: Festschrift für Rochus Zuurmond.* Edited by Karel A. Deurollo and Bernd J. Diebner. Heidelberg: Selbstverlag der Dielheimer Blätter zum Alten Testament, 1996.

Himmelfarb, Martha. "Judaism and Hellenism in 2 Maccabees." *Poetics Today* 19, no. 1 (1998): 19–40.

Hornblower, Simon, ed. *Herodotus: Histories, Book V.* Cambridge Greek and Latin Classics. Cambridge: Cambridge University Press, 2013.

Hornblower, Simon, Antony Spawforth, and Esther Eidinow. *The Oxford Classical Dictionary.* 4th ed. Oxford: Oxford University Press, 2012.

Horrocks, Geoffrey. *Greek: A History of the Language and Its Speakers.* 2nd ed. West Sussex: Wiley & Sons, 2010.

Horsley, G. H. R. *New Documents Illustrating Early Christianity,* vol. 1: *A Review of the Greek Inscriptions and Papyri Published in 1976.* North Ryde: Macquarie University, 1981.

Ilan, Tal. *Lexicon of Jewish Names in Late Antiquity,* I. Texte und Studien zum antiken Judentum, 91. Tübingen: Mohr Siebeck, 2002.

Jannaris, A. N. *An Historical Greek Grammar Chiefly of the Attic Dialect as Written and Spoken from Classical Antiquity Down to the Present Time.* New York: Macmillan, 1897.

Jobes, Karen H., and Moisés Silva. *Invitation to the Septuagint.* 2nd ed. Grand Rapids: Baker, 2015.

Kappler, Werner, ed. *Maccabaeorum liber I.* Copiis usus quas reliquit Werner Kappler. Septuaginta: Vetus Testamentum Graecum, vol. IX/1. Dritte Auflage. Göttingen: Vandenhoeck & Ruprecht, 1990.

Kappler, Werner. *De memoria alterius libri Maccabeorum.* PhD diss., Göttingen, 1929.

Katz, Peter. "Eleazar's Martyrdom in 2 Maccabees: The Latin Evidence for a Point of the Story." *Studia Patristica* 4 (1961): 118–24.

———. "The Text of 2 Maccabees Reconsidered." *Zeitschrift für die neutestamentliche Wissenschaft und die Kunde der älteren Kirche* 51 (1960): 10–30.

Kemmer, Suzanne. *The Middle Voice.* Typological Studies in Language, 23. Amsterdam: John Benjamins, 1993.

Kennell, N. M. "New Light on 2 Maccabees 4:7-15." *Journal of Jewish Studies* 56 (2005): 10–24.

Klauck, Hans-Josef. *Ancient Letters and the New Testament: A Guide to Context and Exegesis*. Waco, Tex.: Baylor University Press, 2006.

Koehler, Ludwig, and Walter Baumgartner. *The Hebrew and Aramaic Lexicon of the Old Testament*. Translated by M. E. J. Richardson. 5 vols. Leiden: Brill, 1994–2000.

Lange, Armin. "2 Maccabees 2:13-15: Library or Canon?" Pages 155–67 in *The Books of the Maccabees: History, Theology, Ideology: Papers of the Second International Conference on the Deuterocanonical Books, Pápa, Hungary, 9-11 June, 2005*. Edited by G. G. Xeravits and József Zsengellér. Journal for the Study of Judaism Supplement Series, 118. Leiden: Brill, 2007.

——, ed. *Textual History of the Bible*, vol. 2C: *Deuterocanonical Scriptures*. Leiden: Brill, 2019.

Lee, John A. L. *The Greek of the Pentateuch: Grinfield Lectures on the Septuagint 2011-2012*. Oxford: Oxford University Press, 2018.

——. "The Present State of Lexicography of Ancient Greek." Pages 66–74 in *Biblical Greek Language and Lexicography: Essays in Honor of Frederick W. Danker*. Edited by Bernard A. Taylor. Grand Rapids: Eerdmans, 2004.

Le Moigne, Philippe. "Le caractère hétérogène du grec de la LXX: l'example de 2M." Pages 249–72 in *Die Septuaginta – Entstehung, Sprache, Geschichte*. Edited by Siegfried Kreuzer, Martin Meiser, and Marcus Sigismund. Wissenschaftliche Untersuchungen zum Neuen Testament, 1/286. Tübingen: Mohr Siebeck, 2012.

Levinsohn, Stephen H. *Discourse Features of New Testament Greek: A Coursebook on the Information Structure of New Testament Greek*. 2nd ed. Dallas: SIL International, 2000.

——. "Functions of Copula-Participle Combinations ('Periphrastics')." Pages 307–26 in *The Greek Verb Revisited: A Fresh Approach for Biblical Exegesis*. Edited by Steven E. Runge and Christopher J. Fresch. Bellingham, Wash.: Lexham Press, 2016.

——. "'Therefore' or 'Wherefore': What's the Difference?" Pages 325–43 in *Reflections on Lexicography: Explorations in Ancient Syriac, Hebrew and Greek Sources*. Edited by Richard A. Taylor and Craig E. Morrison. Perspectives on Linguistics and Ancient Languages, 4. Piscataway, N.J.: Gorgias Press, 2014.

Liddell, Henry George, and Robert Scott. *A Greek-English Lexicon with a Revised Supplement*. Revised by Henry Stuart Jones. Oxford: Clarendon Press, 1996.

Louw, Johannes P., and Eugene A. Nida. *Greek-English Lexicon of the New Testament Based on Semantic Domains*. 2 vols. New York: United Bible Societies, 1988.

Luraghi, Silvia. *On the Meaning of Prepositions and Cases: The Expression of Semantic Roles in Ancient Greek*. Studies in Language Companion Series, 67. Philadelphia: John Benjamins, 2003.

Lust, Johan, Erik Eynikel, and Katrin Hauspie. *A Greek-English Lexicon of the Septuagint*. Rev. ed. Stuttgart: Deutsche Bibelgesellschaft, 2003.

Marcus, Ralph. "Divine Names and Attributes in Hellenistic Jewish Literature." *Proceedings of the American Academy of Jewish Research* 3 (1931–1932): 43–129.

Markovic, Daniel. "Hyperbaton in the Greek Literary Sentence." *Greek, Roman, and Byzantine Studies* 46 (2006): 127–45.

Mason, Steve. "Jews, Judaeans, Judaizing, Judaism: Problems of Categorization in Ancient History." *Journal for the Study of Judaism* 38 (2007): 457–512.

———. *Orientation to the History of Roman Judaea*. Eugene, Ore.: Cascade, 2016.

Mayser, Edwin. *Grammatik der griechischen Papyri aus der Ptolemäerzeit mit Einschluss der gleichzeitigen Ostraka und der in Ägypten verfassten Inschriften*. Band II Satzlehre. Berlin/Leipzig, 1926–1934.

McKay, Kenneth L. *A New Syntax of the Verb in New Testament Greek: An Aspectual Approach*. Studies in Biblical Greek, 5. Bern: Lang, 1994.

Miller, Marvin Lloyd. *Performances of Ancient Jewish Letters: From Elephantine to MMT*. Journal of Ancient Judaism Supplements, 20. Göttingen: Vandenhoeck & Ruprecht, 2015.

Miller, Neva F. "Appendix 2: A Theory of Deponent Verbs." Pages 423–30 in *Analytical Lexicon of the Greek New Testament*. Edited by T. Friberg, B. Friberg, and N. Miller. Grand Rapids: Baker, 2000.

Montanari, Franco. *The Brill Dictionary of Ancient Greek*. Leiden: Brill, 2015.

Moulton, J. H. *A Grammar of New Testament Greek*, vol. 1: *Prolegomena*. Edinburgh: T&T Clark, 1908.

Moulton, J. H., and Nigel Turner. *A Grammar of New Testament Greek*, vol. 3: *Syntax*. Edinburgh: T&T Clark, 1963.

Moulton, J. H., and W. F. Howard. *A Grammar of New Testament Greek*, vol. 2: *Accidence and Word-Formation*. Edinburgh: T&T Clark, 1929.

Mounce, William D. *The Morphology of Biblical Greek*. Grand Rapids: Zondervan, 1994.

Muraoka, T. *A Greek-English Lexicon of the Septuagint*. Leuven: Peeters, 2009.

———. "Septuagintal Lexicography: Some General Issues." Pages 17–47 in *Melbourne Symposium on Septuagint Lexicography*. Septuagint and Cognate Studies, 28. Edited by T. Muraoka. Atlanta: Scholars Press, 1990.

———. *A Syntax of Septuagint Greek*. Leuven: Peeters, 2016.

Newman, Judith H. *Praying by the Book: The Scripturalization of Prayer in Second Temple Judaism*. Atlanta: Scholars Press, 1999.

Nicklas, Tobias. *Makkabaion II. Das 2. Buch der Makkabäer*. Pages 1376–1416 in *Die Septuaginta deutsch: Erläuterungen und Kommentare I: Genesis bis Makkabäer*. Edited by Martin Karrer and Wolfgang Kraus. Stuttgart: Deutsche Bibelgesellschaft, 2011.

———. "Makkabaion II / 2 Maccabees." Pages 271–77 in *Introduction to the Septuagint*. Edited by Siegfried Kreuzer. Waco, Tex.: Baylor University Press, 2019.

———. "Makkabaion II / Das zweite Buch der Makkabäer." Pages 306–13 in *Handbuch zur Septuaginta: Einleitung in die Septuaginta*. Edited by Siegfried Kreuzer. Gütersloh: Gütersloher Verlaghaus, 2016.

———. "Metaphern im 2. Makkabäerbuch." Pages 173–84 in *The Metaphorical Use of Language in Deuterocanonical and Cognate Literature*. Edited by Markus Witte and Sven Behnke. Deuterocanonical and Cognate Literature. Berlin: de Gruyter, 2015.

Niese, Benedikt. "Kritik der beiden Makkabäerbücher nebst Beiträgen zur Geschichte der makkabäischen Erhebung." *Hermes* 35 (1900): 268–307, 453–527.

Nordgren, Lars. *Greek Interjections: Syntax, Semantics and Pragmatics*. Trends in Linguistics, 273. Berlin: de Gruyter, 2015.

Novenson, Matthew V. *Christ among the Messiahs: Christ Language in Paul and Messiah Language in Ancient Judaism*. Oxford: Oxford University Press, 2012.

———. "'God is Witness'": A Classical Rhetorical Idiom in Its Pauline Usage." *Novum Testamentum* 52, no. 4 (2010): 355–75.

———. "Paul's Former Occupation in Ioudaismos." Pages 24–39 in *Galatians and Christian Theology: Justification, the Gospel, and Ethics in Paul's Letter*. Edited by Mark Elliott, Scott Hafemann, N. T. Wright, and John Frederick. Grand Rapids: Baker, 2014.

Olmstead, Wesley G. *Matthew 1–14: A Handbook on the Greek Text*. Baylor Handbook on the Greek New Testament. Waco, Tex.: Baylor University Press, 2019.

Palmer, Leonard R. *A Grammar of the Post-Ptolemaic Papyri*, vol. 1: *Accidence and Word-Formation*. London: Oxford University Press, 1946.

Parente, F. "ΤΟΥΣ ΕΝ ΙΕΡΟΣΟΛΥΜΟΙΣ ΑΝΤΙΟΧΕΙΣ ΑΝΑΓΡΑΨΑΙ (II Macc. IV, 9): Gerusalemme è mai stata una ΠΟΛΙΣ?" *Rivista di storia e letteratura religiosa* 30 (1994): 3–38.

Parker, Victor. "The Letters in II Maccabees: Reflections on the Book's Composition." *Zeitschrift für die alttestamentliche Wissenschaft* 119 (2007): 386–402.

Penner, Ken W., ed. *The Lexham English Septuagint*. Bellingham, Wash.: Lexham Press, 2019.

Perry, Peter S. *The Rhetoric of Digressions: Revelation 7:1-17 and 10:1–11:13 and Ancient Communication*. Wissenschaftliche Untersuchungen zum Neuen Testament 2/268. Tübingen: Mohr Siebeck, 2009.

Pietersma, A., and B. G. Wright III, eds. *A New English Translation of the Septuagint*. Oxford: Oxford University Press, 2007.

Porter, Stanley E. *Idioms of the Greek New Testament*. 2nd ed. Sheffield: Sheffield Academic, 1999.

———. *Καταλλάσσω in Ancient Greek Literature, with Reference to the Pauline Writings*. Estudios de filología neotestamentaria, 5. Córdoba: Ediciones El Almendro, 1994.

———. *Verbal Aspect in the Greek of the New Testament with Reference to Tense and Mood*. Studies in Biblical Greek, 1. New York: Lang, 1989.

Rahlfs, Alfred, and Robert Hanhart. *Septuaginta: Editio Altera*. 2nd rev. ed. Stuttgart: Deutsche Bibelgesellschaft, 2006.

Rajak, Tessa. *Translation as Survival: The Greek Bible of the Ancient Jewish Diaspora*. Oxford: Oxford University Press, 2009.

Reed, Jeffrey T. *A Discourse Analysis of Philippians: Method and Rhetoric in Debate over Literary Integrity*. Journal for the Study of the New Testament Supplement Series, 136. Sheffield: Sheffield Academic, 1997.

Regev, Eyal. "Hanukkah and the Temple of the Maccabees: Ritual and Ideology from Judas Maccabeus to Simon." *Jewish Studies Quarterly* 13 (2006): 1–28.

Rigsby, Kent J. *Asylia: Territorial Inviolability in the Hellenistic World*. Berkeley: University of California Press, 1996.

Rijksbaron, Albert. *The Syntax and Semantics of the Verb in Classical Greek: An Introduction*. 3rd ed. Chicago: University of Chicago Press, 2002.

Risberg, Bernhard. "Textkritische und exegetishe Anmerkungen zu den Makkabäerbüchern." *Beiträge zur Religionswissenschaft* 27 (1918): 6–31.

Roberts, Colin H., and T. C. Skeat. *The Birth of the Codex*. Oxford: Oxford University Press, 1987.

Robertson, A. T. *A Grammar of the Greek New Testament in the Light of Historical Research*. 4th ed. Nashville: Broadman & Holman, 1934.

Rolle, Renate. *The World of the Scythians*. Berkeley: University of California Press, 1989.

Rosenblum, Jordan D. *The Jewish Dietary Laws in the Ancient World*. Cambridge: Cambridge University Press, 2016.

Royse, James. "The Early Text of Paul (and Hebrews)." Pages 175–203 in *The Early Text of the New Testament*. Edited by C. Hill and M. Kruger. Oxford: Oxford University Press, 2012.

Runge, Steven E. *Discourse Grammar of the Greek New Testament: A Practical Introduction for Teaching and Exegesis*. Bellingham, Wash.: Lexham Press, 2010.

Runge, Steven E., and Christopher J. Fresch, eds. *The Greek Verb Revisited: A Fresh Approach for Biblical Exegesis*. Bellingham, Wash.: Lexham Press, 2015.

Sanders, E. P. *Judaism: Practice and Belief 63 BCE – 66 CE*. London: SCM Press, 1992.

Schams, Christine. *Jewish Scribes in the Second-Temple Period*. Journal for the Study of the Old Testament Supplement Series, 291. Sheffield: Sheffield Academic, 1998.

Schaper, Joachim. "Translating 2 Maccabees for NETS." Pages 225–32 in *XII Congress of the International Organization for Septuagint and Cognate Studies: Leiden, 2004*. Septuagint and Cognate Studies, 54. Edited by Melvin K. H. Peters. Leiden: Brill, 2006.

Schmid, W. *Der Atticismus in seinen Hauptvertretern von Dionysius von Halikarnass bis auf den zweiten Philostratus*. 5 vols. Stuttgart: Kohlhammer, 1887–1897.

Schnocks, Johannes. "2 Maccabees." Pages 142–53 in *Textual History of the Bible*, vol. 2: *Deuterocanonical Scriptures*. Edited by Frank Feder and Matthias Henze. Leiden: Brill, 2019.

Schwartz, Daniel R. *2 Maccabees*. Commentaries on Early Jewish Literature. Berlin: de Gruyter, 2008.

Schwartz, Seth. "How Many Judaisms Were There?" *Journal of Ancient Judaism* 2 (2011): 208–38.

Sharon, Nadav. *Judea under Roman Domination: The First Generation of Statelessness and Its Legacy*. Early Judaism and Its Literature; 46. Atlanta: Society of Biblical Literature, 2017.

Shaw, Frank. "2 Maccabees." Pages 273–91 in *The T&T Clark Companion to the Septuagint*. Edited by James K. Aitken. London: Bloomsbury T&T Clark, 2015.

―――. "The Language of 2 Maccabees." Pages 407–15 in *Die Sprache der Septuaginta / The Language of the Septuagint*. Edited by Eberhard Bons and Jan Joosten. Gütersloh: Gütersloher Verlaghaus, 2016.

von Siebenthal, Heinrich. *Ancient Greek Grammar for the Study of the New Testament*. New York: Lang, 2019.

Sievers, Joseph. *Synopsis of the Greek Sources for the Hasmonean Period: 1–2 Maccabees and Josephus, War 1 and Antiquities 12–14*. Subsidia Biblica, 20. Rome: Pontifico Istituto Biblico, 2001.

Sim, Margaret G. *A Relevant Way to Read: A New Approach to Exegesis and Communication*. Eugene, Ore.: Pickwick, 2016.

Simkovich, Malka Zeiger. "Greek Influence on the Composition of 2 Maccabees." *Journal for the Study of Judaism* 42 (2011): 293–310.

Smyth, Herbert Weir. *Greek Grammar*. Cambridge, Mass.: Harvard University Press, 1956.

Stemberger, Günter. "Forbidden Gentile Food in Early Rabbinic Writings." Pages 209–24 in *Jewish Identity and Politics between the Maccabees and Bar Kokhba: Groups, Normativity, and Rituals*. Edited by Benedikt Eckhardt. Journal for the Study of Judaism Supplement Series, 155. Leiden: Brill, 2012.

Swete, Henry Barclay. *The Old Testament in Greek According to the Septuagint*, vol. 3: *Hosea–4 Maccabees, Psalms of Solomon, Enoch, The Odes*. Cambridge: Cambridge University Press, 1905.

Thackeray, Henry St. John. *A Grammar of the Old Testament in Greek According to the Septuagint*. Cambridge: Cambridge University Press, 1909.

Theophilos, Michael P. "John 15.14 and the ΦΙΛ- Lexeme in Light of Numismatic Evidence: Friendship or Obedience?" *New Testament Studies* 64 (2018): 33–43.

―――. "Κτίστης (1 Peter 4:19) in Light of the Numismatic Record." Pages 191–205 in *Biblical Greek in Context: Essays in Honour of John A. L. Lee*. Edited by T. Evans and J. Aitken. Leuven: Peeters, 2015.

Thomson, Christopher J. "What Is Aspect?: Contrasting Definitions in General Linguistics and New Testament Studies." Pages 13–80 in *The Greek Verb Revisited: A Fresh Approach for Biblical Exegesis*. Edited by Steven E. Runge and Christopher J. Fresch. Bellingham, Wash.: Lexham Press, 2015.

Thrall, Margaret E. *Greek Particles in the New Testament: Linguistic and Exegetical Studies*. New Testament Tools and Studies, 3. Leiden: Brill, 1962.

Torrey, C. C. "The Letters Prefixed to Second Maccabees." *Journal of the American Oriental Society* 60 (1940): 119–50.

VanderKam, James C. *From Joshua to Caiaphas: High Priests after the Exile*. Minneapolis: Fortress, 2004.

———. "Hanukkah: Its Timing and Significance according to 1 and 2 Maccabees." *Journal for the Study of the Pseudepigrapha* 1 (1987): 23–40.

Wallace, Daniel B. *Greek Grammar beyond the Basics: An Exegetical Syntax of the New Testament*. Grand Rapids: Zondervan, 1996.

Wheaton, Gerry. "The Festival of Hanukkah in 2 Maccabees: Its Meaning and Function." *Catholic Biblical Quarterly* 74 (2012): 247–62.

White, John L. *Light from Ancient Letters*. Philadelphia: Fortress, 1986.

Wilhelm, Adolf. "Zu einigen Stellen." *Akademie der Wissenschaften in Wien, Philosophisch-historische Klasse: Anzeiger* 74 (1937): 15–30.

Williams, Margaret H. "The Use of Alternate Names by Diaspora Jews in Graeco-Roman Antiquity." Pages 317–31 in *Jews in a Greco-Roman Environment*. Wissenschaftliche Untersuchungen zum Neuen Testament, 1/312. Tübingen: Mohr Siebeck, 2013.

Wilson, Robert D. "Royal Titles in Antiquity: An Essay in Criticism, Article Four: The Titles of the Greek Kings." *Princeton Theological Review* 3 (1905): 238–67.

Zeitlin, Solomon, and Sidney Tedesche. *The Second Book of Maccabees: With Introduction and Commentary*. New York: Dropsie College, 1954.

Zerwick, Maximilian. *Biblical Greek: Illustrated by Examples*. Rome: Pontificii Instituti Biblici, 1963.

GRAMMAR INDEX

Superscript indicates the number of times an element
appears within a verse.

This index covers only *2 Maccabees 1–7*. See the Grammar Index in
2 Maccabees 8–15 for a comprehensive index of 2 Maccabees.

accusative (adverbial), 3:16, 4:26,
5:1, 5:7^2, 5:11, 6:10, 6:13, 7:5,
7:18, 7:26, 7:27^2, 7:34
accusative absolute, 7:5
accusative complement, 3:28, 5:3^5
accusative direct object, 1:3^2, 1:4^2,
1:5, 1:8^5, 1:9, 1:12, 1:14, 1:15^2,
1:16^5, 1:17, 1:18^4, 1:19, 1:20^4,
1:21^3, 1:23, 1:24, 1:25^3, 1:26^2,
1:27^4, 1:28^2, 1:29, 1:30, 1:31, 1:33^2,
1:34^2, 1:35, 1:36, 2:2^3, 2:3, 2:4,
2:5^4, 2:6, 2:7, 2:8, 2:9^2, 2:10^2, 2:12,
2:13^4, 2:14, 2:15^2, 2:16^2, 2:17^3,
2:18^3, 2:19, 2:21^2, 2:22^3, 2:24^2,
2:25^3, 2:26, 2:27^3, 2:29, 2:30, 2:31^3,
2:32^3, 3:2^2, 3:3, 3:5, 3:7^3, 3:8^3, 3:13,
3:14^2, 3:15^3, 3:16^2, 3:19, 3:20^2,
3:22^3, 3:23, 3:24, 3:25^3, 3:26^2,
3:28^2, 3:30^2, 3:31, 3:32^2, 3:33^2,
3:34^2, 3:35^3, 3:36^2, 3:37, 3:38^4,

3:39^2, 4:1^2, 4:4^3, 4:5, 4:6, 4:7^3,
4:8^2, 4:9^4, 4:10, 4:11^4, 4:12^2, 4:15^2,
4:16^2, 4:17, 4:19^3, 4:23^3, 4:24^3,
4:25^4, 4:26, 4:27, 4:28, 4:31, 4:32^3,
4:33, 4:34^5, 4:36, 4:38^4, 4:40^2,
4:41^3, 4:42^4, 4:44, 4:45^2, 4:46,
4:47^2, 4:48, 5:2^2, 5:5^3, 5:6^2, 5:7, 5:8,
5:9, 5:10, 5:11, 5:12^2, 5:15, 5:16^2,
5:17, 5:19^2, 5:21, 5:22^4, 5:23^4,
5:24^4, 5:25^2, 5:26^2, 5:27, 6:2^3, 6:4,
6:6, 6:7, 6:8, 6:9^2, 6:10^3, 6:11, 6:12,
6:13, 6:14, 6:15, 6:16^2, 6:18, 6:19^2,
6:21^3, 6:22^2, 6:23, 6:25^4, 6:26^2,
6:27, 6:28^2, 6:29, 6:30^3, 7:2^2, 7:3^2,
7:4, 7:7^3, 7:8, 7:9^3, 7:10^2, 7:11^3,
7:12^2, 7:13, 7:14, 7:15, 7:16^2, 7:17^2,
7:18^2, 7:20, 7:21^2, 7:22^3, 7:23^5,
7:24^5, 7:25, 7:26^2, 7:27^4, 7:28^3,
7:29^3, 7:30, 7:31, 7:34, 7:35, 7:36^2,
7:37^2, 7:42^2

AUTHOR INDEX

313